PSYCHOLOGY
THE
EASY
WAY

Nancy J. Melucci, Ph.D.
Long Beach City College
Long Beach, CA

BARRON'S

All inquiries should be addressed to:
Barron's Educational Series, Inc.
250 Wireless Boulevard
Hauppauge, NY 11788
http://www.barronseduc.com

International Standard Book No. 0-7641-2393-9

Library of Congress Catalog Card No. 2003056296

Library of Congress Cataloging-in-Publication Data

Melucci, Nancy J.
    Psychology the easy way / Nancy J. Melucci.
        p. cm. — (Easy way)
    Includes bibliographical references and index.
    ISBN 0-7641-2393-9
        1. Psychology. I. Title. II. Series.

    BF121.M45   2004
    150—dc22   2003056296

PRINTED IN THE UNITED STATES OF AMERICA

9 8 7 6 5 4 3 2

CONTENTS

PREFACE

*P*sychology the Easy Way presents a detailed yet concise overview of important theories, concepts, and facts in behavioral science as we begin the twenty-first century. The past two decades have seen a revolution in our understanding of human behavior, based on technological advances in medical science that permit us to study the nervous system more accurately and thoroughly than ever before.

Because of the expanding knowledge base, introductory psychology textbooks for high school and lower division college courses are becoming larger, denser, and more costly. Whether you seek an inexpensive alternative to your course's recommended textbook or you need a supplement for study and review for your final exam or a major standardized exam such as the Advanced Placement, GRE subject exam, or professional licensing test, *Psychology the Easy Way* will assist you in developing a full understanding and appreciation of this most useful of the sciences. Concise wording is used throughout the book, and when the required technical terms and jargon are presented, they are accompanied by simple explanations to help clarify difficult concepts. Terms that may be unfamiliar are italicized, defined, and listed at the end of each chapter.

Psychology the Easy Way is divided into fifteen chapters that roughly parallel a standard introductory psychology textbook. I say "roughly" because there tends to be some differences in the order of chapters from textbook to textbook, but in the *Easy Way* you will find all the major topic areas you need to match the content of the standard general introductory course. You will also find many types of review questions including fill-in-the-blank, multiple choice, true and false, tables/matching columns, essays, glossary, and answer key.

I thank the following individuals for their outstanding and patient help: Anna Damaskos for her efficient and knowledgeable oversight of the production process and Susan Farruggia for her assistance in generating ideas for end of chapter exercises. I also thank my good friend Naidine Adams for emotional support as I worked hard to make the manuscript deadline!

You have the book, your instructor, and your course in General Introductory Psychology. Please refer to the next section for suggestions on how to use *Psychology the Easy Way* to achieve the best possible results. I hope you will find this book to be a valuable tool in achieving your goal—whether that is an A in your Psych course, an excellent exam score, or both.

I am interested in your opinions on the book. If you wish to provide me with specific feedback and suggestions for future editions, please contact me at: Psychology Department, Business and Social Sciences Division, Long Beach City College, 4901 East Carson Street, Long Beach, CA 90808. My voice mail number is (562) 938-4097, but you can get the fastest response by emailing me at nmelucci@lbcc.edu.

For little Hannah, the best daughter a mom could ask for . . .
NJM

HOW TO GET THE MOST OUT OF THIS BOOK

Psychology the Easy Way is an easy-to-use yet rich and detailed overview of material covered in a standard two-semester high school or one-semester, lower division course in general introductory psychology. It provides a simple and clear introduction to major theories and concepts, along with definitions of any technical terms that must be understood by the student.

You may attend your class faithfully and take notes diligently, but to cement your understanding, you must attend your own self-study sessions without fail. How can you use your own precious time to your best advantage?

- *Clarify your learning goals* and set deadlines for achieving them. You can use your instructor's syllabus to help you, but remember that most instructors will deviate from the syllabus or course schedule at some point. You can use this book along with the syllabus to establish the order in which you want to master each content area, and date by which you wish to do so.
- *Find a study area* that will allow you to attend to your studies fully. Most students find studying at home very difficult because of the enormous number of distractions. If you study at home, be prepared to turn off all electronic noise-producing devices (TV, radio, music players, computer), to let the telephone ring or let voice mail handle the calls, and to ask your family to support your efforts by being as quiet as possible. If your school library is available or a public library is nearby, you may want to consider studying there.
- *Establish a study schedule.* In general, as you will see in Chapter 7, short, frequent practice is more effective for learning and retention than "cramming" study marathons are. Plan to use this book at least four times a week, for one to two hours instead of once a week for five to eight. You'll get more out of it.
- *Read each chapter more than once.* The first time, read it to get acquainted with the material, the second time read and take notes, and the third time, read without taking notes, but see if you can write a quick summary of what you learned.
- *Review using the word-study connection.* Buy a large supply of index cards and make flash cards using the words in this list. Use these cards to memorize each word, its meaning, and its significance for your understanding of psychological science.
- *Do the chapter review exercises.* The objective questions are provided to help you over-learn the material. The "Connecting to Concepts" essays provide both a review and a chance to relate the facts and theories you are learning to everyday life and the "outside world." The more meaningful the material is, the more likely you are to remember it.

Psychology is an amazingly useful course because it helps us to understand our daily lives and manage them better. This book, if you make the commitment to study smart and use it wisely, will help the facts "come to life." If you make the effort, you will find connections between the book, your course, and the whole world of human behavior, every day.

Nancy J. Melucci, Ph.D.
June 2003

Chapter 1

PSYCHOLOGY: AN INTRODUCTION

In this chapter you will be introduced to the science of psychology, its history, and its methods.

Psychology: The Quest to Understand the Mind

What is psychology? Those who practice and teach in the discipline call it *the scientific study of mental processes and behavior.* Psychology is a "young science." It emerged from the combined influence of other scholarly and scientific fields, especially medicine, biology, and philosophy. Psychology has grown rapidly over the past 150 years as a discipline in its own right. It also has become an applied science that works alongside a wide variety of other fields: health sciences, education, management, and law, just to name a few. Psychologists—those who specialize in psychology—are found primarily in academic and clinical settings, but they are also commonly found working in some places where you would not expect to find them (unless you took a good psychology course!).

Just as the true science of astronomy gradually separated itself from the pseudoscience of astrology over the ages, psychology has struggled since its beginnings to distinguish itself from superstition and nonsense. Through observation and research, psychologists have tried to present reliable information and distinguish well-supported conclusions about the way organisms behave and experience consciousness, emotions, and thought from misconceptions and false beliefs about "what makes people tick" that are based on unreliable casual observations, prejudices, and preconceived but untested notions.

Making the distinction between the valid and the invalid in psychology is quite challenging. Many concepts in psychology require that we design research studies that enable us to investigate and measure constructs—abstract concepts that are assumed to influence behavior and experience. Because psychologists must develop ways to infer the presence of these constructs from measuring subject expressions, language, and behavior, the general public tends to view it as one of the "soft" (contestable or debatable) sciences.

Even the so-called hard sciences have some ambiguous and abstract aspects. Similarly, psychology also describes and investigates many directly measurable phenomena. Recent technological breakthroughs in the life sciences have permitted observation of the brain at work in living organisms, and new research in *neuroscience* (the study of the nervous system) has provided interesting findings that are dramatically changing what is known about mental processes.

The Ancient Roots of Psychology

"The unexamined life is not worth living." *Socrates*

The ancient Greek philosophers were very interested in understanding mental processes and the various influences on human behavior. The word *psychology* reflects the origins of the science—it is made of two Greek words *psyche* (mind or soul) and *logos* (study). Socrates (quoted above) and his student Plato viewed the body and mind as separate but constantly interacting with each other. The ancient Greeks thought and debated about how information taken in through the physical senses changed the nature of mental processes (which, being good dualists, they believed to be occurring in the nonmaterial soul of the human being). *Dualism* holds that the mind exists somehow separately from the body and controls it through the brain. Aristotle was one of the first empiricists who tried to link physical cause with effect. He was also interested in the process of perception. He believed in the existence of the soul and thought about how its existence might be proven. His ideas later influenced key figures in psychology, such as Sigmund Freud.

Psychology has grown out of the methods of philosophy. In the nineteenth century, psychology became a science and incorporated the methods of scientific inquiry. The following philosophical debates continue to be relevant, and you will encounter them periodically in this book and in your psychology course:

- *Free Will Versus Determinism.* The question is: Do people freely choose to behave as they do, or is behavior driven by powerful forces that cannot be controlled?
- *Nature and Nurture.* The question is: To what degree are our tendencies and differences between people and groups of people a product of heredity or the environment? (Although it is widely accepted that both do contribute, there is often a great deal of disagreement about the degree to which each contributes.)
- *The Mind-Body Problem.* The question is: Is the mind a product of the brain *or* is the mind separate from the body, controlling it through the brain (see *dualism,* earlier.)

Early Milestones in Psychology

As interesting as the speculations of the ancient Greeks were, such thoughts often resulted in conclusions about the nature of behavior and experience that were inaccurate or downright laughable. By the mid-nineteenth century, the emergence of an organized medical science and the lasting impact of Darwin's theory of natural selection helped to push psychology into the realm of science. Table 1-1 chronicles the work of the earliest pioneers of the new science from the late 1870s to 1920.

TABLE 1-1
EARLY ACHIEVEMENTS IN PSYCHOLOGY

Year	Pioneer	Achievements	Area of Psychology Influenced
1879	Wilhelm Wundt	Established the first psychology laboratory at the University of Leipzig	Wundt's work forms the basis for experimental psychology (structuralism)
1885	Hermann Ebbinghaus	Performed the first experiments on memory	Cognitive psychology (the study of thought)
1890	William James	Published *Principles of Psychologist*	James was a functionalist; his work forms the basis for applied forms of psychology such as educational and industrial organizational psychology
1898	Edward Thorndike	Conducted the first experiments on animal learning	Behaviorism—he proposed the law of effect that forms the basis of operant conditioning
1900	Sigmund Freud	Published *The Interpretation of Dreams*	Psychodynamic and clinical psychology
1905	Alfred Binet/ Theophile Simon	Devised the first IQ test for use in French public schools	Wide range of influence in education, learning, and cognition (thinking)
1906	Ivan Pavlov	Described simple associative learning processes in animals	Behaviorism
1912	Max Wertheimer	Presented the experiment that demonstrated the phi phenomenon	Gestalt psychology and perception
1920	John Watson	Wrote an essay that established the importance of the behaviorist view; performed conditioning experiments with humans	Behaviorism

These are just some of the achievements by early researchers in psychology. You can see by studying Table 1-1 that there arose quickly a variety of schools of psychology, or perspectives (frameworks) used to characterize and understand behavior and mental processes. Although it would be too simplistic to characterize them as competing frameworks, they can be sorted by fundamental differences in their unique views of human nature and what drives it. In Table 1-1, three schools are mentioned. They are primarily of historical influences (for our purposes) in over-viewing the science of psychology.

- *Structuralism.* The school founded by Edward Titchener, a student of Wilhelm Wundt. Structuralism focused on analyzing the basic elements that comprise the structure of consciousness primarily through the use of the technique called introspection in which the subject examines his or her conscious process and describes them for the researcher.
- *Functionalism.* The school founded by William James. Compared to structuralism, this school was primarily concerned with how mental processes influence behavior in order to help the organism to adapt and to function more effectively in its environment.

- *Gestalt*. A school concerned primarily with the processes of perception. It is related to structuralism in its interest in the parts that comprise the structure of consciousness. The Gestalt psychologists believed that the greatest significance lay in understanding how the mind organizes objects and patterns into unified, integrated, whole units of meaningful information—"the sum is greater than the parts."

TABLE 1-2
PERSPECTIVES IN PSYCHOLOGY

Perspective	View of Human Nature	Major Influence(s) upon Behavior	Seeks to Understand
Biological (neuroscience)	Behavior and experience are the result of biochemical processes originating at the cellular level.	Electrochemical processes in the nervous system, hormones secreted by the endocrine glands	How does the brain and body create sensory, feeling thought processes and behaviors?
Evolutionary	Behavior is the result of selection over the course of millions of years for the most adaptive strategies leading to survival and reproduction.	The drive to perpetuate the genes by surviving and reproducing	In what ways does natural selection influence behavioral tendencies?
Cognitive	Behavior is influenced by how organisms remember, process and organize information and how they make decisions and solve problems.	The way in which an organism understands and interprets information	In what ways do we use information in remembering, deciding, reasoning, and solving problems?
Psychodynamic	Behavior is driven by unconscious forces that come into conflict with conscious motives and the demands of the environment.	How a person manages the strong unconscious forces while getting some needs met appropriately	How do unconscious forces and early experiences shape behavior in the present?
Behavioral	Behavior is shaped by the ways in which the organism learns.	The contingencies and observational experiences that shape an organism's responses	How can we use associations and contingencies to influence learning and behavior?
Humanistic	Behavior is driven by a need to grow and reach full potential.	An inner need for self-actualization and a need for positive regard from others	How can we understand subjective experience in order to help people to achieve their potential?
Sociocultural	Behavior can only be understood in a broad cultural or societal context.	The demands, expectations, and assumptions of the culture in which one lives	What are the common behavioral tendencies and experiences across cultures? What are the unique ones?
Behavioral genetics	Behavior is a product of the interaction between genes and environment.	The interaction between genetic tendencies and environmental forces	How can we separate the influences on behavior that are mostly genetic from those that are mostly environmental?

Recently psychology has been criticized for presenting a narrow view of the world rooted only in the values and traditions of the Western world. Prejudice and ignorance certainly played a role in excluding a wide range of voices from contributing to the new science. In the late nineteenth century, Christine Ladd-Franklin (who studied the evolutionary roots of color vision) and Mary Calkins (the first female president of the American Psychological Association) attained the same scholarly and scientific credentials as their male counterparts and were not even granted degrees until late in their lives (Gerrig & Zimbardo, 2002). Due to racial prejudice and poverty, Francis Sumner had to educate himself to the high school level. In spite of the enormous obstacles, he became the first African American to earn a PhD and went on to chair the psychology department at Howard University (Wood & Wood, 2000). One of the first important American structuralists was another African American, J. Henry Alston (Lahey, 2001). These are only a few of the women and ethnic minorities who fought to contribute despite the adversity they faced. Happily, now young psychologists from a variety of backgrounds are encouraged to work and expand the knowledge base and perspective of the science to be more accurate and to include a wider range of human experience. Table 1-2 outlines the most widely used perspectives in psychology.

We now understand and accept that it is impossible to interpret and understand behavior and thought outside of the cultural context. The sociocultural perspective improves our knowledge of psychology by making comparisons across cultures and situations.

The Work of Psychologists

Psychology is an academic discipline that is allied with health and human services, education, business, and many other fields. The requirements for working as a psychologist vary from country to country. In the United States, there are many possible jobs for a person with a BS/BA degree in psychology, but few of them are within the field of psychology. Most college students considering a career directly related to psychology will need at least a master's degree. Having earned a master's degree (MS) one can practice psychotherapy as a Marriage and Family Therapist or Clinical Social Worker or teach in many two-year colleges. A doctorate is required for teaching at the university level (PhD) and entering private practice as a psychologist in most states (PhD or PsyD).

TABLE 1-3
MOST COMMON SPECIALTIES OF PSYCHOLOGISTS

Specialty	Percent Employed
Clinical	36
Neuroscience	7
Counseling	18
Industrial/organizational	5
Social/personality	6
School/educational	5
Developmental	9
Other (Forensic, etc.)	19

The stereotypical view of the work of psychologists is in the role of the "shrink"—the therapist who treats emotional and mental illnesses. This narrow view does not capture the enormous diversity of contributions that psychologists make in a wide variety of professional capacities. Table 1-3 breaks down specialties in which psychologists are employed, based on data collected by the American Psychological Association (2003).

The Scientific Method in Psychology

Despite the difficulties presented by abstract concepts such as "intelligence," "memory," and "personality," these things can be investigated scientifically. This is the work of modern research psychologists. The scientific method presents the guidelines for our investigation. They include the assumptions, perspectives, and procedures that are used in the research process. Many research questions are grounded in a theory, which is a broad principle that explains how a set of separate facts are related.

Basic (also called pure) *research* is done in psychology to expand the knowledge base in the science. *Applied research* is done (sometimes on a foundation laid by basic research) to address practical issues related to behavior and experience. Whatever the type of research, the ultimate goal is to find the right answers.

In psychological research, we use a scientific approach to obtain answers related to any or all of the following four goals. We are striving to

- Describe behavior and mental processes.
- Explain the reasons for behavior and mental activities.
- Predict the expected behavior or experience of the organism(s).
- When desirable or appropriate, influence or control the behavior or mental process under investigation.

Whatever our goals are, we must begin by creating a clear and specific research question, our research *hypothesis*. To be a true hypothesis it must be testable; thus, the question "Do maintenance rehearsal strategies improve working memory?" is not a perfect hypothesis, but it is a good start. Once we define our variables in the most specific terms possible, we will be able to test this question. We can choose a specific maintenance rehearsal strategy, select an adequate number of subjects, and find or create a valid way to measure working memory using an *operational definition* (a definition that allows us to measure a construct of interest.) The question "Are people reincarnated after death?" is very intriguing, but it cannot be tested using empirical means. *Empirical* means that we can somehow measure or experience a phenomenon using our physical senses. Questions such as life-after-death, the existence of a soul, and the existence of astral planes cannot be experienced in an empirical way and are best left for philosophy and theology classes.

Our next step is to design a good study. The appropriate design for our study depends on our goals and the nature of the variables (constructs or qualities that change from observation to observation or subject to subject) we are investigating. We will do *descriptive* study if our goal is to observe and describe behavioral or mental processes. We will do an *experimental* study if we want to predict how one variable will be influenced by changes in another.

Table 1-4 summarizes the features of the most common research designs employed in psychology.

TABLE 1-4
EXPERIMENTAL METHODS IN PSYCHOLOGY

Type	Method	Strengths	Weaknesses
Experimental	Experiment (manipulate one variable and measure changes in another) and quasi experiment (version in which researcher studies naturally occurring variations linked to a subject variable such as age, and sex)	Some degree of control over extraneous variables; may be able to infer cause and effect	Artificial situation, hard to generalize results
Descriptive	Correlation (working with archival, demographic, or other preexisting data)	Allows for quantitative analysis of relationships between some variables	Can't control some extraneous variables, can't determine order of occurrence, can't infer cause and effect
Descriptive	Survey (asking questions through use of a structured format)	Economical method of gathering large amounts of data	Problems with sampling and selection; problems caused by respondent distortions, memory lapses and dishonesty; can't infer cause and effect
Descriptive	Field study or naturalistic observation (making careful observations in a natural setting)	Results can be generalized more easily than those of lab studies	Little control over variables or observers, unintended effects from expectations; can't infer cause and effect
Descriptive	Case study (detailed investigation of a single subject	Can be used to generate hypotheses	Only appropriate for unusual cases

As you can see, each of these research methods has its good points and weaknesses. All things being equal, psychological investigators prefer to do true experiments when feasible. Despite the difficulty with generalizing from the artificial setting of the laboratory or research center, this design offers the greatest degree of confidence conclusions regarding cause-and-effect relationships between variables.

Table 1-5 provides a brief glossary of the language of the true experiment.

TABLE 1-5
EXPERIMENTAL JARGON

Independent variable (IV)—The construct that is applied, changed, or manipulated; the treatment or change effected by the researcher. If a researcher gives a new medication for anxiety to some people in a research study, and gives others a fake pill or placebo, the medication is the independent variable.

Subject variable—The variable of interest in a quasi-experimental study, when it is not possible for the researcher to change it deliberately. A researcher wishes to study the difference in mathematics achievement between men and women. Sex is the variable of interest. The researcher cannot change the sex of the people in the research study.

Dependent variable (DV)—The reaction, quality, or construct that is measured after the manipulation of the independent variable. After the researcher gives the anxiety medication to the people in the study, the level of anxiety of the subjects is measured with an anxiety questionnaire and various medical monitoring devices. The scores and readings provided by these tools are assumed to represent the dependent variable.

Random sample—A set of subjects chosen *randomly*—by chance (not self-selected, selected because they are available, or selected because they belong to a particular group). The Centers for Disease Control contacts U.S. citizens for a health survey using a computerized program based on a random number table in order to generate names and addresses of people from all fifty states and the territories.

Random assignment—Placing subjects into the experimental groups *randomly*. College freshmen volunteering for a university research study are selected for either a memory-training group or no training group by having their names drawn out of a hat.

Conditions—The type of group to which subjects are assigned in a research study depending on whether or not a change is made (in an experiment) or depending on an already existing classification (in a quasi experiment). The treatment condition received the new anxiety medication; the control condition received a fake pill (placebo.)

Placebo—A fake pill or phony treatment given to subjects in one or more experimental conditions to help researchers separate the real effects of the treatment apart from the "placebo effects" that people experience when they think they are being given a treatment of some type. The control group received a pill made of an inert substance while the treatment group got the real medication.

Control group—The group in a research study that receives no treatment or a placebo. The researcher had the control subjects in the memory experiment spend one hour in the waiting room while the treatment subjects received the special memory training.

Exp group

A single research study cannot prove or disprove a hypothesis; rather, a single study forms part of the body of research on a topic. After the results of a study are published, other researchers will repeat the original investigation or a version of it to see if the results are replicable. Replication, which is the ability to reproduce results consistently, is a key part of the scientific method. If the results reoccur when several other investigators repeat the study, we can feel more certain that the information provided by the study will be useful in helping us to accomplish any of the four goals of the science of psychology.

TIP BOX
A Simple Example of a Research Study

Jennifer and Tasha want to know if gingko biloba pills can help improve memory for college students. They administer a quick memory test to 100 volunteer student participants. Using a lottery system, the researchers randomly assign the 100 student volunteers to one of two conditions—those who will receive the treatment of ginko biloba, and those who will receive a placebo (the control condition). The student volunteers take pills once a day for six weeks. The volunteers are then given an alternate version of the memory test, and their scores are compared to the first set of scores.

This is a true experiment. The two researchers control who gets the treatment and who does not (who receives ginko biloba and who gets a placebo). Thus, there is a real independent variable in this study. The dependent variable is memory as measured by the test that the researchers administer at the beginning and the end of the study.

Connecting Through Chapter Review

WORD-STUDY CONNECTION

Write each of these words on index cards, and write their definitions on the opposite side.

applied research
basic research
behavioral genetics
behaviorism
biological
case study
clinical
cognitive
conditions
control group
correlation
dependent variable
descriptive
determinism
dualism
empirical

evolutionary
experimental
field study
free will
functionalism
Gestalt
humanistic
hypothesis
independent variable
mind-body problem
nature
natural selection
neuroscience
nurture
operational definition
perception

placebo
psychodynamic
psychology
random assignment
random sample
quasi experiment
research design
self-actualization
sociocultural
subject variable
survey
structuralism

SELF-TEST CONNECTION

PART A. *Completion*
Write in the word that correctly completes each statement.

1. The scientific study of behavior and experience is called _____ .
2. An intangible concept that is assumed to influence behavior and mental processes is a _____ .
3. The belief that the mind and the body are separate entities is referred to as _____ .
4. Freud believed that powerful, unconscious internal forces drive human behavior. This belief is sometimes referred to as _____ .
5. _____ performed the first experiments in memory.
6. The first IQ tests were developed by _____ and _____ for use in the French public school system.
7. _____ is the early school of psychology that later influenced applied areas such as industrial organizational and educational psychology.
8. The study of perception and how the mind organizes and integrates information about the world into whole, meaningful units of information is closely associated with the early school of _____ psychology.
9. Processes in the nervous and endocrine systems are the main focus of the modern perspective called _____ psychology.
10. Psychodynamic psychologists are interested in early experiences and _____ forces and how these factors influence personality and development.
11. Memory and problem solving would be of great interest to a(n) _____ psychologist.
12. According to recent data from the American Psychological Association, about 3 percent of psychologists work as _____ .
13. About _____ percent of psychologists are specialists in neuroscience.
14. The assumptions, perspectives, and procedures that are used as guidelines for investigation in psychology are collectively referred to as the _____ .
15. _____ research is done to address practical issues related to behavior and experience.
16. The clear, specific, and testable research question that we wish to investigate is called the _____ .
17. If our goal is to observe and describe human behavior, we are most likely to do _____ research.
18. A(n) _____ is a research study in which we change one variable and measure changes in another.
19. A(n) _____ _____ can be done if we are studying an unusual event or rare disorder.
20. The variable that is manipulated in a true experiment is referred to as the _____ variable.

PART B. Multiple Choice
Circle the letter of the item that correctly completes the statement.

1. A clear and specific research question is referred to as a(n) _____ .
   (a) theory   (b) hypothesis
   (c) independent variable   (d) experiment
2. The first psychology research laboratory was established by _____ .
   (a) Freud   (b) Pavlov
   (c) Watson   (d) Wundt
3. A research design that allows the investigator to infer a cause-and-effect relationship between variables is called a(n) _____ .
   (a) correlation   (b) survey
   (c) experiment   (d) case study
4. Which of the following is *not* an example of a psychological construct?
   (a) Aggression   (b) Memory
   (c) Weight   (d) Personality
5. Those who try to link physical causes with effects in the sciences are known as _____ .
   (a) behaviorists   (b) dualists
   (c) Freudians   (d) empiricists
6. The theory of _____ proposed by Darwin had a major impact on the development of psychology in the nineteenth century.
   (a) natural selection   (b) empiricism
   (c) free will   (d) nurture
7. Early experiments on the process of memory were performed by _____ .
   (a) James   (b) Ebbinghaus
   (c) Aristotle   (d) Freud
8. Simple associative learning processes were demonstrated by the laboratory work of _____ .
   (a) Freud   (b) Pavlov
   (c) Binet and Simon   (d) Wundt
9. _____ psychologists believe that the need for positive regard from others is a major influence on human behavior.
   (a) Humanistic   (b) Psychodynamic
   (c) Empirical   (d) Cognitive
10. Which of the following is *not* a common professional specialization of psychologists?
    (a) Neuroscience   (b) Counseling
    (c) Education   (d) Political
11. People who practice as Marriage and Family Therapists commonly hold _____ degrees.
    (a) PhD   (b) BA
    (c) MS   (d) PsyD
12. Research that is done with the goal of expanding the knowledge base of psychology is referred to as _____ .
    (a) applied   (b) basic
    (c) clinical   (d) inferential

13. In order to measure a variable in a research study, we must develop _____ for it.
    (a) a hypothetical definition   (b) a descriptive definition
    (c) an independent definition   (d) an operational definition
14. In an experiment to measure the effectiveness of a new medication for Attention Deficit Disorder some participants are given the medication and some are given an inert pill. The group that got the inert pill is referred to as the _____ group.
    (a) treatment   (b) placebo control
    (c) independent   (d) manipulated
15. A construct or quality that changes from subject to subject is referred to as a(n) _____ .
    (a) variable   (b) definition
    (c) experiment   (d) hypothesis
16. _____ studied the evolutionary roots of color vision.
    (a) Calkins   (b) Ladd-Franklin
    (c) Wundt   (d) Sumner
17. The "old school" of psychology known as _____ concerned itself primarily with the process of perception.
    (a) psychodynamic   (b) functionalism
    (c) behavioral   (d) gestalt
18. The _____ perspective is concerned with how behavior changes across broader contexts.
    (a) humanistic   (b) cognitive
    (c) sociocultural   (d) observational
19. Which of the following is *not* one of the four main goals of psychological research?
    (a) Description   (b) Prediction
    (c) Innovation   (d) Explanation
20. Which of the following constructs *cannot* be measured empirically?
    (a) Intelligence   (b) Reincarnation
    (c) Memory   (d) Speed

PART C. Modified True-False

If the statement is true, write "T" for the answer. If the statement is incorrect, change the underlined expression to one that will make the statement true.

1. Aristotle was one of the first true empiricists.
2. In a true experiment, the research manipulates the dependent variable.
3. Most psychologists are employed in the field of neuroscience.
4. A theory is a testable proposition.
5. William James was the founder of the functionalist school of psychology.
6. The evolutionary framework of psychology is particularly concerned with describing the structure and function of the brain and nervous system.
7. A dependent variable must be operationalized in order to make it measurable.
8. Sigmund Freud performed conditioning experiments with "Little Albert."
9. A psychologist who believes that behavior is driven by the need to achieve one's full potential would be called a humanistic psychologist.
10. A research psychologist who wishes to use study results to improve the motivation level of factory workers is doing applied research.

PART D. Is it a question for science?

After the research question, write "yes" if it is possible to use empirical methods to investigate it, or "no" if it is not an appropriate question for investigation by the scientific method.

1. Men are more likely than women to report fantasies of achieving celebrity status.
2. Animals are born with an innate sense of sin.
3. Gingko biloba improves memory function in elderly women.
4. Every human will be reincarnated at least 100 times.
5. The typical adolescent clique is comprised of four to seven persons.
6. Babies who hear classical music during the first two years of life will have higher IQ scores than those who do not hear classical music.
7. The soul forms in a human fetus when the brain reaches a weight of one-half pound.
8. Seven-year-olds understand the concept of "justice."
9. Handwriting analysis is a reliable way to screen for honesty in future employees.
10. During the human sleep cycle, our dream activity is a by-product of our souls' out-of-body experiences.
11. During the human sleep cycle, our brain undergoes physical changes that reflect our learning of new information during the day.
12. Sleep deprivation results in a reduction of reflex speed and diminished judgment.

CONNECTING TO CONCEPTS

Review the chapter and then write down your thoughts about the following questions.

1. Why do many people have difficulty understanding that psychology is a science?
2. Create a hypothesis related to human behavior. Briefly describe how you would use one research method described in this chapter to investigate your hypothesis.
3. Choose two pioneers from the early history of psychology. Describe their achievements during their own lifetimes, and discuss the contributions that they made to the field of psychology that lasted beyond their own lifetimes.
4. Discuss how the self-sacrificing behavior of a humanitarian such as Mother Teresa or Martin Luther King would be explained by any two of the current perspectives in the science of psychology.
5. Discuss how a professional from any area of psychological practice might utilize theory and research based upon the assumptions of any current perspective in the science of the psychology.

CONNECTING TO LIFE/JOB SKILLS

Critical Thinking Skills

"Thinking like a scientist" does not require a PhD nor does it require you to choose a scientific career. To do good scientific thinking, all that is required is that you have a reasonably open mind and require good evidence of any claim that is made to you. To have an open mind is not the same thing as believing whatever you are told (which is called gullibility); rather, it means that you will consider any claim based on the evidence presented to support the claim. Scientific thinking requires that you resist emotional reasoning—believing what you wish to believe because it makes you happy, rejecting the information that displeases you.

The best quality evidence is gained through studies that use experimental controls with the largest samples possible. The popular claim that the full moon causes behavioral instability in humans, for example, is based on people's anecdotal recollections. As convinced as some people are of this claim, the fact is that when you subject the claim to scientific scrutiny, for example, by having police and emergency workers keep detailed logs of accidents and crimes during all phases of the moon, this relationship is not borne out. Behavioral instability in humans is not connected in any way to the phases of the moon. Yet even those who have participated in such studies continue to hold the belief because it gives a comforting though false feeling of predictability.

WHAT'S HAPPENING!

Cross-Cultural Psychology

An ongoing area that opens up new perspectives on psychology is the sociocultural perspective, also called cross-cultural psychology. The roots of psychology can be found in many global cultures, but the science has evolved most quickly in the West and, therefore has carried a heavily Western view of human behavior up until recently.

Through the influence of researchers and scholars such as Matsumoto, Ekman, Fernandez-Dols, and Sue, psychology is being transformed. Without such scholarship and research, psychology cannot become a global force. Culture has a pervasive influence on human existence. Cultural context has an impact on development and values and what constitutes "normal." Culture dictates rules for communication and emotional expression. With an understanding of the impact of culture, we can raise our chances of increasing understanding and knowledge for all people.

Visit these links for more information on the cross-cultural perspective in modern psychology:

www.psichi.org/pubs/article.asp?article_id=82

teachpsych.lemoyne.edu/teachpsych/faces/text/Ch05.htm

www.ac.wwu.edu/~culture/readings.htm

OTHER USEFUL WEB SITES

AMOEBAWEB

www.vanguard.edu/faculty/ddegelman/amoebaweb/

This comprehensive site is sponsored and maintained by psychology faculty at Vanguard University. Visiting it will expand your knowledge of topics covered in this first chapter: history and systems, philosophical issues, and careers in psychology.

ENCYCLOPEDIA OF PSYCHOLOGY

www.psychology.org/links/

Jacksonville State University's Psychology Department created and maintains this web site.

PSYCHWEB

www.psywww.com/index.html

This site was created and is maintained by Russ Dewey PhD. It includes a link to Dr. Marky Lloyd's very helpful *Careers in Psychology* page.

AMERICAN PSYCHOLOGICAL ASSOCIATION

www.apa.org

This is the homepage of the American Psychological Association, a great resource for anyone who is curious about psychology.

AMERICAN PSYCHOLOGICAL SOCIETY

www.psychologicalscience.org/

This is the homepage of the American Psychological Society, another good resource, especially for those who are very interested in psychological research.

REFERENCES

American Psychological Association (2003) *Where Are the New Psychologists Going? Employment, Debt and Salary Information.* Washington, DC: American Psychological Association Research Office.

Gerrig, R. J. & Zimbardo, P .G. (2002) Psychology and Life. Boston: Allyn & Bacon.

Lahey, B. (2001) Psychology: An Introduction. New York: McGraw-Hill.

Wood, S. E. & Wood, E. G. (2000) The Essential World of Psychology. Boston: Allyn & Bacon.

Chapter 2

THE GENETIC BASIS OF BEHAVIOR AND EXPERIENCE

In this chapter you will become acquainted with some basic principles of genetics and the connection between genes and behavior.

Genes, Evolution, and Psychology

It is clear that many aspects of human appearance are inherited: eye color, hair color, height, and body build, to name just a few. It is also true that some aspects of behavior are inherited, although you are more likely to find some level of disagreement among scientists about the number, types, and nature of such inherited tendencies. For example, while almost all psychologists agree that males as a group are more aggressive than females and that biology must play a role, some believe that this aggression is primarily learned through observation and socialization with just a little help from genes. Others feel that it is primarily a biologically based tendency that is supported by experience. Still others now argue that the barrier between biology and aspects of the environment, such as culture, is ever shifting and complex and that it is overly simplistic to try to divide the influence provided by each into some exact proportion.

Heredity refers to the characteristics or traits passed from parents to offspring. The direct mechanism of transmission for these characteristics is the *chromosome*, a microscopic thread composed of *genes*. Each gene is a unit composed of a series of *nucleotides* forming strands of *deoxyribonucleic acid* or *DNA*—special combinations of sugars and proteins that work to direct chemical processes at the cellular level through an intermediary (go-between) chemical called *ribonucleic acid* or *RNA*. This chain of chemical messengers regulates the processes that control that individual organism's growth and functioning.

Each organism grows according to the instructions of a set number and unique combination of chromosomes. Humans possess forty-six chromosomes, inheriting twenty-three from each parent when the *sex cells* of mother and father unite. Each pair of chromosomes has many pairs of genes that code for characteristics. Whether the individual inherits a characteristic or particular version of the characteristic depends upon the combination of *dominant* and *recessive* genes created by the uniting of egg and sperm. Recessive genes will exert their influence only when both mother and father contribute one of them, while a dominant trait will tend be manifested even when only one dominant gene is present.

I say "tend" because it is not only the gene that matters, but also the environment in which the organism lives. You may get the gene for freckles (a dominant gene) but if you live in a frequently cloudy region of the world, you may not get many (or any) freckles. It is important to remember that *genotype* (the exact instructions for an organism) does not completely determine how the individual turns out. Certain features of the environment will interact with the biological development of the organism, resulting in a final outcome of appearance, ability, and health called a *phenotype* (the actual traits manifested by the individual organism). Genotype does not equal phenotype.

Behavioral Genetics

Recently a new field of study in psychology has emerged: *behavioral genetics*. This field blends an understanding of *genetics* with psychology to attempt to study and predict the influence of heredity on behavior.

Strategies that are used in the field of behavioral genetics include:

- *Twin studies.* Since *monozygotic* (identical) twins are essentially nature's clones, two individual organisms with identical genotypes are uniquely well suited for study of the contributions of heredity and experience. Although *dizygotic* (fraternal) twins are (in terms of heredity) ordinary siblings who happen to be born at the same time, such pairs are also useful for observing the effects of shared environment.
- *Adoption studies.* Studies of children who are adopted and their biological and adoptive parents can also be informative—Do adopted children resemble their birth parents or the parents who reared them? Most studies suggest that although adoptive parents and their environment *do* have an impact, heredity ultimately exerts a greater influence. "Separated at birth" twin studies (identical twins, each of whom are reared in a different home) combine the best features of twin and adoption studies.
- *Family studies.* In-depth studies of persons from the same bloodline who share the potential to inherit or pass on a certain trait are time-consuming and difficult to carry out from a practical standpoint. Such studies are often worth the trouble though as they yield very interesting results about the possible influence of heredity on behavior.
- *Genetic diseases.* Studies of disorders such as color-blindness, hemophilia, PKU, and Down's syndrome are very informative and often provide strong cause-and-effect evidence for the contributions of heredity. As psychologists have observed and learned from studies of genetic disorders, we have begun to develop research that is revealing the role that genetics plays in disorders such as schizophrenia, autism, and Alzheimer's dementia.

Behavioral geneticists often refer to the *hereditability* of a trait. The term "hereditability" is often misunderstood by nonscientists and misused by scientists who should know better. Hereditability is an index of the differences among members of a population that can be attributed *only* to the effects of heredity. For example, if I raised 100 pea plants in a large tub of soil and, through sheer determination and watchfulness, was able to hold all the conditions affecting my pea plants completely constant (temperature, light, moisture, soil composition, and the like), I could safely assume that the variations that arise among the members of my pea plant crop were wholly the result of genetic differences between the plants. It is important to keep in mind when you read the word "hereditability" that what is challenging but possible to accomplish with plants is much less feasible with humans and most other animals. Hereditability refers only to estimates of traits in groups and should only be used to describe groups. That a certain trait is found to be 60 percent hereditable in a certain species or group provides little meaningful information about an individual's potential in that area.

The Role of Environmental Influences

In most situations, heredity and experience are difficult or impossible to separate. Height is strongly influenced by genes, but you cannot count on achievement of a certain height from a high hereditability estimate. The child of parents whose heights both exceed six feet may not reach that level given the wrong set of circumstances (for example, if born into a situation where he or she is malnourished and receives little health care).

PKU (phenylketonuria) is an interesting example of the weakness of the assumption that genes and environment play opposing roles in development and behavior. Although the disorder is entirely genetic in origin (either you get the pair of recessive genes that cause it, and get the disease, or you don't), most of its damaging effects can be controlled through dietary restrictions.

Most behavioral geneticists, and psychologists who utilize information gained through research in this area, take care to avoid overly simplistic assumptions about the relationship between genes and environment.

Evolutionary Psychology

Evolution is the theory stating that species inheriting the traits that best enable survival and reproduction in their environments will thrive and flourish. Charles Darwin (1859) is primarily credited with developing this theory. Over time, natural selection will promote certain adaptations to the environment and eliminate traits that are not as adaptive. Gradual change, creation of new species, and extinction all occur through this mechanism.

The theory of evolution has had a profound impact on all life and social sciences. *Evolutionary psychology* attempts to describe how the processes of genetic mutation and natural selection may have influenced behavior and mental functioning. Evolutionary psychologists assume that the brain and nervous system that we now possess are the products of a long history of gradual genetic change. The arrangement of the four lobes of the cerebral cortex, which we will learn about in the next chapter, is the result of genetic mutations that eventually produced this particular arrangement, with visual processing in the back, judgment and forethought in the front, body sensation along the top of the back, and hearing at the sides of the brain. Evolutionary psychologists also propose that various psychological mechanisms (called *modules*) were selected for over long spans of time because of utility in helping us to survive and bear offspring; in other words, these modules contributed to our evolutionary fitness. Fitness is a misunderstood concept because of most people's associations of the term with strength or exercise and diet. In evolutionary terms, fitness refers strictly to the ability to produce offspring; who survive to reproductive age and have their own offspring—it describes success in spreading and perpetuating one's genes. To an evolutionary psychologist, the fact that humans possess a vast intelligence compared to most other animals, along with diverse and interesting personality traits such as extroversion and determination, is explained most accurately by the fact that these qualities helped us to thrive as a species and therefore were "selected" over the course of evolutionary time. Those who had the traits were able to reproduce more successfully than those who lacked them.

Sociobiology, a field related to evolutionary psychology, examines how individual behavior occurring within the group or community, as well as group behavior, contribute to reproductive success and survival. Sociobiologists argue that the tendency to engage in certain social behaviors is genetic in origin because these behaviors will increase the odds of successfully passing on one's genes. For example, an animal may engage in parental care-taking behaviors because such behavior maximizes the odds that offspring will survive to reproduce.

Some psychologists have proposed that because it is likely that social and cultural influences have an impact on evolution, thoughts and ideas may be passed along from mind to mind in a way that roughly parallels genetic evolution. The units of this process of sociocultural evolution are called *memes* (Pinker 1999). According to *meme theory,* building blocks of thought and culture are transmitted and changed over the course of time. This idea is highly novel and controversial.

Nature and Nurture

Most psychologists now understand that the influence of genes and environment on development and behavior is not an "either-or" dilemma. A complex interaction of genes and environment has shaped our nervous systems, thoughts, feelings, and behaviors. As was stated at the beginning of this chapter, psychologists do not necessarily agree about the degree to which nature and nurture influence mental processes and behaviors.

Some psychologists give the greater weight to genes, pointing out how strong and commonplace selected behaviors are in animals and humans, the obvious resemblances that exist between family members in intelligence and physical appearance, and the sometimes eerie similarities that sometimes are found to exist in twins that are separated at birth. Other psychologists, although they do not reject the influence of genes, tend to view genes as playing a secondary role to environment. For example, a psychologist who argues for the strong role of environment would say that family resemblances in intelligence, personality, and physical appearance might be a result of shared environment—socioeconomic status, climate, diet, and such—as well as genes. He or she might point out that eerie similarities can sometimes be found between pairs of randomly selected strangers.

Identical twins inherit the same genes and therefore will powerfully resemble each other in appearance, behavior, and potential. On the other hand, they are not merely carbon copies of each other and anyone who knows both members of a pair of identical twins knows that they can be very different in terms of their individual behaviors, accomplishments, and ways of self-expression. As scientists struggle to determine the degree of contribution made by nature and nurture, it is probably most useful for you, as you learn about behaviors, emotions, and experience, to view these two major influences as always acting in combination, perhaps with one or the other dominating in certain circumstances.

Connecting Through Chapter Review

WORD-STUDY CONNECTION

Write each of these words on index cards and write their definitions on the opposite side.

adoption studies	genetic	nucleotides
behavioral genetics	genetic disease	PKU
chromosome	genotype	phenotype
DNA	hereditability	RNA
dizygotic	heredity	recessive
dominant	memes	sex cells
evolutionary psychology	meme theory	sociobiology
family studies	modules	traits
genes	monozygotic	twin studies

SELF-TEST CONNECTION

PART A. Completion

Write in the word that correctly completes each statement.

1. Aggression and dominance are behavioral tendencies that some psychologists believe may be _____ .
2. _____ refers to all the traits that may be passed from parents to offspring.
3. A gene is composed of a series of _____ that are arranged in sequences referred to as _____ strands.
4. The manufacture of protein in a cell is directed by DNA working through an intermediary chemical called _____ .
5. Human heredity is controlled by a total of _____ chromosomes.
6. _____ genes will exert their influence only when both parents contribute one of each.
7. The exact genetic instructions for an organism are called the _____ ; the traits that actually appear as the organism matures are called the _____ .
8. _____ is a new field of psychology that attempts to explain how heredity influences behavior.
9. _____ or identical twins have exactly the same genotype.
10. Color-blindness and PKU are examples of _____ diseases.
11. _____ is an index of differences in a certain trait among members of a population—differences that are attributable only to the effects of heredity.

12. _____ attempts to describe how selection pressures and mutations might have influenced the development of behaviors and mental processes.
13. Psychological mechanisms are called _____ by evolutionary psychologists.
14. "Fitness" in terms of natural selection refers to an organism's ability to pass on its _____ by having many _____ .
15. _____ claim that the tendency to engage in certain behaviors is genetic in origin because such behaviors increase an organism's fitness.
16. The idea that certain aspects of culture and thought are transmitted and mutate across evolutionary time is referred to as _____ theory.
17. Although psychologists don't always agree as to the proportion of the contribution of _____ and _____ , most agree that both of these combine to influence almost all psychological processes and behaviors.

PART B. Multiple Choice
Circle the letter of the item that correctly completes the statement.

1. The mechanisms of transmission of inherited characteristics are called _____ .
   (a) RNA   (b) chromosomes
   (c) ribosomes   (d) cells
2. Genes are composed of a series of _____ composing strands of _____ .
   (a) nucleotides; DNA   (b) chromosomes; cells
   (c) ribosomes; RNA   (d) genetic mutations; traits
3. _____ only exert their influence when an organism inherits one from each parent.
   (a) Dominant genes   (b) Ribosomal genes
   (c) Recessive genes   (d) Mutation genes
4. Sara got a dominant gene for curly hair from her mother and a recessive gene for straight hair from her father. Her hair will most likely be _____ .
   (a) curly   (b) wavy
   (c) straight   (d) curly at first but straight later
5. Jerry's family carries the "thrifty gene" that tends to cause obesity. Jerry's mother puts him on a low-fat diet and enrolls him in two after-school athletic programs. Jerry's weight remains in the high normal range for his height. Jerry's current weight is his
   (a) genotype   (b) phenotype
   (c) mutation   (d) dominant trait
6. Another term for monozygotic twins is
   (a) dizygotic   (b) fraternal
   (c) genotype   (d) identical
7. Adoption studies provide evidence that _____ has greater influence on traits that we develop in life.
   (a) environment   (b) heredity
   (c) learning   (d) mutation
8. Intensive studies of the history of certain traits in persons who share the same bloodline are called _____ .
   (a) twin studies   (b) adoption studies
   (c) family studies   (d) genotype histories

9. According to current research in behavioral genetics, it appears likely that _____ is influenced by heredity.
   - (a) autism
   - (b) Alzheimer's dementia
   - (c) schizophrenia
   - (d) All of the above
10. _____ is an index of the degree to which a particular trait is influenced by genetic factors.
    - (a) Inheritance
    - (b) Heredity
    - (c) Genotype
    - (d) Hereditability
11. Studies of genetic disorders such as PKU provide evidence that it is probably over-simplistic and inaccurate to view genes and environment as playing _____ roles in development.
    - (a) complimentary
    - (b) equal
    - (c) opposing
    - (d) unpredictable
12. _____ is the theory that species and their traits have changed as a result of forces of heredity, selection, and mutation over the course of time.
    - (a) Hereditability
    - (b) Behavioral genetics
    - (c) Evolution
    - (d) Memetics
13. Evolutionary psychologists use the term _____ to refer to mental processes and behavioral patterns that help organisms to survive and flourish.
    - (a) genes
    - (b) chromosomes
    - (c) modules
    - (d) fitness strategies
14. In evolutionary terms, fitness means (most nearly) _____ .
    - (a) strength
    - (b) reproductive success
    - (c) health
    - (d) brute force
15. A _____ would be most interested in how group behavior contributes to reproductive success in species.
    - (a) sociobiologist
    - (b) memeticist
    - (c) geneticist
    - (d) clinical psychologist
16. According to some scientists, human sociocultural behavior undergoes a process of evolution. The basic unit of transmission of sociocultural information is called a _____ .
    - (a) gene
    - (b) nucleotide
    - (c) meme
    - (d) DNA strand

PART C. Modified True-False

If the statement is true, write "T" for the answer. If the statement is incorrect, change the underlined expression to one that will make the statement true.

1. The degrees of influence that biology and environment exert on psychological processes are easy to distinguish.
2. Chromosomes are made up of genes.
3. DNA is the intermediary for instructions from the genes to the cell.
4. Dominant genes will exert their influence only if an organism inherits one from each parent.
5. The genotype is the set of inherited instructions for the organism.
6. Dizygotic twins are essentially clones, being genetically identical.

7. Adoption studies provide evidence that <u>environment</u> exerts a more powerful influence on development and behavior.

8. <u>Down's syndrome</u> is an example of a genetic disorder.

9. <u>Hereditability</u> refers to the amount of variation among organisms that is caused by genes when the environment is held constant.

10. It is probably true that genes and environment are <u>opposing</u> forces in development and behavior.

11. Fitness refers to an organism's <u>strength, nutrition, and overall health</u>.

12. <u>Sociobiologists</u> argue that the tendency to engage in certain social behaviors increases fitness in a species.

13. According to <u>gene theory</u>, building blocks of thought and culture are passed down from generation to generation.

14. Most psychologists agree that genes and environment exert their influence on an "<u>either-or</u>" basis.

15. To some degree, a trait like extroversion is probably a result of <u>the influence of genes only</u>.

CONNECTING TO CONCEPTS

Review the chapter and then write down your thoughts about the following questions.

1. In the first chapter you considered the fact that some humans engage in self-sacrificing behavior. How would a sociobiologist explain the fact that some humans engage in these behaviors?

2. Name one human trait related to psychological processes about which you are curious. Discuss how you would study the degree to which genes and environment contribute to this trait using one of the types of study described in this chapter.

3. Think of your own family, or a family with whom you are well acquainted. Name a physical trait and a psychological trait that the members of the family appear to hold in common. See if you can identify a physical trait and a psychological trait in which the members seem to differ to some degree.

4. Think of an aspect of your culture for which you suspect that a meme exists (assuming for the sake of argument that memes are real). Describe the mechanisms by which this meme would be passed along from generation to generation.

CONNECTING TO LIFE/JOB SKILLS

Behavioral Genetics

Behavioral genetics offers a dynamic and fascinating career path for those who are interested in learning more about the human genome, and how knowledge of the genome can enhance our ability to predict and change aspects of human development and behavior. It is becoming increasingly evident that this information can be used to prevent and cure serious mental illnesses and developmental deviations (see the information in "What's Happening!" regarding the latest findings on the autism spectrum disorders).

Behavioral genetics is primarily a research career (basic research). A behavioral geneticist utilizes genetic research methods and concepts to discern and understand how genes contribute to the origin and extent of individual differences in behavior and functioning. If you wish to pursue a career in behavioral genetics, you will obtain a PhD in psychology (essential for a research career) but also take a large compliment of biology courses, especially those related to genetics.

If you are interested in learning more about this area of psychology, a good starting point for the web site of the Behavior Genetics Association at *www.bga.org*.

WHAT'S HAPPENING!

The Genetic Basis of Autism

Tragically for some parents in the mid-twentieth century, autism once was thought to be caused by "bad parents" and "refrigerator mothers." As brain-imaging techniques have improved, evidence of an organic basis for autism has become more compelling. Our new knowledge of the genetic influences on human development and behavior has yielded a great deal of value in the effort to clarify the causes of the autism spectrum disorders. This is the term used to refer to autism, the pervasive developmental disorders, and Asperger's disorder (a milder form of autism). Those who have Asperger's disorder are generally normal intellectually but have a great deal of difficulty with social and emotional functioning. Evidence from various studies points strongly toward autism being a congenital (present from birth) illness involving damage to structures in the brainstem and limbic system that has a genetic origin.

Visit the following links to learn about some of the research studies that are in progress, and what psychologists and medical doctors are learning from the research.

www.exploringautism.org/genetics/index.htm

depts.washington.edu/autism/

faculty.washington.edu/dawson/CurrentResearchActivities/Genetic.html

OTHER USEFUL WEB SITES

HOW STUFF WORKS—DNA AND GENETICS

www.howstuffworks.com/category.htm?cat=Cell

Visiting Marshall Brain's wonderful site is a great way to consolidate your learning for this fundamental chapter.

GENETICS VIRTUAL LIBRARY

www.ornl.gov/TechResources/Human_Genome/genetics.html

Comprehensive online library of genetic information, affiliated with the Human Genome Project.

NATIONAL INSTITUTE OF MENTAL HEALTH—GENETICS AND MENTAL ILLNESS

www.nimh.nih.gov/research/genetics.htm

This site has more information on one of the most useful and potentially beneficial applications of genetic information to the science of human behavior.

HUMAN GENOME PROJECT

www.ornl.gov/TechResources/Human_Genome/home.html

This is the homepage of the most comprehensive and ambitious project undertaken to map the human genome.

NATIONAL HUMAN GENOME RESEARCH INSTITUTE

www.genome.gov/

This research institute is part of the National Institutes of Health and is dedicated to using genomic information to discover the causes and cures of major genetic diseases.

REFERENCES

Darwin, C. (1859) *On the Origin of Species.* London: Oxford University Press.

Pinker, S. (1999) *How the Mind Works.* New York: W.W. Norton & Company.

Chapter 3

THE NERVOUS SYSTEM AND BEHAVIOR

In this chapter you will become acquainted with the biological basis of mind and behavior.

Communication: The Divisions of the Nervous System

The nervous system is one of the most amazing bodily systems, comprised of cells that are specialized to communicate, called *neurons,* and a number of different kinds of supporting cells, known collectively as *glia* or *glial cells.*

Before we look at the structure and function of the nervous system at the cellular level, it is useful to look at the organization of this bodily communication system briefly. We will start with the two functional divisions of the nervous system—the *central nervous system* (CNS) and the *peripheral nervous system* (PNS). These are two separate anatomical systems that are highly interdependent, constantly exchanging information.

Command Center: The Central Nervous System

The central nervous system is comprised of two major structures, the *brain* and the *spinal cord.* The brain is the bodily organ in which all mental, emotional, and behavioral activity originates. There are specialized areas in the human brain for organizing, interpretating, processing, and storing information, which comes in through all the sense channels. Structures in the brain issue orders to the glands, organs, muscles, and joints.

The brain is protected from injury and damage by several structures. Internally, a *blood-brain barrier* prevents some toxins and poisonous substances from being transmitted into brain tissue by blood vessels. Over the brain, there is a system of protective layers. The *skull* is the outermost and strongest of these layers; its purpose is to lessen the likelihood that blows and insults will injure the brain. Under the skull, two layers of tissue protect the brain from hitting the skull, called the *pia mater* and the *dura mater* (literally the "soft mother" and the "tough mother").

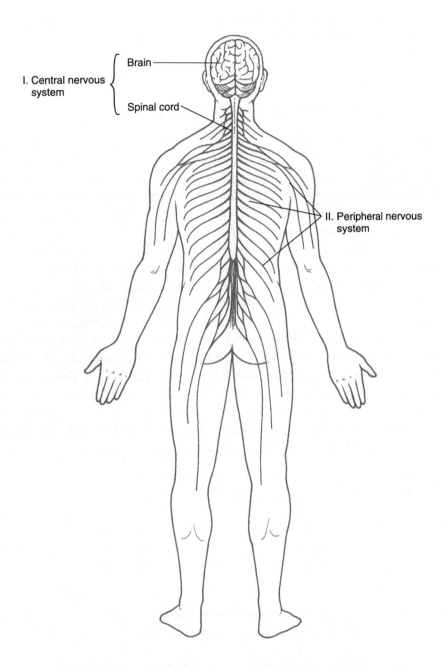

Figure 3.1 The two principal divisions of the human nervous system.

The brain is a marvel of design for many reasons. For example, you have certainly noticed the characteristic wrinkly appearance. The brain is a lot of tissue in a small space. The gray and wrinkled cortex allows room for a great deal of higher cognitive processing—thinking and remembering. Under the cortex are structures responsible for emotion, memory, physical drives, and vital life support functions.

The spinal cord connects the brain to the peripheral nervous system. Not only does it send messages to the organs, muscles, and glands, but it also sends information from the sensory receptor cells and organs to the brain. When the spinal cord is broken, the resulting paralysis is evidence that the brain is no longer receiving information from the regions of the body below the injury. The spinal cord is capable of issuing orders for *reflex* actions but not for *voluntary* (under conscious control) behavior—this type of behavior originates in the brain.

The Peripheral Nervous System

"Peripheral" is derived from the Latin word for "edges." Through a system of spinal and cranial nerves, the peripheral nervous system sends information to and receives information from the brain and spinal cord. The tracts that carry information from the receptors to the spinal cord and brain (the central nervous system) are called *afferent* (roughly equivalent to "sensory") nerves, and those that carry information from the CNS to the muscles and other body structures are called *efferent* (roughly equivalent to "motor") nerves.

The PNS is composed of a series of subdivisions. The broadest division is between the *somatic* and *autonomic nervous systems* (ANS). Most though not all of the somatic tracts are involved in the transmission of information related to voluntary movements or reflexes. The receptors and tracts of the somatic system are found in the skin, muscles, and joints. If you decide to catch or throw a ball, or if your friend tries to give you an affectionate "dope slap" and you duck out of the way spontaneously, the information that allows these actions to occur travels through the somatic tracts. As you can probably tell from the "auto" part of the word "autonomic" the ANS is the main pathway for information going from and to the parts of the body that seem to operate in a "self-regulating" manner—the respiratory, circulatory, digestive, and other systems. That "full feeling" after dinner is a result of autonomic nerves in your stomach sending information to your brain about the distended state of your stomach muscles.

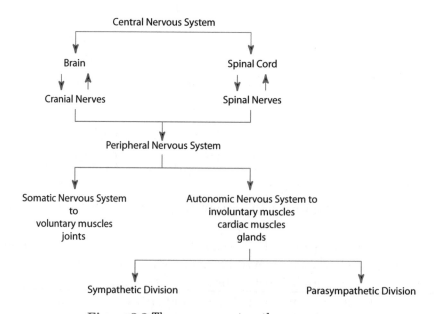

Figure 3.2 The nervous system the easy way

The autonomic nervous system has two of its own subdivisions—the *sympathetic* and *parasympathetic nervous systems*. Both of these divisions manage important, survival-related functions.

To distinguish between the two, think of the sympathetic nervous system as the "crisis-management" division that prepares the body to react to a potentially life-threatening emergency. When you sense that you may be in danger, the sympathetic nervous system uses chemical and electrical signals to organs and glands to make your heart beat faster, the pupils of your eyes dilate, and your respiratory system speed up—all changes that will help you respond to a direct threat. These same changes may also be initiated to a lesser degree by other emotional situations—good or bad.

The parasympathetic nervous system, on the other hand, can be thought of as the system that promotes life-sustaining processes—just as crucial to survival, but survival in a more long-term sense. The parasympathetic nervous system sends messages to glands and internal organs that promote digestion, rest, and other restorative functions.

Communication I: The Endocrine System

In discussing communications within the body, some mention must be given to the *endocrine* system. It is a system of specialized glands that secretes chemicals (hormones) that influence mood, body structure, and behavior. (If you are having a hard time imagining this, just think of the changes that puberty brings, all of which are a result of changes in and secretions from endocrine glands.) There are three varieties of hormones:

- *Steroids*. Chemicals synthesized from cholesterol that promote growth (think of the illicit steroid drugs that some people take to build muscles), sexual and reproductive functions, and healing of body tissues.
- *Peptides*. A hormone that functions to stimulate the production of other hormones. Oxytocin is a well-known peptide hormone that stimulates the start of labor and lactation in pregnant females.
- *Amino acids*. Amino acids are a class of simple organic compound based on carbon, oxygen, hydrogen, and nitrogen—often these compounds are referred to as "the building blocks of life." Adrenaline is one of the amino-acid-derived hormones.

Some peptides and amino-acid-derived hormones lead an interesting "double life"—they can function in the bloodstream as hormones or in the nervous system as neurotransmitters (discussed at length shortly.) The major glands of the endocrine system are listed in Table 3-1, along with a brief description of the hormones that they secrete and the actions of those hormones.

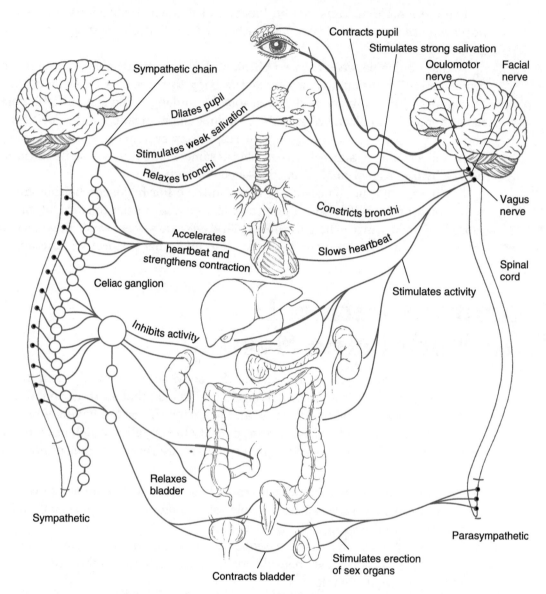

Figure 3.3 The two branches of the autonomic nervous system. Nerves of the sympathetic system (left) prepare the body for an emergency. Note that the system consists of nerves before the sympathetic chain of ganglia (preganglionic nerves) and after the sympathetic chain (postganglionic nerves). Nerves of the parasympathetic system (right) return the body to normal. Many of these nerves arise from cranial nerves at the upper spinal cord.

TABLE 3-1
THE ENDOCRINE SYSTEM

Gland and Hormone Produced/Secreted	Function(s) of Gland and Hormone
Pineal Melatonin	Regulates circadian (daily) cycles of sleep and wakefulness
Pituitary Growth hormone Prolactin Oxytocin Follicle stimulating hormone (FSH)/ Luteinizing hormone (LH)	Regulates several other glands (sex glands). Promotes growth in childhood Stimulates milk production in pregnant females Causes muscle contractions (milk let-down, labor) Functions in both males and females in the generation of gametes (sex cells) and reproductive function
Thyroid Thyroxin	Regulates body metabolism
Parathyroid Parathormone	Regulates metabolism of calcium and phosphate (important for the function of nervous system and other organs)
Thymus Thymosin	Establishes immunity, processes immune system cells (lymphocytes; t-cells)
Adrenal Adrenaline (epinephrine) Norepinephrine	Regulation of stress response; interacts with immune system Both of these act simultaneously as hormones and neurotransmitters and influence the stress reaction, mood, and immune function
Pancreas Insulin	Regulates blood-sugar levels and influences hunger and eating behavior
Ovary Estrogen Progesterone	Produces ova (egg cells) Both of these act in the female reproductive system to generate and promote reproductive function
Testes Testosterone	Regulates male secondary sex characteristics; influences sex drive in males and females

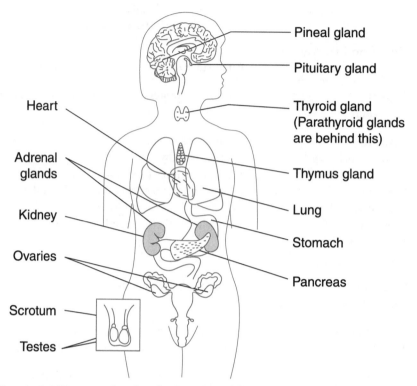

Figure 3.4 Diagram showing the location of the major endocrine glands: pineal, pituitary, thyroid, parathyroid, thymus, pancreas (part), lining of the small intestine, adrenal glands, and sex glands.

Communication II: Fundamental Components of the Nervous System

The nervous system manages the task of communication not through a relatively simple use of tissue and chemicals (as does the endocrine system) but through a more complex set-up comprised of specialized cells able to generate both chemicals and electric impulses.

If you have taken a biology course, you may already be familiar with the neuron—the key cellular component in the nervous system. This cell is able to receive and send information to other cells. Neurons form long chains and networks that conduct information in the form of electrochemical messages between the brain and the rest of the body. There are many, many types of neurons in the brain and body, but they can be broadly classified in three major varieties:

- *Sensory neurons* convert physical energy into one of eight types of sense messages (see Chapter 4) and carry that information to the brain. Your brain does not know or understand any information from the environment directly. When light strikes one of the millions of cells that makes up your retina, that light is converted into an electrochemical impulse that your brain can understand. The sensory neurons make up the afferent tracts in the nervous system, mentioned earlier in this chapter.

- *Motor neurons* convey information from the brain to the muscles and organs, and as you can now probably guess, make up the previously mentioned efferent tracts of the nervous system. When you use your fingers to type a paper or an e-mail to a friend, millions of motor neurons are activated.
- *Interneurons,* by far the most plentiful of the three types of neurons, carry on communication *between* neurons. Most of the neurons in your brain, for example, are interneurons.

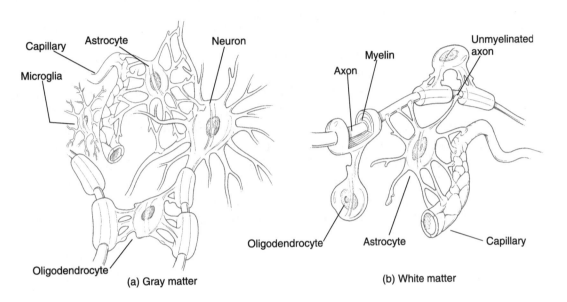

Figure 3.5 The neurons and glial cells of the nervous system. (a) The relationships of the two cell types in the gray matter of the brain and spinal cord. (b) The relationships in the white matter.

Neurons are the "stars of the show," but every star depends upon a good supporting cast. The supporting cast in this show outnumbers the stars by a ratio of almost ten to one. These cells in the nervous system are the glia (plural form) also known as glial cells and they are composed mainly of fat. These cells have little direct involvement in the sending or receiving of information but perform a variety of important support functions, which include

- Providing structural support.
- Speeding up communications from neuron to neuron (glia that produce a substance called *myelin* help with this).
- Healing injuries and fighting infection.
- Removing waste products and dead neurons.

The Structure and Function of a Typical Neuron

Part 1: Structure—Neural Anatomy

There are many types of neurons in the body. All neurons share some features in common with other body cells including:

- A *cell membrane,* to hold the neuron together.
- A *nucleus,* containing the chromosomes and genetic material of the cell. Most neurons are created before birth, and as far as we know most do not undergo *mitosis* ("splitting") and reproduction after the prenatal period. You are born with almost all the neurons you will ever have. Growth does continue, though. The human brain and nervous system are highly *plastic* during the first eight years of life, developing many new synaptic connections to allow for learning, memory, and development of new functions.
- *Organelles* are the small structures that carry out the basic life processes of a cell, including protein production, metabolism, and excretion of waste products. Mitochondria and Golgi bodies are two types of organelles. These are mainly contained in the *cell body* or *soma* (see Figure 3.6).

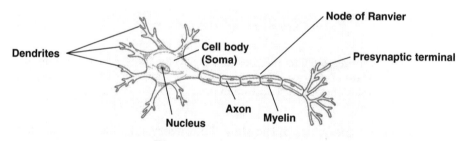

Figure 3.6 A motor neuron.

Neurons are also highly specialized for communication and therefore are very different from other body cells in some key ways as well:

- Neurons have specialized extensions for receiving information—these are called *dendrites*. They are attached to the cell body, as you can see from Figure 3.6. The dendrites have special openings on their surfaces, called *receptors*, which can receive chemical messages from neighboring neurons.
- Neurons also have specialized extensions for sending information, called *axons*. The axon is a single, extra-long "arm." Some axons are coated with myelin, the fatty substance produced by glia that helps to speed transmission of messages. Motor neurons, for example, commonly have myelin on their axons. (The disease known as *multiple sclerosis* is directly caused by a deterioration of this substance.) There are nodes or gaps in the myelin, called *nodes of Ranvier,* and the electrical signal jumps from node to node on its way to the synapse.

- The ends of the axons form junctions with the dendrites of adjoining neurons. A very tiny gap separates the axon of the sending neuron from the dendrite of the receiving neuron. These are called *synapses*. The presynaptic ends of the axon contain tiny sacs of chemicals (*vesicles*) that will be transmitted across the synapse to the receptors in the dendrites of the postsynaptic cell (see Figure 3.7.) These chemicals are called *neurotransmitters*.

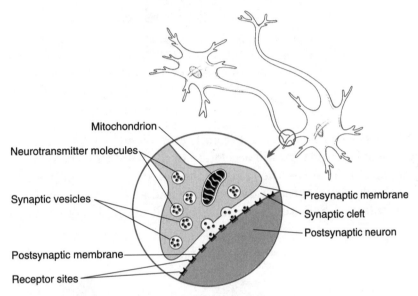

Figure 3.7 An axon releases neurotransmitters at the synapse.

The whole design of the neuron facilitates a process of electrochemical communication, which is described next.

Part 2: Function—The Action Potential

The neuron is designed to communicate—to send and receive information, to and from other neurons and other parts of the body. The communication is an *electrochemical process*; that is, it depends on the activity of electrically charged chemicals in the nervous system. In most parts of the nervous system, the chemicals involved in transmission are sodium, potassium, chloride, and calcium.

We say that the chemicals in the nervous system are electrically charged because the atoms that compose the chemicals are in an *ionic* state. Recall from introductory chemistry that ions are atoms that either lack one or more electrons (which causes them to be positively charged) or have one or more extra electrons (causing a negative charge.)

Neurons that are not transmitting or receiving information are said to be in a state of *resting potential*, and their internal electrochemical state is oppositely charged relative the surrounding outside area. Typically, the internal charge of the neuron is negative. This state of resting potential is maintained by a very slow exchange of ions through openings in the cell membrane—a few ions drift in and out, but not enough to change this *polarization* (opposing charge) of the inside relative to the outside of the cell.

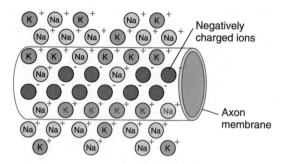

Figure 3.8 The ionic imbalance between the inside and outside environments of the resting nerve cell. The large number of negatively charged ions within the cell is attributed to protein molecules. The number of sodium ions outside the cells is greater than the number of potassium ions, thereby contributing to the overall positive charge.

When a resting neuron is sufficiently stimulated by adjacent neurons, it will *depolarize*—the rate of ion exchange will accelerate to the point that the internal charge of the cell will be changed to positive, the same as the outside. This brief positive charge, which travels from the dendrite, through the cell body and axon, and down to the synapse, is called the *action potential*. Sometimes psychologists call this *firing*—they say that the neuron "fires."

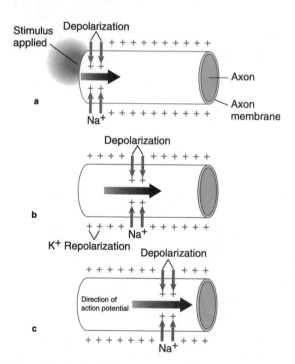

Figure 3.9 The action potential in a nerve cell. (a) A stimulus is applied to the membrane, and sodium ions (+) rush into the cell; the membrane loses its polarity, thereby generating an action potential. (b) The adjacent membrane area is depolarized by this action, and the action potential is propagated; meanwhile the original area undergoes repolarization with the accumulation of potassium ions (+) so it can "fire" again. (c) The action potential continues down the axon as successive areas undergo depolarization. Eventually, the action potential will pass into another nerve cell or a muscle cell.

Here are three important facts to know about the action potential:

- It is referred to as an all-or-nothing process. There is no such thing as firing weakly or strongly. Either the neuron will fire or it won't. This is the *all-or-none law*. The level of stimulation required for the action potential to occur is called the *stimulus threshold*. Think of a row of dominos lined up on one edge—if you blow on the first domino hard enough, it will fall, causing all the others to fall afterward. If you do not blow on it with sufficient strength, nothing will happen.
- The action potential is always followed by a brief resting period—called a *refractory period*. During the refractory period, no amount of stimulation will cause the neuron to fire. The neuron is said to be *hyperpolarized* (very strongly polarized). It is reestablishing its normal resting polarized levels of ions.
- The action potential enables the chemical messengers, the neurotransmitters to be released from the vesicles and travel from the presynaptic (sending) neuron to the receptors of the postsynaptic (receiving) neuron. This is called *synaptic transmission*. When the action potential ends, most of the molecules of the neurotransmitter are reabsorbed by the presynaptic neuron in a process called *reuptake*. They are recycled—used again and again.

The neurotransmitters *are* the messages being sent from neuron to neuron. There are about sixty different types of neurotransmitters. Depending on the situation in which the action potential occurs, the effect of the neurotransmitter on the neighboring neuron can be either *excitatory* (promoting the firing of the receiving cell) or *inhibitory* (preventing the firing of the receiving cell). Table 3-2 below provides you with basic information about the most important neurotransmitters.

TABLE 3-2
NEUROTRANSMITTERS AND THEIR ROLES

Neurotransmitter	Role	Lack of Causes	Oversupply Causes
Acetylcholine	Muscle function (contraction); memory	Dementia (Alzheimer's Disease)	Convulsions (spider bite/nerve gas)
Dopamine	Movement; sensory processes; cognition	Tremors/sensory deficits (Parkinson's Disease)	Hallucinations/delusions (methamphetamine addiction)
Endorphins	Inhibit pain; promote good feelings	Stress; pain	Euphoria; dependence (opiate addiction)
Gaba	Lowers activity levels in brain; involved in visual processing	Visual deficits (fetal alcohol syndrome); anxiety disorders	Sedation (alcohol/sedative addiction)
Norepinephrine	Memory; learning; "fight or flight" reaction	Depression	Anxiety
Serotonin	Mood and sleep regulation	Depression; aggression	Mood problems (manic episodes)
Substance P	Transmits pain information	Lack of sensitivity to tissue damage	Pain; stress

Imaging the Brain

Some modern brain scientists have proposed that the human brain actually arose from the integration of function of several primitive organs. In other words, it would be in a sense more appropriate to think of the brain (so to speak) as a complex yet smoothly integrated *organ system*. This view opens up some useful avenues for practical application. Consider the possibility, for example, that some of the serious mental illnesses (such as schizophrenia) are caused by disruptions in the communications between the components of the system. This is but one of the possibilities that the scientific study of the brain allows us to test. Our chances of bringing relief to those who suffer from such illnesses have improved greatly over the last fifty years because of innovations in our ability to study the brain.

In fact, the greatest gift of our modern technology of brain imaging has been to allow us to know better how parts of the brain impact our functioning in daily life. The most commonly used brain imaging techniques are mentioned in Table 3-3.

TABLE 3-3
METHODS FOR IMAGING THE BRAIN

Technique	How It Works	Can Be Used For
EEG/MEG (Electroencephalography/ Magnetoencephalography	Electrodes are placed on the scalp. These provide a real-time log of brain wave activity.	Studying brain activity changes during sleep
CAT (computerized axial tomography)	Uses an X-ray tube that rotates around the patient taking many pictures. The pictures are reconstructed by a computer in axial slices (like slices of bread).	Detecting lesions or tumors of the brain
PET (positron emission tomography)	A very low level of radioactive substance is injected into the bloodstream. A scanner is used to detect the activity in the brain by tracking the radiation produced.	Determining areas of the brain that may be highly active during cognitive tasks, emotional reactions, or physical processes
MRI/fMRI (magnetic resonance imaging/ functional magnetic resonance imaging	Using a powerful magnet, it tracks and images the protons in the nuclei of hydrogen atoms in the water that makes up most of the body.	Making detailed images of brain structures and determining which areas of the brain are most active in cognition, emotion and physical processes.
DTI (diffusion tensor imaging)	Similar to MRI but also tracks the random motion of the water molecules in the body.	Tracking the communications between different areas of the brain during cognition, emotion, and physical processes.

The Structures and Functions of the Brain

Psychologists typically divide the brain into three major regions:

- The *brainstem*. This area, the lowest part of the brain (or the top of the spinal cord, depending on how you look at it) contains basic structures of life support along with nuclei (clusters of neurons) that control sensory/motor integration.
- The *limbic system*. Several structures on each side of the brain involved in producing life-sustaining drives, emotion, and memory.
- The *cerebral cortex or cerebrum*. When you think of the brain, you most likely think of this region, split into two specialized hemispheres, subdivided into four primary regions (lobes), and involved in most complex thinking processes, remembering and interpreting emotions.

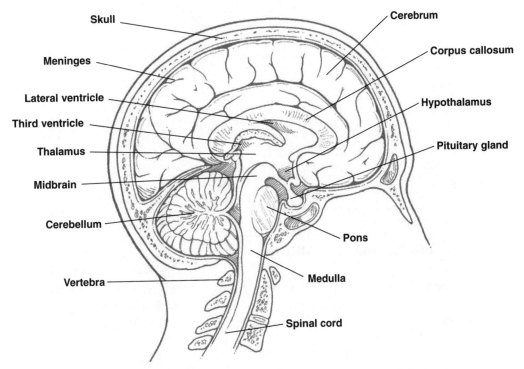

Figure 3.10 Cross section showing the major structures of the brain.

What's in the Brainstem?

The brainstem is subdivided into two regions, the *hindbrain* and the *midbrain*. For ease of reference, the important brainstem structures and the subdivision in which they are located are listed in Table 3-4.

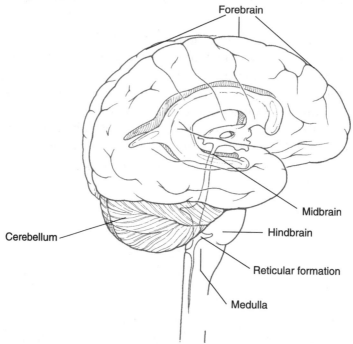

Figure 3.11 The brain viewed from an evolutionary perspective.

TABLE 3-4
STRUCTURES IN THE BRAINSTEM

Brainstem Structure	Subdivision	Function
Medulla (medulla oblongata)	Hindbrain	Controls basic autonomic functions—circulation, breathing, digestion
Pons ("bridge")	Hindbrain	Relay station to hindbrain from forebrain (cerebral cortex)
Cerebellum	Hindbrain	Coordination of motor function, integration of multiple sensory stimuli (the ability to drive depends heavily on the cerebellum)
Reticular formation (reticular activating system or RAS)	Hindbrain	Reticular means netlike—this network of neurons is involved in producing the general level of arousal experienced during stages of consciousness from deep sleep to wide awake
Substantia nigra	Midbrain	Through the action of dopamine, is crucial for control of motor function.
Tectum ("roof")	Midbrain	Orientation of response to sensory stimuli.
Superior and inferior colliculi	Midbrain	Responses to auditory and visual stimuli
Nucleus ruber ("red nucleus")	Midbrain	Integration of voluntary motor functioning (i.e., walking)

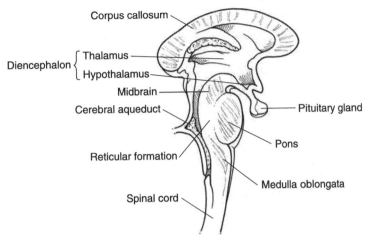

Figure 3.12 Structures of the human brain stem. The major structures in descending order are the diencephalon, midbrain, pons, and medulla oblongata.

The Limbic System

You may have noticed that the brainstem is divided into hindbrain and midbrain and wondered about the location of the forebrain. Everything else in the brain is classified the *forebrain*, which has two major regions, the limbic system and the cerebral cortex.

The limbic system has been called the reptilian brain by scientists of a bygone era. This is because the structures of the limbic system are the essential structures for animal survival—satisfying biological needs (eating and drinking), fostering reproduction to continue the genetic line (sex), and self-preservation (aggression and memory). You have probably heard the incorrect generalization about the "walnut-sized" brain of the dinosaur. This is not strictly true, but the brains of these ancient reptiles were comprised of little more than a limbic system and a very small amount of higher cortical tissue. The brain of a modern reptile is not radically different.

The limbic system is organized bilaterally and symmetrically under the two halves of the cerebral cortex and consists of the following structures:

- *Hypothalamus.* A vital regulatory structure in charge of the autonomic nervous system; physical drives such as hunger, thirst, and the sex drive; the pituitary gland; and our cycles of consciousness. (The hypothalamus contains the *suprachiasmic nucleus*, which is connected to the *pineal gland*, both of which work together to regulate our patterns of sleep and wakefulness.)
- *Thalamus.* Structure that processes, integrates, and distributes all sensory information (except olfactory, or smell, stimuli) to the cerebral cortex. The thalamus also influences attention and is one of the brain regions that have been implicated as a possible site of damage that brings about the potentially very debilitating autism spectrum disorders.
- *Hippocampus.* Vital structure in the formation and storage of new memories. The protagonist of the popular recent movie *Memento* is a fairly accurate representation of some of the possible consequences of damage to the hippocampus.
- *Amygdala.* An almond-shaped structure implicated in a number of crucial emotion-memory responses. For example, the amygdala promotes the associations between

unpleasant emotions—fear, sadness, anger, and memory for the stimuli that induced those emotions. It is easy to see how this would be useful for an organism's survival.

- *Basal ganglia.* A ganglion (plural: ganglia) is a group of neurons working together. The basal ganglia are involved in planning and producing movement. When they are damaged, as is the case in Parkinson's disease, movements may become jerky, hampered by tremors or impossible due to muscular rigidity.

The Cerebral Cortex

The uppermost, and by far the largest region of the brain, is the cerebrum. In human beings, this is an enormous region, about a quarter of an inch thick and about nine square feet in area. It fits within the confines of our very small skulls by virtue of the complicated folding that we see as gyri (bumps) and sulci (folds). The outer layer of the cortex is the *gray matter*. Gray matter is mostly glia, neuronal cell bodies, and axons. Under the gray matter is the *white matter*—myelinated axons that reach between the lobes of the cerebral cortex and other parts of the brain.

The cerebral cortex has been studied and divided into four lobes, based primarily upon the functions of each (see Figure 3.13).

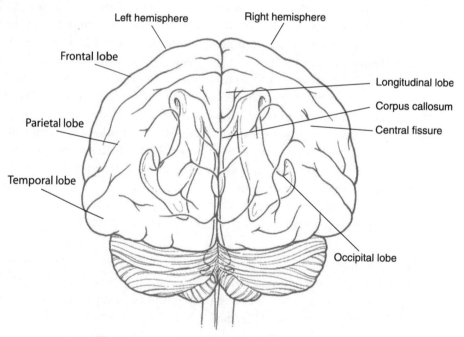

Figure 3.13 The anatomy of the cerebral cortex.

From the back to the front, these are the lobes of the cerebral cortex:

- *Occipital lobes.* The human brain dedicates about 40 percent of its tissue mass to the processing of vision. The occipital lobes are entirely devoted to this sense and contain the *primary visual cortex.*

- *Temporal lobes.* These lobes contain additional visual processing areas, along with the *primary auditory cortex.* Toward the front part of the brain, the temporal lobes contain important language processing areas also.
- *Parietal lobes.* These lobes contain an interest area devoted to processing touch information from the rest of the body—the *primary somatosensory cortex.* The primary somatosensory cortex possesses an interesting configuration for the body, devoting the largest share of its area to the hands, fingers, face, and lips. This makes sense because in fact we use and move these parts of our body much more than the other parts.
- *Frontal lobes.* Human beings possess the largest frontal lobes of all animals on the planet. This area of the brain is specialized for planning and exercising voluntary movement (the *primary motor cortex* is located here). On the left side of the brain, along its border with the temporal lobe, the frontal lobe contains important language processing areas. About 30 percent of our brains is the very foremost part of the frontal lobes, the *prefrontal cortex.* This region appears to be crucial in the management of many processes that drive human intelligence—focusing and maintaining attention, interpreting social information, and interpreting our own emotions.

Scattered across the cerebral cortex are several important *association areas.* In the association areas, complex sensory processing occurs, and sensory and motor information is combined.

The Two-Sided Brain

Many people who have not taken psychology in school and are not otherwise knowledgeable about the brain know that the brain is divided into right and left hemispheres, that the right side of the brain controls motor and sensory function on the left and the left side controls the same processes on the right, and that the right and left sides play different roles in our cognitive processing. These things are all true. Many people have the mistaken idea that some people are "left-brained" (the logical people) and others are "right-brained" (the artistic people). This is not true.

The cerebral cortex is divided into two *hemispheres.* These hemispheres are in constant communication through the function of a large bundle of axons running between them, the *corpus callosum.* The left hemisphere of the brain is almost entirely responsible for language functioning, speech abilities, and verbal memory. The right hemisphere handles nonverbal data, pattern and face recognition, spatial information, and interpreting emotional cues. Through the study of persons who have had their corpus callosa severed for control of severe seizures, we know that the right brain cannot read words because it needs to communicate with the left side of the brain to retrieve the meaning of the word from memory (Sperry 1967). We know from studying a small group of people who have had strokes in the right temporal lobe that the ability to recognize faces is located there (Humphreys 1999). These individuals cannot recognize photos of familiar people or even their own faces unless they are looking in a mirror—because they see the mirror, not because they recognize their own faces.

It is clear that no one depends more on one hemisphere than the other—normal brain function depends on an integrated operation of all regions of the brain. We use all of our brains (not just 10 percent) and we use both sides to know and experience the world and to learn from our experience.

Connecting Through Chapter Review

WORD-STUDY CONNECTION

Write each of these words on index cards and write their definitions on the opposite side. Use them to memorize the information in the chapter, and try to sort them into piles based on relationships (parts of the cerebrum, parts and functions of the neuron, etc.).

action potential
adrenaline
afferent
all-or-none law
amino acids
amygdala
association areas
axon
autonomic nervous system
basal ganglia
blood-brain barrier
brain
brainstem
cell body
central nervous system
cerebral cortex
cerebrum
cerebellum
colliculi
corpus callosum
dendrite
depolarize
dura mater
efferent
electrochemical process
endocrine gland
excitatory
firing
forebrain
frontal lobes
glia/glial cells
gray matter
hemisphere

hindbrain
hippocampus
hormone
hyperpolarized
hypothalamus
inhibitory
interneuron
ionic
limbic system
medulla
mitosis
midbrain
motor neuron
multiple sclerosis
myelin
neuron
neurotransmitters
nodes of Ranvier
nucleus ruber (red nucleus)
occipital lobes
organelles
organ system
parasympathetic nervous
  system
parietal lobes
peptides
peripheral nervous system
pia mater
pineal gland
plastic/plasticity
polarization
pons
prefrontal cortex

primary auditory cortex
primary motor cortex
primary somatosensory
  cortex
primary visual cortex
receptors
reflex
refractory period
resting potential
reticular activating system
  (RAS)
reuptake
sensory neuron
skull
soma
somatic nervous system
spinal cord
steroids
stimulus threshold
substantia nigra
suprachiasmic nucleus
sympathetic nervous
  system
synapse
synaptic transmission
tectum
temporal lobes
thalamus
vesicles
voluntary
white matter

SELF-TEST CONNECTION

PART A. *Completion*
Write in the word that correctly completes each statement.

1. _____ are the supporting cells of the nervous system, and _____ are the cells that are specialized for communication with the body.
2. The central nervous system is composed of two major structures, the _____ and the _____ .
3. The _____ helps to prevent toxins and other dangerous substances from reaching and damaging the delicate tissues of the brain.
4. The _____ is designed to protect the brain from injury from blows and insults.
5. The spinal cord controls _____—actions that are *not* under conscious control.
6. The _____ tracts of the peripheral nervous system carry sensory information from the sense receptors into the central nervous system.
7. The skin, muscles, and joints of the body contain the tracts of the _____ nervous system.
8. Digestion is a self-regulating process and therefore is under the control of the _____ nervous system.
9. The _____ nervous system promotes rest and restorative functions.
10. The glands of the _____ system secrete hormones into the bloodstream.
11. The three types of hormones are steroids, amino acids, and _____ .
12. _____ is a hormone that can also act as a neurotransmitter.
13. _____ neurons convey electrochemical information from the muscles and joints to the spinal cord and brain.
14. _____ are the most plentiful type of neuron in the nervous system.
15. The _____ in a neuron manufacture protein, control cellular metabolism, and remove waste products.
16. Some axons are coated with _____ , a fatty substance that speeds transmission and is manufactured by the glial cells.
17. Neurotransmitters are held within the _____ of the neuron and are released when a(n) _____ occurs.
18. Charged _____ of sodium and potassium drift slowly in and out of the cell membrane of the neuron when the neuron is in a state of _____ .
19. For an action potential to occur, the neuron must _____ so that the electrical charge is the same on the inside and the outside of the cell.
20. For an action potential to occur, the stimulation of the neuron must exceed the _____ .
21. An _____ neurotransmitter will work to prevent the receiving cell from firing.
22. _____ is a neurotransmitter that is needed for visual processing.
23. _____ uses X-rays to take pictures of the brain in axial "slices."
24. The _____ is the structure located in the brainstem that acts as a "bridge" to other regions of the brain.
25. The _____ is heavily involved in activities that require the management of multiple sensory stimuli such as driving.
26. The structure that is in charge of the pituitary gland is the _____ .
27. The thalamus integrates information from every sense except _____ .

28. Severe amnesia is one possible result of damage to the limbic system structure called the _____ .

29. The _____ is the limbic system structure that is involved in the planning and production of movement.

30. The _____ is composed of myelinated axons that help to connect the lobes of the cerebral cortex.

31. The primary visual cortex is located in the _____ lobes.

32. The _____ in the parietal lobes gives most of its tissue to processing the sensations of the hands and face.

33. The _____ makes up about 30 percent of the human brain.

34. Sensory and motor functions are combined in the _____ of the cerebral cortex.

35. Language functions are located almost entirely in the _____ .

36. A stroke that occurs in the right temporal lobe can cause an individual to lose his or her ability to _____ .

PART B. Multiple Choice
Circle the letter of the item that correctly completes the statement.

1. A specialized cell that allows communication between different parts of the body is called a _____ .
   (a) a glial cell   (b) a neuron
   (c) a neurotransmitter   (d) a gland

2. The _____ nervous system is the command center of the body.
   (a) peripheral   (b) central
   (c) somatic   (d) autonomic

3. The _____ literally means "tough mother." It protects the brain from the skull.
   (a) glial mater   (b) pineal mater
   (c) dura mater   (d) pia mater

4. The _____ tracts of the peripheral nervous system carry information from the brain to the muscles and joints.
   (a) efferent   (b) afferent
   (c) parasympathetic   (d) autonomic

5. When a crisis occurs, the sympathetic nervous system will make all of the following happen except _____ .
   (a) a faster heartbeat   (b) dilated pupils
   (c) increased respiration   (d) faster digestion

6. Hormones that the body synthesizes from cholesterol are classified as _____ .
   (a) amino acids   (b) steroids
   (c) peptides   (d) GABAs

7. The pineal gland produces a hormone called _____ that is important for the regulation of sleep-wake cycles.
   (a) FHS   (b) parathormone
   (c) melatonin   (d) oxytocin

8. _____ neurons convert physical stimuli into electrochemical messages.
   (a) Motor   (b) Glial
   (c) Inter   (d) Sensory

9. All of the following are functions of glial cells *except* _____ .
   (a) removing waste
   (b) releasing neurotransmitters
   (c) providing support
   (d) speeding up messages
10. Regular body cells and neurons *both* have _____ .
    (a) mitochondria
    (b) dendrites
    (c) myelin
    (d) axons
11. _____ is also referred to as the "firing" of the neuron.
    (a) Reuptake
    (b) An action potential
    (c) An emission
    (d) A polarization
12. A deficiency of _____ can cause symptoms very similar to those experienced by persons with Parkinson's disease.
    (a) acetylcholine
    (b) substance P
    (c) dopamine
    (d) GABA
13. The brain-imaging technique that works by tracking a weakly radioactive substance as it travels through the bloodstream is called _____ .
    (a) PET
    (b) fMRI
    (c) CAT
    (d) MEG
14. The area of the brain that contains the structures responsible for maintaining basic life support functions such as respiration is the _____ .
    (a) limbic system
    (b) brainstem
    (c) basal ganglia
    (d) cerebrum
15. The _____ controls motor coordination and tasks that require the management of multiple sensory stimuli.
    (a) hypothalamus
    (b) medulla
    (c) reticular formation
    (d) cerebellum
16. The general level of arousal during various states of consciousness is controlled by the _____ .
    (a) reticular formation
    (b) basal ganglia
    (c) amygdala
    (d) red nucleus
17. The substantia nigra is found in the _____ and depends heavily on the action of the neurotransmitter _____ .
    (a) hindbrain; acetylcholine
    (b) hindbrain; substance P
    (c) midbrain; dopamine
    (d) midbrain; GABA
18. The _____ or "roof" of the brainstem is responsible for helping an organism to orient to sensory stimuli.
    (a) red nucleus
    (b) tectum
    (c) pons
    (d) medulla
19. The _____ processes and integrates stimuli from all of our senses except smell.
    (a) amygdala
    (b) hypothalamus
    (c) thalamus
    (d) tectum
20. The hypothalamus contains the _____ , which contributes to the regulation of our sleep-wake cycles.
    (a) red nucleus
    (b) basal ganglia
    (c) pons
    (d) suprachiasmic nucleus
21. Damage to the _____ can cause amnesia.
    (a) occipital lobes
    (b) hippocampus
    (c) hypothalamus
    (d) basal ganglia

22. Damage to the _____ can cause symptoms very similar to those experienced by persons with Parkinson's disease.
    (a) hippocampus   (b) medulla
    (c) hypothalamus   (d) basal ganglia
23. The _____ is divided into four lobes based on function.
    (a) limbic system   (b) cerebral cortex
    (c) cerebellum   (d) brainstem
24. The primary visual cortex is located in the _____ .
    (a) frontal lobes   (b) parietal lobes
    (c) temporal lobes   (d) occipital lobes
25. The _____ contain areas for auditory and visual processing.
    (a) frontal lobes   (b) parietal lobes
    (c) temporal lobes   (d) occipital lobes

PART C. Modified True-False

If the statement is true, write "T" for the answer. If the statement is incorrect, change the underlined expression to one that will make the statement true.

1. The nervous system is comprised of cells that are specialized to communicate, called neurons.
2. The two major functional divisions of the nervous system are the somatic nervous system (SNS) and the sympathetic nervous system (SPNS).
3. The peripheral nervous system is comprised of two major structures, the brain and the spinal cord.
4. The dura mater is the outermost and strongest of the layers that protect the brain from outside injury.
5. The tracts that carry information from the receptors to the central nervous system are referred to as the afferent tracts.
6. The parasympathetic nervous system is like the "crisis-management" division that prepares the body to react to life-threatening emergencies.
7. Oxytocin is a peptide hormone that helps to stimulate the start of labor and lactation in females.
8. The thymus is the gland that produces thyroxin, a hormone that helps to regulate metabolism.
9. Adrenaline can act as both a hormone in the bloodstream and a neurotransmitter in the nervous system.
10. Sensory neurons convey information from the brain to the muscles and organs and make up the efferent tracts of the nervous system.
11. In the nervous system neurons outnumber glia by a ratio of almost ten to one.
12. The human nervous system is highly plastic during the first years of life, developing many new neurons to allow for the development of new functions.
13. Neurons have specialized extensions for receiving information called dendrites.
14. Motor neurons commonly have myelin on their axons.
15. A very tiny gap called a synapse separates the dendrite of the sending neuron from the axon of the receiving neuron.
16. The inside of a neuron that is in resting potential has the same charge as the outside.
17. The all-or-none law states that neurons fire either weakly or strongly.

18. When the action potential reaches the synapse, the vesicles release <u>hormones</u> in order to send the electrochemical message to the next neuron.
19. <u>GABA</u> is the neurotransmitter that is important for lowering levels of activity in the brain.
20. MRI uses a <u>magnet</u> to make pictures of the brain.
21. The <u>cerebral cortex</u> is involved in producing life-sustaining drives, emotion, and memory.
22. The medulla oblongata controls <u>basic life support functions</u>.
23. <u>The substantia nigra, the red nucleus, and the tectum are all</u> located in the hindbrain.
24. The <u>hypothalamus</u> is in charge of the pituitary gland.
25. <u>The hippocampus, amygdala, and basal ganglia</u> are parts of they limbic system.
26. <u>Gray matter</u> is made of myelinated axons that reach between the lobes of the cerebral cortex and other parts of the brain.
27. The <u>temporal</u> lobes contain visual and language processing areas and the primary auditory cortex.
28. The primary somatosensory cortex devotes the largest share of its area to the <u>arms, legs, and torso of the human body</u>.
29. Human beings possess the largest <u>parietal lobes</u>—the areas specialized for planning and exercising voluntary movement—of all animals.
30. Humans <u>prefer to use one hemisphere of the cerebral cortex over the other</u> in thinking and processing sensory inputs.

PART D. Chart Completions

Fill in the missing information in each of the charts. One row is completed in each chart as an example

PARTS AND SUBDIVISIONS OF THE NERVOUS SYSTEM

Structure or Subdivision	Located in	Function
Spinal Cord	Central nervous system	Controls reflex functions and conduit to the brain
		Controls all divisions and functions of the nervous system
Autonomic Nervous System		
	Peripheral nervous system	Controls most voluntary movements
Sympathetic Nervous System	Autonomic nervous system	
		Controls long-term, life-sustaining bodily functions

PARTS AND FUNCTIONS OF THE NEURON

Part	Function
Cell body	Contains nucleus and organelles
Dendrite	
	Sends information to neighboring neurons
	Speeds transmission of messages from neuron to neuron
Vesicles	
Synapse	
	Chemical messenger contained in the neuron

NEUROTRANSMITTER OR HORMONE?

Chemical Name	Classification	Function
GABA	Neurotransmitter	Lowers brain activity; visual processing
Thyroxin		Regulates metabolic processes
	Hormone	Produces sex cells
Dopamine		
		Inhibits pain, promotes good feelings
		Muscle contractions—labor, milk let-down
Serotonin		
Melatonin		
Insulin	Hormone	
		Transmits sensations of pain
Acetylcholine		
	Neurotransmitter/hormone	

BRAIN ANATOMY

Structure	Location	Function
Amygdala	Forebrain/limbic system	Enhances memory for emotional stimuli; generates aggressive impulses
	Hindbrain/brainstem	"Bridge" from cerebral cortex to hindbrain
Red nucleus	Midbrain/brainstem	
	Forebrain/cerebral cortex	Location of the primary visual cortex
Reticular Formation		Regulates brain arousal for different states of consciousness
		Formation and storage of new memories
Cerebellum		
		Planning and exercising voluntary movement
Thalamus		
Medulla	Hindbrain/brainstem	
		Location of primary auditory cortex
Basal ganglia	Forebrain/limbic system	

CONNECTING TO CONCEPTS

Review the chapter and then write down your thoughts about the following questions.

1. Imagine that you are walking to the bus stop on your way to school and you see the last bus that will get you there on time pulling up. You are almost a block away. How will the divisions and parts of your nervous system function in helping you to reach the bus in time to get to school?
2. A neuron in the basal ganglia is just about to receive a signal from a neighboring neuron. Describe the process of its action potential, and be sure to include the neurotransmitter that is involved in the firing of this neuron.
3. List three facts that you have learned in this chapter about the brain and nervous system that you think are important and/or are especially interesting to you.
4. Describe one of the new brain-imaging technologies, and list at least two questions you would like to see this kind of technology used to help to answer in the next decade or two.

5. You are starting to get hungry. Describe how your brain operates in generating this feeling and how it will help you to satisfy the need for food.

CONNECTING TO LIFE/JOB SKILLS

Careers That Require Neuroscience Knowledge

Many careers are founded upon a solid understanding of the functioning of the human nervous system. We will mention just two here, but you can use the career-related web sites provided in this book to find information on many other careers that require or seek to expand our knowledge of the nervous system.

An *occupational therapist* (OT) helps to retrain those with disabilities to live independently and reenter school or the work force. To understand and fully utilize the patient's capabilities, the OT must know the brain and nervous system. Courses in introductory psychology, human development, and abnormal psychology are required in almost all OT programs. To find out more about this career, go to the web site of the American Occupational Therapy Association: *www.aota.org*.

You can also be a brain surgeon. Seriously! A *neurosurgeon* is an MD who possesses a detailed knowledge of brain and nervous system anatomy. There are a number of different paths to a career as a neurosurgeon, depending on subspecialty (in the complex geography of the brain). For the inspirational story of Dr. Benjamin Carson, one of our leading pediatric neurosurgeons, check out this web page: *express.howstuffworks.com/extraordinary-carson.htm* or his homepage at Johns Hopkins University: *www.neuro.jhmi.edu/profiles/carson.html*.

WHAT'S HAPPENING!

Hemispherectomies

In the "Connecting to Life/Job Skills" section, you learned about Dr. Ben Carson and some of his contributions to pediatric neuropsychology. One of the groundbreaking procedures that Carson and other brain science innovators have pioneered has been the *hemispherectomy*—the removal of one of the two halves of the brain, usually done for very young children who suffer from uncontrollable seizures. These seizures cannot be effectively controlled using medication or less radical surgery and can be fatal if untreated.

This procedure of last resort has been made safer and more effective through a combination of advanced medical technology and brain science knowledge. Specifically, the knowledge that the brain is "plastic" and able to rewire itself—forming new synaptic connections—in response to some kinds of damage. The brains of children up to about age 15 are especially able to do this, and some very young hemispherectomy patients (under age 5) resume almost completely normal functioning within a year or two of the surgery.

To learn more about this innovative brain surgery visit the following links:

www.drbencarson.com/hem-facts.html

teacher.scholastic.com/researchtools/articlearchives/humanbody/lifewithhalfabrain.htm

www.pbs.org/wnet/brain/episode2/faq/page2.html

OTHER USEFUL WEB SITES

THE WHOLE BRAIN ATLAS

www.med.harvard.edu/AANLIB/home.html

Visit Harvard's wonderful web site to see beautiful pictures of the structures discussed in this chapter and to use the many resources provided here for your study!

BRAIN MODEL TUTORIAL

pegasus.cc.ucf.edu/~Brainmd1/brain.html

This interactive site created by Mark Darty is also useful for your further learning and study.

NEUROSCIENCE FOR KIDS

faculty.washington.edu/chudler/neurok.html

Not necessarily for kids, frequently updated, and amazingly helpful, this site maintained by Dr. Eric Chudler of the University of Washington.

BASIC NEURAL PROCESSES TUTORIALS

psych.hanover.edu/Krantz/neurotut.html

John Krantz of Hanover College sponsors and updates this comprehensive neurosciences tutorial page.

NEUROPSYCHOLOGY CENTRAL

www.neuropsychologycentral.com/index.html

If you develop a serious interest in neurosciences, you will want to visit this site, which features up-to-date information on imaging, assessment, and activities at various research laboratories.

NEUROSCIENCES ON THE INTERNET

www.neuroguide.com/

This searchable site is similar to Neuropsychology Central and is an excellent alternative or supplementary source of information.

REFERENCES

Humphreys, G. W. (1999) *Case Studies in the Neuropsychology of Vision*. UK: The Psychology Press.

Sperry, R. (1967) Split-brain approach to learning problems. In G. C. Quarton, T. Melnechuk, & F. O. Schmitt (Eds.) *The Neurosciences: A Study Program*. (714–722). New York: Rockefeller University Press.

Chapter 4

SENSATION AND PERCEPTION

In this chapter you will become acquainted with how the brain is connected to and interprets the physical world.

What Is Sensation?

Now that you have learned that the nervous system manages and performs thousands of essential bodily functions, we are going to explore a specific subset of the nervous system's functions, which are crucial to survival. These are the workings of the various sensory systems. There are six to eight of these, depending on whom you ask. None of them are paranormal, but some may surprise you. You know these:

- Vision
- Hearing
- Taste
- Smell
- Touch

But these are probably new to you (at least as separate systems):

- Balance
- Kinesthetic (the sense of the weight, strain, and position of your joints and muscles in space)
- Pain

Some psychologists group various senses together by common features:

- The chemical senses: Smell and taste, because these senses involve the detection of molecules of odor and flavor.
- The body senses (touch, pain, balance, and kinesthetic) because they alert the brain to vital information about the conditions to which the organism is being subjected.

This chapter will cover the eight senses listed here, organized according to the preceding grouping scheme.

These diverse sensory systems have one crucial feature in common. The brain does not know the taste of pizza, the sight of a sunset, or the sound of Beethoven and R&B music. It only knows the firing of neurons—action potentials. *Sensation* is the process by which any physical stimulus (sound, light, texture, flavor, etc.) is transformed into action potentials by the workings of specialized *receptor* cells that operate in the peripheral nervous system. The process by which the delicious smell of a stew cooking or the fuzzy and warm feeling of your pet cat rubbing against your leg is made into the firings of neurons is called *transduction*.

To prevent a possible overload of sensory stimuli, several processes occur at the levels of the peripheral and central nervous systems. At the level of the peripheral system, we have certain *thresholds* for detecting the initiation of or a change in a stimulus. An *absolute threshold* is the point at which, under ideal conditions (all other sensory input at a minimum), a specific sensory stimulus can be detected at least 50 percent of the time. If a sensory input cannot be detected at least 50 percent of the time, it is said to be *subliminal*, from the Latin for "below the threshold." Contrary to what urban legends and the media project to the public, it is not possible to manipulate human behavior in any significant way using subliminal stimuli, although subtle changes in mood may occur upon exposure to them. If you buy popcorn at the movie theatre, you were tempted by your own hunger and a completely obvious and appealing advertisement that was designed to encourage you to do so. A *difference threshold* is the smallest difference or change in an ongoing stimulus that can be detected at least 50 percent of the time. This is also referred to as the *JND*, or the *just noticeable difference*. The greater the strength of the stimulus is, the greater the change that will be needed for the change to be detected. (If you are bench-pressing 100 pounds and someone adds 2 pounds to each side, you probably won't notice the difference. If you are holding a 5-pound weight in each hand and someone hands you an additional 2 pounds for each hand, you almost certainly will feel the change.) A rule proposed by a German physiologist—*Weber's law*—hypothesized that the change needed for detection is proportional to the strength of the original stimulus. This has turned out not to be strictly true, but it does work as a rule of thumb. The stronger the stimulus is, the larger the increase that will be needed to detect the change.

In the central nervous system, structures in the brainstem and midbrain allow us to orient and focus on particular stimuli, and help us to integrate and process them. The brain can lower the priority of messages through *sensory adaptation* ("getting used to it" as we do after a few minutes in a cool swimming pool) and/or raise their priority through voluntary processes of focus and attention. The seemingly mysterious process of *hypnosis* is in actuality a power possessed by the person undergoing the procedure, not by the hypnotist. The person uses the guidance of the hypnotist to focus on some sensations or thoughts, ignoring others. A hypnotizable person can use this skill to manage pain, for example, by learning to pay less attention to the signals. This is one of the few legitimate and valid uses for this procedure (see the information in Chapter 5).

The central nervous system is also responsible for *perception*, the processing and interpretation of the messages that are made from the sensory stimuli. A one-week-old infant can *see* a new toy (if it is held very close) or the face of a caregiver but will not be able to *perceive* these things until their significance becomes clear through daily experience. The brain is a meaning-making organ. Perception is the crucial process that allows us to determine the significance of our experiences. We do not always interpret sensory inputs accurately, as we will see later on in this chapter.

Before we meet each of the eight senses individually, please keep in mind that the senses almost always work together, through the smooth integration provided by the central nervous system. Life is a multisensory experience. We take this for granted when our nervous systems work properly. We now understand that individuals with some developmental disabilities do not have the same smooth sensory experience. This may be the problem at least in part for those who suffer from some types of autism and the pervasive developmental disorders.

The Eight Senses

We will now overview each of the separate sensory systems, in terms of

- The type of physical stimulus the system detects.
- The equipment (that is neurons and structures) in the peripheral nervous system that transduces the stimulus.
- The involvement of the brain in the integration and perception of the information about the stimulus.

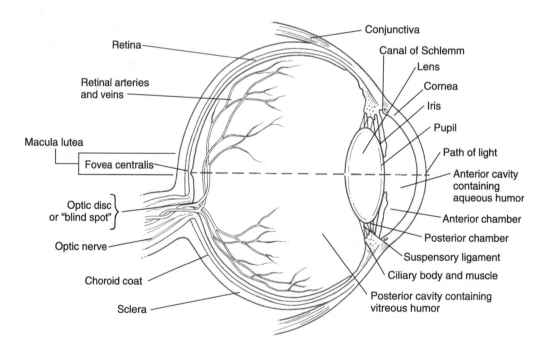

Figure 4.1 Anatomy of the eye.

Vision

Physical Stimulus

The human eye is able to detect a very narrow portion of the electromagnetic spectrum, the "rainbow" of colors from red to violet.

Equipment

The eyes are the light-gathering and processing extensions of the nervous system. Figure 4.1 displays all major structures in the eye. The outermost layer of the eye is the *cornea*, which serves both to protect the eye and start the light-gathering process. The cornea directs the light through the *sclera* (white) and the *aqueous humor* (liquid in the portion of the outer eye) to the *pupil*, which is a hole in the eye itself. The *iris* is the muscle that gives your eye its color and controls the dilation (enlargement) and constriction (shrinking) of the size of the pupil, depending on the level of light available and the amount of activation in the sympathetic nervous system. The lower the level of light, the greater the size of the pupil. When you are experiencing strong stress or emotion, your pupils will typically be more widely dilated than when you are calm.

The light then hits the *lens*, which is able to change its size and thickness through a process called *accommodation*. This ability of the lens enables the light entering the eye to be focused properly, to travel through the *vitreous humor* (the jelly-like fluid in the center of the eyeball), and to fall on the *retina*. The retina is a thin layer of neurons that covers the back of the eye and it is the location where the actual transduction of the light energy will occur.

The Structure of the Retina

The retina has an interesting configuration (see Figure 4.2)—three separate layers comprise the retina, and the light travels all the way to the back layer to be processed and then is transmitted forward through the outer two layers. Two types of *photoreceptors* make up the back layer—*rods*, thin neurons that only fire in conditions of very low or dim light; and *cones*, short, thickly built neurons, that fire in bright light and are responsible for our ability to see color and detail (crucial for daytime vision). Rods far outnumber cones; in each retina it is estimated that there are between 120 million and 125 million rods and between 6 million and 7 million cones. (Animals such as dogs and cats, which do not have good color vision, have retinas that are mainly composed of rods.) Both the rods and cones use specialized chemicals called *photopigments* to begin the process of turning light energy into action potentials. Rods tend to be most dense at the edges of the retina, while cones are most dense toward the center, in the area called the *fovea* where our visual acuity—our ability to detect fine detail—is strongest.

The middle layer of the retina both continues the process of transduction and begins to gather the impulses to send them out of the eyes and back to the visual-processing regions of the brain. This layer is made of three specialized types of cells—*bipolar neurons, horizontal cells,* and *amacrine cells.* The action potential then proceeds to the outermost layer of neurons in the retina. These are the *ganglion cells.* The axons of the ganglion cells make a U-turn, converging to exit the eye at the *blind spot* (because there are no photoreceptors at this point in the eye) and forming the beginning of the *optic nerve.*

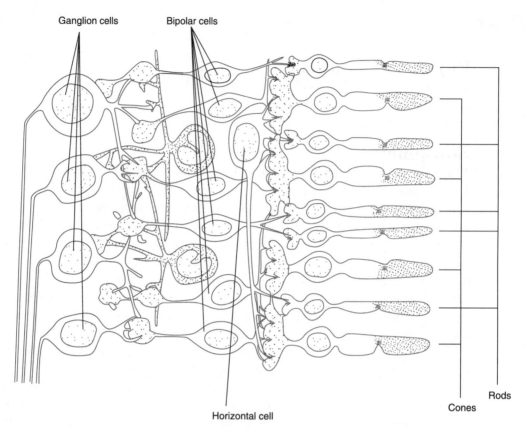

Ganglion cells   Bipolar cells

Rods

Cones

Horizontal cell

Figure 4.2 The layers of the retina.

The Role of the Brain

All the information from the left and right visual fields in each eye travels to a crossover point called the *optic chiasm.* At this point, the projections of the optic nerve from the left fields of each retina cross over to the right hemisphere, and the projections from the right fields cross over to the left hemisphere. Figure 4.3 shows the path traveled by information leaving the eye.

After the crossover, the visual information travels to a region of the thalamus—the *lateral geniculate nucleus*—for initial processing and then on to the primary *visual cortex* in the *occipital lobe,* and the visual association areas of the temporal lobe, for further processing.

As mentioned earlier, the 10 percent myth is untrue; in fact 40 percent of the human brain is devoted to visual processing. Your brain is a vision machine. Besides the amazing eye and visual tract, your occipital and temporal lobes perform an incredible amount of fine processing using neurons called *feature detectors.* These neurons are so specialized that each type fires for only one type of visual stimulus—an angle of a certain size, a curve, or a contour. The retina is also designed to assist in the process of detecting edges, boundaries, and motion. The phenomenon of *lateral inhibition,* which causes objects to look brighter when seen against a dark background than they do when seen against a light background, is the result of cells in adjacent regions of the retina preventing each other's activity, the net result being that contrasting areas are especially easy to detect.

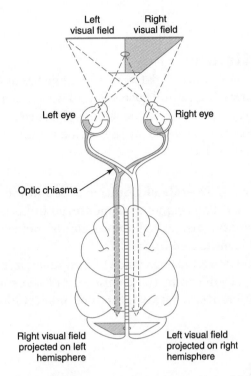

Figure 4.3 Visual pathways and the optic chiasma.

Three Theories of Color Vision

The Trichromatic Theory. There are three types of cones in the retina—red-sensitive, green-sensitive, and blue-sensitive. These roughly correspond to short, medium, and long waves of light, and the cells primarily respond to these types of light waves. Any other wavelength will trigger a combined reaction (so purple light triggers a mixed reaction of red and blue cones, or short and long wave cones). This explanation is favored because it also provides a good functional explanation for color blindness—a lack of one of the three types of cones. One problem with the explanation is that it does not account for afterimages.

The Opponent Process Theory. If you stare at a green object for a long time, and then look at a white wall or paper, you will see a red afterimage. The opponent process theory proposes that cones work in pairs—specifically red-green and blue-yellow. These pairs work in opposition to each other. Seeing blue light generates a response from the blue members of the pairs but none from the yellow members. Other colors stimulate combinations across the pairs (blue stimulates red in the red-green pairs and blue in the blue-yellow pairs).

Integrated Theory. A theory that simply states that both the trichromatic and opponent process theories work together at different stages of visual processing. The trichromatic theory is thought to apply to additional processing that occurs in the ganglion cells, using information from the red, blue, and green cones. Opponent processing may occur not in the retina itself but in the thalamus and occipital lobes. The neurons in these regions may work in an opponent manner.

Hearing

Physical Stimulus

The ear detects sound waves—patterns of change (compression and expansion) in air pressure traveling through time and space. Sound waves carry important information—spoken words, a baby's cry, an alarm, or the simple pleasure of music.

The differences in the quality of the various sound waves that we detect depend on a number of important features.

- *Frequency of cycles*. The rate of vibration of sound waves determines the *pitch* (how high or low a sound is). The frequency is measured in hertz.
- *Intensity*. Loudness, (also called *amplitude*) is indicated by the density of vibrating air molecules and is measured in *decibels*.
- *Timbre*. Since most sounds are made of a complex mix of waves, the characteristic quality of a sound, results from the complexity of the sound waves that comprise it. This allows us to differentiate between types of musical instruments, voices, and the like.

Equipment

We hear through a process known as *bone conduction hearing*. Your ear accomplishes a large part of this job, and the parts that you can't see are most crucial in performing the tasks that comprise the process. The ear is divided into three regions—outer, middle, and inner.

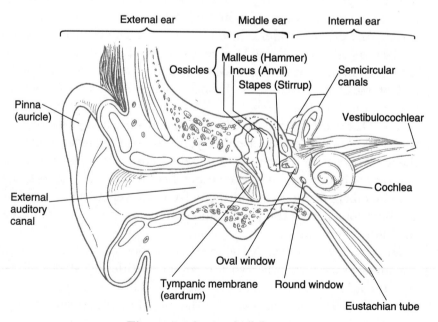

Figure 4.4 Anatomy of the ear.

The Outer Ear. What you think of as your ear is only the external ear. The technical term for this highly recognizable structure is the *pinna*. The pinna is the gathering device for the sound waves, channeling them into the *external auditory canal*. After this, the sound waves are directed into the chambers in which they will be transduced into action potentials. Figure 4.4 shows all major structures of the ear.

The Middle Ear. The major organ of transduction is a part with which you are most likely familiar (at least you have heard of it, so to speak!). The *eardrum* (in medical literature the term used actually means "drum" in Latin—the *tympanic* membrane). Three *ossicles*—movable, interconnected bones—work together with the eardrum—the *malleus* (hammer), the *incus* (anvil), and the *stapes* (stirrup). The vibration of these three very tiny bones sends the transduced energy on its way to the inner ear.

The Inner Ear. The *cochlea* (literally "snail") is the major structure of the inner ear. The vibrations from the middle ear pass through the *oval window* into this fluid-filled, convoluted structure. The pressure created by the vibrations in the cochlea is relieved by the presence of another membrane, the *round window*, on the other end of the cochlea. The *basilar membrane* and the *organ of Corti* are the major subdivisions of the cochlea. The membrane separates the two tubes of the cochlea, and both the membrane and the organ are lined with hairlike receptors. When these receptors are disturbed by the incoming transduced sound energy, the conduction of the sound information along the *auditory nerve* to the *auditory cortex* begins.

The Role of the Brain

The temporal lobes, located at the sides of the head right by your ears, contain most of the cortical tissue devoted to processing auditory input. The journey of the auditory nerves takes them through the midbrain region of the brainstem and finally to the *primary* auditory cortex. Studies have shown that the processing of auditory information in the temporal lobes happens in a manner that somewhat parallels the processing of visual information in the occipital lobes. Certain groups of neurons in the cortex are specialized for designated, narrow frequency ranges and will fire only when the sound falls within those ranges. This is the same type of highly structured neuronal organization that produces feature detection in the visual system.

Theories of Hearing

The range of human hearing is about 20 hertz to about 20,000 hertz. Pitch perception changes over the lifecycle. Thus, children are able to hear higher frequencies than adults are able to hear. The way we hear low-pitched sounds differs from the way we hear high-pitched-sounds. The lower pitches (20 to 4000 hertz) cause the basilar membrane to vibrate in synchrony with the sound waves, and the action potentials in the sensory neurons are the same frequency as the sound. This is sometimes referred to as *temporal coding* or the *frequency principle*. At higher pitches, the basilar membrane remains in sync with sound waves, but the individual hair cells can't keep up. So selected groups of them respond instead. The highest frequency sounds operate through this mechanism called *place coding* or the *place principle*. Sound waves of different frequencies cause different places on the basilar membrane to vibrate. This is true at any frequency, but because the temporal coding works well at lower frequency, place coding is only crucial for detection at the higher frequencies (over 5000 hertz) There is an overlap in the use of temporal and place coding between 1000 and 5000 hertz, the range into which most of human speech falls.

Theories of Hearing Loss

Conduction deafness is a result of the failure of the bones in the middle ear (can you name them?) The h_____, the a_____ , and the s____ to transmit the sound waves properly to the inner ear. This can be corrected sometimes by surgery. People who suffer conduction deafness can hear their own voices.

Nerve deafness is a direct result of damage to the cochlea, the hair cells, or the auditory nerve. This is the kind of deafness that your parent is warning you about when they tell you to turn down that "racket." It can also result from heredity, and from disease processes such as multiple sclerosis, which causes deterioration in the myelin of the nerve cells that are transmitting the auditory information.

The Chemical Senses

The next two senses are responsible for the transduction of molecules of chemicals (odor and flavor), have some similarity in the functioning of their receptors, and are interdependent to some extent (How does your food taste when you have a cold?). So *olfaction* (smell) and *gustation* (taste) are usually discussed together as the *chemical senses*.

Smell

Physical Stimulus. The sensation of smell is produced by detecting chemical molecules in the air. These have been given off by a particular substance and have traveled through the air to our vicinity.

Equipment. We inhale the molecules through our nostrils and mouth. (There is an opening in the palate—the roof of the mouth leading up to the nose). Once in the nasal cavity, they land on the *olfactory epithelium*. The olfactory epithelium is covered with tiny hair cells—the *olfactory receptors*. There are thousands of types of olfactory receptors; this sense is much more complex than taste with its five channels. In fact, most of the really interesting food flavors are actually being smelled, not tasted. The odor molecules are dissolved by chemicals in the epithelium, and as they dissolve, they trigger the receptors to create action potentials. This message makes a very short trip via the olfactory nerve tracts to the brain. Figure 4.5 shows the anatomy of the olfactory system.

The Role of the Brain. The *olfactory bulb* is a small structure, very close to the frontal lobes (just beneath them). It is the brain center for smell, and it routes the neural messages *directly* to the temporal lobes and limbic system. Recall from Chapter 3 that the thalamus integrates every sense except smell, which travels directly into the drive and emotion centers of the brain. The axons from the olfactory tracts in the peripheral nervous system go directly into the higher areas of the brain—there is no "middle person." This is one reason why it is not unusual to become deeply emotional or nostalgic when encountering a familiar smell (a dish your grandmother used to cook, for example).

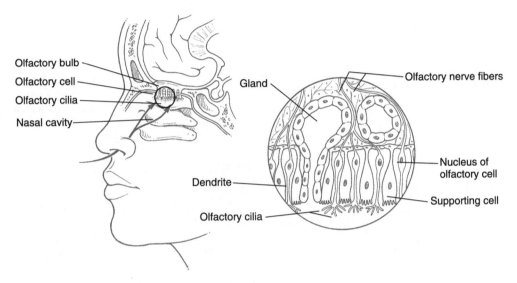

Figure 4.5 The sense of smell.

Taste

Physical Stimulus. The sensation of taste is produced by the detection of chemical molecules in the mouth, which are emitted by any substance that we eat or ingest. The basic design of this system helps us to detect whether a substance is potentially toxic or unhealthy for consumption (bitter/sour) or nutritious (sweet/salty). A fifth taste channel, *umami* has been proposed to exist based on research into the flavor of some Asian cuisines, but the evidence for this taste type has not been found consistently.

Equipment. The *fungiform papilla,* or *taste bud,* is the basic unit in the peripheral region of the taste system. (Some views of the tongue and taste bud are shown in Figure 4.6.) Each papilla holds between 50 and 150 receptor cells with hairlike tips (called the *microvilli*) within it. Most taste buds are found on the surface of the tongue (in the middle and along the sides), but some are also found in the cheeks, the roof of the mouth and the back of the throat. It has been thought that different tastes dominate in different regions of the tongue and mouth, but this has not been substantiated by research. The chart from your elementary school science book of the four taste types located in specific regions on your tongue was almost certainly incorrect. There is a great deal of individual variation in the sense of taste, depending on how many taste buds a person has. Children generally have more taste buds than adults, so their sense of taste is more sensitive than that of adults. Some adults have relatively few taste buds, and others have many more than average, so sensitivity levels range from *nontaster* to *supertaster* (Bartoshuk 2000).

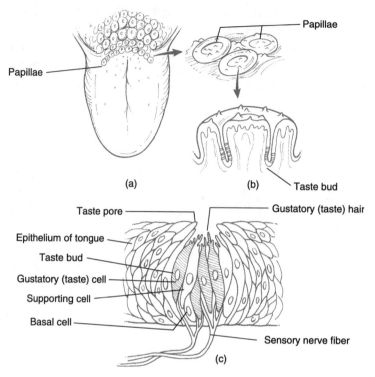

Figure 4.6 Taste buds.

The Role of the Brain. Despite the similarities between smell and taste at the peripheral level, taste makes a more complex journey to the brain. The action potentials travel to the brainstem via two of the cranial *nerves* (numbers 7 and 9), through the medulla and the thalamus, and finally to the limbic system and cerebral cortex.

The Body Senses

Touch

Physical Stimuli. The skin is referred to as "the largest organ of your body." An average adult has about 20 square feet of skin. The skin is where our bodies meet the environment, and it has its own set of sense receptors (sometimes referred to as *cutaneous receptors*) to keep that environment from damaging the body contained within. In contrast to the eye, with a relatively simple set of receptors in the peripheral nervous system and an impressively complex system of processing in the central nervous system, the skin has a fairly complex set of peripheral receptors and a relatively simple processing system in the brain. There are specialized receptors in the skin to transduce diverse stimuli such as hair displacement, several types of pressure, several ranges (in hertz) of vibration, heat, and cold.

Equipment. Table 4-1 briefly presents the various types of receptors in the skin. Figure 4.7 shows a section of skin with an assortment of these receptors.

The action potentials generated by these receptors travel through afferent nerve tracts to the spinal column, the thalamus, and the *parietal lobes* of the cerebral cortex.

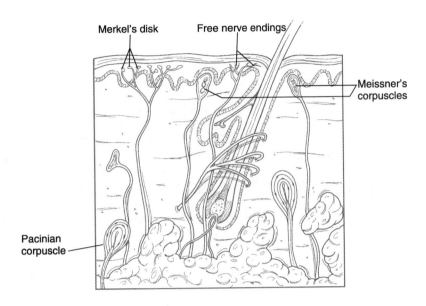

Figure 4.7 A selection of touch senses in the human skin.

TABLE 4-1
TOUCH RECEPTORS

Receptor	Location	Function
Hair follicle ending	Surrounds hair follicle in the skin	Detects hair displacement
Ruffini endings	Under epidermis all over body	Detects pressure
Krause corpuscle	Lips, tongue, genitals	Detects pressure
Pacinian corpuscle	Deep layers of skin all over body	Detects vibration (150–300 Hz)
Meissner corpuscle	Deep layers of hairless skin	Detects vibration (20–40 Hz)
Merkel discs	Top layer of hairless skin	Detects pressure
Thermoreceptors	Under epidermis all over body	Detects temperatures between 30 and 43°C
Cold receptors	Under epidermis all over body	Detects temperatures between 20 and 35°C

The Role of the Brain. The layout of the parietal lobes' processing areas for the perception of touch information is called the *primary somatosensory cortex* and is a fascinating area of the brain. (Figure 4.8 shows the structure of this area.) You may have noticed that your back and forearm are not nearly as sensitive as your fingers and lips. This is because, in fact, your brain has dedicated a great deal more tissue to the detection of stimuli in the hands and face (especially the fingertips and lips) than to the limbs and torso. The layout, if drawn according to the space allotted, makes a funny looking human figure, called the *sensory homunculus,* with a huge face, lips, feet, and hands. (See Figure 4.9.)

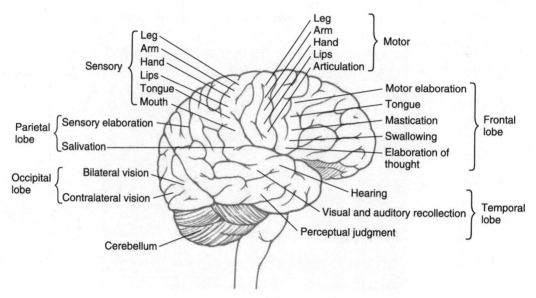

Figure 4.8 The primary somotosensory and motor cortex.

Those who have lost a limb after early childhood will often report that they still feel as if the limb is there—even reporting pain at times. This is called a *phantom limb*. Before advanced brain imaging, these persons were thought to have an emotional or mental disorder, but we now understand that once the brain has dedicated space to the limb, any stimulation in neighboring regions of the brain may result in real physical sensation for the person. Our experience of the world is happening in our brains, after all.

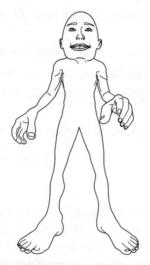

Figure 4.9 The sensory homunculus.

Pain

Physical Stimuli. Pain is an unpleasant response generated by a combination of tissue damage and emotional reaction. The sensations detected by the pain system are warning messages. Those few unfortunate persons who are born with no pain detection system are doomed to die at relatively young ages, no matter how carefully they are watched by family or medical personnel. We need those unpleasant messages to help us avoid self-injury, a constant danger when moving through the physical environment.

Equipment. *Nocioreceptors*, or free nerve endings that exist in all body tissues, are responsible for transducing the sensory portion of the pain message. The action potentials generated by the nocioreceptors travel through afferent nerve tracts to the spinal cord. Then, according to a leading theory of pain sensation, the *gate control theory*, pain messages must pass through a neuronal gateway that either allows the message to proceed to the brain or blocks the message. Neurotransmitters also influence the sensory experience of pain. When *substance P* is released, pain signals increase in strength, but when *endorphins* (chemically identical to opiate drugs) are present, substance P's effects will be reduced. People who run in triathlons and marathons can often do so despite the wear and tear on muscles and joints because of the "runner's high"—caused in part by the release of endorphins in response to the stress of running such a long distance.

The Role of the Brain. The pain messages end up in the primary somatosensory cortex as do other touch messages. The brain also contributes emotional responses to pain. Since emotion is generated along with memory in the limbic system, this enhances our ability to recall and avoid future contact with pain-inducing stimuli. Because emotion influences the perception of pain, the experience of pain can be manipulated to some degree. Hypnosis can be used to alleviate pain—a real benefit for some women in childbirth and for some chronic pain patients. If a person possesses the ability to distract him- or herself through hypnosis, he or she can experience significant pain relief without the use of medication. This also explains the *placebo effect*, at least in part. The expectation of relief may be part of the reason that we experience a lessening of pain when we take an analgesic (pain-reducing) medication.

Balance

Physical Stimuli. Balance is also called the *vestibular sense*. It informs the brain of the position of the head relative to the ground, and the speed at which the head and body are moving.

Equipment. The reception system for balance lives alongside the system responsible for hearing. There are three *semicircular canals*, each oriented in a different direction, and each filled with a jelly-like fluid and lined with hair cells. When the head moves, so does the fluid, which in turn moves the hair cells. The motion of the hair cells creates action potentials. There is another set of hair cells in the two *otolith organs*. Calcium carbonate particles called *otoliths* move in response to the tilt of the head and excite the hair cells in the otolith organs. One of the cranial nerves (number 8) sends the information to the brain for processing.

The Role of the Brain. Balance information is crucial for many functions and activities—maintaining posture, planning and executing movements, and protecting oneself. It is processed throughout the brain. Balance is interdependent with vision. The common and disturbing problem of *motion sickness* tends to arise most frequently when the information from the balance system ("there is no motion") conflicts with the information from the visual system ("there is motion").

Kinesthetic

Physical Stimulus. Motion of the limbs and joints and the amount of weight that is placed upon the joints are the two types of information processed by this sensory system. We tend to take this system for granted. It is trained very early in our lives through processes of implicit and procedural memory (see Chapter 7), and unless we experience severe injury or neurological disorder, it operates smoothly as long as we are healthy and active.

Equipment. As one would expect, the receptors for this system are found in the joints, muscles, and tendons. They are also known as *proprioceptors* or *mechanoreceptors*. There are three basic types of kinesthetic receptors, shown in Table 4-2.

TABLE 4-2
THE KINESTHETIC RECEPTORS

Receptor	Location	Function
Muscle spindle	All skeletal muscles	Detects degree of stretching in muscle
Golgi tendon organs	All tendons	Detects amount of tension
Joint receptors	All tissues that surround joints	Detects range of motion in joints

The Role of the Brain. Much like balance, the information from the kinesthetic system is crucial to activities we plan and carry out almost constantly during our waking lives. Together with information from the balance and visual systems, information from the muscles, tendons, and joints is processed in many regions of the brain.

Perceptual Organization, Interpretation, and Misinterpretation

As was mentioned earlier, perception is a complex process, strongly related to sensation but fundamentally different in that it *starts* in the brain. Sensation starts with inputs detected by neural receptors; perception often starts with concepts, expectations, and knowledge stored in the higher cortical regions of the brain. We have already discussed the process of perception by reviewing the higher cortical areas involved in processing sensory inputs and the psychophysical laws that attempt to explain when and how we sense a physical stimulus.

The power of hypnosis to influence pain is in fact evidence of the brain's (at least the brains of some individuals) power to manipulate the perception of a stimulus.

Perceptual set is what laypeople often refer to as a "frame of mind," and it is one of the easiest perceptual processes to understand. Expectations influence how we interpret sensory inputs. If you are walking home at night after having seen a rowdy comedy movie, you will be less likely to interpret the footsteps behind you as a threat than you will if you have just seen *Friday the 13th Part 24* or some other movie featuring massive amounts of homicidal mayhem.

Gestalt Laws of Perception

One of the most thorough attempts to explain human perceptual processes in terms of laws was made by those psychologists of the *Gestalt* school, which was founded by the early twentieth century psychologist Max Wertheimer. "Gestalt" is one of those hard-to-translate words from the German language, but it means, roughly, "whole unified form/pattern." The underlying philosophy of this school of perceptual psychology is that the whole does not necessarily equal the sum of the parts. Gestalt psychologists would argue that these tendencies are innate and found in all normal human brains.

Most of the Gestalt laws apply primarily to vision, but a few can also be applied to hearing. The Gestalt psychologists believed that, above all, *shape* is fundamental to how we perceive objects and situations in the world. They did clever studies to show that even young children will continue to recognize a familiar object if its color, size, or material composition was changed, but if the shape was altered in any substantial way, the children no longer recognized it.

Related to the central importance of shape, the Gestalt laws of *closure* proposes that if a shape or figure is broken, our brains will "close" the figure in order to make sense of it, even filling in missing pieces if necessary. You see the triangles in Figure 4.10, don't you? The law of *good continuation* states that objects connected by or arranged as a smooth curve tend to be seen as a continuous contour. There is no reason why the lines in Figure 4.11 aren't actually drawn from a to d or c to b but you and I will almost certainly perceive them as going from a to b and c to d.

Figure 4.10 The law of closure.

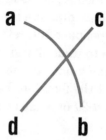

Figure 4.11 The law of good continuation.

Another fundamental law of the Gestalt school is the *figure-and-ground relationship law*. A reversible figure such as that in Figure 4.12 shows us how we need to decide what part of a picture is the background and which part or parts are the figure or foreground. In this famous illusion (Figure 4.12), although you may know that there are both a pair of faces and a vase, you will only see either the faces or the vase as you determine what is background and what is figure in the picture. You can see either the vase or the faces, but only by switching your designations of what is figure and what is background.

Figure 4.12 Figure-foreground.

Grouping is also important in the Gestalt school. The law of *proximity* states that objects that are grouped near to each other will be perceived as having some relationship to each other. Similarly, the law of *common fate* proposes that objects moving at the same speed and in the same general direction will be interpreted as parts of a greater unit. Both laws would be illustrated when you see three or four people arrive together at a party, and even though they all arrived separately at the same time you keep thinking of them as a group of friends. Finally, the law of *similarity* dictates that a group of objects that resemble each other with respect to some major characteristic (color, size, or shape) will be grouped together as a unit. Tell the truth now—isn't it much easier to see the rectangle in Figure 4.13 as composed of rows of diamonds and rows of clubs than it is to see it as made of columns of interspersed diamonds and clubs?

Figure 4.13 The Law of Similarity.

The "ease" issue is not trivial to the Gestalt school. Simplicity or *Prägnanz* states that, above all, the brain seeks to process and organize information and produce the simplest and most stable interpretation. If you have to work too hard to see it (as when you try to see the columns in Figure 4.13), you will resist or reject the stimulus. This is a central Gestalt law.

Motion Perception

We take this element of perception for granted because we do it so effortlessly. As we watch a moving object, the image of the object is cast upon the retina. The size of the image is our cue for its distance from us. If the image is expanding, we interpret the object as heading toward us, and if the image is contracting, we perceive that the object is moving away. We compare the object to the background against which it appears to be moving. The brain also factors in the sounds that appear to be made by the object (getting louder and higher pitched signifies motion toward us, while getting softer and lower pitched signifies motion away from us).

We begin to learn how to interpret the distance to and direction of moving objects long before our first conscious memories develop. Studies of young infants, persons with congenital blindness whose vision is restored, and the extremely rare case of brain injury that results in "motion blindness" suggest that motion perception is learned and depends on the interpretation of subtle cues and the effects of the standard assumptions that humans tend to make when viewing a moving object. This results in some interesting misinterpretations and illusions, which include the following:

- *The stroboscopic effect.* Two small lights, adjacent to each other, are flashed just a tenth of a second apart. Although each light is stationary, the retinal image is interpreted as one light moving back and forth very quickly. One of the most common forms of entertainment, movies, relies heavily on this visual illusion. The *phi phenomenon* is a similar illusion in which the color of the light changes also.
- *Induced motion.* By moving the background instead of the figure, one can create the appearance that the figure is moving. This is because humans are almost always functioning under the assumption that the background stands still.
- *Perceptual constancies.* When we watch an object move toward us or away from us, we tend to perceive its size, brightness, and shape as remaining the same. These are complex phenomena, but all of them hinge on the fact that through the use of other cues (such as other stationary objects and acquired knowledge of the physical world) your brain interprets an object as moving toward or away from you, not merely increasing or decreasing in size. This process also contributes to the influence of cultural background (which determines some of what you learn) on perception (see following discussion.)

TABLE 4-3
DEPTH PERCEPTION CUES

Name of Cue	Type (Monocular/Binocular)	How It Works
Aerial perspective	Monocular	Knowledge that it is more difficult to see the details of faraway objects.
Convergence	Binocular	The more strain felt in the eye muscles due to inward rotation, the closer the object is seen to be (interaction of visual and kinesthetic senses).
Linear perspective	Monocular	Parallel lines seem to converge as they run farther away from you. The closer together they are, the more distant they appear to be from you.
Motion parallax	Monocular	Judgment about the meaning of the speed of a passing object—the faster it passes you, the closer you judge it to be (think of how slowly an airplane appears to move overhead, yet its flight speed is hundreds of miles an hour).
Overlap	Monocular	If one object blocks the view of another, we perceive the blocking object as closer to us.
Relative size	Monocular	If we assume that two objects are similar in size, the larger one is judged to be closer to us.
Retinal disparity	Binocular	The two retinas are physically not exactly lined up (the sides of the face are not symmetrical.) This covers the blind spot and gives us an ability to judge distance. The farther away an object is, the less disparity is experienced.
Texture gradient	Monocular	Fuzziness and lack of definition are perceived as signs of great distance.

Depth and Distance Perception

Our ability to experience the three-dimensional world allows us to enjoy its beauty and flee or protect ourselves from its dangers. This ability depends mainly upon a combination of *monocular* (one eye) and *binocular* (two eye) *cues*. Monocular cues are the type that artists exploit to create the illusion of a three-dimensional landscape on a two-dimensional canvas. Binocular cues depend upon the interacting work of the two retinas. Both types are influenced by knowledge stored in and assumptions made at the cortical level. The depth perception cues are listed for you in Table 4-3.

Culture and Perception

The illusion reproduced in Figure 4.14 is known as the *Müller-Lyer Illusion*. The presence of the arrows at the ends of the lines makes it very hard to detect the fact that the two lines are equal in length. If you are having a hard time believing this, use a ruler or straight edge to confirm it.

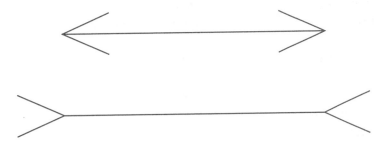

Figure 4.14 The Müller-Lyer Illusion.

Most people have a hard time seeing the equal length of the lines—most people raised in industrialized, urban environments, that is. People from agrarian and simple societies, who are not exposed to a great deal of rectangular architecture (think of huts and other dome-shaped structures as opposed to houses and office buildings) typically are *not* fooled by the illusion and detect fairly quickly that the lines are in fact the same length (Segall et al. 1966).

This finding has been well researched and provides evidence that there are many cultural and environmental influences on perception. Other examples of cultural influences include the *Moon Illusion*—the fact that the moon looks so much larger when it is at the horizon, because we see it among visual cues of objects that are much closer, such as trees and rooftops. People who live in the rain forest often do not develop the kind of distance vision that those who are raised in other environments do—large objects far away are often misinterpreted as small objects that are nearby. As is the case with almost everything else in psychology, how we perceive the world is likely a result of nature (the design of the sensory receptors and brain and the Gestalt laws) and nurture working together with, rather than in opposition to, each other.

Connecting Through Chapter Review

WORD-STUDY CONNECTION

Write each of these words on index cards, and write their definitions on the opposite side. Use them to memorize the information in the chapter, and try to sort them into piles based on relationships (parts of the cerebrum, parts and functions of the neuron, etc.).

absolute threshold
accommodation
aqueous humor
amacrine cells
amplitude (loudness)
auditory cortex
auditory nerve
basilar membrane
binocular cue
bipolar neurons
blind spot
bone conduction hearing
chemical senses
closure
cochlea
common fate
cones
conduction deafness
cornea
cranial nerve
cutaneous receptor
decibel
difference threshold
eardrum
endorphins
external auditory canal
feature detectors

figure-and-ground
  relationship
fovea
frequency principle
fungiform papillae
ganglion cells
gate control theory
Gestalt
good continuation
gustation
hearing
hertz
horizontal cells
hypnosis
integrated theory
incus (anvil)
induced motion
iris
just noticeable difference
  (JND)
kinesthetic
lateral geniculate nucleus
lateral inhibition
lens
malleus (hammer)
mechanoreceptors
microvilius/microvilli

Moon Illusion
monocular cue
motion sickness
Müller-Lyer Illusion
nerve deafness
nocioreceptors
nontaster
olfaction
occipital lobes
olfactory epithelium
olfactory bulb
olfactory receptors
organ of Corti
opponent process theory
optic chiasm
optic nerve
ossicles
otoliths
otolith organs
oval window
parietal lobe
perception
perceptual constancies
perceptual set
phantom limb
phi phenomenon
photopigments

photoreceptors
placebo effect
pinna
pitch (frequency)
place coding/place principle
  primary auditory cortex
primary somatosensory
  cortex
primary visual cortex
proprioceptors
Prägnanz
proximity
pupil
receptor

retina
rods
round window
semicircular canal
sensation
sensory adaptation
sensory homunculus
sclera
shape
similarity
stapes (stirrup)
stroboscopic effect
substance P
subliminal

supertaster
taste bud
temporal coding
temporal lobes
threshold
timbre (complexity)
touch
trichromatic theory
transduction
tympanic
umami
vestibular sense
vitreous humor
Weber's law

SELF-TEST CONNECTION

PART A. *Completion*
Write in the word that correctly completes each statement.

1. _____ is the sense that informs your brain of the position of your limbs and the strain on your joints and muscles.
2. _____ and _____ are known as the *chemical senses*.
3. _____ is the process that converts physical stimuli into action potentials.
4. The _____ is the point at which a specific sensory stimulus can be detected at least 50 percent of the time.
5. The term "_____" literally means "below the threshold."
6. "Getting used to the stimulus" is a nonscientific way to describe the process of _____ .
7. _____ is the process of organizing, integrating, and interpreting sensory stimuli.
8. _____ is the sense that tranduces waves of light into nerve signals and sends them to the brain for processing.
9. The _____ is the outermost layer of the eyeball that protects it and begins the light gathering process.
10. The _____ changes size and shape through a process called *accommodation*.
11. The jelly-like substance in the center of the eyeball is called the _____ .
12. The _____ is the thin layer of neurons that covers the back of the eyeballs.
13. The _____ are the visual receptors that only function at low levels of light.
14. _____ are the specialized chemicals that help to start the process of turning waves of light into action potentials.

15. The middle layer of the retina is made up of three types of cells: bipolar neurons, _____ and _____ .

16. The _____ is located in the occipital lobes.

17. Fine processing in the visual cortex is partly a result of the functioning of many highly specialized brain cells called _____ .

18. The _____ of color vision combines features of the trichromatic and opponent process theories.

19. The rate of vibration of sound waves is referred to as a sound's _____ .

20. The _____ is the technical term for the outermost part of the human ear.

21. Within the eardrum, three small, movable bones called _____ vibrate together in order to facilitate to transduce the sound waves. This process is called _____ hearing.

22. The basilar membrane and the organ of Corti are the major subdivisions of the _____ .

23. Higher frequency sounds are detected through a process called _____ .

24. The inner lining of the nasal cavity is covered by the _____ epithelium.

25. Smell is experienced as a highly emotional sense because the olfactory tract takes signals directly into the _____ .

26. _____ is a technical term for what most people call a "taste bud."

27. _____ corpuscles are one type of touch receptor that detect vibrations against the skin.

28. The parietal lobes are laid out with a great deal of tissue devoted to the face and the _____ .

29. _____ is the neurotransmitter that is thought to be involved in the transmission of pain messages.

30. The _____ canals in the ears help to transduce information about the position and speed of the head as it moves through space.

31. _____ are the mechanoreceptors that detect the degree of stretch in the muscles.

32. A "frame of mind" that might influence perception is referred to as a _____ .

33. The Gestalt psychologists believed that an object's _____ is fundamental in how it is perceived.

34. The faces-and-vase illusion is a good illustration of the Gestalt law of _____ .

35. Because we assume that the background of a scene remains stationary, we are subject to the _____ illusion.

36. Convergence is an example of a _____ depth or distance perception cue.

37. The _____ provides evidence of the influence of culture on the process of perception.

PART B. Multiple Choice

Circle the letter of the item that correctly completes the statement.

1. All of the following are usually classified as "body senses" *except* _____ .
   - (a) vision
   - (b) touch
   - (c) kinesthetic
   - (d) pain

2. Physical stimuli are changed into neural messages through a process called _____ .
   - (a) perception
   - (b) the JND
   - (c) transduction
   - (d) translation

3. _____ is the idea that the change in stimulus strength needed for a detection of the change is proportional to the strength of the ongoing stimulus.
   (a) Weber's law
   (b) Subliminal perception
   (c) Sensory adaptation
   (d) Transduction

4. The _____ is the muscle that controls the size of the pupil and gives the eye its color.
   (a) cornea
   (b) iris
   (c) lens
   (d) retina

5. _____ are the photoreceptors that are responsible for color and other facets of daytime vision.
   (a) Amacrine cells
   (b) Rods
   (c) Horizontal cells
   (d) Cones

6. The _____ is the area of the retina that possesses the greatest visual acuity.
   (a) iris
   (b) lens
   (c) fovea
   (d) photopigment

7. _____ cells are those possessing long axons that exit the eyeball at the blind spot and form the beginning of the optic tract.
   (a) Bipolar
   (b) Ganglion
   (c) Horizontal
   (d) Amacrine

8. The optic nerve passes through the thalamus at the _____ .
   (a) temporal lobe
   (b) medulla
   (c) optic chiasm
   (d) lateral geniculate nucleus

9. Objects look brighter when placed against a dark background owing to the process of _____ .
   (a) feature detection
   (b) lateral inhibition
   (c) transduction
   (d) sensory adaptation

10. All of the following are theories of color vision *except* _____ .
    (a) trichromatic
    (b) integrated
    (c) place principle
    (d) opponent process

11. The complexity of sound waves that give a sound its special quality is referred to as _____ .
    (a) pitch
    (b) timbre
    (c) decibel range
    (d) amplitude

12. Pick the one that is *not* the name of one of the ossicles in the eardrum.
    (a) Incus
    (b) Malleus
    (c) Stapes
    (d) Cochlea

13. The _____ is the major structure of the inner ear.
    (a) tympanic membrane
    (b) oval window
    (c) cochlea
    (d) primary auditory cortex

14. If the bones in the middle ear fail to vibrate, _____ deafness will usually be the result.
    (a) nerve
    (b) conduction
    (c) tone
    (d) pitch

15. The _____ is the major brain structure involved in the sense of smell.
    (a) olfactory bulb
    (b) olfactory epithelium
    (c) fungiform papilla
    (d) thalamus

16. _____ contains between 50 and 150 individual taste receptor cells or microvilli.
    (a) A tympanic membrane   (b) An olfactory bulb
    (c) A fungiform papilla   (d) A tongue

17. Ruffini endings, Merkel discs, and Meissner corpucles are different kinds of _____ .
    (a) touch receptors   (b) pain receptors
    (c) mechanoreceptors   (d) balance organs

18. The primary somatosensory cortex is located in the _____ .
    (a) temporal lobes   (b) parietal lobes
    (c) limbic system   (d) frontal lobes

19. Free nerve endings are also known as _____ . They tranduce pain signals.
    (a) proprioreceptors   (b) nocioreceptors
    (c) dodidodoreceptors   (d) mechanoreceptors

20. The vestibular sense is another term for _____ .
    (a) pain   (b) touch
    (c) balance   (d) kinesthetic

21. Calcium carbonate particles that are responsible in part for the transduction of balance information are called _____ .
    (a) olfactory bones   (b) ossicles
    (c) oracles   (d) otoliths

22. _____ or mechanoreceptors are found in the muscles and joints.
    (a) Free nerve endings   (b) Proprioreceptors
    (c) Thermoreceptors   (d) Nocioreceptors

23. Which of the following is not a type of mechanoreceptor?
    (a) Muscle spindles   (b) Golgi tendon organs
    (c) Merkel discs   (d) Joint receptors

24. _____ psychologists believe that the brain seeks to make the simplest and most stable interpretation of stimuli.
    (a) Psychophysical   (b) Experimental
    (c) Gestalt   (d) Cross cultural

25. We tend to interpret objects moving together and in the same general direction as a unit. This is the law of _____ .
    (a) common fate   (b) good continuation
    (c) proximity   (d) Prägnanz

26. We perceive movement in movies as a result of the illusion called _____ .
    (a) induced motion   (b) perceptual constancy
    (c) figure and ground   (d) the stroboscopic effect

27. Which of the following is not one of the perceptual constancies listed in this chapter?
    (a) Size   (b) Brightness
    (c) Background   (d) Color

28. Which of the following is not a monocular cue for depth perception?
    (a) Convergence   (b) Motion parallax
    (c) Texture gradient   (d) Overlap

29. _____ is the depth cue that results from the slight difference in the placement of our two retinas owing to facial asymmetry.
    (a) Convergence   (b) Overlap
    (c) Retinal disparity   (d) Relative size

30. The _____ illusion provides evidence that perception is at least partly influenced by the culture in which we are reared.
    (a) Müller-Lyer   (b) vase-and-faces
    (c) negative afterimage   (d) ball-and-triangle

PART C. Modified True-False

If the statement is true, write "T" for the answer. If the statement is incorrect, change the underlined expression to one that will make the statement true.

1. Vision and hearing are collectively referred to as the chemical senses.
2. An absolute threshold is the point at which under ideal conditions a stimulus can be detected at least 50 percent of the time.
3. Weber's law describes the process of sensory adaptation.
4. Perception is the detection of sensory stimuli by special receptor cells in the peripheral nervous system.
5. Vitreous humor is the fluid in front of the iris and pupil.
6. The lens changes shape through a process called accommodation.
7. Rods and cones are the two types of photoreceptors that make up the retina.
8. Cones outnumber rods by about 26 to 1.
9. The middle layer of the retina is composed of three types of cells: bipolar, amacrine, and ganglion.
10. 40 percent of the human brain is dedicated to vision.
11. The density of vibrating air molecules determines amplitude, or loudness.
12. The tympanic membrane is commonly referred to as the eardrum.
13. The basilar membrane and the stapes are the major subdivisions of the cochlea.
14. The parietal lobes hold most of the auditory cortex.
15. Low-frequency sounds are heard mainly through the operation of the frequency principle.
16. The olfactory bulb lies very close to the occipital lobes.
17. Fungiform papillae are the basic unit of the peripheral division of the taste system.
18. Compared to taste, smell is the chemical sense with the more complex route to the brain.
19. Cutaneous receptors include those that detect pressure, vibration, and temperature.
20. Krause corpuscles, Ruffini endings, and Merkel discs are all skin receptors that detect the sensation of pressure.
21. The primary somatosensory cortex is laid out with the greatest amount of tissue dedicated to information coming from the hands and arms.
22. The gate control theory is a leading theory that attempts to explain how organisms experience the sensation of pain.
23. Dopamine is the neurotransmitter that blocks the effects of substance P.
24. Expectations and emotions may influence our experience of pain, as demonstrated by the occurrence of pain relief through the placebo effect.
25. The motion of the semicircular canals produces the action potentials for the sense of balance.
26. Motion sickness usually results from a clash of information coming from the visual and kinesthetic systems.

27. The kinesthetic system is the sensory apparatus for communicating information about the position of the limbs and amount of muscle strain experienced by the body to the brain.
28. Meissner corpuscles and Golgi tendon organs are two examples of proprioreceptors or mechanoreceptors.
29. Perceptual set refers to your expectations that may influence how you interpret incoming sensory information.
30. Gestalt is a term that refers to the whole image or experience being greater than or different from the sum of the parts.
31. Gestalt psychologists believe that above all color is central to the meaning that we make in perceiving objects in our environments.
32. The law of closure refers to our brains' tendency to fill in the missing or broken parts of an image.
33. By moving the background instead of the picture, one can create an illusion of motion called the stroboscopic effect.
34. Convergence is an example of a monocular depth cue.
35. A talented artist would make use of texture and linear perspective to create the illusion of depth in a painting on a two-dimensional canvas surface.

PART D. Chart Completions

Fill in the missing information in each of the charts. One row is completed in each chart as an example.

THE EIGHT SENSES

Sense	Physical Stimulus/Stimuli	Receptor(s)
Vision	Light waves	Rods and cones
Hearing		Cochlea: basilar membrane, organ of corti and hair cells contained within
		Olfactory receptors
	Chemical molecules	
Touch		
		Free nerve endings
	Position and speed of head	
Kinesthetic		

THE VISUAL SYSTEM

Structure	Location	Function
Cornea	Outer layer of eyeball	Protects eye and gathers light waves
Pupil	Under aqueous humor and cornea	
		Muscles that causes pupil to dilate and constrict
		Focuses light on the retina
Retina		
	Exits eyeball at the blind spot	
Lateral geniculate nucleus	Part of thalamus	
		Primary sight for processing of visual information
Temporal lobes		

THE AUDITORY SYSTEM

Structure	Location	Function
Pinna	Outside of head	Gathers sound waves
Tympanic membrane		Contains the ossicles that vibrate in response to sound waves
Cochlea		
Hair cells		
	Temporal lobes	

THE CHEMICAL SENSES

Structure	Location	Function
Olfactory epithelium	Inside of nasal cavity	Contains olfactory receptors
	Right below the frontal cortex	
Tongue		
	On the surface of the tongue, in the cheeks, and in roof of the mouth	
Thalamus		Begins processing and integration of taste information
Limbic system and cerebral cortex		

THE BODY SENSES

Structure	Location	Function
Skin	Covers entire body	Contains various types of cutaneous receptors
Primary somatosensory cortex		
	Skin and other body tissues	Transduce information related to pain and other unpleasant sensations
Substance P		
Semicircular canals		
		Contain otoliths
Cerebellum		
	Joints, muscles, and tendons	

CONNECTING TO CONCEPTS

Review the chapter and then write down your thoughts about the following questions.

1. Define and distinguish between sensation and perception. Describe how each process would be carried out as you look at an impressionist painting or listen to a piece of music that you enjoy.
2. Your friend is concerned about possible manipulation by subliminal messages. What would you tell him or her about the meaning of the word "subliminal" and the actual power of subliminal stimuli?
3. A person is looking at a beautiful sunset. Describe the pathway taken by the light waves entering the eyes of this individual and the processing of these waves in the brain.
4. At the end of this chapter, the impact of culture upon visual processing and perception is discussed. Using either the sense of hearing or the chemical senses, discuss the possible impact of culture on perception of other sensory stimuli.
5. Describe how the body senses would interact for an athlete playing or participating in a sport of your choosing.
6. Describe the Gestalt school of psychology and its explanation of visual perception. Explain how the law of closure might prevent you from seeing your own typographical errors in a homework assignment that you are proofreading.

CONNECTING TO LIFE/JOB SKILLS

Optometry

As with Chapter 3, there are many interesting and exciting careers that involve working knowledge of the senses. An *optometrist* uses knowledge of the visual system, optics, and the brain to diagnose and correct problems with vision. Along with a standard selection of premedical courses, a preoptometry student is typically expected to take several classes in psychology and research methods. To obtain more information on this career, visit the web site of the American Academy of Optometry's page for students at *www.aaopt.org/students* or the web page of the American Optometric Association at *www.aoanet.org*.

Knowledge of perception and misperception is crucial to the science of *ergonomics*. Ergonomics seeks to optimize working conditions for maximum efficiency. Vision is an essential ergonomic aspect of the work of pilots and air traffic controllers. Recent research has suggested that misperceptions of panel information may have been responsible for airplane crashes, some of which have resulted in great loss of life. Knowledge of other senses also comes into play—*haptics*, for example, is the science of understanding body sensations and mechanics and is based in part on the human body senses. Knowledge of haptics helps ergonomists make workstations more comfortable and efficient. To learn more about human factors and ergonomics, go to *http://hfes.org/*.

WHAT'S HAPPENING!

Restoring Vision

Our increased understanding of the circuitry of the visual system has been one of the great blessings of the new brain science. Along with breakthroughs in computer and optical technology, ways for the brain and machines to interface are being brought closer to reality every day. The ultimate goal is to restore vision for the millions of persons who live with significant visual impairments or total blindness. Three variations are being explored: an artificial retina, retinal implants, and implants placed directly in the occipital lobes of the brain.

Restoring sight is only part of the battle, because vision is partly learned. If you saw the 1997 movie *At First Sight* you saw a fictionalized but essentially accurate depiction of some of the problems that arise for a person who has been blind from early life and who needs to learn how to use the visual system to understand the world. Restoring visual perception is a more complex problem.

Those individuals who have lost the sense of sight as adults would not face the same challenges in learning to use an artificial visual system. And, with continued time and innovation, perhaps we can restore sight early enough in life to avoid this problem entirely.

Visit these sites to learn more about this new and exciting sensory technology.

www.optobionics.com/

jollyroger.com/retina/

abcnews.go.com/sections/GMA/GoodMorningAmerica/GMA020508ArtificialRetina.html

OTHER USEFUL WEB SITES

HOWARD HUGHES MEDICAL INSTITUTE: SEEING, HEARING AND SMELLING THE WORLD

www.hhmi.org/senses/

Visit this site for interesting updates on research into the senses, as well as a review of what you have already learned.

GALLERY OF ILLUSIONS

dragon.uml.edu/psych/illusion.html

This site was created and is maintained by Dr. David Landrigan of the University of Massachusetts at Lowell. It contains versions of some illusions included in this book, and others that may be new to you.

THE EXPLORATORIUM ONLINE

www.exploratorium.edu/exhibits/f_exhibits.html

This is the web site of the wonderful San Francisco Science Museum—a collection of cyber exhibits that are updated on a regular basis.

SENSATION AND PERCEPTION TUTORIAL

psych.hanover.edu/Krantz/sen_tut.html

It's a great introduction to the senses and a place to practice what you are learning here. This is also a good "jumping off" page to surf the net for more information on sensation and perceptual illusions.

REFERENCES

Bartoshuk, L.M. (2000) Psychophysical advances in the study of genetic variations in taste. *Appetite,* 34, 105.

Segall, M., Campbell, D.T. & Herslovits, M.J. (1966) *The Influence of Culture on Visual Perception.* Indianapolis, IN: Bobbs-Merrill.

Chapter 5

STATES OF CONSCIOUSNESS

In this chapter you will consider the problem of defining consciousness and its different stages and states.

What Is Consciousness?

There is only one person who you can be 100 percent sure is conscious—you.

Because of this fact, consciousness continues to be a fascinating yet extremely challenging aspect of behavior to investigate. If we define *consciousness* as "awareness of internal and external stimuli"—it sounds simple—but we are referring to an ever-shifting yet seemingly continuous stream. Many psychological researchers suspect that the "continuity" is an illusion, given the variety of states one can experience even in a short span of time. In five minutes, an average person may shift from daydreaming to intent focus on an external sound to problem solving to listening to music in his or her head. And all of us have had that strange experience (at least a few times) of sustaining a minor injury (like a cut) and not realizing it until minutes after it occurred because we were so focused on the activity of the moment (perhaps the game or task that caused the injury).

In this chapter we will examine all the possible states of consciousness—our daily cycle of sleep and wakefulness, mildly altered states such as hypnotic trance and daydreaming, and alterations of consciousness that are induced by the use of psychoactive drugs.

Circadian Rhythms: The Internal Clock

Circadian rhythm refers to daily cycles of mental alertness and wakefulness that we all experience. You probably call yourself a "morning person" or an "evening person" on the basis of your preferred patterns getting out of and going to bed, and you probably know at which time(s) of day you feel at your best. Circadian rhythms are experienced in almost all body systems.

The brain structures involved in generating the circadian rhythm and levels of alertness are found in the brainstem and limbic system. They are

- The *suprachiasmic nucleus* (SCN)—a small cluster of neurons in the hypothalamus.
- The *pineal gland*—an endocrine gland located near the hypothalamus.
- The reticular formation or *reticular activating system* (RAS)—a network of neurons in the brainstem.

The SCN responds to levels of sunlight and influences the production of the hormone *melatonin* by the pineal gland (Turek & Czeisler 1999). Melatonin levels are lowest in the early morning. As the day progresses, activity in the SCN is triggered by signals from the visual system. The SCN signals the pineal gland to produce melatonin, and as the day progresses (and especially as evening draws near) the melatonin levels in the bloodstream gradually rise and drowsiness tends to increase. The levels of the hormone continue to rise until the middle of the night when we are most likely to be asleep. As the night progresses, melatonin levels drop. In addition to the influence of melatonin levels, the RAS is thought to be responsible for periodically "activating" the higher regions of the brain; this function is believed to result in periods of REM during the sleep cycle, and variations in alertness during the day.

Although these mechanisms explain *how* sleep happens, the question remains: "*Why* do we sleep?" It is clear that adequate daily sleep is necessary for good health and that the optimum time for that sleep is late at night/early in the morning (see the following discussion.) Animals that are deprived of sleep eventually die. Humans have been able to force themselves to remain awake for days but eventually they begin to experience sensory and cognitive disruptions. This fits with *restorative theory* of sleep. Sleep is refreshing and necessary for optimal functioning. This theory is supported by the declines in total sleep and REM sleep that are observed during the lifespan (see the following discussion.)

Sleep also appears to have an adaptive function. You can see this by noting the sleep patterns of animals that are typically "prey animals"—the animals that carnivores prefer to eat. They need to be able to move quickly under threat, so they tend to sleep sporadically and lightly. Predators, on the other hand tend to sleep a larger proportion of every twenty-four-hour period and sleep more deeply (think of your pet cat) partly because they can usually afford the luxury. Animals that hibernate (for example, most bears) sleep for weeks when the environment is least hospitable. These patterns prevent animals from interacting with the environment when the most threats to survival are present. This is the *evolutionary theory* of sleep—that sleep patterns represent an adaptation to an animal's niche.

Most humans do not keep a regular sleep-wake schedule—we tend to go to bed early and get up early on workdays and sleep in/go to bed late on our days off. When we travel by airplane, we often experience some degree of *jet lag* because of the stress involved in rapidly changing time zones. Additionally, many people do *shift work* out of societal necessity (we can't close the hospital and send everyone home at 5 P.M.); others, because of sheer busy-ness, don't get enough sleep. Both the amount of sleep and the regularity of its occurrence are important to maintaining a healthy "sleep style." The amounts of sleep that are appropriate may vary from person to person, but *all* people need to keep a regular schedule. The mechanisms described above are designed to maintain a regular pattern for sleeping and waking up. It is possible that some sleep disorders, brain fogginess, depression, and accidents that occur are partly caused by our society's tendency not to promote regular sleep-wake schedules and to keep people awake at a time when our brains are preparing for sleep. For example, most automobile accidents occur late at night and early in the morning, and some major industrial accidents (Chernobyl, Three Mile Island) occurred during the "graveyard" shift. This is probably no "accident."

Table 5-1 lists the names and symptoms of some of the most common sleep disorders and other unusual events related to sleep.

TABLE 5-1
SLEEP DISORDERS

Disorder/ Unusual Behavior	Symptoms	Connection/ Consequence	Treatments
Insomnia	Inability to get to sleep or waking very early and being unable to get back to sleep	May be either related to or caused by depression and stress; can cause mental/physical fatigue in the short term and compromise physical health in the long term	Behavior therapies based on classical conditioning; relaxation training; medication
Periodic Limb Movement Disorder/ Restless Legs Syndrome	Unpleasant sensations in legs; sudden movements of legs, knees, and hips during sleep	Same as insomnia	Same as insomnia
Sleep apnea	Repeated episodes of breathing cessation during the night	Found in males over 50 and severely overweight persons; potentially fatal	Mouthpieces, surgery, lifestyle changes (nutrition and exercise)
Parasomnias (sleepwalking, night terrors, bruxism); sleep paralysis	Poorly coordinated walking, sudden waking in a panic, grinding of the teeth, waking and being unable to move for short period of time	All the parasomnias are much more common in children than in adults; sleep paralysis occurs in adulthood	Parasomnias usually stop in adulthood; since all of these unusual events may be related to high levels of fatigue and stress, lifestyle changes and relaxation training may help
REM Sleep Behavior Disorder	Thrashing, punching, and acting out activity in dreams	As opposed to sleep paralysis, this is the failure of the process of REM sleep to induce paralysis—most sufferers are elderly males; danger of injury to sufferer and bed partner	Seems to be associated with degeneration of brainstem, currently untreatable
Narcolepsy	Excessive daytime sleepiness; "sleep attacks" in which person enters REM sleep immediately	Runs in families, genes have been implicated in laboratory studies, very dangerous in some situations	Sleep attacks can be controlled with medication

Sleep and Dreaming

Sleep research was facilitated by the invention of the EEG (electroencephalogram). Both systematic and accidental events in laboratories during physiological research using the EEG led to the realization that sleep was not, in fact, a time of continuous unconsciousness or "brain shut-down" but was actually a dynamic series of states. Combining an EEG with various other types of physiological monitors created the machine that is now used specifically to monitor the sleep cycle—the *polysomnograph*.

Good quality observational and experimental research on sleep took off in the mid-1950s. Scientists working in the United States (Aserinsky and Kleitman, Dement) and France (Jouvet) published their work on *rapid eye movement* or *REM* sleep, known as active or paradoxical sleep. The activity or "paradox" is that while the person is still deeply asleep, the brain waves tracked by the EEG are identical to those of a person who is awake and alert (though most of the body is held in a state of gross motor paralysis, which protects us from acting out our dreams and injuring others and ourselves). This is the stage of sleep in which most dreaming (and the most vivid dreaming) occurs. REM sleep was named so because even without any hi-tech equipment it is easy to observe the eyes darting back and forth under the eyelids, perhaps following the action of a dream. Physiological arousal states during this phase of sleep follow a waking pattern, with increased heart rate, blood pressure, and respiration. There may be some muscle twitches in spite of the overall paralysis. The work of the first sleep scientists also revealed that, like REM, each stage of sleep has its own distinct brain wave pattern, and that stages of sleep evolve through the night in ninety-minute cycles.

Based on this early work, modern sleep scientists now distinguish between two broad categories of sleep, *NREM* or non-REM (four separate stages) and REM. NREM is also called "quiet sleep"—people toss and turn in these stages but report only transient dream activity. The brain waves that are produced during NREM sleep tend to be lower frequency and relatively synchronized (alpha, theta, and delta), and those produced during REM and the fully awake state are higher frequency and relatively desynchronized (beta or "sawtooth" waves).

Table 5-2 lists the chief characteristics of the five stages of sleep.

As you pass through your first ninety minutes of sleep, you go through stages 1, 2, 3, and 4. At the end of this first period, you don't go directly from stage 4 to REM; rather, you cycle back from stage 4 to stage 2, and then enter your first episode of REM sleep instead of returning to stage 1. Figure 5.1 depicts the patterns of the sleep cycle.

The first stage of REM is brief, typically lasting between five to fifteen minutes. Over the course of the rest of the night, the NREM cycles become shorter, and REM becomes longer. Stages 3 and 4 typically do not appear at all during the second half of the night, and the pattern shows an alternation between stage 2 and REM. Because we awaken in the morning during this pattern, it is more likely that we will remember the content of our dreams at the end of our sleep.

Over the course of the human lifespan there are changes in our sleep stage patterns and sleeping habits. Overall, the actual time sleeping appears to decrease, although during growth spurts (such as adolescence) this trend may briefly reverse. By the time we reach our 60s, sleep averages about six hours a night and is generally shallower. It appears that all fetal brain activity is similar to REM sleep. A newborn sleeps about sixteen hours a day, and spends about 80 percent of its sleep time in REM. The proportion of the sleep cycle that is spent in REM declines throughout the lifespan. These patterns may indicate that REM is necessary for growth and rejuvenation of the brain and its functioning and may account for some of the mild cognitive decline experienced in older adults.

TABLE 5-2
STAGES OF SLEEP

Sleep Stage	Brain Waves	Characteristics	Apparent Benefits
Stage 1 NREM	Transition of alpha to theta	Light sleep, hallucinations, sleeper is easily awoken	
Stage 2 NREM	Theta with sleep spindles and k-complexes	Deeper sleep, less sensory awareness	Need to pass through and finish this stage to get full benefit of sleep
Stage 3 NREM	Transition of theta to delta (20–50% delta)	Deep sleep	See Stage 4
Stage 4 NREM	Mostly delta (50–100%)	Deep sleep; it can take 10 to 20 minutes to wake up from Stage 4 fully	Important for growth, healing, restoration; also important for consolidation of learning during the day
REM	Beta waves	Gross motor paralysis; vivid dreaming; hallucinations may be experienced when awoken from REM	Central nervous system rest/growth; consolidation of learning that occurs during the day

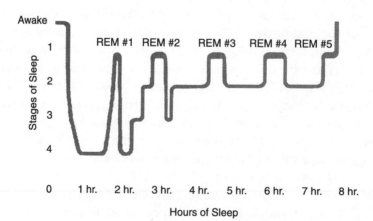

Figure 5.1 The human sleep cycle.

Dreaming

Dreaming can occur during any phase of sleep, but it is most commonly reported during REM sleep. The high level of activity in the brain makes these dreams by far the most vivid. Some people believe that they do not dream, but in fact is it is probably true that everyone dreams to some extent. Even during the active REM period, most dreaming probably consists of a relatively uninteresting kind of dwelling on everyday problems (material that is called *day residue*) and is referred to as *sleep thinking*. This kind of dreaming is not emotional or bizarre, and so it is very likely to be forgotten. One of the more popular theories about dreaming is the *neurocognitive theory*. This theory holds that dreaming is the thinking that we do during sleep. Psychologists still hold a wide variety of views of dreaming. The Freudian view that dreams represent some type of desire for wish fulfillment is rejected by a majority of modern psychologists as too limited and lacking in scientific support. Some psychologists believe that dreams are completely without significance. Others propose that dreams begin as random signals from the limbic system and brainstem onto which the cerebral cortex imposes meaning by drawing connections between the images. (Some sleep researchers propose that these connections may have meaning.) This is called the *activation-synthesis hypothesis* (Hobson & McCarley 1977). Some psychologists are investigating whether dreaming and REM are useful for learning (by helping us to consolidate information taken in during the day.) (Stickgold et al. 2001). Still others are investigating whether dreams are a kind of helpful thought about significant personal problems that may be in need of some kind of attention (Cartwright. & Lamberg 1992).

Hypnosis, Meditation, and Daydreaming

Hypnosis, meditation, and daydreaming can all best be understood as mildly altered states of consciousness. When we daydream, we turn our thoughts inward and often appear to effectively "tune out" at least some external stimuli. This is a very different state than the fully alert and in-tune condition that characterizes most of our non-sleeping time.

Hypnosis was first practiced in the late eighteenth century. Anton Mesmer and others popularized it, practicing it in royal courts of western Europe (thus the term "mesmerized" is used as an expression for hypnosis because he was one of the first to practice it). From the outset, very questionable claims were made about its uses, and this trend continues to the current era. Hypnosis is *not* a form of "mind control," and it is not "sleep." On the contrary, hypnosis depends primarily on the cooperation and suggestibility of the person who is being hypnotized. It appears to involve some division or refocusing of attention and concentration. The hypnotist provides little more than coaching or direction. For many people, a hypnotist is not even necessary in the achievement of a hypnotic trance. People vary in their individual degrees of hypnotizability, but even the most hypnotizable person will not do anything under hypnosis that he or she is not willing or able to do when not under hypnosis. So, there are no special powers granted in hypnosis, and, with all due respect to Hollywood, it is extremely unlikely that anyone would commit murder or other crimes while in this state (unless they were already very much inclined to do so). Similarly, although some clinical practitioners use hypnosis for the purpose of "recovering blocked memories," there is no evidence to support its effectiveness for this purpose. Memories recovered under hypnosis are just as likely to be incorrect as those recovered in a fully alert state. Hypnosis can be easily faked; even experts often cannot tell a genuinely hypnotized person from a person who is pretending.

Hypnosis is not "bunk." Hypnotizability is a quality that all people probably possess to some greater or lesser degree. An ability to divide attention is necessary in order for people to drive cars and perform other activities, so the skill that forms the basis of hypnosis is probably a fundamental human cognitive (thinking) ability. Highly hypnotizable people appear to experience sensory distortions and be open to posthypnotic suggestions (Nash 2001). Many people are able to use hypnosis or self-hypnosis for pain management. (Lamaze training is a good example of a hypnotic pain management system—it does not work for everyone, but many have used it successfully to deal with the pain that normally accompanies childbirth.) Hypnosis can be used for stress management and is employed by some sports psychologists to enhance the concentration and performance of athletes.

Meditation can be understood as a form of self-hypnosis. It involves the focusing of attention and intense concentration while promoting relaxation. EEG readouts taken during meditation show that alpha waves are generated, very similar to the state of the brain just before the onset of sleep. Meditation techniques have been utilized for centuries in many world cultures and religions, although the practice was not necessarily referred to as meditation. There are a number of forms of meditation practiced worldwide; TM (transcendental meditation) is probably the best known of all forms.

Psychoactive Drugs and Their Effects on Consciousness and the Brain

The use of substances to alter consciousness is probably as old as humankind itself. Psychoactive substances have been used for religious rituals, celebrations, and medical treatments for most of human history. Although people will debate vigorously about many aspects of substance use, it is now well understood that the use of *psychoactive* (mood and behavior altering) substances has real effects on the physical functioning of the brain and nervous system, usually through manipulation of the effects of naturally occurring neurotransmitters. Sometimes the effects linger weeks or months after the person ceases to use the drug. Sometimes, the effects are permanent or even fatal.

People often discuss patterns of drug use without using the terminology correctly. *Abuse* refers to a pattern of drug use that is not compulsive (no cravings) but has negative consequences for the user (job or personal difficulties). *Dependence* or *addiction* refers to compulsive use. The hallmark symptoms are an increasing *tolerance* for the drug and *withdrawal* symptoms. Tolerance develops as the nervous system cuts off the receptors for neurotransmitters, with the net effect that the user needs more of the drug to experience its effects. Withdrawal is associated with tolerance; the user is hypersensitive to the lack of the drug, even using less than a typical amount will produce unpleasant symptoms or a *rebound* effect—a dramatic state opposite from the one the drug produces. Treatment of drug dependence can be unpleasant and costly for the user and society.

Because the public health costs of substance abuse and addiction are so high, it is of great interest to all those who make and evaluate social policy to know what makes some people so vulnerable to substance abuse and addiction. We have been used to viewing substance misuse as purely a moral issue, but there is evidence that some people are more vulnerable. For example, there is a very high rate of substance dependence in certain ethnic groups; this suggests that social factors and genetic factors may also play a role. A model of alcoholism that specifies two different types of alcohol dependence has been proposed. Type 1 alcoholism tends to begin in adulthood and typically features milder mood and behavior changes and involves an easier recovery. Type 2 alcoholism arises in adolescence, is typified by more dramatic mood alterations, and more commonly features violent behavior. Recovery is more difficult. Type 2 alcoholism appears to have a genetic or familial component (McGue 1999). A person who suffers from Type 2 alcoholism is much more likely to have relatives with alcoholism that a person who suffers from the Type 1 variety.

Table 5-3 summarizes the major classes of psychoactive substances.

TABLE 5-3
PSYCHOACTIVE DRUGS AND THEIR EFFECTS

Drug Class	Examples	Short-Term Effects	Long-Term Effects
Central nervous system depressants	Alcohol; barbiturates such as Quaaludes and Seconal; minor tranquilizers such as Xanax and Valium	Sleepiness; slurred speech; poor coordination; violent behavior (alcohol only)	Dependence, withdrawal symptoms; convulsions; impotence; damage to multiple organ systems; dementia
Narcotics	Natural opiates drugs such as heroin, morphine, and codeine; synethic verions such as methadone	Euphoria; lethargy; drowsiness; constipation	Dependence; withdrawal symptoms; health problems associated with lifestyle, HIV/AIDS, and hepatitis
Inhalants	Glue; solvents such as nail polish remover and paint thinner; gasoline	Euphoria, intoxication	Brain damage, respiratory failure, and sudden death
Stimulants	Amphetamines, methamphetamine, cocaine, nicotine, ephedrine, caffeine	Increased energy, alertness, euphoria, "crashes," violent behavior	Craving, dependence, exhaustion, weight loss/weight gain (when discontinued), sexual dysfunction, heart attacks
Hallucinogens	LSD, peyote, mescaline, "mushrooms"	Hallucinations, perceptual and time distortions, dreamlike changes in internal and external experience, "bad trips"	Flashbacks, long-term psychotic reactions occur in those who use hallucinogens with other drugs (polydrug use) or have a mental illness

TABLE 5-3 (Continued)
PSYCHOACTIVE DRUGS AND THEIR EFFECTS

Drug Class	Examples	Short-Term Effects	Long-Term Effects
Cannabinoids	Cannabis (marijuana); hashish	Mild sedation, appetite increase, jitters, time distortion	Many alleged long-term effects, none determined—research is inconclusive; heavy daily use may lead to dependence
Miscellaneous and "designer drugs"	MDMA, PCP	Hallucinations, lack of inhibition, euphoria, violent behavior	Depression, immune system suppression

Connecting Through Chapter Review

WORD-STUDY CONNECTION

Write each of these words on index cards and write their definitions on the opposite side.

abuse	insomnia	rapid eye movement (REM)
activation-synthesis hypothesis	jet lag	rebound
addiction	k-complexes	REM sleep behavior disorder
alpha waves	MDMA	reticular activating system
beta waves	meditation	restorative theory
bruxism	melatonin	shift work
cannabinoids	narcolepsy	sleep apnea
consciousness	narcotics	sleep paralysis
circadian rhythm	neurocognitive theory	sleep spindles
CNS depressants	NREM	sleep thinking
day residue	parasomnia	stimulants
delta waves	PCP	theta waves
dependence	periodic limb movement disorder	tolerance
evolutionary theory	pineal gland	Type 1 alcoholism
hallucinogens	polysomnograph	Type 2 alcoholism
hypnosis	psychoactive	withdrawal
inhalants	suprachiasmic nucleus	

SELF-TEST CONNECTION

PART A. Completion
Write in the word that correctly completes each statement.

1. A person's awareness of internal and external stimuli is referred to as _____ .
2. _____ are daily cycles of wakefulness and mental alertness.
3. The parts of the brain that generate sleep and circadian rhythms are found in the _____ and the _____ .
4. The pineal gland is part of the _____ system and is found near the hypothalamus.
5. The _____ is thought to play a role in generating periods of REM sleep.
6. _____ levels are lowest in the early morning.
7. The idea that sleep is necessary for healing, growth, and optimal functioning is known as the _____ theory.
8. Statistics kept on accident rates suggest that it is most dangerous to work the _____ shift.
9. _____ is a syndrome that involves repeated cessation of breathing during the night.
10. The sleep disorders known collectively as _____ are more common in children than in adults.
11. _____ seems to be related to degeneration of the brainstem.
12. _____ is also known as active or paradoxical sleep. It appears to be associated with certain aspects of learning and memory.
13. There are _____ stages of quiet or non-REM (NREM) sleep.
14. _____ is the sleep stage in which the EEG readout consists mainly of delta waves. It is associated with healing, growth, and certain aspects of learning.
15. "Dreaming is a form of thinking." This statement summarizes the _____ theory of dreaming.
16. _____ depends mainly on the cooperation and suggestibility of the subject.
17. One legitimate use of hypnosis is to help to reduce _____ .
18. _____ can be considered a form of self-hypnosis.
19. _____ and _____ are the two major symptoms of substance dependence.
20. _____ alcoholism appears to have a genetic or familial component.
21. _____ is an example of a central nervous system depressant drug.
22. Chronic use of _____ drugs can result in heart attacks and loss of sexual function.
23. Use of _____ drugs can alter one's sense of time and produce a nervous, jittery feeling.

PART B. Multiple Choice
Circle the letter of the item that correctly completes the statement.

1. Almost all organ systems in the human body experience daily variations of activity that are called _____ .
   (a) hypnosis
   (b) REM sleep
   (c) consciousness
   (d) circadian rhythms

2. The _____ is a small cluster of neurons in the hypothalamus that respond to levels of sunlight.
   - (a) SCN
   - (b) REM
   - (c) RAS
   - (d) NREM

3. The _____ produces melatonin in response to signals from the suprachiasmic nucleus.
   - (a) thyroid gland
   - (b) hypothalamus
   - (c) pineal gland
   - (d) RAS

4. Animals appear to have sleep patterns that minimize their exposure to dangers in the environment. This is referred to as the _____ theory of sleep.
   - (a) restorative
   - (b) hibernating
   - (c) evolutionary
   - (d) circadian

5. _____ is a harmless phenomenon that sometimes occurs as people wake up out of REM sleep.
   - (a) Bruxism
   - (b) Sleep paralysis
   - (c) Insomnia
   - (d) Sleep behavior disorder

6. _____ can be controlled in part with medication.
   - (a) Insomnia
   - (b) Narcolepsy
   - (c) Restless legs syndrome
   - (d) All of the above

7. An EEG combined with various types of physiological monitors is referred to as a _____ .
   - (a) DTI machine
   - (b) CAT scan
   - (c) polysomnograph
   - (d) PET scanner

8. During _____ sleep, the body is almost entirely paralyzed.
   - (a) Stage 1 NREM
   - (b) REM
   - (c) Stage 2 NREM
   - (d) Stage 4 NREM

9. _____ sleep is also referred to as quiet sleep.
   - (a) REM
   - (b) NREM
   - (c) Narcoleptic
   - (d) Nonspecific

10. It can take up to 20 minutes to fully awaken from _____ sleep.
    - (a) Stage 1 NREM
    - (b) REM
    - (c) Stage 2 NREM
    - (d) Stage 4 NREM

11. Toward the end of a typical night or period of sleep, the EEG read out indicates an alternation between _____ sleep and _____ sleep.
    - (a) Stage 1 NREM; Stage 3 NREM
    - (b) REM; Stage 2NREM
    - (c) Stage 2 NREM; Stage 4 NREM
    - (d) Stage 4 NREM; REM

12. Humans get the most REM sleep relative to the rest of their sleep time during which stage of the lifespan?
    - (a) Infancy
    - (b) Adolescence
    - (c) Early adulthood
    - (d) Late adulthood

13. Most of human dreaming could accurately be described as _____ .
    - (a) bizarre and frightening imagery
    - (b) fulfilled wishes
    - (c) day residue and sleep thinking
    - (d) visions of the future

14. The cerebral cortex struggles to make meaning out of random signals from the brain-stem and limbic system. This sentence briefly summarizes the _____ view of dreaming.
    - (a) psychodynamic
    - (b) activation-synthesis
    - (c) behavioral
    - (d) neurocognitive

15. In the eighteenth century, _____ helped to popularize the practice of hypnosis.
    - (a) Sigmund Freud
    - (b) William Wundt
    - (c) John Watson
    - (d) Anton Mesmer
16. Which of the following is *not* a valid use for clinical hypnosis?
    - (a) Pain reduction
    - (b) Enhanced concentration
    - (c) Recovering memories
    - (d) Stress management
17. Meditation is most accurately viewed as a form of _____ .
    - (a) NREM sleep
    - (b) self-hypnosis
    - (c) REM sleep
    - (d) hallucination
18. A pattern of substance use that is noncompulsive but has negative interpersonal or social consequences is called _____ .
    - (a) abuse
    - (b) dependence
    - (c) tolerance
    - (d) withdrawal
19. Which of the following is *not* classified as a stimulant drug?
    - (a) Methamphetamine
    - (b) Cocaine
    - (c) Nicotine
    - (d) Solvents
20. Flashbacks may result from previous use of _____ .
    - (a) hallucinogens
    - (b) marijuana
    - (c) cocaine
    - (d) heroin

PART C. Modified True-False

If the statement is true, write "T" for the answer. If the statement is incorrect, change the underlined expression to one that will make the statement true.

1. <u>Daydreaming</u> is an example of a mildly altered state of consciousness.
2. An individual's daily cycles of consciousness, alertness, and sleep are referred to as the <u>sleep cycle</u>.
3. The <u>pituitary gland</u> produces melatonin. It is a small endocrine gland located near the hypothalamus.
4. Levels of melatonin in the bloodstream <u>rise</u> until late into the nighttime.
5. Scientists believe that the <u>RAS</u> is responsible for periodically "activating" the higher regions of the brain.
6. The basic idea of the <u>evolutionary theory</u> of sleep is that sleep is necessary for rest, healing, and the optimum functioning of an organism.
7. REM sleep behavior disorder is associated with deterioration of the <u>cerebral cortex</u>.
8. To track the changes that occur during the course of the sleep cycle, scientists use a <u>simple EEG</u> machine.
9. REM sleep is also known as <u>active or paradoxical sleep</u>.
10. Hallucinations and the beginning of the production of theta waves are characteristics of <u>Stage 1 NREM</u> sleep.
11. <u>Stage 2 NREM and Stage 3 NREM</u> are the stages that are associated with consolidation of learning.
12. During <u>late adulthood</u>, human sleep is typically shallowest, and individuals tend to get less sleep on average than at any other time of life.
13. The <u>psychodynamic</u> theory of dreaming states that most dreaming is simply a form of thinking.

14. It is very <u>hard</u> to tell if someone is faking a state of hypnosis.
15. <u>Lamaze</u> is an example of a hypnotic technique used to help to reduce pain.
16. <u>Dependence</u> is the term for compulsive use of any psychoactive substance including the development of tolerance and withdrawal symptoms.
17. A rebound effect is <u>an extreme overreaction similar to</u> that produced by a psychoactive drug.
18. <u>Type 1 alcoholism is milder and easier to treat than Type 2.</u>
19. Use of <u>inhalants</u> can result in death due to respiratory failure.
20. Research has not produced any consistent evidence of long-term negative effects from the use of <u>cannabis</u>.

PART D. "Your Naïve Friends"—Some Critical Thinking Questions
Write brief essay-type responses to the following questions.

1. Your friend asks you if he should spend $250 on a CD-ROM that promises to help him learn to speak and understand Spanish in his sleep. The program involves playing Spanish words and phrases over and over for six hours during the night. The program does not include Spanish grammar or vocabulary practice during the day. What would you tell your friend about the connection between sleep and learning? Would you advise him to buy the CD-ROM?
2. The following week, another friend asks you about hypnosis. She says that she saw a hypnotist at work on the *Rikki Lake Show*. She said that people lost control and clucked like chickens on command. She also tells you how the hypnotist was able to make people remember past lives from the Middle Ages and Civil War, as well as traumatic experiences from the infancy and early childhood in their "present" lives. Based on what you have learned, what would you tell your friend about the degree of authenticity of the hypnotism featured on the show?
3. One month later, a friend of yours shows you a bottle of a new "all-natural" herbal weight loss supplement. He has just bought a $500 supply of this supplement. You look at the bottle closely and read that one of the ingredients is ephedrine. What would you tell your friend about the quality and safety of this all-natural supplement?

CONNECTING TO CONCEPTS
Review the chapter and then write down your thoughts about the following questions.

1. Define the term circadian rhythm. Discuss some of the health and safety problems that appear to arise as a result of modern human habits as they conflict with biologically based circadian cycles.
2. Write a description of a ninety-minute human sleep cycle, including information about the physiological and psychological aspects of each of the five stages.
3. Define hypnosis and discuss some of the valid and legitimate uses of this altered state. Compare hypnosis with meditation and daydreaming.
4. Define and compare psychoactive substance use, abuse, and dependence. Select any one class of drugs, describe the effects, and list the most common examples of drugs from the class.

CONNECTING TO LIFE/JOB SKILLS

The Value of Good Sleep Hygiene

"You should get more sleep." Most of us have heard this statement. Why? It is generally true for most adolescent and adults in our society that we need more sleep than we get. We experience what Dr. William Dement, noted sleep researcher, refers to as "the sleep debt." There is a pervasive attitude of "who needs sleep, anyway?" The answer is—all of us. The debt generates an enormous cost to society—poor sleep hygiene and sleep deprivation affects our immune systems, raises our accident rates, and may have psychological consequences that touch on our ability to learn, remember, and relate to others.

One product of the boom in sleep research has been a new understanding of the changes in circadian rhythm brought on by puberty. A variety of laboratory studies have provided evidence that puberty resets the child's circadian rhythms. Melatonin production and release occurs later in the evening. So, teenagers become sleepy later than do children or adults. They now need a little less sleep than younger children, but they still need on average about one hour more sleep than adults do.

The teen sleep pattern does not fit well with what society expects from them. There may be serious consequences for school performance (learning and memory may be affected) and mental health (depression and irritability). Many schools begin classes between 7 and 8 A.M. Results of a recent study in a Minnesota public high school district showed significant benefits to student GPAs and morale when school began later and ended later. Other school districts have been responding to this data, although slowly.

A recent National Sleep Foundation poll confirmed that sleep deprivation is a significant economic problem, especially for businesses that rely on shift workers. Of course, shift work is a necessity in many industries. One solution under study involves the scheduling of a consistent period of "anchor sleep" sometimes combined with multiple short naps in situations where eight consecutive hours may not possible (in the military for example). Anchor sleep is a period during the day that occurs consistently whether the person is on his or her shift or not. Thus, a person sleeps from 8 A.M. to 4 P.M. when she is scheduled for night shift, and sleeps from 4 A.M. to 12 P.M. on her day off. She is always asleep between 8 A.M. and 12 P.M. This consistency of sleep time appears to have many benefits, including improved mental acuity, stamina, and better all-around health. Once again, we have found that the consistency of sleep pattern is just as important as the amount obtained.

National Space Biomedical Research Institute Web Site: Human Factors, Performance, and Chronobiology (2002) *Technical Summary*—Research of David Dinges, PhD

www.nsbri.org/Research/2001-2003/SleepProj3.html

Sleep Quest Web Site: Archived Columns (2000)—*Sleep Debt* by William Dement, MD, PhD

www.sleepquest.com/d_column_archive6.html

APA Monitor Online (2001)—*Sleep deprivation may be undermining teen health* by Siri Carpenter

www.apa.org/monitor/oct01/sleepteen.html

WHAT'S HAPPENING!

Progress in treatment of drug addiction

Drug abuse and addiction continue to take a substantial toll on society in lives and dollars. Scientists continue to investigate safer and more effective means to end dependence on powerfully addictive drugs such as heroin and nicotine. Pharmaceutical methods are improving. In the treatment of opiate addiction, buprenorphine has shown promise as a replacement for the more dangerous methadone therapy that has been standard over the past generation. Buprenorphine is a drug that mimics the effects of heroin at the synapses with far fewer side effects. It satisfies the craving without the level of euphoria or depression of the central nervous system.

The most popular pharmacological strategies for treatment of nicotine dependence have been replacement strategies (patches and gum) and low-dose prescriptions for antidepressants such as bupropion (called Zyban). Recovering smokers tend to be more successful when their treatment includes group support and behavioral counseling to promote resistance to cues for use and enhance motivation to succeed. Unlike the heroin user, nicotine, being legal, is widely advertised. An ex-heroin user may face temptation to use, but the scale of the temptation is somewhat smaller. It is more easily managed through lifestyle changes than the stress faced by the ex-nicotine user who is more constantly exposed to cues for using through advertising and the more open and widespread use of the drug by others in the environment.

On the horizon, behavioral genetics has provided information regarding familial vulnerability to drug dependence. Alcoholism appears to have a very strong genetic component. The University of Colorado as well as other major universities and research centers worldwide continue to investigate the role of heredity in addiction. Perhaps we will have ways to prevent or control this problem at the genetic level in the not too distant future.

OTHER USEFUL WEB SITES

NATIONAL CENTER ON SLEEP DISORDERS

rover.nhlbi.nih.gov/about/ncsdr/

Affiliated with the National Institutes of Health, this informative site presents the latest scientific research on sleep-related disorders and difficulties.

SLEEPNET

www.sleepnet.com

Although it is a .com domain, this is a noncommercial site with abundant information on the science of sleep and sleep hygiene.

UNIVERSITY OF ARIZONA CENTER FOR CONSCIOUSNESS STUDIES

www.consciousness.arizona.edu/

This site presents an interesting combination of scientific and philosophical viewpoints and studies on the nature of consciousness.

THE ASSOCIATION FOR THE STUDY OF DREAMS

www.asdreams.org/

This site is the main web site of a multidisciplinary association for the study of dreams and processes of dreaming.

SOCIETY FOR CLINICAL AND EXPERIMENTAL HYPNOSIS

sunsite.utk.edu/IJCEH/scehframe.htm

This is the homepage of a leading organization for the scientific study of hypnosis and its applications.

NATIONAL INSTITUTE ON DRUG ABUSE

www.nida.nih.gov/

This is the homepage of a leading governmental organization dedicated to education on all legal and illegal drugs of abuse, prevention, and treatment of substance-related disorders.

VAULTS OF EROWID

www.erowid.org/index.shtml

This web site provides a great deal of information about psychoactive substances and explores the cultural and historical aspects of substance use and abuse.

REFERENCES

Cartwright, R. & Lamberg, L. (1992) *Crisis Dreaming: Using Your Dreams to Solve Your Problems*. New York: HarperCollins.

Hobson, J. A. & McCarley, R. W. (1977) The brain as a dream state generator: An activation-synthesis hypothesis of the dream process. *American Journal of Psychiatry,* 134, 1335–1348.

McGue, M. (1999) The behavioral genetics of alcoholism. *Current Directions in Psychological Science,* 8, 109–115.

Nash, D. (2001) The truth and the hype of hypnosis. Scientific American, July (Online) *www.sciam.com/issue.cfm?issuedate=Jul-01*

Stickgold, R., Hobson, J. A., Fosse, R. & Fosse, M. (2001) Sleep, learning and dreams: Off-line memory reprocessing. *Science,* 294, 1052–1057.

Turek F. W. and Czeisler C. (1999) "Role of melatonin in the regulation of sleep," Chapter 6. In: *Regulation of Sleep and Circadian Rhythms* (F. W. Turek and P. C. Zee, eds.) Marcel Dekker, Inc., New York, pp. 181–195.

Chapter 6

LEARNING

In this chapter you will become acquainted with the major theories of learning.

What Is Learning?

There's more than one correct definition for *learning*. For our purposes, one comprehensive yet brief definition is: "Any relatively permanent change in behavior resulting from experience." There are three different types of process that can bring about permanent changes in behavior and three major types of learning. Learning seems to be something that most animals are "born" to do. If animals did not learn, they could not adapt successfully to changes in their environment, and they would not survive.

The school of psychology that is most closely associated with learning theory is the *behaviorist* school, as you may remember from Chapter 1. The scientists in this school vary in their perspectives on the process of learning, some being more "strict" in counting only behaviors that can be observed and measured as evidence of learning. Others believe that learning takes place when mental processes are changed—these are the *cognitive-behaviorists*.

Classical Conditioning

Classical conditioning is about the formation of associations between stimuli and responses. The responses that are learned (conditioned) are reflexive or involuntary. No new voluntary behavior is learned; rather, a new association is established between a formerly neutral stimulus and an old, involuntary response.

The Legacy of Pavlov

Ivan Pavlov (1849–1936) was a physiologist by training and profession. Before his groundbreaking work on classical conditioning, he had won a Nobel Prize for his work on digestion (1904). His discovery of the mechanisms of associative learning and classical conditioning were, as has been the case with many other great scientific discoveries, accidental—a product of serendipity. He had no interest in processes of learning, until a process of learning threatened to ruin his latest set of experiments.

Pavlov, an expert on digestive processes, was studying salivation in dogs. He needed to take precise measurements of their salivation rates, but unfortunately, the dogs were starting to salivate before he had a chance to set up the measuring equipment—long before the food was served to them. By making various changes in the experimental conditions, Pavlov eventually was able to make a correct inference about the cues that alerted the dogs that a feeding was about to take place. The laboratory procedures that signaled the start of the experiment were reliable cues to the animals that food was coming; therefore, strong *associations* formed to the arrival of the laboratory staff, Pavlov's footsteps, and other events that the dogs had started to recognize as predictable, reliable signals. Pavlov then replicated the effects deliberately to verify that he was indeed correct. Any *neutral stimulus* (such as a bell or a buzzer) that was paired with the presentation of the food would become a signal that food was on its way, and the dogs would salivate.

John B. Watson and "Little Albert"

John Broadus Watson (1878–1958) was one of the first American promoters of the behaviorist perspective in psychology. He held very some very radical ideas about human experience. As was the case with so many other behaviorists, he believed that consciousness was almost impossible to study, that all there was that could be studied *was* behavior. His most famous case study has come to be known as "Little Albert," in which he set out to provide solid evidence of his theory that all emotions and reactions in humans were learned, not innate. He did so by teaching a 9-month-old infant, Albert, to fear white bunny rabbits, white rats, and, by extension, all manner of white, fuzzy things (including a Santa Claus beard). He made a loud, unpleasant sound each and every time Albert was given the rat or rabbit with which to play. Eventually Albert did show fear when the animals were present. The Little Albert research study is no longer well regarded as scientific evidence. Case study methodology is usually only considered appropriate for use in studying unique or rare disorders or phenomena. There is substantial evidence from biological, evolutionary, and cross-cultural psychology to suggest that the brain is wired for certain emotions from birth, and that people across all world cultures recognize a basic set of emotions, so that it can be reasonably inferred that these are innate emotions. Evidence also suggests that at least some fears exhibited by humans and other animals may be instinctual—it is much easier to teach an animal to fear a spider than to fear a rock, for example.

The Language and Processes of Classical Conditioning

- An *unconditioned stimulus (UCS)* is an event, object, or substance that naturally evokes a response. For example,
  - *Pizza* makes a person hungry.
  - A *shark* is scary.
  - A *trip on an ocean liner* makes you sick.
- The *unconditioned response (UCR)* is the reaction to the unconditioned stimulus.
  - Pizza makes a person *hungry*.
  - A shark is *scary*.
  - A trip on an ocean liner makes you *sick*.

- The *neutral stimulus* under normal circumstances does not give you a distinct reaction.
  - A *doorbell* doesn't usually make you hungry.
  - *Music* doesn't usually scare you.
  - *The sound of a foghorn* doesn't make you sick.
- The neutral stimulus is paired with the unconditioned stimulus.
  - The *doorbell* rings when the *pizza* delivery person arrives.
  - The *music* plays when the *shark* is approaching.
  - The *foghorn is blowing* while you are on the *ocean liner getting sick*.
- The *association* is formed.
  - Doorbell = pizza
  - Music = shark
  - Foghorn = ocean liner
- The *neutral stimulus* now elicits the same response as the *unconditioned stimulus*.
  - The *doorbell* rings, and you get *hungry*.
  - The *music* plays, and you get *nervous*.
  - The *foghorn blows,* and you want to *throw up*.

The neutral stimulus is now called a *conditioned stimulus (CS)*, and the response it evokes is called the *conditioned response (CR)*.

Practice on these examples.* See if you can name the UCS, UCR, neutral stimulus, and the newly paired CS/CR.

1. Every time the funny theme song to a certain animated movie plays, an FBI performance rights warning screen (a dark screen with white print) precedes it. Ten-month-old Gabe loves to hear the theme song and laughs and laughs at it. After awhile, his parents notice that Gabe laughs when the warning screen appears.
2. John's mother was a great baker. When he was a boy, she would spend all afternoon on Saturdays baking while listening to opera on the radio. The smell of the cakes, breads, and cookies and the sound of the music, would fill the house. Twenty years later, John can't listen to opera music without getting hungry.
3. Jeannie was sitting in a Chinese restaurant with her fiancé when he told her he was leaving her for a chorus girl from Las Vegas named Cherries Flambé. Now, whenever she walks past a Chinese restaurant, she gets very, very sad.

Some Other Important Concepts Related to Classical Conditioning

Stimulus Generalization

If an organism begins to produce the conditioned response when stimuli that are similar but not exactly the same as the original conditioned stimulus, *stimulus generalization* has occurred. If Gabe starts to laugh anytime the screen on the TV becomes dark, if John gets

*Answers appear at the end of the chapter.

hungry when he hears any type of classical vocal or choral music, stimulus generalization has occurred. When little Albert began to exhibit fear of white stuffed animals or Watson when he put on a fake white beard, he may have been exhibiting generalization.

Extinction

Extinction is the loss of the response to the neutral or conditioned stimulus. It can be achieved in two ways. The circumstance or the experimenter might cease to pair the neutral stimulus with the unconditioned stimulus, causing the eventual unlearning of the association. Or, the organism might be exposed to the conditioned stimulus for such frequent and/or prolonged periods that it becomes *desensitized* and loses the reaction.

Avoidance Prevents Extinction

This crucial principle of classical conditioning—avoidance prevents extinction—has some important practical and clinical applications. The tendency exhibited by most organisms is to avoid stimuli that bring on unpleasant feelings. It makes sense to do this if we are dealing with events or things that are clearly and imminently dangerous. However the tendency to avoid certain stimuli can work against us. The more you avoid a stimulus that evokes a strong emotional or reflex response, the more the strong feeling associated with that stimulus will be perpetuated. For a businessperson who is so frightened of airplanes that she can't take a one-hour flight for an important trip, the fear reaction could be a threat to her career. She must find a way to "get over it." This process also holds true for stimuli that evoke pleasant reactions. If you don't eat potato chips, which you love, because someone told you that they were bad for you and would make you fat, you will likely begin to think a great deal about potato chips. The most effective way to stop wanting potato chips would be to eat *nothing* but potato chips until you get sick of them (desensitized). In our modern junk-food-saturated environment, you would likely soon find a replacement treat. Avoidance is generally not an effective dieting strategy. It is probably best that you allow yourself to eat a small number of chips whenever you crave them, eat a more balanced diet overall, and increase your daily exercise.

Systematic Desensitization

Systematic desensitization is a type of psychotherapy that uses the avoidance-prevents-retardation principle to help people overcome phobias by gradually helping them to spend more and more time in the presence of the stimulus that is the source of the difficulty. If our business traveler gradually spent more and more time exposed to objects and activities associated with airline travel, she would eventually feel ready to get on a plane, first with her therapist, and then by herself. *Virtual reality* technology is now being used creatively in this type of therapy. It lowers the cost and decreases some of the practical difficulties—such as time and expense—that have been associated with the treatment.

Spontaneous Recovery

For reasons that are not yet quite fully understood by psychologists, a response to a conditioned stimulus sometimes will reappear suddenly after extinction has been achieved.

Spontaneous recovery happens even in cases where a long period of time has elapsed since the extinction of the conditioned response.

Aversive Counterconditioning

Aversive conditioning is another type of therapy based on the principles of classical conditioning. In this treatment, a stimulus that is pleasurable to the individual or organism is paired with a painful or noxious stimulus. The goal is, through the pairing, to form an unpleasant association that will discourage pursuit of that stimulus. This treatment has been used in the treatment of child molesters and others with serious or dangerous problems. The use of the drug *Antabuse* in the treatment of alcoholics is based on this principle. The drug is taken daily by the patient and induces nausea whenever he or she ingests alcohol. This technique has shown only limited effectiveness according to follow-up studies. The infliction of pain and suffering in this manner also presents some ethical difficulties even if the goal is to cure the problem.

Operant Conditioning

Operant conditioning is used to shape voluntary behavior through the use of contingencies or consequences, called reinforcers (to make a behavior happen more) and punishers (to make a behavior decrease or disappear).

Edward Thorndike (1874–1949) was the first psychologist to study animal learning in a systematic fashion. Specifically, he examined how voluntary behavior is learned or unlearned through consequences. In the simplest terms, he studied learning through trial and error. He worked with cats that had to figure out an escape from "puzzle boxes." Thorndike observed that the cats were most likely to repeat the behaviors that led to escape and a reward of food. On the basis of these experiments, he formulated the law of effect.

Thorndike's Law of Effect: Responses that are followed by pleasant consequences are more likely to be strengthened and are likely to reoccur in a similar situation. Responses that are followed by unpleasant consequences are weakened. In other words, behavior that produces good effects tends to become more frequent over time; behavior that produces bad effects tends to become less frequent.

Further work on the law of effect produced reformulation that took into account the importance of cues that precede behavior as well as its contingencies or consequences.

Behavior is influenced not only by the effects that follow it but also by the situational cues that precede it.

Although B. F. Skinner (1904–1990) did not discover the principles on which operant conditioning is founded, he is one of the most well-known behaviorists in the history of psychology.

* Skinner followed Thorndike's principles and developed into a staunch "radical" behaviorist. He promoted the principles of operant conditioning as an effective way to improve the human condition.
* He expanded the study of conditioning and showed that it can be used as a process to induce an organism to engage actively in new behaviors.
* It was he who coined the term "operant" to describe these active behaviors that operate on the organism's environment, and he created most of the language that is used to describe the process of operant conditioning.

For example, Skinner trained a pigeon to turn 360° by a gradual process of reinforcement that he called *shaping*. He rewarded the pigeon for making small portions of the full motion at first, and then larger and larger ones, thus demonstrating the principle that behavior could be shaped by "successive approximations" through the use of reinforcement. Shaping is used in a variety of settings to create complex behaviors in very small steps. Animal training is one of the most popular and effective uses of the technique.

Again, Don't Forget! The basic premise of operant conditioning is that behavior is shaped and maintained by its consequences.

There Are Two Basic Types of Consequences

Reinforcers

The term "reinforcement" is roughly synonymous with the term "reward." A *reinforcer* is a consequence that strengthens a behavior and makes it more likely to occur. *This can involve either providing a pleasant stimulus or taking away an aversive or unpleasant one.* Reinforcers come in two basic varieties:

* Primary (natural) reinforcers. Food, warmth, water, sexual contact.
* Secondary (conditioned) reinforcers. Reinforcing value acquired by association with primary reinforcers. For example, what makes money a reinforcer? The answer may seem obvious to you, but keep in mind that you have been raised with the association between money and more basic resources. The paper out of which the money is made is not reinforcing; it's the stuff you can get with money. There can be many steps or links between a primary and secondary reinforcer—like your college degree and its rewards.

The process of *reinforcement* occurs if a stimulus or event that follows an operant increases the likelihood of the operant being repeated. Reinforcement is defined by the effect it produces. If it doesn't cause the behavior to occur more frequently, it's not reinforcement. We can reinforce by presenting (application) or withdrawing (removing) a stimulus.

Punishers

A *punisher* is a type of consequence that causes a behavior to become less frequent. This can involve removing a pleasant stimulus or applying an unpleasant one. The process of *punishment* occurs when an event that follows an operant decreases the likelihood of the operant being repeated. As is true of reinforcement, we also punish by application or removal.

To understand operant conditioning fully, you must also commit to memory a different definition for "positive" and "negative." Refer to Figure 6.1 for more clarification of the mechanism of operant conditioning.

Positive: Refers to application or giving something.
Negative: Refers to removing something or taking it away.

Positive Reinforcement (*Reinforcement by Application*). *Positive reinforcement* follows an operant behavior with the addition of a reinforcing stimulus—in other words, a reward. Application of the stimulus results in an increase in the target behavior.

For the following examples, name the stimulus that is applied and the desired behavior that is facilitated or strengthened.

Example: The pigeon pecks the lever to receive a pellet of food.

Example: Your kid takes out the garbage; you take him/her out for ice cream.

Example: The soda machine eats your money without giving you the longed-for soda, so you hit it and receive a can of soda. What are you going to do next time a soda machine eats your money?

Negative Reinforcement (*Reinforcement by Removal*). *Negative reinforcement* follows an operant behavior, wherein a stimulus (typically unpleasant) is removed.

In the following examples, name the stimulus that is withdrawn and the desired behavior that is facilitated or strengthened.

Example: Your spouse nags you until you clean the living room just to make him/her shut up.

Example: You give your kid a cookie before dinner to stop him/her from whining.

Example: You decide to divulge the location of a rival school's kidnapped mascot in order to stop the students from that school who abducted you from playing nothing but elevator music.

Most people find negative reinforcement to be an especially confusing concept. Try the following examples for additional practice. Identify the stimuli that has been removed and the strengthened behaviors.

- Taking an aspirin to relieve a headache.
- Hurrying home in a thunderstorm to get out of the rain.
- Giving in to a dog's begging and whining for a potato chip.
- Pulling up the covers on the bed in order to avoid feeling cold.
- Leaving a movie theatre when the movie is a real turkey.
- Smoking a cigarette to relieve the craving.
- Feigning a stomachache in order to avoid a morning psychology class.
- Putting on a car seat belt to avoid the irritating buzz.
- Turning the dial when the radio is playing music that you hate.
- Saying "uncle" to stop being beaten.

INTENTION

	Increase Behavior	Decrease Behavior
Present	Positive Reinforcement	Positive Punishment
Remove	Negative Punishment	Negative Reinforcement

Figure 6.1 Operant conditioning contingencies.

Positive Punishment *(Punishment by Application)*. *Positive punishment* involves the presentation of an stimulus (usually unpleasant) or event following a behavior. The stimulus/event acts to decrease the likelihood of the behavior being repeated.

In the following examples, name the stimulus that is applied and the behavior that it is intended to discourage or extinguish.

Example: The rat runs into the wrong (dead-end) section of a maze and receives a mild shock. The rat no longer runs there.

Example: You arrive at school one-half-hour late and receive one hour's detention. You arrive on time after this.

Example: You forget to pay your credit card bill on time and are assessed a $25.00 late fee. You pay it on time from that time on.

Negative Punishment *(Punishment by Removal).* *Negative punishment* involves the removal of stimulus or event (usually pleasant) following a behavior. The removal acts to decrease the likelihood of the behavior being repeated.

Name the stimulus and the behavior that its removal is intended to discourage or extinguish.

Example: A teenager breaks his/her curfew and is forbidden to drive the family car for two weeks.

Example: A child goes bicycle riding without a helmet and is forbidden to ride the bicycle for two weeks.

Example: A child in a kindergarten classroom throws a building block and is sent to time out for five minutes.

Some Other Important Concepts Related to Operant Conditioning

Extinction

Extinction refers to the ending of a behavior—desirable, undesirable, or neutral. We can achieve this by failing to reinforce the target behavior. For example, we can ignore a four year old who tries to shock us by using a naughty word or we can negatively punish the behavior (by placing the child in time out).

Maintaining Behaviors

Because extinction occurs if we stop reinforcing a behavior, we must continue to reinforce it in order to keep it going. There are five patterns or *schedules of reinforcement.* A schedule of reinforcement refers to the delivery of reinforcers according to a preset pattern based on the number of responses or the time interval between responses.

1. *Continuous reinforcement* simply means that we reinforce the behavior every time it occurs. From a practical standpoint, it can be difficult, and it is not necessarily the most effective way to maintain behavior.
2. *Partial reinforcement schedules* come in two general varieties: the ratio-based schedules, where the reinforcement pattern is based on the number of responses produced, and the interval-based schedules, in which the pattern of reinforcement depends upon lengths of time. Additionally, these schedules are termed either *fixed* because the number of responses or length of time does not vary or *variable* because either the responses or time does vary.

- *The fixed-ratio (FR) schedule.* Reinforcement occurs after a fixed number of responses. An example would be a ten to one schedule. A pigeon needs to peck the lever ten times to get one pellet of food. This schedule usually produces a high rate of responding that follows a burst-pause-burst pattern. Some real-life, human examples are doing piecework and collecting green stamps, coupons, box tops, or those cards you get from the coffee shop (if you buy nine drinks, you get the tenth for free).
- *The variable-ratio (VR) schedule.* Reinforcement occurs after an average number of responses that varies from trial to trial. A pigeon presses the lever eight times to get the first reward, ten to get the second, seven for the third, and so on. The number that is required on any one specific trial is unpredictable. All forms of gambling offer this type of reinforcement, which is evidence of its great power in maintaining behavior. It produces high, steady rates of response—think of the mesmerized person standing in front of the slot machine.
- *The fixed-interval (FI) schedule.* Reinforcement occurs after a preset time, not number of reinforcements. The pigeon gets the pellet after successive three-minute intervals have elapsed, for any lever pecks given during that interval. This produces a pattern of responses that tend to increase as the time for the reinforcement draws near. If a teacher gives a test every four weeks, students' studying behavior will likely follow this response trend as well.
- *The variable-interval (VI) schedule.* Reinforcement occurs after an average amount of time has elapsed, and the interval varies from trial to trial. Over a set of trials it works out to a predetermined average interval. If a pigeon is placed on a VI-10 schedule, it gets a reinforcer after 8, 12, 11, and 9 seconds. Over the long run, it produces a moderate but steady rate of response. This schedule, when reinforcements ends, tends to produce the quickest rate of extinction. A variable-interval schedule is seen in any real-life situation in which one awaits events that follows an approximate but nonprecise schedule. Fishing is a very good example of a VI schedule, and people who enjoy fishing tend to be very patient about receiving their reinforcements!

Observational Learning

Observational learning is the learning of new, voluntary behaviors takes place simply through processes of observation and imitation, and without the use of any direct consequences to shape or maintain it.

A central debate in learning theory revolves around the degree to which cognition (thinking) plays a role in shaping and maintaining new behaviors. Traditionally, behaviorists tend to downplay the influence of thought on learning, while cognitive psychologists view it as a major force in producing new voluntary behaviors. Strict behaviorists reject changes in mental processes as impossible to measure and therefore unscientific.

Some of the earliest evidence for cognitive learning comes from the work of psychologists observing and testing animals. Comparative psychologists (those who study the similarities and differences between humans and other animals) have watched primates learn to use objects as tools either by observing members of their own species, or by what appears to be moments of "insight." *Edward Tolman* (1886–1959) directly challenged Skinner's claim that consequences were essential for shaping behavior. Tolman supported his own view by allowing rats to spend time in mazes and then comparing the time it took to train these rats using rewards to the time necessary to train rats that were unfamiliar with the same mazes. The rats that had just "hung out" in the mazes learned to solve them correctly in a shorter time. He proposed that as animals explore environments, they form *cognitive maps*—mental representations of the features that allow them to know where they are and how to get from place to place. As an organism moves through an environment, each point passed serves as a stimulus or reminder of the next step or turn. Cognitive maps also allow the formulation of alternative routes when a path is blocked off. Thus Tolman claimed that learning can takes place in a *latent* fashion—in the absence of a reward or reinforcement. The learning will not be demonstrated until the reinforcement is presented, but that does not mean that it has not occurred. Left on their own, rats will explore a maze. Students will read and study their psychology texts (we hope). But the rats won't run the maze for you unless you present the possibility of a positive reinforcement— a reward of food. Many students will not display their learning until the possibility of reinforcement exists—through a test, quiz, or assignment.

Social Learning Theory

Over the course of the twentieth century, many researchers demonstrated that humans, and many other animals, are able to learn by watching the behavior of others, as long as they can remember what they saw and are motivated to imitate those actions. This body of research forms the basis for *social learning theory*. Albert Bandura (b.1925) used the work of Tolman and others to form a new theory of learning—that learning takes place primarily through observation of others' behavior and also the consequences that other individuals experience in response to their behavior. Observation of consequences is called *vicarious conditioning*. If a student sees that two other students are given detention for smoking cigarettes on school property, he or she may be less likely to attempt the same behavior in the future.

In real-life most people can easily identify cases in which they have learned directly either from watching role models—parents, peers, and others or from watching the consequences experienced by other individuals.

Bandura's classic study of social learning is referred to informally as the "Bobo doll" experiment (Bandura et al. 1963). The study was done in response to public concern that violent television and movies could promote real violent behavior. In the experiment, 4-year-olds watched three different versions of a film with adults treating an inflatable, round-based, self-righting "Bobo doll" aggressively.

- In one version, the adult was rewarded with candy and soda afterwards.
- In a second version, the adult was punished after hurting the Bobo doll.
- In a third version, nothing at all happened after the Bobo doll abuse.

Each child was given access to a Bobo doll after viewing one version of the film. The effects of vicarious conditioning, as well as observational learning, were obvious. The children who saw the reward versions were more likely to imitate aggressive behavior with the Bobo doll than were the children who saw the no-consequence or punishment versions. And (more disturbingly) all the children, no matter what version of the film they saw, would repeat the behaviors at the request of the experimenter for a reward of candy or soda.

On the basis of this study and other research, Bandura concluded that thinking is affected by observation, and that direct consequences are *not* necessary for learning—knowledge of the mere *possibility* of reinforcement or punishment may be enough to promote or suppress behavior.

Connecting Through Chapter Review

WORD-STUDY CONNECTION
Write each of these words on index cards and write their definitions on the opposite side.

Antabuse
aversive counterconditioning
associations
behaviorist
classical conditioning
cognitive-behaviorist
cognitive maps
conditioned response (CR)
conditioned stimulus (CS)
continuous
desensitization
extinction
fixed interval (FI)
fixed ratio (FR)
latent
law of effect
learning
Little Albert

negative
negative punishment
negative reinforcement
neutral stimulus
observational learning
operant conditioning
partial
Ivan Pavlov
positive
positive punishment
positive reinforcement
primary reinforcer
punisher
reinforcement
reinforcer
schedule of reinforcement
secondary reinforcer
shaping

B. F. Skinner
social learning theory
spontaneous recovery
stimulus generalization
systematic desensitization
Edward Thorndike
Edward Tolman
unconditioned response (UCR)
unconditioned stimulus (UCS)
variable interval (VI)
variable ratio (VR)
vicarious conditioning
virtual reality
John Broadus Watson

SELF-TEST CONNECTION

PART A. Completion
Write in the word that correctly completes each statement.

1. _____ is any relatively permanent change in behavior that results from experience.
2. The _____ school of psychology is most closely associated with learning theory.
3. _____ conditioning involves learning simple associations between stimuli and responses.
4. The Russian physiologist _____ is credited with first describing simple stimulus-response associations in the laboratory.
5. A(n) _____ stimulus is one that is not connected to any automatic or innate response.

6. A response becomes classically conditioned when the neutral stimulus is reliably presented _____ the unconditioned stimulus.

7. A juicy hamburger that makes you hungry is a good example of a(n) _____ stimulus.

8. Your hunger when you see the hamburger is a(n) _____ response.

9. The "Burger Baron" jingle that plays when the hamburger is shown on TV has started to make you feel hungry. It was once a _____ stimulus, it is now a _____ stimulus.

10. _____ is the loss of the response to the neutral or conditioned stimulus.

11. Operant conditioning is used to create, shape, and eliminate _____ behavior.

12. _____ systematically studied trial-and-error learning in animals and formulated the law of effect.

13. B. F. Skinner showed that complex voluntary behaviors could be _____ through reinforcement of successive approximations.

14. A(n) _____ is a consequence that tends to increase the frequency of a behavior.

15. The word _____ in operant conditioning is used to signify "applied" or "given."

16. Money is a common form of _____ or indirect reinforcement.

17. _____ reinforcement increases behavior through the removal of a stimulus. When a child whines at a parent until he receives a cookie, this form of reinforcement has motivated the parent's behavior.

18. A teenager who is grounded for breaking curfew has experienced negative _____ .

19. To maintain a behavior after it is learned, we can use various _____ of reinforcement.

20. If you receive a reward after emitting a set number of responses, you are being reinforced on a(n) _____ schedule.

21. There is an ongoing debate about the degree to which _____ is involved in the process of learning.

22. _____ disputed Skinner's position that consequences were vital for learning processes.

23. An organism's mental representation of the features of an environment is called a(n) _____ .

24. In the well-known "Bobo doll" study, _____ provided evidence that observing aggressive behaviors might make children act more aggressively.

PART B. Multiple Choice
Circle the letter of the item that correctly completes the statement.

1. Which of the following is *not* one of the three major kinds of learning processes?
   (a) Operant conditioning   (b) Routine conditioning
   (c) Observational learning   (d) Classical conditioning

2. The responses that are learned through classical conditioning are
   (a) involuntary   (b) voluntary
   (c) permanent   (d) general

3. _____ first described the process of classical conditioning, which he discovered by accident.
   (a) Watson   (b) Skinner
   (c) Pavlov   (d) Thorndike

4. Pavlov's dogs learned to associate _____ stimulus such as footsteps or a bell with an unconditioned stimulus.
   - (a) an unconditioned
   - (b) a natural
   - (c) a neutral
   - (d) a general

5. After being paired repeatedly with the _____ stimulus, the neutral stimulus becomes conditioned.
   - (a) response
   - (b) predictive
   - (c) classical
   - (d) unconditioned

6. If a song reminds you of your first crush, it has become _____ stimulus.
   - (a) an unconditioned
   - (b) a natural
   - (c) a neutral
   - (d) a conditioned

7. _____ believed that all behaviors and experiences, including intense emotional reactions, were learned.
   - (a) Watson
   - (b) Skinner
   - (c) Pavlov
   - (d) Tolman

8. If an organism produces the conditioned response to stimuli that are similar but not exactly the same as the conditioned stimulus, _____ has occurred.
   - (a) generalization
   - (b) extinction
   - (c) neutralization
   - (d) counterconditioning

9. _____ is the loss of the response to the neutral or conditioned stimulus.
   - (a) Generalization
   - (b) Extinction
   - (c) Neutralization
   - (d) Reinforcement

10. _____ prevents extinction.
   - (a) Punishment
   - (b) Counterconditioning
   - (c) Avoidance
   - (d) Desensitization

11. Spending longer and longer times in the presence of frogs in order to overcome your intense fear of them would be an example of a _____ procedure.
   - (a) systematic desensitization
   - (b) stimulus generalization
   - (c) spontaneous recovery
   - (d) positive reinforcement

12. _____ is the sudden reappearance of a conditioned response after its extinction.
   - (a) Systematic desensitization
   - (b) Stimulus generalization
   - (c) Spontaneous recovery
   - (d) Positive reinforcement

13. Operant conditioning is the shaping, maintenance, and reduction of _____ behaviors.
   - (a) voluntary
   - (b) involuntary
   - (c) innate
   - (d) cognitive

14. _____ was the first psychologist to study animal learning in a systematic fashion.
   - (a) Skinner
   - (b) Watson
   - (c) Thorndike
   - (d) Tolman

15. Skinner taught a pigeon to turn in circles using a procedure that he called _____ .
   - (a) desensitization
   - (b) generalization
   - (c) shaping
   - (d) punishment

16. If a consequence increases the frequency of a behavior, it is called a(n) _____ .
   - (a) punisher
   - (b) reinforcer
   - (c) operant
   - (d) generalizer

17. The word _____ refers to the removal of a stimulus as the consequence in operant conditioning.
   (a) reinforcement   (b) punishment
   (c) positive   (d) negative

18. A child sits in his room whining until his babysitter lets him stay up for another half
hour. The babysitter has been _____ .
   (a) positively punished   (b) positively reinforced
   (c) negatively reinforced   (d) negatively punished

19. A man who vandalized a store is sentenced to work at the local animal shelter for two
weeks. He has been _____ .
   (a) negatively reinforced   (b) negatively punished
   (c) positively reinforced   (d) positively punished

20. Gambling is a good example of a _____ schedule of reinforcement.
   (a) variable-interval   (b) variable-ratio
   (c) fixed-ratio   (d) fixed-interval

21. The activity of bird watching is probably maintained by a _____ schedule of
reinforcement.
   (a) variable-interval   (b) variable-ratio
   (c) fixed-ratio   (d) fixed-interval

22. Tolman's research provided evidence of the existence of _____ .
   (a) reinforcement schedules   (b) stimulus generalization
   (c) learned aggression   (d) cognitive maps

23. The idea that animals may learn simply by watching each other's behaviors forms the
basis of _____ theory.
   (a) classical learning   (b) operant conditioning
   (c) social learning   (d) universal learning

24. In Bandura's "Bobo doll" experiment, the children who were most likely to repeat the
behaviors were those who saw the _____ version of the film.
   (a) reward   (b) punishment
   (c) no consequence   (d) All were equally likely to imitate it.

25. A little girl sees her classmate receive a gold star for cleaning up her work area. She
imitates this behavior by cleaning up her own desk. This is an example of _____ .
   (a) extinction   (b) reinforcement schedule
   (c) generalization   (d) vicarious conditioning

PART C. Modified True-False

If the statement is true, write "T" for the answer. If the statement is incorrect, change the
underlined expression to one that will make the statement true.

1. Learning can be defined as any relatively permanent change in an organism's behavior that occurs as a result of experience.

2. The school of psychology that is most closely associated with learning theory is the
cognitive school.

3. Watson inadvertently trained his dogs to salivate upon his arrival in the laboratory.

4. Pavlov was the first scientist to describe the process of operant conditioning.

5. In Pavlov's procedure, the dogs learned to associate a neutral stimulus with an
unconditioned or involuntary response.

6. When a neutral stimulus becomes reliably associated with an involuntary response, it becomes a <u>conditioned</u> stimulus.
7. If a certain perfume makes you anxious because the smell reminds you of an elementary school teacher who was strict and unpleasant, you have been <u>classically conditioned</u>.
8. <u>Stimulus generalization</u> occurs when the organism no longer responds to the conditioned stimulus.
9. Use of the drug Antabuse is an example of <u>aversive counterconditioning</u>.
10. Avoidance <u>promotes</u> extinction.
11. <u>Thorndike's</u> studies of trial-and-error learning form the basis of the theory of operant conditioning.
12. Operant conditioning methods are used to shape, maintain, and eliminate <u>voluntary behaviors</u>.
13. <u>B.F. Skinner</u> first described the law of effect.
14. Animal training procedures often include <u>shaping complex behaviors by successive approximations.</u>
15. The word "negative" in operant conditioning signifies "<u>bad" or "unpleasant."</u>
16. Receiving a reward for returning a lost wallet is an example of <u>positive reinforcement</u>.
17. A speeding ticket is an example of <u>positive punishment</u>.
18. When a child has been sent to his room for disobeying his parent, he has been <u>negatively reinforced</u>.
19. When your driver's license is suspended for speeding, you have been <u>negatively punished</u>.
20. Receiving a paycheck every month is an example of a <u>variable interval</u> schedule of reinforcement.
21. If you receive a free flight for every 10,000 miles that you travel with a certain airline, you are reinforced on a <u>fixed ratio</u> schedule.
22. <u>Albert Bandura</u> challenged the radical behaviorist view and did the first experiments to demonstrate the existence of latent learning processes.
23. A <u>cognitive map</u> is an animal's internal representation of the environment.
24. The "Bobo doll" experiments provided evidence that children <u>do not learn aggression</u> by observation.
25. All the children <u>would imitate the aggression</u> they saw in the films if they were rewarded, no matter which film they saw.

PART D. Practical Applications of Learning Theory

The following essay questions ask you to think about the uses of learning theory in everyday life. Respond accordingly.

1. Provide one example of how you would use at least two of the three major learning theories (classical conditioning, operant conditioning, social learning) in the following contexts:
   a. You are a *parent* trying to teach your child good manners.
   b. You are a *teacher* trying to encourage your students to succeed academically.
   c. You are an *animal trainer* developing techniques for teaching dog obedience.
   d. You are an *athletic coach* who wishes to get the best performance from your team members.
   e. You are a *manager* who wishes to promote good work habits and productivity in your office.

2. One criticism of operant conditioning is based on the fact that sometimes positive reinforcement doesn't seem to motivate humans in the intended way. For example, most teachers will say that the prospect of achieving good grades does not appear to motivate all capable students to study hard. Think of three examples of rewards that you have been offered in your everyday life. List them and describe briefly how well they motivated you to perform the desired behavior. If you did not receive the reward, describe the factors that might have contributed to your lack of interest in the reward or in performing the activity that was going to be positively reinforced. If you did receive the reward, describe the extent to which the prospect of the reward played a role in influencing you.

3. Many learning theorists believe that punishment is problematic and often ineffective. They propose that it is easier to teach with positive reinforcement, and that (when necessary) the most effective punishments should be mild, logical, and consistent. Harsh punishment may actually interfere with learning because of the biological reactions to pain and distress. A logical punishment should have some connection to the behavior that is to be reduced or eliminated. It is almost certain that in real life settings most punishment is administered inconsistently (leading to unintended rewards when a behavior is not punished—the feeling that one "gets away with it"). For each of the following behaviors, see if you can devise a plan for using punishment (and positive reinforcement) in an effective manner to teach and promote good behavior.

   a. A 7-year-old has shoplifted a candy bar from the local convenience store.
   b. Police pick up two 11-year-old boys for spray painting their names on the wall of an office building.
   c. An office manager wants to reduce the number of office supplies that are being removed from the workplace by her staff.

CONNECTING TO CONCEPTS

Review the chapter and then write down your thoughts in response to the following questions.

1. Define classical conditioning. Using an everyday situation, describe how the process occurs, defining the steps (UC, UR, Neutral Stimulus, CS, CR).
2. Define operant conditioning. Define the four contingencies (positive and negative reinforcement, positive and negative punishment) in general terms and then again using real-life examples.
3. Discuss the evidence that thinking does play a role in learning. What do you think? Given your opinion regarding the role of cognition in learning would you say you are a "radical" or "cognitive" behaviorist? Why?
4. Define social learning. Describe the procedures and findings from Bandura's classic "Bobo doll" experiment. Provide two real-life examples of animals or humans learning from watching role models.

CONNECTING TO LIFE/JOB SKILLS

Behavior Modification, Wellness, and the Workplace

Behavior modification is a technique for changing behavior based on simple principles of operant conditioning. It involves six steps.

- Choosing a target behavior that would be beneficial to change.
- Counting the number of times the behavior occurs in a specified period. This is called establishing a baseline. If the target behavior is smoking, the baseline might be established by counting the number of cigarettes an individual smokes per day. As part of this process, a journal or other record might be kept so that the events that precede the target behavior (the antecedents) are also identified. For example, the individual might "light up" before a meeting with the boss, when he or she is nervous, or perhaps when he or she feels relieved.
- A structured series of steps or program is created to help the person eliminate or replace the target behavior. Let's say that instead of smoking in response to the antecedent behaviors identified in the baseline, our soon-to-be ex-smoker would like to take a five minute walk or chew a piece of sugar-free gum if taking a walk is not possible.
- Since this program is based on operant conditioning principles, the person needs to choose a reinforcer—a reward. So, every time the recovering smoker walks, or pops a piece of gum, he or she receives a small incentive from the employer—fifteen minutes' worth of hourly pay, an hour added to vacation or personal time, a chance for a drawing to be held at the company party, among others.
- A specified time is set for the behavior modification program. The individual's goal is to fully stop smoking within six months. For this purpose, it is good to use a written contract for the program. A human resources employee or other co-worker might witness the contract or even help to write it.
- At the end of the program, the individual evaluates his or her progress, and either decides to continue (with or without changes) or ends the program if the goal has been met.

Behavior modification programs are becoming more popular and commonplace in the world of work. Employers now realize that improving workplace safety, reducing employee stress, and encouraging employee wellness (such as using incentives to help employees stop smoking, begin exercising, and eat more balanced diets) can have a very beneficial effect on profit margins. Employees who are physical healthy and work in safe environments are much less likely to cost the company sick time and disability leave. Healthy, relaxed workers are more likely to be productive. Behavior modification and similar incentive-based programs are tools that can be used for this purpose.

WHAT'S HAPPENING!

Applied Behavior Analysis and Functional Behavior Assessment

Widespread use of *applied behavior analysis* is relatively new in the world of psychology and represents some of the most innovative clinical applications of behaviorism. It is used to help improve the functioning of children who suffer from autism spectrum disorders, attention deficit-hyperactivity disorder, and other mental illnesses that cause several behavioral difficulties. Applied behavior analysis involves the following:

- Observing the child and noting the antecedents of the problem behavior, the behavior itself, and the consequences.
- Performing a functional behavioral assessment—determining what function the behavior serves for the child. For example, especially in a classroom or group care situation, a problem behavior results in increased attention for a child. A child with limited verbal and social skills may use problem behaviors, for example, tantrums or aggressive behaviors, for this purpose.
- Finding a way to eliminate the problem behavior to prevent it from serving the identified function.
- Finding a different, harmless, or positive behavior and providing reinforcement to the child for engaging in that behavior. Ideally, the reinforcement would be similar to the function that the problem behavior served for that child. So the child is removed from the classroom when the tantrum begins, and he is rewarded with attention when he remains in control.

Two crucial elements of the treatment are: understanding the function of the problem behavior and identifying effective consequences. Versions of applied behavior analysis have been in use since the late 1930s, but the technique did not really become popular until the early 1990s. Children with autism appear to benefit substantially from intensive versions of this treatment, and their parents have been energetic in spreading the word. Many programs for children with severe developmental disabilities now offer functional assessments so that the treatment plan is truly individualized for each child.

Visit the following web sites to learn more about applied behavior analysis:

A physician explains the philosophy behind the treatment:

www.ddleadership.org/events/conference/Videos/WhatIsABA.pdf

The web site of the Institute for Applied Behavior Analysis:

www.iaba.net/

The web site of the Association for Behavioral Analysis:

www.abainternational.org/

OTHER USEFUL WEB SITES

CLASSICAL CONDITIONING OVERVIEW

www.as.wvu.edu/~sbb/comm221/chapters/pavlov.htm

This is West Virginia University's Communication department web site. In a section on persuasion and influence techniques, there is a useful summary of classical conditioning.

VIRTUAL REALITY THERAPY

www.cc.gatech.edu/gvu/virtual/Phobia/

Georgia Tech's web site describes an innovative treatment for phobia based on classical conditioning techniques.

CLICKER TRAINING: INTRODUCTION TO OPERANT AND CLASSICAL CONDITIONING

www.wagntrain.com/OC/

Even though this website is commercial and targets animal trainers, it has a great explanation of operant conditioning.

OPERANT CONDITIONING AND BEHAVIORISM: A HISTORICAL OUTLINE

www.biozentrum.uni-wuerzburg.de/genetics/behavior/learning/behaviorism.html

This web site features a chronicle of the major events and figures in the development of operant conditioning techniques.

ALBERT BANDURA'S PERSONALITY THEORY

www.ship.edu/~cgboeree/bandura.html

At this informative web site, C. George Boeree presents Bandura's theory of observational learning.

OBSERVATIONAL LEARNING

chiron.valdosta.edu/whuitt/col/soccog/soclrn.html

At this Valdosta State University web site, you can find a nice description of the famous Bobo doll study done by Albert Bandura.

REFERENCES
Bandura, A., Ross, D. & Ross, S. A. (1963) Imitation of film-mediated aggressive models. *Journal of Abnormal and Social Psychology, 66,* 3–11.

Chapter 7

MEMORY

In this chapter you will become acquainted with current theory regarding the processes and functioning of memory.

What Is Memory?

In general, memory is defined as the ability to retain and recall various types and pieces of information. It is measured through the demonstration of retention—the ability to recall. This definition is very simple and doesn't fully reveal the complexities of memory in all of its forms and fallibility. Memory does not operate like recording equipment; it is a reconstructive process, leading us frequently to remember only partially or entirely incorrectly. There is no such thing as a "photographic memory." Even our most vivid memories of crucial events such as the Space Shuttle tragedy (so called *flashbulb memories*) are usually inaccurate to some degree—usually a large degree.

There appear to be separate memory systems for activities or procedures requiring motor skills, for information, and for events. Remembering is far from a simple yes-or-no process; it is possible to "know that you know it" but be unable to recall something on demand. A memory expert can develop strategies to recall lists of fifty random numbers but have trouble remembering where she put her keys. Memory is a complex and tricky system.

One of the first scientists to study memory systematically was *Hermann Ebbinghaus* (1850–1909). He used himself as a subject, and memorized vast lists of nonsense syllables, in order to test his own retention. He concluded, based on his own performance, that people quickly forget about 90 percent of the information that they have learned within a month.

Although forgetting *is* a significant problem for most all people, there are a couple of points to keep in mind regarding the generalizability of Ebbinghaus's conclusions. We must take into account that usually when we learn material and try to remember it, we are not trying to remember nonsense syllables but rather something meaningful. Although you may feel overwhelmed by the amount of information in your psychology course, you can relate it to your own life and to your other studies to some extent. Ebbinghaus's performance in the memory task also demonstrates the interesting problem of *interference* or *blocking*—memories getting in the way of other memories. This is a practical difficulty that can be managed using a variety of *mnemonic* strategies, as you will see.

The Stages of Memory

One model of memory describes the process of acquiring and storing information as a series of stages—two or three stages—depending on whose opinion you ask. Most scientists are in agreement regarding the first stage:

- *Sensory memory.* Through a series of clever experiments, George Sperling demonstrated that much more information registers than can be retained for more than a few seconds. The stage of memory in which this occurs, in which information is held for a very brief period of time, is called sensory memory. This is the stage in which everything "registers" (so it is sometimes also referred to as the sensory register).

Only a very small amount of what registers in sensory memory will make it to the next stage. *Attention* is the crucial factor in determining the amount and kind of information that is retained. You are most likely to retain that information to which you are paying attention. While you read this book, many things are registering, but if you are reading attentively, the information in this book is by far more likely to be transferred to the next stage of memory.

There is some disagreement regarding the model as to what occurs next. To some neuroscientists, there are two separate stages.

- *Short-term memory.* The active stage of memory in which information is stored and processed for about thirty to forty-five seconds. The process that occurs in short-term memory is *encoding* or *consolidation*. This is the transference of memory into permanent storage. The storage capacity of short-term memory is estimated to be 7 ± 2 bits of information (roughly the length of a phone number without the area code).
- *Long-term memory.* The stage of memory that represents the long-term storage of information. There are two types of long-term memory—*procedural (implicit)* and *declarative (explicit)*.

Figure 7.1 illustrates the process of memory in three stages.

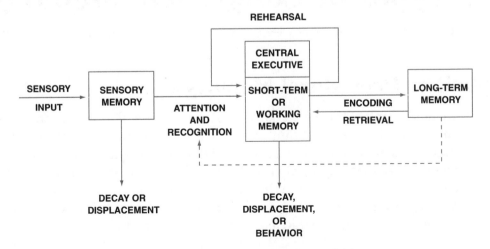

Figure 7.1 The three stages of memory acquisition.

124MEMORY

To other scientists, there is only one stage following sensory memory—long-term memory. In this alternative model, the stage called short-term memory is referred to as *working memory*. The argument is that in order to encode new memories, long-term memory is almost always accessed. The information about memory that you are learning at this moment is being related to previously stored memory; the words that you are reading are already part of long-term memory. Working memory is characterized as the beginning of the process of acquiring long-term memories and, therefore is not considered a discrete stage. Even those scientists who subscribe to the three-stage memory model often refer to short-term as working memory because it is a very active memory-processing stage.

The Process of Memory Acquisiton

- When you see a visual image (let's say an image of your favorite tennis player walking off the court, in defeat, after a hard match), the whole scene registers briefly in sensory memory. You are focused on the tennis player, although you also detected the court, the line judge, and the fans in the stands.
- You only really paid attention to the tennis player, though, so this is the information that is transferred to short-term or working memory. *The other details of the scene will be forgotten, although if someone asks you about them, you will be able* reconstruct *them plausibly using your schema or mental template for a "tennis match."*
- If you thought about the end of the tennis match and talked about it with other people, some version of the image will make it into long-term memory. You will have *encoded* it. We encode in all of our senses (but especially through sight and sound) and semantically.
- To continue to retain the memory of this event, you will need to retrieve it periodically.

As you will see, memory is truly a "use it or lose it" process. We appear to be able to remember an enormous amount of information, provided that we periodically access it and relate it to other learning or new memories.

The Types of Long-Term Memory

There are two broad categories of long-term memory, as you can see from Figure 7.2.

Implicit or Procedural Memory

We don't think of this vital type of recall as memory. This is your storage of all the things you do seemingly without thinking; all learned in early infancy, the basic activities that we need to learn in order to function in day-to-day life—like working our limbs, hands, and mouth. Also, many things that we learn to do later in life, such as typing and driving, are also tasks that are stored in procedural memory. This type of long-term memory begins forming at birth. Of course, you can't remember how you learned to walk because that is a type of explicit or declarative memory (see next section.)

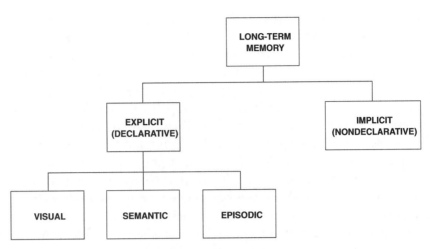

Figure 7.2 Modes of long-term memory storage.

Explicit or Declarative Memory

We think of explicit or declarative memory as conscious memory. Declarative memory may begin forming shortly after birth, but our earliest memories are inaccessible. This is most likely the result of the relative immaturity of the brain systems for memory and the lack of sufficient language ability. Without language, it appears to be impossible to remember because language gives our experience meaning. Meaning is an enormous asset in retention and recall of information and experience. There are two subdivisions of this kind of memory. *Semantic memory* contains all kinds of general knowledge of the world. As you read this book and do the exercises at the end of each chapter, you are increasing your semantic knowledge. *Episodic* or *autobiographical memory* is that which contains the events and experiences that make up your life.

The Biology of Memory

Memory is a *biological* process. Technological advances in cognitive neuroscience have allowed us to observe activity in different parts of the brain as memories are formed, stored, and recalled. We have also discovered that, except for the simplest associative memories, most information is stored globally (all over the brain). *Karl Lashley* (1890–1958) spent a major portion of his career searching for an *engram* or memory trace in a rat's brain that could be related to a specific event or piece of information. He never found it. Later, several other scientists confirmed that although classically conditioned responses are stored locally, more complex memories are not. Thus your flinching reaction when a fly buzzes near your face is a locally stored memory; your knowledge of how to get from your home to school is stored all over your brain.

Because of the instantaneous nature of sensory memory, our sense receptors (in the peripheral nervous system), the cerebellum, and the association areas of the cortex can be characterized as sensory memory centers. The processing of memories beyond this level involves a complex interaction between the limbic system and cerebral cortex. The limbic system contains the *hippocampus*. This structure has been identified as the place where memories are encoded, where short-term memories or working memories are consolidated into long-term memories. Individual nerve cells throughout the body may have the ability to change the shape of their axon and dendrite endings in response to learning, but the hippocampus grows new cells, a quality that makes it unique and interesting.

The *frontal lobes* appear to function mostly as a file clerk or a kind of Windows Explorer program; they help you to organize and retrieve information stored in other areas of the brain. Some studies have shown that information can be remembered by human beings—even decades after it was learned—if the right *retrieval cues* are used.

Neurotransmitters such as epinephrine *(adrenaline)* and, as mentioned previously, the limbic system (particularly the hippocampus and the *amygdala*) play important roles in memory formation. We appear to be much better able to remember strongly emotional or stress-related information compared to emotionally neutral information. In evolutionary terms, our ancestors needed to remember where the dangers were and how to escape from them to have a better chance of avoiding and escaping from them later. For modern humans, this mechanism is less adaptive. All people tend to remember unpleasant occurrences vividly. A person who lives through a terrible car crash or violent crime may be plagued by strong memories of the event. Such maladaptive symptoms of posttraumatic stress may have their roots in our formerly adaptive memory circuits, which at one time helped us to survive.

It must be noted that too much stress and chronic stress have been shown to be detrimental to overall memory function. When animals experience prolonged periods of severe stress, the constant production of gluticosteroid hormones (a by-product of sympathetic nervous system activation) may damage the hippocampus. Cortisol is an example of such a hormone. The long-term results of prolonged cortisol release include decreased ability to encode and store new information owing to hippocampal damage.

Memories that have been consolidated in the limbic system are stored in the cortex. Neuroscientists theorized that the formation of a long-term memory involved either a change in structure or function of neurons. By studying the acquisition of simple classically conditioned responses by animals (first simple invertebrate animals, later mammals and birds), they found evidence to support this hypothesis. Learning and new memories change the cortical tissue at the synaptic level and increase the amount of neurotransmitters that are released.

How We Remember

Since memory storage is not localized, it appears that the bits and pieces of memories that have been stored all over the brain are brought back together when you try to recall something. The details are not always reassembled correctly; thus, memory is fundamentally *reconstructive* and prone to be inaccurate.

Access, Retrieval, and Retrieval Cues

Retrieval is the act of remembering, or bringing forward information from memory. A retrieval cue is a bit of information that assists us in this process of *accessing* stored memories. Usually, the cue is information that helps to make the stored information more meaningful, and therefore more memorable. If you are trying to remember the name of a famous actor, it might help retrieval if you first think of the name of a movie in which he or she starred. Sometimes this process occurs without our conscious awareness, or any intent. As thoughts come to mind, or as we encounter information in our environment, memories we weren't trying to recall are triggered. Cognitive psychologists call such "spreading" of thoughts and memories *priming*.

How information is retrieved is in part a function of the nature of the memory task with which we are faced. The easiest type of remembering or retrieval is *recognition memory*—you are given several options; all you need to do is recognize one (as is the case of the game show *Who Wants to Be a Millionaire?* or a typical multiple-choice exam). A more difficult retrieval task requires you to bring forth the correct answer from long-term memory with only one clue (think of the television program *Jeopardy!,* a relatively difficult game show). This is the easiest type of *recall memory* item—a fill-in-the-blank exercise. More challenging types of recall questions require accessing a large amount of information from one short prompt or question. An essay test (more commonly given at advanced levels of education, such as college) requires this type of more difficult recall memory.

Ordinary Forgetting

As you have seen, memory is a fallible system, and forgetting is a common experience. And as there are various types of memory, there are also several varieties of forgetting and memory distortion. There are three broad categories of memory failure are

- Failure to encode
- Failure to retain
- Failure to retrieve

Failure to Encode

Much day-to-day information requires only the briefest and most effortless sort of recognition memory. You don't need to remember the details of the cover of your mathematics textbook; the color, size, shape, and title are more than sufficient for helping you to locate the book when you need it. If someone asked you for a detailed description, you might not be able to provide it.

We never encoded the information that this task demands because generally we don't need it. We cannot possibly pay attention to everything that hits the sensory register, and we usually cannot process everything that is held in short-term memory. For the sake of efficiency, we try to take in only what is necessary to perform everyday tasks; the rest is lost. If the information is never fully processed through working memory, it is forgotten as a result of *encoding failure*.

Failure to Retain—Use It or Lose It!

Encoding failure occurs when information that is not transferred from short-term to long-term memory—it decays very quickly. Similarly, if we do not access, review, connect to, or use the information stored in long-term memory occasionally, it also starts to fade or decay. *Decay theory* proposes that the synaptic and functional changes in neurons that are created by new memories will eventually deteriorate unless the new information or skill is used on a regular basis. The reason you cannot remember the date of the Battle of the Bulge is because (since you have not thought about World War II since your junior year of high school) the synaptic changes formed when you learned this information have been reabsorbed—they no longer exist.

Failure to Retrieve

We all have experienced the (very unpleasant) failure to retrieve information. There are many ways in which this can occur. These mishaps, though inconvenient, teach us much about the nature of memory.

TOT (Tip of the Tongue) *phenomenon* is the common term for the inability to access retrieval cues. You know that you know the information, but you can't summon it forth from semantic long-term memory. And you say, "It's on the tip of my tongue!"

What is happening? One model proposes that your retrieval cues are failing you, or you are just missing the right one. It may seem that you can remember all kinds of related information (though it may be of little help to you). In some instances, these related bits of information will act like retrieval cues and you will finally be able to overcome the TOT—drawing the material that you seek out long-term memory.

Such an ordinary form of forgetting teaches us great deal about the nature of memory. It is not the case that you either remember it or you don't. You can know that you know something, but not be able to recall it at the moment. There is some logic and order to how we store information in our brains. It seems that retrieval cues are so crucial that you may not be able to remember information without them.

"Memories get in the way"—so the song goes. Sometimes memories *do* get in the way of other memories. This is a common and frustrating type of forgetting called interference. The most critical factor in determining whether interference does or does not occur is the degree of similarity between items of information. Researchers have repeatedly demonstrated that the more similar the information in the two memories is, the more they will interfere with each other. A good example would be telephone numbers. A person who receives a new cell phone with a phone number very similar to his or her home number may have trouble giving out either number for weeks. He or she is likely to confuse the two numbers, especially while retrieving them or processing them in working memory, and could experience one of two types of interference (see Figure 7.3). There are two specific types of interference. *Retroactive interference* occurs when new information blocks your ability to remember old information. So, for the proud new owner of the cell phone, the number of the new phone is making it hard to remember the home phone number. *Proactive interference* occurs when old memory interferes with a new memory. The cell phone owner is also having difficulty remembering the cell phone number because it is similar to the home phone number. The classic and tragic romantic version of this glitch is calling a new love interest by the name of an "ex."

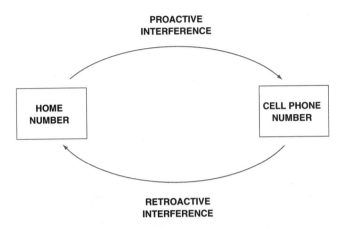

Figure 7.3 Proactive and retroactive interference.

The two types of *serial order effect* (also known as serial position effect) are special subtypes of interference. *Primacy effect* occurs when the beginning of a list or other mass of information is learned and remembered, but the material that follows it is not. *Recency effect* occurs when the end of the list or last part of the material is recalled, but what precedes it is not. See Figure 7.4 for a graph that illustrates the relative retention rate when serial order effect is taken into account.

Schacter's (2001) Seven Sins of Memory

Interference is a type of *blocking*—one of seven memory problems summarized by cognitive psychologist Daniel Schacter (2001) in his book *The Seven Sins of Memory*. The "sins" of memory do make our lives more challenging, but they also reflect its adaptive aspects—the priority of messages related to threats and stress, for example, and our advanced ability to assemble information in a meaningful way, even if that meaning is sometimes incorrect or distorted. (See Table 7-1 for a complete list of the seven sins of memory.)

TABLE 7-1
THE SEVEN SINS OF MEMORY

Sin	Description	Associated Problem(s)
Blocking	Information that is known cannot be recalled.	Tip-of-the-Tongue phenomenon; interference; serial order effect (primacy/recency)
Misattribution	A memory or piece of information is associated with the wrong source.	Memory distortion; source amnesia (forgetting where you learned something)
Transience	Information that was learned fades over time.	Memory decay ("use it or lose it!")
Absent-mindedness	Information is not attended to long enough to process and consolidate it in short-term memory.	Encoding failure

TABLE 7-1 (Continued)
THE SEVEN SINS OF MEMORY

Sin	Description	Associated Problem(s)
Bias	Attitudes and beliefs about aspects of a situation distort how the details are recalled.	Confirmation bias (remembering details that support our beliefs, forgetting those that do not); self-consistency bias (forgetting attitudes and behaviors that are inconsistent with our beliefs); memory distortion
Suggestibility	Questions and materials presented during an interview influence how the details are recalled.	Memory distortion, creation of false memories
Persistence	Memories of events that evoke unpleasant emotions are recalled regardless of whether we wish to think about them.	Intrusive thoughts and flashbacks (as seen in Posttraumatic Stress Disorder); phobic reactions, stress

Amnesia and Forgetting

Dissociation and Repression

When the word "amnesia" is mentioned, most people envision the case of a person whose facilities are essentially intact but who cannot remember his or her own identity, often as a result of some emotional trauma or extreme stress. This stereotypical vision is based on a few sensational case reports ("Jane Doe") and on the idea that people sometimes suffer from *dissociative amnesia*. Although some people do still receive this diagnosis, most psychologists, especially those who are well grounded in the biology of behavior and neuroscience, are skeptical. To these scientists, dissociative amnesia and related disorders are more likely kinds of malingering behaviors or factitious disorders. (*Malingering* refers to the faking of a disorder in order to gain monetary advantage or avoid consequences of past behavior; *factitious* disorders are disorders that are simulated for the purpose of receiving attention and sympathy.) Still other skeptics believe that dissociative amnesia, multiple personality disorder, and similar illnesses are culture-specific disorders, products of the sensational presentation of such cases in movies, TV shows, and popular journalism.

Psychodynamic and psychoanalytic psychologists are more likely to consider dissociative amnesia real because they view the mind as a dynamic system with forces that can work to *repress* material that is unpleasant or traumatic. Repression is a popular concept with many psychologists inside and outside of the psychoanalytic school, but there is virtually no empirical evidence to support its existence. Other psychologists have proposed that it is possible to *suppress* information that we wish to forget. Again, this idea is not empirically supported nor does it fit with the current biological model of memory—as you have seen, unpleasant, emotional, or stress-inducing memories are much harder to forget than more neutral or trivial ones.

False Memories and Recovered Memories

An enormous controversy has brewed during the past two decades over the idea that repressed (as opposed to forgotten) traumatic memories can be recovered through methods such as psychotherapy, interviewing, and hypnosis. In several well-publicized court cases, young women and men were able to reopen for prosecution decades-old murder and child abuse cases based on memories recovered in psychotherapy. Sometimes the plaintiffs in these cases claim to be recalling memories from very early ages, as early as 3 to 5 years old.

As scientists have come to better understand the process of memory formation and retrieval, several facts have become apparent:

- Memories are subject to a great deal of distortion (see Table 7-1).
- Stressful memories would be more likely to be remembered because of the influence of the limbic systems and stress-generated hormones and neurotransmitters in memory consolidation.
- It is very unlikely that any person possesses episodic memories from an age younger than 2.5 to 3 years. Although this is a normal condition, it is often referred to as if it were a disorder—*infantile amnesia*. This forgetting is likely caused by the immaturity of the brain and memory systems *and* a lack of language abilities sufficient to give meaning to and thread together our experiences in a "story" form. When people claim to have very early memories (even up to age 5) it is more likely that what is being remembered is a retelling of the event. For example, if your aunt delights in repeatedly telling how you ran in fright from the clown your parents hired for your second birthday party, you will likely develop a vivid—but false—memory based on her story as opposed to the actual event.
- Suggestive interviewing can cause people to change details of their memories. Because memory is *reconstructive* (as opposed to photographic) we typically forget many details of any event or scene. When we are pressed for details, we tend to fill them in according to our schema. A *schema* is a set of instructions or a framework for an event. As a result, your memory for an event (such as a wedding) might feature details that you associate with what is typical for such an occasion (flowers might be substituted in for crepe streamers that were actually used that day because the florist failed to make the delivery on time). Or, suggestions given in the course of clinical and police interviews can change the details of people's memories. In one classic and controversial study *Lost in a Shopping Mall,* Loftus and Pickrell (1995) were able to create false memories in a sample of college-aged adults.
- As mentioned in Chapter 5, hypnosis is not a reliable tool for the recovery of memories. It should not be used for this purpose.

You have learned that the system for retrieving memories can be unreliable in many ways. It is possible to forget an event and be reminded about it later by an event, person, or object that acts as a retrieval cue or reminder. A number of memories recovered in therapy or in the course of daily life certainly are true. It is still impossible to know whether these memories were repressed or merely forgotten. At this time, while most psychologists accept that it is possible for true memories to be recovered, it is also certain that some recovered memories are false, and that anyone who interviews or examines people in search of memories must be cautious in this process by, for example, using open-ended questions that do not suggest anything in particular about events or people.

Organic Amnesia

Apart from dissociation, the term "amnesia" is used to refer to the loss of explicit memory, especially episodic memory. Procedural or implicit memories do not seem to be subject to this type of destruction—evidence that such memories are stored in a different system or way than explicit memories.

Amnesia can be caused by traumatic brain injuries, disease processes (such as stroke), or brain surgery performed to remedy other harmful conditions. There are two major types of organically induced amnesia.

Retrograde Amnesia

In *retrograde amnesia,* memories from the period preceding the injury are lost. Sometimes this is a very brief period, only minutes or hours in the case of a minor head injury causing a brief period of unconsciousness. It is similar to losing unsaved data when the power fails on your computer. Sometimes, in the wake of a stroke or an infection of the brain tissue, the memory loss can be much more dramatic and debilitating, deleting years of experience and knowledge from the brain's "hard drive." It is not necessarily true that the person will forget who he or she is; in fact, this is a relatively rare outcome. A case study in retrograde amnesia is Clive Wearing, a British conductor whose untreated viral encephalitis robbed him of most of his memories of the events of his own life, although he retains the ability to play and sing music (because such memories are stored in the implicit or procedural system.)

Anterograde Amnesia

Anterograde amnesia involves the inability to form new memories. Old memories may remain completely intact. The most famous patient with this type of amnesia is known in medical annals as *H.M.* H.M. had serious epileptic seizures, untreatable with standard drug therapies. As a last resort, doctors removed both of H.M.'s temporal lobes and his hippocampus. After the surgery, he seemed normal enough in all everyday interactions. He retained some memories of youth, before the onset of his seizure disorder, but could remember nothing occurring after his operation. If asked for his current address, he would give the one he had at the time of the operation. He had to be reminded that his mother was dead. He continued to demonstrate capability to form new procedural or implicit memories. He could be taught new skills, but he could not form any new episodic or semantic memories. He could learn to solve puzzles but would have no memory of being taught or struggling to learn the skill. Since H.M. many other cases of anterograde amnesia have been studied, and an excellent cinematic example of the disorder is portrayed in the movie *Memento.*

Aging and Memory

Because of the influence of media stereotyping, most people assume that the normal processes of aging include dramatic memory loss. The good news is, although minor memory loss and behavioral slowing do have some small detrimental effects, a healthy older person can retain much of his or her ability to remember, learn, and remember information. Research results do show that some memory abilities decline, but not all of these deteriorate to the same degree. Knowledge and experience (semantic and autobiographical memory) that are retrieved and used regularly are as accurate as they were in young and middle adulthood. New implicit memories continue to be formed and retained. Problems with *prospective memory*—that is, keeping track of appointments and future events or responsibilities—can be easily managed using appointment books and other reminder strategies.

The degree to which some of the declines occur is influenced both by genes and lifestyle. Simple steps such as maintaining a healthy diet, limiting or avoiding use of all drugs (including alcohol and cigarettes), and avoiding head injury (for example, wearing a helmet when playing contact sports) are all ways to lower one's chances of experiencing severe memory loss or dementias such as *Alzheimer's* disease. Also, chronic alcohol use has been linked to a form of anterograde amnesia called *Korsakoff's syndrome* (this is another good reason to limit the intake of alcohol). Additionally, new and creative research studies have produced evidence that keeping both mentally and physically active may have protective effects. The longitudinal *Nun Study* conducted by David Snowdon (2001) has provided evidence that learning and complexity of thought create additional synaptic connections in the brain. These connections act as a buffer against dementia when neurons die off in later life. They provide crucial protection against Alzheimer's and other dementias.

Other recent research has demonstrated that acetylcholine is important for memory processing in the brain. The brains of Alzheimer's sufferers, upon autopsy, show a marked lack of *acetylcholine*. Moderate, regular exercise increases the amount of acetylcholine in the synapses. It is a small investment that we can make in our youth to raise the chances of having a healthier, happier, and more productive old age.

Alzheimer's disease, like cancer and many other devastating illnesses, is a disorder to which we become more vulnerable as we age. It is a progressive fatal loss of memory, starting with higher cognitive processes (semantic and episodic). Eventually even procedural memory is lost. There is a genetic component to the disorder; however, there have also been case studies of identical twins in which one begins to manifest the disorder while the other remains healthy. So there is good reason to suspect that we can help ourselves postpone or avoid this, even if there is a history of the disorder in the family, through lifestyle choices. Find an exercise that you enjoy doing (so that you will be motivated to do it), and keep on learning!

Connecting Through Chapter Review

WORD-STUDY CONNECTION
Write each of these words on index cards and write their definitions on the opposite side.

absent-mindedness
accessing
acetylcholine
adrenaline
Alzheimer's disease
amnesia
amygdala
anterograde amnesia
attention
bias
blocking
consolidation
decay theory
declarative
dissociative amnesia
Hermann Ebbinghaus
encoding
encoding failure
engram
episodic memory
explicit
factitious

false memories
flashbulb memory
frontal lobes
H.M.
hippocampus
implicit
infantile amnesia
interference
Korsakoff's syndrome
Karl Lashley
Loftus and Pickrell
long-term memory
malingering
misattribution
mnemonic
persistence
primacy effect
priming
proactive interference
procedural
prospective memory
recall memory

recency effect
recognition memory
reconstructive
recovered memories
repress
retrieval
retrieval cues
retroactive interference
retrograde amnesia
schema
semantic memory
sensory memory
serial order effect
short-term memory
David Snowdon
George Sperling
suggestibility
suppress
TOT phenomena
transience
working memory

SELF-TEST CONNECTION

PART A. Completion
Write in the word that correctly completes each statement.

1. _____ is the ability to retain and recall information.
2. Memory is a _____ process, not a photographic process.
3. _____ was one of the first scientists to study memory systematically. He memorized and tried to recall long lists of random syllables.
4. The work of _____ demonstrated the processes that occur in the first stage of memory.
5. The first stage of memory is called _____ memory, and it lasts about ½ second.
6. _____ limits the amount of information that is transferred from the first to second stage of memory.

7. _____ memory, also referred to as *working memory,* is the active second stage in which information is processed for storage in long-term memory. Processing in working memory is referred to as _____ or consolidation.

8. _____ long-term memory is the type that stores activities that we do "without thinking" such as typing or riding a bicycle.

9. _____ long-term memory is what we typically think of as conscious memory.

10. There are two major types of _____ long-term memory—semantic and episodic.

11. _____ memory is like the knowledge base that we carry in our brains.

12. Your memory for your elementary school graduation is stored in _____ memory.

13. Recent advances in neuroscience have provided evidence that memory is a _____ process.

14. _____ searched in vain for the precise location of a stored memory or "engram."

15. The _____ has been identified as the structure in the limbic system that encodes new memories.

16. The _____ of the brain help you to organize and retrieve memories.

17. Release of the neurotransmitter _____ may facilitate the processes of encoding storing memories.

18. Formation of a long-term memory probably involves a change in the structure or functioning of _____ .

19. _____ is the act of remembering, or bringing forward information from memory.

20. The spreading or triggering of memories by others that are recalled is referred to as _____ .

21. Multiple-choice exams involve the easiest type of remembering called _____ memory.

22. These fill-in-the-blank items require _____ memory.

23. Forgetting owing to failure to process information in working memory is called _____ .

24. Inability to access retrieval cues is referred to as the _____ phenomenon.

25. If you can't remember your new phone number and keep thinking about your old phone number, you are experiencing _____ .

26. When you can't stop thinking about the way you froze during a classroom presentation, you are experiencing the sin of memory called _____ .

27. _____ is said to occur when unconscious forces work to remove material that is unpleasant or threatening from memory.

28. A person who suffers hippocampal damage may not be able to form any new memories. This is referred to as _____ amnesia.

29. A _____ is a mental template or framework for an event.

PART B. Multiple Choice

Circle the letter of the item that correctly completes the statement.

1. Memory is most accurately described as _____ .
   - (a) photographic
   - (b) reconstructive
   - (c) infallible
   - (d) an all-or-nothing process

2. Ebbinghaus's problems retaining the syllables that he tried to memorize demonstrated the memory problem known as _____ .
   (a) decay
   (b) persistence
   (c) interference
   (d) bias

3. Which of the following is *not* one of the three stages of memory acquisition?
   (a) short-term
   (b) sensory
   (c) long-term
   (d) retrieval

4. _____ studied the processes of sensory memory.
   (a) Ebbinghaus
   (b) Sperling
   (c) Lashley
   (d) Schacter

5. _____ limits the amount of information that enters working memory.
   (a) Attention
   (b) Encoding
   (c) Blocking
   (d) Interference

6. How to write and walk are examples of _____ long-term memories.
   (a) declarative
   (b) procedural
   (c) sensory
   (d) flashbulb

7. In seventh grade you memorized the capitals of all the European countries. This information is now part of your _____ memory.
   (a) implicit
   (b) episodic
   (c) photographic
   (d) semantic

8. Your high school graduation dance is part of your _____ memory.
   (a) implicit
   (b) episodic
   (c) photographic
   (d) semantic

9. Karl Lashley searched for the _____ but never found it.
   (a) engram
   (b) hippocampus
   (c) primacy effect
   (d) amygdala

10. The _____ consolidates new memories.
    (a) engram
    (b) hippocampus
    (c) frontal lobes
    (d) amygdala

11. The _____ helps to retrieve stored memories.
    (a) engram
    (b) hippocampus
    (c) frontal lobe
    (d) amygdala

12. Memory storage is *not* _____ .
    (a) cortical
    (b) permanent
    (c) biological
    (d) localized

13. The activation or spreading of new thoughts and memories as we recall information is called _____ .
    (a) blocking
    (b) priming
    (c) primacy effect
    (d) persistence

14. Answering this question requires you to use _____ .
    (a) recall
    (b) priming
    (c) recognition
    (d) blocking

15. Which of the following is *not* a category of ordinary forgetting?
    (a) Failure to retain
    (b) Failure to encode
    (c) Failure to retrieve
    (d) Failure to spread

16. You don't remember exactly what a nickel looks like. This is an example of _____ .
    (a) TOT
    (b) encoding failure
    (c) bias
    (d) transience

17. Retrieval cue failure is commonly called _____ .
    (a) TOT
    (b) amnesia
    (c) transience
    (d) absent-mindedness
18. You can't remember where you put your keys. This is a typical example of _____ .
    (a) transience
    (b) absent-mindedness
    (c) persistence
    (d) misattribution
19. During questioning by a homicide detective, an eyewitness changes her story to match crime details that the investigator mentions. This is an example of the sin of memory called _____ .
    (a) blocking
    (b) priming
    (c) suggestibility
    (d) misattribution
20. There is no real empirical evidence to support the existence of forgetting owing to _____ .
    (a) repression
    (b) interference
    (c) anterograde amnesia
    (d) encoding failure
21. Blackboard, desks, chalk, and a podium are parts of your _____ for a classroom.
    (a) engram
    (b) retrieval cue
    (c) false memory
    (d) schema
22. Traumatic injury to, diseases of, and surgery on the brain all can potentially cause _____ .
    (a) repression
    (b) blocking
    (c) amnesia
    (d) false memories
23. A man can no longer remember the events of his life before his stroke. This condition is called _____ amnesia.
    (a) anterograde
    (b) retrograde
    (c) dissociative
    (d) temporary
24. Aging inevitably causes _____ memory loss.
    (a) major
    (b) anterograde
    (c) permanent
    (d) minor
25. We become more vulnerable to this form of dementia as we age.
    (a) False memory syndrome
    (b) Dissociative amnesia
    (c) TOT
    (d) Alzheimer's disease

PART C. Modified True-False

If the statement is true, write "T" for the answer. If the statement is incorrect, change the underlined expression to one that will make the statement true.

1. Recognition can be defined as the ability to retain and recall various types and pieces of information.
2. Memory functions photographically, much like a camera.
3. Karl Lashley memorized vast lists of nonsense syllables to test his own retention.
4. Sensory memory is the first, very brief stage of memory in which much information registers but from which very little is retained.
5. Attention is the limiting factor that determines which information is transferred from short-term to long-term memory.
6. Encoding is the transferring of information from short-term memory into long-term memory.

7. There are two types of long-term memory—procedural and <u>implicit</u>.
8. Short-term memory is often referred to as <u>working memory</u> because it is a very active processing stage.
9. Knitting and sewing are activities that are stored in <u>procedural memory</u>.
10. <u>Conscious memory</u> is another term for declarative or explicit memory.
11. <u>The information that you learned on your first day of school</u> is stored in episodic memory.
12. Lashley <u>succeeded</u> in locating the elusive engram.
13. The hippocampus is located in the <u>limbic system</u>.
14. The frontal lobes function as a <u>memory consolidation center</u>.
15. Adrenaline is a <u>hormone</u> that promotes memory storage.
16. Neuroscientists believe that the formation of a long-term memory involves changes in the structure or functioning of <u>neurons</u>.
17. <u>A retrieval cue</u> can help us to access stored memories.
18. <u>Recognition remembering</u> occurs when you respond to a single question or clue—as is the case when you answer a fill-in-the-blank item.
19. <u>The recency effect</u> occurs when you remember end of the list or last part of the material but not what comes before it.
20. <u>David Snowdon</u> is best known for identifying the seven sins of memory.
21. <u>Absent-mindedness</u> is another term for memory decay.
22. There is <u>abundant empirical evidence</u> for the existence of repression.
23. Not remembering the first three years of life is referred to as <u>retrograde amnesia</u>.
24. H.M.'s surgery resulted in permanent <u>anterograde amnesia</u>.
25. Healthy lifestyle and an active life of thinking and learning have <u>no protective effect</u> against dementias such as Alzheimer's disease later in our lives.

PART D. Name That Memory Problem

Identify the memory difficulty described in the vignette. Write a brief definition of the concept.

1. Jason put his keys into his gym bag instead of his jacket pocket as he usually does. Now he cannot remember where the keys are.
2. Annie has always thought that medicine is a "man's job." After a serious car accident, a female trauma doctor treated Annie in the emergency room. She keeps telling people that a wonderful male physician saved her life.
3. Susie memorized all fifty state capitals when she was in eighth grade, but she can only remember twenty-three of them now that she is in graduate school.
4. After receiving a serious concussion in a football scrimmage, Andy can't remember the week before the accident.
5. Kenneth can't forget the day that an earthquake leveled twelve homes in his neighborhood.
6. At age 78, Maurice has begun to experience consistent problems remembering new information.
7. Busy Helen forgot her parent's anniversary for the third year in a row.
8. When opening the door to her classroom. Dr. Robinson needs to check the codes on all of her building keys because she never bothered to memorize the right code.

9. John is convinced that he learned about amnesia by watching the Discovery Channel, although in reality he watched a documentary on PBS.
10. Larry is in the doghouse because he called his new girlfriend by the name of his old flame.

CONNECTING TO CONCEPTS

Review the chapter and then write down your thoughts about the following questions.

1. As you have learned, human memory is *not* photographic, but reconstructive. Discuss how memory really works and identify one implication for real-life situations (such as police work).
2. Name the types of amnesia, and briefly describe each one, including its possible causes.
3. Identify and describe the components of the brain and the nervous system that are most directly involved with acquisition and storage of memories.
4. Summarize the current debates regarding the following concepts:
   a. Repression
   b. Dissociative amnesia
   c. Recovered memories versus false memory syndrome
5. List the seven sins of memory, and try to identify an example of an actual occurrence of each one in your life, or the life of someone you know well.

CONNECTING TO LIFE/JOB SKILLS

Using Psychology to Improve Memory

> The time you spend thinking about material you are reading and relating it to previously stored material is about the most useful thing you can do in learning any new subject matter. (Myers 1998)

As you have seen in this chapter, two of your greatest allies in committing the material from your studies to memory are emotion and meaning. You need to care about what you are learning and understand its relevance to your life. In fact, the more you can see the connection between what you learn and your world, the better your chance of retaining it. This is called the *self-reference effect*. The more you can see concepts from your studies at work in everyday life, the more meaningful they will be to you.

If you are studying a subject that has only limited relevance to your everyday life, you may need to be more creative. A good source of inspiration is found in the "memory Olympians," people who memorize random lists of words, numbers, and other materials. They are not "born gifted" in memorizing; they develop or are taught clever strategies to create context and retrieval cues. For example, they write a story using the one hundred words on a list in order to link them together (*categorical clustering*). And of course, they practice—a lot.

Another technique that can enhance your memory is *chunking*. Look at these letters for fifteen seconds, then cover them and write down as many as you can remember:

XSOSESPIRSNBCX

If you didn't cheat, you probably found it pretty hard to memorize the letters. But if you detected the possibility to form smaller, more meaningful *chunks* of information you probably found it much more doable:

XSOSESPIRSNBCX

X SOS ESP IRS NBC X

Chunking is a great help for organizing information—something your brain is particularly good at, as you will see in the next chapter.

At a certain point, the amount we are trying to memorize may be so great that no matter how many clever cues we have up our sleeves, our cues may fail us. For this reason, whenever possible, *over-learning* the material is recommended. It is much better to space out the memorization process across a longer period of time (so you must not procrastinate). It is better to space your practice into short, frequent sessions. Massed practice, also known as cramming, tends to be a good deal less effective. Allow yourself the time to over-learn the material.

To find out more about the Memory Olympics, visit these web sites:

goodmedicine.ninemsn.com.au/goodmedicine/factsheets/db/body/neurological/1069.asp

archive.abcnews.go.com/onair/DailyNews/2020_000210_mentalolympics_chat.html

The first four web sites listed in "Other Useful Web Sites" section at the end of the chapter are also great sources of tips and strategies to improve your memory.

WHAT'S HAPPENING!

Alzheimer's Research

Some of the most exciting benefits of the neuroscience revolution have emerged in the area of Alzheimer's prevention, early detection, and management.

Studies of identical twins have revealed lifestyle and environmental factors that raise the risk. (As is the case with almost every genetically based mental disorder, in many sets of identical twins only one twin gets the disease, which suggests that environmental factors play a role also.) Because of such studies, we understand that the health of the brain depends on the health of the body in general, so exercising, dieting, exercising moderation in consumption or avoidance of alcohol and other drugs, avoiding head injury, and remaining mentally active all play a role in forestalling or preventing the progress of organic dementias such as Alzheimer's.

In the area of early detection, those persons who have increased vulnerability as a result of family history can now be carefully monitored so that the earliest signs and symptoms are noted. Unfortunately, up until recently, a definitive diagnosis of Alzheimer's could only be made at death. But this is changing—brain-imaging technology (EEG PET and fMRI) is being used to reveal specific areas of the cortex and limbic system that undergo subtle changes before behavioral symptoms begin to emerge. In Alzheimer's, the earlier we detect the disease the more that can be done to slow its progress.

Our improved knowledge of neurotransmitters and the cellular structure of the brain has led to some first attempts to slow the progress of deterioration. We know now that acetylcholine is in short supply in the brains of Alzheimer's sufferers. Drugs that promote the production of acetylcholine appear to slow the progress of the disease somewhat and provide some symptom relief. We have seen the formation of beta-amyloid (a type of protein) plaques on dying cortical cells of those who develop the disease. Although the relationship of these plaques to the disease is not yet fully understood, new drugs to slow the formation of these plaques, or eliminate them entirely, are also under development in animal research.

To learn more about the latest developments in research on Alzheimer's disease and other dementias visit these sites:

www.alzforum.org/home.asp

www.dukehealth.org/news/healthbrief_oct02_3.asp

www.sciencedaily.com/releases/2003/01/030108071621.htm

OTHER USEFUL WEB SITES

Memory Improvement Sites

memory.uva.nl/memimprovement/eng/

This is a University of Virginia-sponsored web site that features a variety of helpful mnemonic strategies.

www.studyhall.com/MEM/memory.html

This site is generally dedicated to helping secondary school and college students. This section of the site features various memory improvement tips.

www.thememorypage.net/

Here you will find tutorials that help you to learn about how memory works and to improve your memory.

matthew-leitch.supanet.com/memory/

This is a great resource for gaining practice in the use of chunking and categorical clustering for memory improvement.

Other Sites About Remembering and Forgetting

ALZHEIMER'S ASSOCIATION

www.alz.org/

This is the homepage of the major education and advocacy group helping Alzheimer's sufferers and their families.

BOOK EXCERPT: SEVEN SINS OF MEMORY

www.2think.org/memory_sins.shtml

At this site you can read an excerpt from Daniel Schacter's book about everyday memory problems.

HOW STUFF WORKS

science.howstuffworks.com/question672.htm

This site presents a nice, easy-to-read summary of the latest findings on anterograde and retrograde amnesia.

MEMORY DISORDERS PROJECT

www.memorylossonline.com/index.htm

Memory Disorders Project at Rutgers University shares its newsletters at this site. Check here for updates in research on amnesia and dementia. It also features information that helps to "separate fact from fiction"—encouraging critical thinking about amnesia and organic brain disorders.

REFERENCES

Loftus, E. F. & Pickrell, J. E. (1995) The formation of false memories. *Psychiatric Annals,* 25, 720–725.

Myers, D. (1998) *Psychology* New York: Worth.

Schacter, D. (2001) *The Seven Sins of Memory: How the Mind Forgets and Remembers.* Boston: Houghton Mifflin.

Snowdon, D. (2001) *Aging with Grace: What the Nun Study Teaches Us About Leading Longer, Healthier, and More Meaningful Lives.* New York: Doubleday.

Zacks, R. T., Hasher, L. & Li, K. Z. H. L. (2000) Human memory. In TA Salthouse & F.I.M. Craik (Eds.), *Handbook of Aging and Cognition,* 2nd edition (293–357). Mahwah, NJ: Lawrence Erlbaum.

Chapter 8

THINKING, LANGUAGE, AND INTELLIGENCE

In this chapter you will become acquainted with some basic theory and current findings in three major areas of cognitive science.

Mental Processes (Cognition)

The terms "mental processes" and "cognition" are merely fancy ways to say that this chapter is about "what goes on inside your head." No jargon can fully capture the complex nature of thought. There are many definitions of "thinking" and almost none of them are satisfying. What is thinking, anyway? You probably have some idea already (because you are thinking about it!). The activities of cognition include

- Understanding
- Remembering
- Interpreting
- Organizing
- Problem solving
- Decision making
- Creating

To accomplish these tasks, our brain works with various types of *mental representations*—symbols, language, concepts, and images. Thinking takes place on multiple levels. Just as there is more than one kind of memory, there is probably more than one kind of thinking. There is your memory of yesterday's breakfast (episodic), for what you read in the paper while you ate (semantic), and for how to use the utensils in order to eat (procedural). Likewise, there is the kind of automatic or associative thinking that you do when you perform a procedural task such as driving to a familiar location, and the thinking you do when you are taking the written portion of the driver's test. It is apparent that these are not the same kind of thinking. The ease with which we drive is limited by an all-important resource—*attention*. It also depends upon the level of familiarity or amount of rehearsal. If a hailstorm begins, or if you are driving to an unfamiliar location, driving becomes a more conscious, declarative task (sometimes called a *controlled* or *cognitive task*) that requires more focused attention and mental effort.

The Tools of Thought

In Chapter 6 we introduced one fundamental tool of thought. The theory of *observational learning* relies on the assumption that we construct a type of mental image, a *cognitive map*. These images are usually visual, but they may also include other sensory features of the place, event, or object about which we are thinking. We can problem-solve, navigate, and perform other thinking tasks using cognitive maps. We can manipulate the images themselves, changing their positions through rotation or altering certain aspects of their features.

Concepts are another basic cognitive tool. They are essential for organizing our knowledge base. Concepts are mental categories, collections of events, people, objects, or other entities that share some important quality or feature. It is interesting to note that although many concepts are universal among cultures, there is some variation in concept formation from culture to culture. For example, aboriginal Australians have a concept that includes "women, fire and all dangerous things" (Lakoff 1990) based on a grouping scheme most people raised in other cultures find hard to grasp. In essence, they perceive the sun as made of fire, the sun gives life, women give life, fire burns, and it is also dangerous. It is hard to follow though, unless you were raised to see it this way. Color categories also reveal differences in concept formation. The Dani of New Guinea have no color words except for "light" and "dark." The Native American people known as the Zuni use the same word for "orange" and "yellow." These differences are very hard for us to grasp. In the same vein, modern American concepts (such as the many words that refer to a "car") might be hard for a person from a less technological society to comprehend.

There are two kinds of concepts. *Natural* (or "fuzzy") *concepts* are learned from experience. Animal, book, and car are all examples of natural concepts. How do we figure out what a "pet" is, for example? As we grow up, we meet friends who own dogs, cats, hamsters, and parrots and eventually even those who have exotic pets such as snakes and tarantulas. We may even have a friend who has a rock for a pet (or we might have if we grew up in the seventies) or an electronic pet (a more recent fad). There are few or no rules for determining what belongs in the category (thus the term "fuzzy concept"). In this case, the only rule would be that if a person takes care of it, it could be a pet. *Artificial* (or formal) *concepts*, on the other hand, are highly specific and based on inflexible rules or characteristics. Most academic subjects are composed of artificial concepts (such as grammar rules or analytic definitions). You learn what entities are sorted into the concept based on training.

A *prototype* is a best or most typical example of a concept. A robin is a prototype of bird. An atypical example is just that, an example of a concept that doesn't strongly resemble other members of that class, but nonetheless, represents that concept. A flamingo, penguin, or ostrich would all be atypical examples of the bird concept. *Stereotypes* are social prototypes. We will examine stereotypes and the problems associated with them further in Chapter 12.

Problem Solving and Decision Making

Nervous systems and brains arose in our world in part because they were useful for problem solving. The problem, for most creatures for most of the vast expanse of evolutionary time, was broadly defined as staying alive; more narrowly, staying alive meant finding food, and avoiding being eaten. Problem solving is a crucial mental process.

There are five categories of decision-making and problem-solving strategies.

- *Compensatory.* There are a few subtypes of this strategy, but they all involve the consideration of aspects or features of the different possible solutions or choices. We may choose the solution that has the greatest number of desirable features, the least number of undesirable features, or the best combination of desirable features with the fewest undesirable ones. Compensatory decision making is typically utilized with nonrisky decisions, for example, making a choice between one of two similar items when shopping.
- *Algorithmic.* An algorithm is a methodical, logical rule or step-by-step procedure that guarantees the solution will be found. The steps for solving an equation such as $2x + 3 = 15$ compose an algorithm, and this is true most of mathematics. Generally, a problem must have a definite solution or solution set if algorithms are to be utilized.
- *Trial and error.* The trial-and-error strategy consists of trying many different solutions and discarding those that don't work. This method is suitable for situations in which time is not a critical factor and there are only a limited number of solutions. Furthermore, the consequences of committing an error cannot be too serious. SWAT team members do not learn to defuse bombs using trial and error (unless the situation can be effectively and safely "simulated.")
- *Heuristic.* Heuristic strategies are referred to as rule-of-thumb strategies that can help us make judgments and solve problems efficiently. They are usually faster to use than algorithms. Unfortunately, they are also less reliable than algorithms. You may wind up with an incorrect solution. Heuristics can also be employed when problems do not have a definite solution. Examples of commonly used heuristics include working backwards, breaking the problem into steps, and working with a similar problem that has a known solution. There are many others. Unlike the compensatory models described earlier, we also prefer to use heuristics for decisions that involve risk of loss or setback (decisions or problems that are more of a "gamble" for us).
- *Insight.* A sudden and novel realization of the solution to a problem or insight can lead to creative solutions, but it usually requires a great deal of experience with the subject area within which the problem falls and the methods and instruments that are typically used.

There are many problems of thinking that may hamper our ability to solve problems and make judgments. Here are some of the most common ones.

- *Representativeness heuristic (or bias).* In the simplest terms, the representativeness heuristic involves using the features of a prototype to make predictions or decisions about people and events. You believe that all men with long hair must be politically liberal "hippie" types based on a prototype (or more accurately stereotype) developed in the 1960s. You may be surprised when you meet a long-haired man who has voted for conservative candidates all his life.
- *Availability heuristic (or bias).* This involves using the information that comes to mind first. Airline accidents are always more vivid in our memories than car accidents. Schoolyard shootings are much more vivid than physical illness. Yet car accidents are far more common and deadly than airline accidents, and many more school-age children die every year from asthma and other serious illnesses than are shot by fellow students. Certainly this misjudgment is related to the powerful emotions that are generated by these events (as you learned in Chapter 7). Our judgment concerning the relative danger is inaccu-

rate given the base-rate of these occurrences. This is the availability bias—what is most easily available to our memory does not always represent the most common occurrence.

- *Confirmation bias.* This could be referred to informally as selective memory. It is easier to remember the evidence that supports our beliefs and assumptions and to forget or discard that which fails to do so. For example, it is easy to disconfirm the myth that people behave erratically when the full moon is out by maintaining records of crimes and disorderly behaviors throughout the lunar cycle for several months (systematic observation). This belief, however, is usually developed based on our casual, less systematic observations. These observations tend to confirm our beliefs. We tend to remember only our "hits" and forget out "misses," thus creating this type of bias in our recollection and decision making (we remember only the nights when the full moon and erratic behavior coincided, and forget all the peaceful nights of full moon light.)

- *Overconfidence.* After we make a decision or adopt a belief, we tend to maintain our confidence that it is the correct one. We tend to overestimate the accuracy of our beliefs and judgments, as well as exaggerate the number of other people who see things as we do. We often hold our position even in the face of a great deal of information suggesting that it is not correct.

- *Anchoring bias or effect.* If we are given a "hint" or are supplied with information while making our decision or choice, the anchoring bias occurs. The information may influence our answer, which may make it more or less accurate. For example, if you are asked whether the distance from New York to Chicago is greater than 200 miles, you most likely will say (correctly) "greater" but your answer will almost certainly underestimate the distance because of the anchoring effect of "200 miles."

- *Functional fixedness.* An inability to think about objects or situations except in terms of their usual function can inhibit problem solving. If you can see, for example, that wax can be used in place of glue for adhesion, or that a nail can be used to etch, you may have greater success in creating or fixing objects.

- *Mental set.* All of us have a mental set, and it isn't an entirely bad thing. Your mental set is your collection of beliefs, assumptions, and perspectives. We need a consistent basis for viewing the world in order to organize our thoughts. Mental set becomes a problem though when it prevents us from viewing a problem in a new way. If you are convinced that men are by nature better at outdoor work than women, you may prevent yourself from hiring a talented new park ranger who happens to be female. (As you can see, this concept is strongly related both to functional fixedness and to prejudice, which will be presented in Chapter 12.)

Language

Language is the primary tool of human thought. We think using language; and arguably language in some way forms the basis of our consciousness (Gazzaniga 2002). It is probably not an accident that our first memories of our lives begin to emerge around the time that our language learning accelerates (at 2½ to 3½ years of age).

Animals communicate using smells, expressions, sounds, primitive gestures, and even human sign language (as some chimpanzees have been taught to do by scientists over the past several decades). These forms of communication are interesting but probably do not qualify as a language, at least not by human standards. What are the special features of language? Which features makes human language unique?

- *Symbols*. Human languages are composed of millions of symbols: letters, phonemes (consonant-vowel combinations), and words. There are also languages based on numbers, signs, sounds, and pictures to represent objects, ideas, and events. The use of symbols is a fundamental part of language. Not only do we use symbols, but we also create new ones constantly. Language is an organic feature of human intelligence. Words are created and fall out of use all the time. For example "groovy" came into the use in the midtwentieth century but is rarely if ever used now. "Cool," on the other hand, is a word that emerged in the same period and continues to be used. Although words may start off as slang, they may gradually become part of the standard vocabulary.
- *Syntax*. Also called grammar, syntax consists of the rules for using the symbols of language. Syntax allows the words to be used in a meaningful fashion. The rules that you were compelled to learn in language arts are not trivial; if your syntax is incorrect you may not convey the correct and intended meaning. Syntax also evolves and changes through the history of a language.
- *Abstraction*. Because language is symbolic, it allows us to not only represent the present but also to refer to the past, the future, and things that never will happen. We can think about and discuss ideas and concepts that are intangible.

So, humans can invent new symbols and syntax and can refer to past, future, and fantasy in thought and discussion. As far as we know, only humans possess these abilities.

Origins of Human Language

Evolutionary psychologists and biologists date the explosion of language in our species to about 50,000 years ago. Of course, other changes occurring millions of years earlier laid the foundation. When our species began to walk upright, our hands were freed not only for using tools but also for signing (so it is likely that human language was originally signed) and our faces and hands became available for more complex communications. Language has given our species an enormous advantage—planning survival related activities such as gathering food, finding shelter, and providing for defense. It is thought that the development of language has driven the evolution of our brains to some extent. *Memes* (mentioned in Chapter 2), if they exist, would be transmitted primarily through language.

Language and the Brain

The *nativist* view of human language development, proposed by Noam Chomsky (1965) states that language is a natural, innate capability of the human brain. He uses the analogy that most birds are born prepared to fly and that humans are born prepared to learn language. In both cases, no training is required. Children learn language at a rate that exceeds the small amount of exposure and teaching they receive in everyday life. This is called the *poverty of stimulus* argument. More recently, Steven Pinker (2000) has promoted this view in his book *The Language Instinct*. As any parent or early childhood educator will attest, a young child is a language learning genius. Between the ages of 2 and 6, a child learns enough vocabulary and syntax to communicate effectively with all adults—tens of thousands of words and a vast number of complex grammar rules. Pinker takes this as evidence that the child's brain is prepared for language from shortly after birth. We will review the specific stages of this process in Chapter 9.

The results of brain research support the nativist view. There appears to be a window of time during which the brain is essentially "wired" for language learning—roughly birth to age 8. Our ability to hear and make all the possible sounds of human language is narrowed over the first year of life, thus increasing the chance that any languages that we learn later in life will be spoken with an accent. Also, during the first six to eight years, two special areas of the left hemisphere (in most people)—*Broca's* and *Wernicke's* areas (see Figure 8.1)—are not yet full set in place. During this period, storage of word meaning and grammar rules is more efficient.

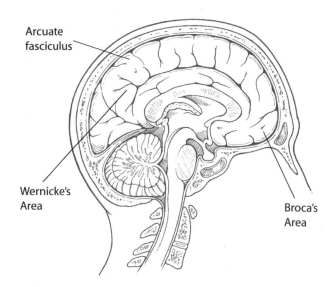

Figure 8.1 Language areas in the left hemisphere of the cortex.

So the brain is "primed" for language learning early in life. Contrary to what most scientists used to think, the best time for a person to learn a second or third language is early childhood, provided that opportunities for regular exposure exist. As we approach adolescence, this efficiency of learning and storage is lost. Although we may still become fluent in other languages, we will never truly "think" in a language learned in adolescence or adulthood.

Language, Thought, and Culture

It is clear that language and thought are intimately connected. In Chapter 7 we touched on the problem of suggestibility in memory. This "sin of memory" can be triggered by language. Loftus and Palmer (1974) demonstrated that changing one word in the description of a car accident could alter people's memories of the accident. The words that we use to describe an event can change how we remember it. In the social sphere, the words we choose to use can influence perceptions of people and events. Using a euphemism such as "passed away" is meant to soften the pain caused by a death; a dysphemism such as "croaked" conveys a lack of respect and may be meant to shock or upset the listener. Other word choices may serve to reinforce or control stereotypes that we hold (for example, "women's rights advocate" versus "feminist" versus "man-hater").

In the early twentieth century, L. S. Vygotsky, (1896–1934), a Russian developmental psychologist, proposed that culture is transmitted through language, that in learning the language of our people we also learn how to think as a member of our society. Working at around the same time as Vygotsky, Edward Sapir (1884–1939) and his student Benjamin Lee Whorf (1897–1941) drew upon early linguistic studies and philosophy proposed two fascinating ideas: *linguistic relativity* (the idea that boundaries between concepts and categories in languages are arbitrary) and *linguistic determinism* (the idea that our native language shapes the way we think, reminiscent of Vygotsky.) Together these two ideas have come to be referred to as the *Sapir-Whorf hypothesis*.

There is a great deal of interesting evidence for relativity—we have already touched upon it in looking at the cultural aspects of concept formation, as with the case of the Dani and the Zuni mentioned earlier. Even in cultures that are less exotic to modern English speakers we can find these differences—there is no exact match for the word "blue" in languages such as Russian and French. Determinism is more actively debated, and there are psychologists and other scientists who simply reject it.

Intelligence

Intelligence is a one of the most interesting and controversial topics in the field of psychology.

Let's start with a crucial distinction. Intelligence is a *construct*—an abstract representation, similar to memory or personality. *IQ* is a score produced by tests that are intended to operationalize (measure) intelligence. There is debate as to whether the current crop of IQ tests actually do so in a completely fair and unbiased manner. Even the moderately strong correlations that IQ tests hold with school and life success are not as impressive as they seem "at face value." Because the data are correlational, cause-and-effect claims made on its basis stand on very shaky ground; for example, does a high IQ cause one to become rich, or does being rich give you better access to resources that allow better nutrition, health care, and educational tools, therefore raising your IQ? It is very hard to know.

Conceptual Definitions of Intelligence

The definition that one chooses for intelligence in part depends on your underlying assumptions about what it is. Here are some possibilities:

- *Behaviorist*. The ability to learn from experience and function successfully in one's environment.
- *Cognitive*. The ability to judge, comprehend, and reason.
- *Utilitarian*. The ability to understand and deal with people, objects, and symbols.

The author of one of the most widely used families of IQ tests (the Wechsler scales), David Wechsler, characterizes it as

- The ability to act purposefully, think rationally, and deal effectively with the environment.

Because we are still in the realm of the conceptual, we must remember that these terms are subject to debate. (What exactly does it mean to "deal effectively"?) To identify intelligent behaviors, we must make intelligence measurable. Intelligence can be operationally defined in different ways depending on culture, context, and other conditions.

Timeline: Intelligence and Intelligence Testing

Intelligence has been examined since long before psychology established itself as a new and separate discipline. (See Table 8-1.) Early philosophers spent the most time contemplating and trying to define it. In the mid-nineteenth century, Darwin's theories added to the already vital interest in intelligence, as it was perceived to be a quality that enhanced an organism's fitness.

TABLE 8-1
THE HISTORY OF INTELLIGENCE TESTING

Period	Contributor	Contribution
Mid-to-late nineteenth century	Frances Galton (1822–1911)	Early proponent of the idea that heredity is primary in determining intelligence. Performed the first twin studies.
Turn of the century (late nineteenth to early twentieth century)	James M. Cattell (1860–1944)	Promoted quantitative methods in psychology (psychometric perspective).
	Charles Spearman (1863–1945)	Proposed the single-factor model of intelligence—g—the general factor important for all intellectual tasks. Any specific intellectual operation requires the influence of g.
	Alfred Binet (1857–1911)	Working with Theodore Simon, created the first intelligence test (for the purpose of identifying children in need of special education).
	Henry Goddard (1866–1957)	Brought intelligence testing to the United States by translating Binet & Simon's test into English. Promoted the idea that intelligence is a unitary entity, strongly hereditary. Believed that those with inferior genes should not be allowed to reproduce (eugenics).
	Robert Yerkes (1876–1956)	Helped to develop the Army Alpha & Beta Intelligence Tests.
	Lewis Terman (1877–1956)	Created IQ scoring index used in modern intelligence testing; studied intelligence in children (especially giftedness).

TABLE 8-1 (Continued)
THE HISTORY OF INTELLIGENCE TESTING

Period	Contributor	Contribution
	Leta S. Hollingsworth (1886–1939)	Performed pioneering research to disprove prejudicial notions regarding the intellect of women; studied giftedness in children.
Mid-twentieth century	Cyril Burt (1883–1971)	Controversial figure who advocated both a hereditarian view of intellectual development and socially progressive policies for identifying and assisting the progress and achievement of bright children from disadvantaged backgrounds.
	L.L. Thurstone (1887–1955)	Performed extensive research that led to the first "multiple factors" theory of intelligence.
	David Wechsler (1896–1981)	Developed one of the most widely administered intelligence scales in current use—the Wechsler test comes in a preschool, children's and adult version.
	J.P. Guilford (1897–1988)	Proponent of "structure-of-intellect" model featuring 120 separate abilities that comprise intelligence. Believed intelligence is far too complex to be characterized by one or two factors.
	Anne Anastasi (1907–2001)	Cataloged and evaluated virtually all intelligence, aptitude, and achievement tests in use in the mid-twentieth centuries—the "test guru."
	Hans J. Eysenck (1916–1997)	Advocated a "hard science" approach to the study of intelligence using rigorous statistics and evidence—*Intelligence: A New Look*—published posthumously.
Recent and current theory and research (late twentieth and early twenty-first centuries.)	Raymond Cattell (1905–1998)	Proposed the existence of two broad categories of intelligence, crystallized and fluid; promoted rigorous statistical analysis in psychological testing.
	Arthur Jensen (1923–)	Major and controversial proponent of the hereditarian view of intelligence. Published book—*Bias in Mental Testing*.
	Leon J Kamin (1924–)	Major critic of hereditarian view, controversial proponent of the influence of environment. Attacked the book *The Bell Curve* (see text.)
	Howard Gardner (1943–)	Proposed a multiple intelligences theory (featuring seven types of intelligence); studied the intellectual development of children.
	Robert Sternberg (1949–)	Proposed the Triarchic theory of intelligence; innovative researcher and theoretician of intelligence and intelligence testing.

For the remainder of this chapter, I will review four debates related to the nature of intelligence.

- Is intelligence best represented as one (or two) numbers or factors that determine different skill and abilities levels across a wide range of talents or are there many different types of intelligence?
- Is intelligence determined primarily by genetic inheritance or to conditions of environment (the nature versus nurture debate)?
- Is one's level of intelligence a fixed or a changeable trait (over the course of a lifetime)?
- Is the perception and definition of what behaviors signify intelligence consistent across all cultures, situations, and contexts, or is it culture/context-dependent?

A Single Intelligence or Many Intelligences?

Chief Advocates of a More "Unitary" Form of Intelligence

Charles Spearman (1863–1945) is remembered as a strong proponent of the *psychometric approach* (simply the idea that intelligence can be measured) and of the theoretical concept he called *g*, which stands for general intelligence factor. He described it as a stable and measurable factor that underlies all skills and performance that requires cognitive ability, from graduating with honors from college to designing skyscrapers to piloting airlines.

Spearman did acknowledge that some people have special abilities that outstrip many of their other skills. An extreme example of this is *savant syndrome*. This syndrome is still a puzzle to cognitive scientists. A person who has savant syndrome has been diagnosed with a organic mental disease (autism) that depresses performance in many, but not all, intellectual performance areas; in fact, the savant is incredibly talented in one or two areas. Another condition that presents evidence against the pervasive influence of a single general intelligence factor is *William's syndrome*, a genetic disease in which the affected person has serious limitations with mathematical and spatial concepts, but also may have amazing verbal fluency and musical ability. Given that these conditions exist in nature, it is difficult to conceive of the consistent and powerful influence of the g factor.

Raymond Cattell (1905–1998) worked with Spearman. He also promoted Spearman's view but, based on psychometric evidence proposed that there were two separate forms of g.

- *Fluid intelligence.* This involves dynamic cognitive processes such as reasoning, seeing patterns and relationships, using information, and finding and applying new knowledge to decision making and problem solving.
- *Crystallized intelligence.* This is acquired knowledge and skills that are applied in a variety of specific contexts, depending on the nature of the activities, demands and environments in which the person functions.

There is some disagreement about where the distinction is drawn in some areas between these two subdivisions. Some cognitive tasks may require both forms.

Chief Advocates of Multiple Intelligences

Thurstone (1887–1955) was the chief opponent of Spearman. He was the originator of the *multiple intelligences* concept. Based on the results of administering a large variety of different abilities tests to many people, he identified seven intellectual skill groups—clusters of abilities that appeared to be interrelated. He designated these as the *primary mental abilities*. There was some variation in patterns of performance on the seven abilities; however, cognitive scientists who have since analyzed Thurstone's work determined that, in general (holding aside savant and related syndromes), most persons who were outstanding in one area tend to be at least higher than average in the other areas. Without a unitary, overriding factor (something like a g factor), this would not be expected to occur. Thurstone later acknowledged the likelihood of influence from an overarching g factor on the primary mental abilities.

Yet Thurstone's theory has had a lasting influence in a number of areas. The measurement procedure underlying Wechsler's widely used intelligence tests is based on the seven primary mental abilities. Also, the creators of two modern theories of intelligence (Gardner and Sternberg) owe a debt to Thurstone.

Howard Gardner proposes the existence of seven separate types of intelligence that, according to cultural dictates are valued and thought of as "smarts." Table 8-2 describes the seven intelligences and some examples of activities that reflect them.

TABLE 8-2
MULTIPLE INTELLIGENCES

Intelligence Type	Skills and Abilities
Logical-mathematical intelligence	Scientific research, mathematical computation, logical reasoning
Linguistic intelligence	Creative and technical writing, teaching and lecturing, storytelling.
Spatial intelligence	Visualizing and manipulating objects and maps, understanding the relationship between positions and things; creating plans for structures and spaces
Kinesthetic intelligence	Ability to move accurately in space, control of body movement, agility and skill in movement as in dancing or playing sports
Musical intelligence	Composition, orchestration, and performance of music
Interpersonal intelligence	Understanding, sensitivity, and ability to interpret other people's thoughts, feelings and motives, social ease and skill
Intrapersonal intelligence	Self-understanding – ability to access and interpret one's own thoughts, feelings, and motivations

Robert Sternberg also supports the multiple intelligences view but he proposes that seven intelligences are too many. He is concerned that such a scheme misidentifies talents as forms of intelligence. He created the *triarchic* (three factor) *theory of intelligence.*

1. *Analytic skills*—cognitive skills important to school, academics, research, and other scholarly pursuits. These can be accurately assessed through IQ, aptitude, and achievement tests.
2. *Practical intelligence*—cognitive skills required for everyday tasks, which are often ambiguous in nature, with changing rules and multiple solutions. Practical intelligence involves flexibility, attentiveness and sensitivity to context.
3. *Creative intelligence*—cognitive skills in managing novel situations and problems, seeing problems in new and different ways, and maintaining an ability to improve and invent. A person who possesses great creative intelligence would rarely suffer from functional fixedness.

A valid criticism of these modern multiple intelligence theories is that they have a generally weak empirical base of support. Sternberg is reportedly working on an IQ test based on his triarchic theory.

Nature and Nurture

The most accurate answer to the question "Is intelligence determined by nature or nurture?" is most likely "yes!" Both play integral parts and interact in complex and fascinating ways.

There is strong evidence of a genetic contribution based on a large body of research. Some examples of this research, in summary form, follow:

- The IQ test scores of identical twins tend to be virtually the same—provided that these twins were reared in the same household. When identical twins are reared in different households, the similarities in IQ scores are great enough that various researchers have estimated a 50–70 percent contribution to IQ scores from genes. A possible weakness of this research that should be noted though, is that it is very hard to find large samples of identical twins.
- Psychological studies of adopted children—on a variety of characteristics, including IQ scores, produce evidence that they favor their biological parents rather than their adoptive parents. Their IQ scores correlate more strongly with those of their biological rather than adoptive siblings.
- Fraternal twins and siblings demonstrate much less similarity in their IQ scores than do those of identical twins.

The Influence of Environment

Just When Do Environmental Effects Begin Anyway?

At conception, the mother's nutrition, health, and level of stress begin to impact the developing fetus. We now understand through witnessing the tragedy of fetal alcohol syndrome and interuterine growth retardation (which can result from use of nicotine or cocaine during pregnancy) that these prenatal environmental influences can be substantial and devastating.

- Interestingly the IQ scores of fraternal twins correlate more highly than those of siblings. Fraternal twins share the *same* relative proportion of genetic material as siblings in the same family, but caregivers tend to treat them in a more similar manner because they are the same age and interestingly their IQ tests are more similar than siblings' are. This suggests the combined effects of shared in utero environment and expectations of people who may assume that twins, even if they are fraternal, are somehow "more similar" than siblings.

- Institutional care—such as early placement in an orphanage—tends to hinder development. A large number of studies have demonstrated this. However, if children are removed early to homes with regular attention and loving care, they do make gains. The earlier this happens, the better. Children in some of these orphanage studies did very poorly on cognitive measures but did improve slightly to moderately if rescued and placed in a more enriched environment. This study suggests that severe disadvantage *does* hurt children, and that nature and nurture interact in an important way in this regard. There are sensitive periods during which children require regular attention and care if they are to reach their full potential.

- The *Flynn Effect* is the intriguing fact that (on a global basis) average IQ has been rising for roughly the past fifty years (Holloway 1999). This rise could be the result of a number of factors, none of which is that we are all growing more brilliant. Nutrition and health care are substantially improved, with major impact on child health—certainly healthy children learn more. We live in information-rich (saturated) societies—print and electronic media are found even in relatively underprivileged households. And finally, we are probably better at fitting various assessments—be they IQ, aptitude, or achievement—to the information we are teaching in our schools.

Hereditability

This term *hereditability* has been widely misused and misunderstood. Hereditability actually refers to the extent to which differences among people (regardless of the trait under discussion) can be linked to the influence of genes. In order to make this determination, the environment must be held constant—made uniform—for all individuals. Then the measurement—in this case IQ—would be made. The amount of variation between individuals who are exposed to the same environmental influences is assumed to be strictly genetic. A major problem with determining hereditability is that, in the natural world, environments are rarely truly uniform, especially for different human population groups.

If you are reading a research review, and find a study suggesting 50 percent heritability for a particular trait—in this case, intelligence—it *does not* mean that genes are responsible for 50 percent of intelligence, and the environment for the rest. We should not use the term "hereditable" to refer to the amount of influence genes have on any trait. In fact, a straightforward, concrete, and easy-to-measure trait such as height is *polygenic* (based on the input from more than one gene), which complicates matters a great deal (Gould 1981). Intelligence, whether it is one thing or many, is probably determined by a diverse combination of genes. There have been multiple genes identified as possibly exerting influence on intellectual functioning. A strongly genetic trait can also be dramatically influenced by environment (see the example of PKU in Chapter 2). Some behavioral geneticists believe that it may well be impossible to know for sure what the exact contribution of genes to an individual's intelligence is, especially given that the scientific community is still in disagreement about the behaviors that signify the presence of this construct.

Is Intelligence Stable, or Does It Change?

For the most part, the scientific evidence suggests that intelligence is stable from about age 7 onward. It can be altered though by insult, injury, or disease processes affecting the brain. It should be noted that there are practical problems with measuring the stability of IQ in very young children—it is hard to know what the reliable indicators of later intelligence are. Many widely used infant intelligence scales—such as the Bayley Scales—appear to measure physical health and development as well as cognitive skills. (Although this may be part of what contributes to IQ.) At this time, quickly becoming bored by images and pictures is the trait that best correlates with later high IQ scores. Case studies of children with exceptional early abilities (for example, early talking) show that they *do not* necessarily grow up to be "rocket scientists." In fact, here is a dramatic though admittedly anecdotal piece of information: Einstein was reported to have been a somewhat speech-delayed child.

So it appears to be safe to assume that intelligence stabilizes around age 7; there are no dramatic changes in the absence of trauma or disease after this (including the effects of old age—healthy older people do not experience IQ declines). Combined with the brain research, we know now that the best time for early environmental intervention on behalf of a child's cognitive development is as *soon* as possible.

Is Intelligence Context-Consistent or "Culture-Bound"?

Although this intriguing question is raised periodically, the debate still appears to be mostly based on opinion. On one hand, it is likely to be true that what a society or culture defines to be crucial for success is likely to be viewed in that culture as also related to essential aspects of intelligence. On the other hand, it is reasonable to suggest that there are numerous cognitive skills that people from diverse backgrounds would recognize as part of intelligence and that contribute to successful functioning in across all environments, cultures, or contexts.

Measuring Intelligence

To fully grasp the process and problems involved in empirically measuring constructs such as intelligence, it is useful to know the terminology of *test construction*. Here is a brief primer.

What Does It Mean for a Test To Be "Standardized"?

In assessment, standardization is assumed to allow us to better discriminate a typical performance from an unusual one. A test is considered "standardized" when all the scores are compared to an original test sample (a *standardization* sample) that was used to establish *norms*. Norms are the scores of the original test sample, analyzed statistically so that each score is compared to the *mean* (average) according to the average deviation from the mean. In other words, it is not good enough to know only what the mean is, when a group of scores has a mean of 50 that doesn't signify that every person in the sample got a 50. The scores clustered around 50, and most of them fall within a range of one *standard* (average) *deviation* unit below or above that point. So any score within that range (almost 70 percent of scores fall here) will be considered average.

What Is the Normal Curve?

The *normal curve* is a theoretical construct—it is generally assumed any common trait (IQ, height, weight, spatial aptitude, etc.) in a large population is normally distributed. When a score is compared to the standardization sample, it can be placed on the normal curve to inform us of how it compares to the entire population. (See Figure 8.2.)

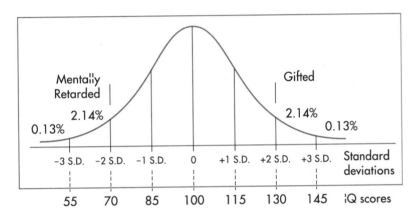

Figure 8.2 The Bell-Shaped Normal Curve.

What About Representativeness?

It is assumed that the sample will be large enough to represent the members of the population who will take the test. The use of norms allows percentiles (a measure of relative position) to be calculated. These percentiles inform us of where a score stands relative to the scores of those persons in the standardization sample. However, if the sample used to standardize the test was not representative, there can be serious implications for interpreting any individual's score.

What Is Reliability and Why Is It Important?

There are other considerations besides the *representativeness* of the standardization sample. The scores produced by the test for any test taker must be consistent or *reliable*. It is relatively simple to detect this problem. The original test (or a different version of it) can be given again to a group of test takers, or a sample test can be divided into two parts and administered to the same group of test takers on different occasions. If the scores fall within a close enough range, the test is considered to be reliable. If a test is not reliable, it is not *valid* (see next question) and therefore essentially useless for assessment purposes.

A test can be reliable but not valid; if it is not reliable it cannot possibly be valid.

What Is Validity?

Validity is the most crucial quality a test offers—the ability truly to assess the presence or level of the construct it claims to test. Simply put, if an IQ or intelligence test is actually testing socioeconomic status (as some critics charge), it is not a valid test. Table 8-3 lists and briefly explains the kinds of validity that are important in psychometrics. You may wish to bookmark this page for easy reference later when we cover personality testing in Chapter 12.

TABLE 8-3
TYPES OF VALIDITY

Type of Validity	Requirement	Example
Face validity	The test should appear to measure what it claims to measure.	A test of religiosity does not have face validity for assessing employee dependability.
Construct validity	Also called operational validity, the test should measure the characteristic or quality that it claims to measure.	A test of memory ability should have questions that actually test recall and retention.
Predictive validity	Performance on a test should correctly predict performance on other outcome measures.	A person who gets a high SAT score should do very well in the first year of college.
Content validity	The test should cover examples of all problems or items in the domain it purports to assess.	An American history achievement test should feature items testing knowledge of history from pre-Columbian to current events.
Criterion validity	A type of predictive validity. The test should predict performance on tasks that fall within the domain that the test purports to measure.	A person who does well on the GRE in mathematics should be able to calculate derivatives and integrals.
Incremental validity	When combined with other measures of the same domain or construct, the test should add information or strengthen predictive and other forms of validity.	A psychological testing battery should increase a clinical psychologist's understanding of a patient's difficulties when combined with interviews and observational reports.
Convergent validity	The tests results should be similar to the results of other tests that measure related constructs or domains.	A high score on a vocabulary test should coincide with high scores on a reading comprehension test and a literature test.

The IQ Testing Controversy

The origins of IQ testing are somewhat checkered. In the nineteenth century (1800s) intelligence testing was relatively unscientific, including such strategies as: measuring the circumference of people's heads, weighing their brains (after death, of course, which posed some problems owing to the effects of disease and decomposition), and comparing the sizes of different brain regions. Whatever the intentions of the researcher, the results almost always were interpreted in ways that suggest that certain groups (women, non-Europeans) had less of the cognitive ability being measured. Much damage was done to scientific credibility through these pseudoscientific strategies of estimating intellectual capacity.

A Brief Historical Overview of IQ Testing

Alfred Binet (1857–1911) developed the first intelligence scale at the request of the French government. At that time, teachers in the public school system were ill-prepared to deal with the wide range of student abilities, especially with students that we would designate in the twenty-first century as in need of special or remedial education. These difficulties would rapidly evolve from academic to classroom behavioral problems (as frustrated teachers interacted with even more frustrated students).

With the assistance of his colleague Theophilus Simon (1873–1961), Binet developed the Binet-Simon test to help the public schools identify students who would require special educational interventions in order to succeed.

Binet believed that he was serving the French public by improving children's chances of achieving school success, even if on a limited basis. He did not believe it was an appropriate use of any test to simply "rank" children according to apparent cognitive ability. After his death, his test was appropriated by a colleague and brought to the United States to form the basis of the Stanford-Binet Intelligence Scale. Further refinements in scoring procedure were made. William Stern, a German psychologist, proposed dividing a child's mental age according to the Binet-Simon test by his or her chronological age. Multiplying the score by 100 (the formula proposed by Lewis Terman; see Table 8-3) led to the familiar IQ score still in use today. Terman and other psychologists working at Stanford University created the *Stanford-Binet Test,* the first individually administered IQ test, with a scoring system based on a sample of 5000 test takers. Robert Yerkes (1876–1956) and other psychometricians working around the same time also developed the first group IQ tests at the request of the U.S. Military, the *Army Alpha* and *Beta tests.*

The next decades saw the gradual development of other types of IQ and achievement tests (see Table 8-4). Unfortunately, it also saw gross misuse of intelligence tests; for example, in the years before World War II, English language intelligence tests were routinely given to non-English speaking immigrants who (surprise, surprise) failed them and were sent back to Europe, in many cases to be slaughtered a few years later. In the past few decades, hard-line hereditarians such as Arthur Jensen and the writers of the controversial book *The Bell Curve* (1994)—Richard Herrstein and Charles Murray—have continued vigorous debate with those who maintain that environmental influences on IQ scores are very strong (Flynn, Gardner and Claude Steele—see the "What's New" section). The controversy, although unpleasant at times, has driven improvements in testing procedure including attempts to control for irrelevant cultural, socioeconomic, and gender-related biases.

To the credit of their profession, most psychometricians have been struggling toward a more accurate understanding of the biases and problems inherent in this testing, and our society for the most part enables an ongoing (if sometimes highly politicized) critical examination of all kinds of tests and assessments. Although the questions and answers often raise a great deal of anxiety, our knowledge base and ability to serve humanity is enhanced by these activities.

How IQ Tests Are Scored

Although there are a number of tests currently in use, the ones that are most widely employed use the following scale for estimating level of cognitive functioning:

IQ Score	Description (Range)
130 and above	Very Superior
120–129	Superior
110–119	High Average
90–109	Average
80–89	Low Average
70–79	Borderline Mental Retardation
55–69	Mild Mental Retardation
40–54	Moderate Mental Retardation
25–39	Severe Mental Retardation
24 and below	Profound Mental Retardation

TABLE 8-4
TABLE OF IQ/COGNITIVE ABILITIES TESTS CURRENTLY IN USE

Test	Description
The Stanford-Binet IQ Test	Requires English language fluency; adaptive method (establishes floors and ceilings for each scale so that test can be used from age 2 to adult); requires individual administration
The Wechsler Scales	English language, available in preschool, school age (6–16—adaptive method), and adult versions, individual administration
Raven's Progressive Matrices	Language and culture-free test of reasoning ability; individual administration
Scholastic Assessment Test	English language; group-administered test that purports to predict performance in the first year of college

Connecting Through Chapter Review

WORD-STUDY CONNECTION
Write each of these words on index cards and write their definitions on the opposite side.

abstraction	hereditability	primary mental abilities
algorithmic	heuristic	prototype
anchoring	insight	psychometric approach
Army Alpha/Beta tests	intelligence	reliable
artificial concepts	IQ	representativeness
attention	linguistic determinism	representativeness bias
availability bias	linguistic relativity	Sapir-Whorf hypothesis
behaviorist	mean	savant syndrome
cognition	memes	standard deviation
cognitive map	mental representations	standardization
cognitive task	mental retardation	Stanford-Binet Test
compensatory	mental set	stereotypes
concepts	multiple intelligences	symbols
confirmation bias	nativist	syntax
construct	natural concepts	test construction
controlled task	normal (bell-shaped) curve	trial and error
crystallized intelligence	norms	triarchic theory of
fluid intelligence	observational learning	intelligence
Flynn effect	overconfidence	utilitarian
functional fixedness	polygenic	valid
g	poverty of stimulus	William's syndrome

SELF-TEST CONNECTION

PART A. Completion
Write in the word that correctly completes each statement.

1. Another term for mental processes is _____ .
2. _____ are mental categories, collections of events, people, objects, or other entities that share some important quality or feature.
3. How to play piano requires _____ memory.
4. _____ concepts are learned from experience.
5. _____ decision making involves the consideration of aspects or features of the different possible solutions or choices.
6. _____ are referred to as rule-of-thumb strategies that can help us make judgments and solve problems efficiently.
7. _____ heuristic (or bias) involves using the information that comes to mind first.

8. Our own overestimating of the accuracy of our beliefs and judgments and exaggerating the number of other people who see things the same way as we do is referred to as _____ .

9. A(n) _____ effect occurs if we are given a "hint" or are supplied with information while making our decision or choice, which may influence our answer and which may make it more or less accurate.

10. _____ is your collection of beliefs, assumptions, and perspectives used to organize your thoughts.

11. The rules for using the symbols of language is _____ ; it is also known as grammar.

12. _____ is a score produced by tests that purport to measure intelligence.

13. _____ created the first intelligence test.

14. Charles Spearman proposed the single-factor model of intelligence referred to as _____ —the general factor important for all intellectual tasks.

15. _____ developed one of the most widely administered intelligence scales in current use. The test comes in a preschool, children's, and adult version.

16. A person who is mentally retarded, but has an extraordinary ability for multiplication, is likely to have _____ .

17. Sternberg's triarchic theory of intelligence includes three types of intelligence, including analytic skills, practical skills, and _____ .

18. Studies of infants raised in orphanages demonstrate the influence of _____ on the development on intelligence.

19. _____ refers to the extent to which differences among people are attributable to genes.

20. Research that suggests that different cultures have different notions of what constitutes intelligence would support the idea that intelligence is culture- _____ .

21. Research that suggests that intelligence in certain domains is important in all cultures would support the notion that intelligence is context- _____ .

22. A test can be reliable but not _____ ; if it is not reliable, it cannot possibly be _____ .

23. A test that appears to measure what it claims to measure has high _____ validity.

24. _____ developed the IQ tests for the U.S. military, known as the Army Alpha and Beta tests.

25. A score in the range of _____ to _____ would be considered low average.

PART B. Multiple Choice

Circle the letter of the item that correctly completes the statement.

1. You will need to pay more attention if you lack _____ a situation.
   (a) familiarity with
   (b) interest in
   (c) novelty in
   (d) none of the above

2. Cognitive maps allow for which of the following types of cognition?
   (a) Creating
   (b) Remembering
   (c) Interpreting
   (d) Problem-solving

3. What types of concepts are learned from experience?
   (a) Mental
   (b) Natural
   (c) Artificial
   (d) Cognitive

4. Which of the following is *not* one of the five categories of decision-making and problem-solving strategies?
   (a) Compensatory   (b) Trial and error
   (c) Heuristic   (d) Prototype

5. What type of bias involves using the features of a prototype to make predictions or decisions about people and events?
   (a) Anchoring bias or effect   (b) Representativeness heuristic
   (c) Confirmation bias   (d) Availability heuristic

6. Which is a special feature of language that makes human language unique?
   (a) Symbols   (b) Abstraction
   (c) Syntax   (d) All of the above

7. Approximately when did language develop in our species?
   (a) 5,000 years ago   (b) 50,000 years ago
   (c) 500,000 years ago   (d) 5 million years ago

8. Who proposed the nativist view of human language development?
   (a) Steven Pinker   (b) Jean Piaget
   (c) Sigmund Freud   (d) Noam Chomsky

9. Which of the following is true about language development?
   (a) Brains appeared to be "wired" for language development.
   (b) Most people have fully developed Broca's and Wernicke's areas at birth, making it easy to learn language.
   (c) Humans have the ability to make all human language sounds through the fifth year of life.
   (d) All of the above are true.

10. The Sapir-Whorf hypothesis combines linguistic relativity (the idea that boundaries between concepts and categories in languages are arbitrary) and _____ .
    (a) linguistic determinism   (b) culture
    (c) language mechanism   (d) cultural mechanism

11. Which view of intelligence is the ability to understand and deal with people, objects, and symbols?
    (a) Behaviorist   (b) Cognitive
    (c) Utilitarian   (d) Cultural relativist

12. Which is an example of crystallized intelligence?
    (a) Reasoning   (b) Problem solving
    (c) Social rules   (d) Applying new knowledge

13. Which of the following is not one of the intelligence types in Gardner's multiple intelligences theory?
    (a) Kinesthetic intelligence   (b) Logical-mathematical intelligence
    (c) General intelligence   (d) Interpersonal intelligence

14. Who of the following did not develop a theory of multiple intelligences?
    (a) Sternberg   (b) Thurstone
    (c) Gardner   (d) Spearman

15. Which of the following have influences on intelligence starting at conception?
    (a) Nutrition   (b) Health
    (c) Stress   (d) All of the above

16. In order to determine heritability, (the) _____ must be held constant for all people.
    (a) genes
    (b) environment
    (c) individual differences
    (d) traits

17. Approximately what percentage of scores fall within one standard deviation of the mean?
    (a) 10 percent
    (b) 30 percent
    (c) 70 percent
    (d) 90 percent

18. What is another word for reliable?
    (a) Consistent
    (b) Independent
    (c) Dependent
    (d) Generalizable

19. A test of mathematical achievement should have questions that actually test all of the following except _____ .
    (a) addition
    (b) engineering
    (c) subtraction
    (d) calculus

20. The test that includes examples of all problems or items in the domain it purports to assess has good _____ validity.
    (a) construct
    (b) content
    (c) predictive
    (d) face

21. Criterion validity is a type of _____ validity.
    (a) construct
    (b) content
    (c) predictive
    (d) face

22. Why did Binet and Simon develop the first IQ tests?
    (a) To provide "evidence" to parents as to why their children were being held back in school
    (b) To help the public schools identify students who would require special educational interventions
    (c) To identity youth who needed accelerated classrooms
    (d) To keep low-achieving youth out of school

23. What is the formula to calculate IQ?
    (a) mental age/100
    (b) mental age × chronological age
    (c) chronological age/100
    (d) mental age/chronological age × 100

24. Who was responsible for updating the Binet-Simon IQ test to the Stanford-Binet IQ Test?
    (a) Terman
    (b) Simon
    (c) Binet
    (d) Freud

25. Which of the following tests is the most culture free?
    (a) Stanford-Binet IQ Test
    (b) The Wechsler Scales
    (c) Scholastic Assessment Test
    (d) Raven's Progressive Matrices

PART C. Modified True-False

If the statement is true, write "T" for the answer. If the statement is incorrect, change the underlined expression to one that will make the statement true.

1. Mental representations are symbols, language, concepts, and images.
2. Remembering what you wore yesterday requires procedural memory.
3. All concepts are universal among cultures.
4. Natural concepts are learned from experience.

5. <u>Insight</u> is a methodical, logical rule or step-by-step procedure that guarantees the solution will be found.
6. The inability to see that a key can be used as a screwdriver is an example of <u>functional fixedness.</u>
7. The argument that children learn language at a rate that exceeds the small amount of exposure and teaching they receive in everyday life is called the <u>poverty of stimulus</u> argument.
8. <u>Jean Piaget</u> proposed that culture is transmitted through language; therefore, in learning the language of our people, we also learn how to think as a member of our society.
9. <u>Linguistic determinism</u> is the idea that that boundaries between concepts and categories in languages are arbitrary.
10. The <u>behaviorist</u> view assumes that mental abilities allow one to learn from experience and function successfully in one's environment.
11. <u>Howard Gardner</u> was an early proponent of the idea that heredity is primary in determining intelligence and performed the first twin studies.
12. Robert Sternberg proposed the <u>triarchic</u> theory of intelligence.
13. Thurstone's concept of g was based on seven intellectual skill groups.
14. <u>Raymond Cattell</u>, in his multiple intelligences theory, suggested that there are seven separate types of intelligence.
15. Studies of twins have demonstrated the possible, strong influence of <u>genetics (nature)</u>.
16. The <u>increaser effect</u> reflects the fact that (on a global basis) average IQ has been rising for roughly the past fifty years.
17. Most scientific evidence suggests that intelligence is stable from about age <u>18</u> onward.
18. Any score that falls within <u>three</u> standard deviation(s) of the mean is considered to be average.
19. A <u>representative</u> sample will be large enough to portray the members of the population that will take the test.
20. A test that indicates how well someone does in his or her first year of graduate school is said to have high <u>construct</u> validity.
21. Combining a test with other measures of the same domain or construct should demonstrate the <u>incremental</u> validity of the test.
22. Test results that are similar to the results of other tests that measure related constructs or domains will have high <u>predictive</u> validity.
23. The controversial book *The Bell Curve* (1994) by Richard Herrstein and Charles Murray take a strong <u>nature</u> stance on intelligence.
24. An IQ score of 115 would typically be considered <u>average</u>.
25. The purpose of the Scholastic Assessment Test (SAT) is to predict <u>high school</u> performance.

PART D. Matching

Place the name of the concept related to thinking next to correct example of that concept.

Thinking

confirmation bias insight   atypical example
algorithm   prototype   representativeness bias
cognitive map   heuristic   availability bias
functional fixedness

1. Someone says "insect," and you think of a fly. _____
2. The way from your house to your best friend's house "in your head." _____
3. Someone says "insect," and you think of a walking stick. _____
4. Your new TV game system came with step-by-step instructions for how to install and operate it. _____
5. Your method for answering multiple-choice questions when you are not sure of the right answer is probably this kind of strategy. _____
6. After thinking about a tough problem for days and days, and doing some research, a good solution "suddenly" occurs to you. _____
7. Your friend thinks that all engineering students are boring and don't like to socialize. _____
8. You thought that the number one cause of death for 30-year-olds was homicide, but it is actually accidents. _____
9. Your friend believes in astrological forecasts because he only remembers the days when they seem to come true. _____
10. You could have used your key to cut the tape on a tightly wrapped package if you'd only thought of it. _____

Language

euphemism   symbols   phonemes
poverty of stimulus suggestibility syntax
abstraction   nativism   memes
linguistic determinism

1. Words, numbers, pictographs, hieroglyphics, sounds, and manual signs are all examples of these. _____
2. You can talk about truth and justice using words, although you can't see them. _____
3. The rules for forming statements in any language are called _____
4. Tra-, sho-, and ma- are all examples of these. _____
5. Language might be the way to transmit these hypothetical units of culture. _____
6. The theory that language is an inborn ability of the human species. _____
7. Children learn an enormous amount of language with very little training. _____
8. A sin of memory that may be triggered by use of language. _____
9. You refer to your friend who helped to start a riot against the World Trade Organization as an "activist." _____
10. Maybe our native language helps to shape the way we think about the world. _____

Scientists in the History of Intelligence Theory and Testing

Sternberg   Spearman   Kamin
Anastasi   Binet   Guilford
Thurstone   Jensen   Gardner
Cattell

1. He was one of the two persons who created the first IQ test. _____
2. He was the person who proposed the existence of the g factor. _____
3. She cataloged a vast number of IQ and other psychological tests. _____
4. He developed the "structure of intellect" model. _____
5. He proposed the existence of two types of g—crystallized and fluid. _____
6. He proposed the existence of eight primary mental abilities. _____
7. He proposed the theory of multiple intelligences. _____
8. He created the triarchic theory of intelligence. _____
9. He was a major critic of the hereditarian (strongly genetic) view of intelligence.

_____
10. He wrote the controversial book *Bias in Mental Testing*. _____

Intelligence Theory and Testing

creative   valid   representative
standard deviation   norms   psychometric
crystallized   g   linguistic
hereditability

1. This is the theory that intelligence can be measured. _____
2. This is the term for a unitary general intelligence factor. _____
3. This is the term for the kind of g that represents acquired knowledge and facts.

_____
4. A person who is good at writing and expression through words would have this kind
   of intelligence according to Gardner. _____
5. This kind of intelligence, according to Sternberg, would be prominent in a person
   who is good with novel environments and problems. _____
6. This is the extent to which differences among individuals related to a specific trait
   are the result of genetic influence only. _____
7. If a test truly tests the construct or quality it was designed to measure, it is said to be

_____
8. These are the scores that are achieved by the original sample that takes a test.

_____
9. If the original sample that took a test does not really resemble the population to
   whom the test will be administered, it is not a _____ sample.
10. This is another term for the typical or "average" difference between a score on test
    and the mean score. _____

CONNECTING TO CONCEPTS

Review the chapter, and then write down your thoughts about the following questions.

1. Define cognitive map, prototype, and algorithm. Describe a real-life example of each of these (one that you use in your everyday life). How does this cognitive tool help you to problem-solve or accomplish your goals?
2. Compare and contrast natural concept and artificial concept using definitions and examples of each.
3. Define heuristic, and give an example of a problem that you face in everyday life that lends itself to the use of heuristics. Which type(s) of heuristics have you used, or might you use?
4. Discuss the evidence for the nativist view of language presented in the book. Describe any evidence for this perspective that you have encountered in your life. How accurate do you think the nativist view of language acquisition is?
5. Outline the debate between the nature and nurture views of intelligence. Do you think that nature predominates, nurture predominates, or both combine in influencing intelligence? Support your position.

CONNECTING TO LIFE/JOB SKILLS

Using Heuristics to Become a Better Test Taker

Test taking is a skill that requires use of many of the tools of thought described in this chapter. You have probably already taken many midterm, final, and standardized tests, and you will probably take many more. Test-taking skills can be improved with practice and with knowledge of helpful heuristics. For example, in a test given by your teacher in the classroom, you might want to look for grammatical "giveaways" such as the word "an" in the question stem and an answer choice that starts with a vowel. Even if only two of the four options start with consonants, you have just increased your chances of picking the right answer substantially.

Standardized tests are screened carefully for errors, but you can still apply heuristics. Before relying on such heuristics though, you should make a commitment to practice as much as you can—take advantage of College Board publication of recent tests or take a test preparation course. The exposure to the material will give you a sense of familiarity with how questions are asked and what right and wrong answers sound like. Guessing may or may not be in your best interest, depending on what kind of guessing penalty is applied. If you can eliminate at least one answer based on knowledge or wording, it is usually in your best interest to take a guess. For more information on heuristics and test preparation strategies, check out these web sites:

TIPS FOR BETTER TEST TAKING: UNIVERSITY OF ST. THOMAS

www.iss.stthomas.edu/studyguides/tsttak1.htm

COLLECTIONS OF TEST PREPARATION LINKS

www.eop.mu.edu/study/index.html
osi.fsu.edu/hot/testtaking/skills.htm

IMPROVING YOUR TEST-TAKING SKILLS

ericae.net/pare/getvn.asp?v=1&n=2

WHAT'S HAPPENING!

The Stereotype Threat

In seeking to address the gaps in performance on standardized tests such as the SATs, a group of social psychologists at Stanford University, led by Claude Steele, PhD, have carried out a series of clever experiments to test the influence of internalized stereotypes on test performance. They have gathered substantial evidence that minorities, women, and even white males may be hampered, depending on context, by their perceptions of their own limitations in performance.

A typical "stereotype threat" experiment would use white male and female students of equal ability (based on previous testing) who would take a math test. There would be two conditions—students are either told that the test is an unimportant research tool that gives no meaningful information about their math ability or that the test is an accurate measure of their math ability. In most cases, the group who has a well-known stereotype about their academic abilities (in this case, "girls are not as good at math as boys are") will perform substantially worse in the latter condition.

Steele and his associates have done many versions of this study pairing black and white students, male and female, white and Asian, even student athletes against nonathletes, and found evidence that stereotypes may become self-fulfilling prophecies in the standardized testing arena. This is a powerful way in which the psychological environment may need to be addressed in order to reduce the potential for bias in these tests.

For more information on stereotype threat research, visit the following web sites:

SOCIAL PSYCHOLOGY NETWORK

steele.socialpsychology.org/

CLAUDE STEELE'S HOMEPAGE

www.stanford.edu/~jbonham/steele/

INTERVIEW WITH CLAUDE STEELE

www.princeton.edu/~vigil/may97/steele.html

OTHER USEFUL WEB SITES

CREATIVITY WEB

www.ozemail.com.au/~caveman/Creative/

This commercial site is a "mental gymnasium" dedicated to the improvement of problems solving and creative thought.

LANGUAGE AND COGNITION LINKS

www.tamiu.edu/coah/psy/langcog.htm

This collection of links relates to topics in this chapter. The site is sponsored by Texas A&M University.

SOCIETY FOR JUDGMENT AND DECISION MAKING HOMEPAGE

www.sjdm.org/

This is the homepage of the Society for Judgment and Decision Making, an interdisciplinary organization devoted to research and improvement of thought processes related to judgment and decision making.

THE ARC HOME PAGE

TheArc.org/

This is the homepage of the Association for Retarded Citizens of the United States, a group of advocates for individuals of all ages who are mentally retarded. They provide education and support.

THE BELL CURVE

www.indiana.edu/~intell/bellcurve.html

This Indiana University web site provides an overview the controversial 1994 book by Murray and Herrstein.

HISTORY OF INTELLIGENCE TESTING

www.indiana.edu/~intell/index.html

Also sponsored by Indiana University, this web site provides comprehensive information about the history of and theory behind IQ testing and psychometrics.

REFERENCES

Chomsky, N. (1965) *Cartesian Linguistics*. New York: Harper and Row.

Gould, S. J. (1981) *The Mismeasure of Man*. New York: W.W. Norton & Co.

Holloway, M. (1999) Flynn's effect. *Scientific American*. January 1999 (accessed online).

Lakoff, G. (1990) *Women, Fire and Dangerous Things*. Chicago: University of Chicago Press.

Loftus E. F., & Palmer, J. C. (1974). Reconstruction of automobile destruction: An example of the interaction between language and memory. *Journal of Learning and Verbal Behavior*. 13, 585–589.

Pinker, S. (2000) *The Language Instinct: How the Mind Creates Language*. Boston: Perennial.

Chapter 9

HUMAN LIFESPAN DEVELOPMENT

In this chapter you will review the major theoretical perspectives and recent scientific findings regarding psychological growth and development—how people grow and change—across the lifespan.

Basic Concepts and Trends in Human Development

Developmental psychology is the branch of psychology that describes and explains change across the lifespan. The two major areas of developmental psychology are *cognitive* (thought and reasoning) and *psychosocial* (personality and behavior in the social context). Until quite recently, the focus of most developmental psychology was the rapid and dramatic changes of infancy, childhood, and adolescence. More recently, developmental theorists have been trying to better understand the changes that occur during adulthood and aging as well.

Central Concepts of Developmental Psychology

- *Critical periods.* Periods of time during which a developing person is maximally sensitive to environmental influences upon development. The first critical periods occur during the *prenatal* period, within days of conception. Environmental contributions during the critical period, whether helpful or harmful, can have a substantial (often permanent) impact on the developing organism. These events can speed up or improve the rate of development and the attainment of developmental milestones, or they can delay or prevent their occurrence entirely. (A milestone is the achievement of a skill or physical characteristic expected within certain timeframes as a part of normal development. A child's first word and puberty are examples of developmental milestones.) It is possible that there are critical periods from conception right up to full biological maturity (and beyond).
- *Sensitive or optimal periods.* An alternative to the critical period view is the sensitive or optimal period view, which states that although there is a best time for certain events and milestones to be reached, gains can be made in other timeframes also. So, although

it is best (or optimal) for the environment to make its contribution during what would be referred to as a critical period, all is not lost if this does not occur. It appears that infants and young children are more resilient than the critical period view would suggest and that later interventions can undo some of the damage of early neglect and abuse. For example, multiple studies of children removed from orphanages suggest that some neglected children who receive educational, nutritional, and psychosocial intervention (adopted and placed in enriched environments) make substantial gains and catch up with their normally developing peers in many ways, if not completely. The early life plasticity of the human brain works in favor of such outcomes (see Chapter 3).

The theme of unfolding changes in development is evident in the major theories that we will look at in this chapter. Whether this is a true description of the process, or an artificial attempt to impose a scheme onto a natural process that has variations and idiosyncrasies, we still can't be sure.

Major Trends of Physical Development

- *Cephalocaudal*. This term literally translates "head to tail." When we observe the human organism developing from conception to middle childhood, growth seems to progress from the head. The head is noticeably larger than other parts of the body from just a few weeks after conception. If you look at pictures of prenatal development—once the embryo has established a relatively human-looking form (5–8 weeks)—the head takes up more than half of the body mass. At birth, a baby's head is roughly one-quarter of his or her body mass. Usually somewhere between 5 and 7 years of age, the human body attains the proportional appearance characteristic of adulthood. Cephalocaudal also refers to the neurological and skeletal and muscular development of the organism. Control of the head must come before control of the rest of the body. An infant must be able to turn and lift his or her head in order to eventually sit, crawl, and walk.
- *Proximodistal*. This is a fancy way to say that development proceeds in a "near to far" pattern. The "near" is the midline of the organism, where the main conduit to and from the brain—the spinal cord—is located. Before the appearance of the distinct head, the embryo looks like a tube—and that tube is the beginning of the central nervous system—the brain and spinal cord. From these structures at midline of our bodies, growth of the limbs proceeds. The torso, limbs, hands/feet, and fingers/toes follow over the course of the first months of prenatal development. And as is the case with the cephalocaudal trend, control of the extremities—the "distal" parts such as the hands and fingers, happens *after* control of parts of the body that are closer to the midline. An 8-month-old infant can barely make a pincer grasp with the thumb and fingers, but by age 6 he or she is writing with crayons and tying shoes like a pro.
- *Differentiation*. As anyone who has witnessed the arrival of a new baby into a family knows, babies don't have a large repertoire of behaviors at first. All they do is cry, eat, sleep, and produce large numbers of soiled diapers. That same child, by age 5 is doing hundreds of complex tasks including drawing, imagining, singing, dancing, throwing . . . the list is enormous. The human child is born more helpless than any other organism on the planet, possibly owing to the relative immaturity of the brain at birth. A fawn or colt can walk and run within minutes of birth. But unlike the human child, its list of skills will not grow very much. This is the payoff for our very long period of childhood dependence.

As you can see, physical growth in infants and toddlers is closely linked to motor and cognitive development, so perhaps it is not useful to view them as separate parts of the overall picture. Physical growth during the first year is intellectual growth, and physical limitations (such as hearing impairment) may have a negative impact on cognitive development if they go undetected. Fortunately, early sensory and other types of health screening (routinely offered as part of well-baby care) can permit early interventions that minimize the impact of such impairments. Besides the effects of congenital (problems present at birth) we can also see the dramatic effects of environment on the growing child. For example, a child who receives poor nutrition will have his or her physical growth detrimentally affected, with a possible delay or loss of motor and cognitive skills as well.

Some Environmental Factors That May Influence Development

- *Socioeconomic status (SES).* More financial resources seems to equal better nutrition and better health care, which equals faster and better growth. Poverty leads to lack of nutrition and health care that can negatively affect development (see next item).
- *Untreated illnesses.* Our relatively advanced medical technology means that the effects of all but a few major childhood illnesses can actually be overcome. This is miraculous given that just four generations ago one-third of all children did not survive past age 10. Timing is everything though and if an illness, such as an ear infection, is not detected quickly, permanent damage can be done to the nervous system and other vital parts.
- *Ethnicity and culture.* There are variations in childrearing practices from culture to culture that sometimes influence the progress of development. For example, Native American children who are carried in a cradleboard may walk later than peers from other cultural backgrounds, but they always "catch up." As is the case with untreated illnesses, this factor may be somewhat influenced by or interact with socioeconomic status. Poor parents have fewer options when it comes to discipline (when there is no allowance to cut off, harsh punishments are more likely to be employed).
- *Emotional disturbance.* This may refer to a condition of the caregiver, the child, or both. If the parent/primary caregiver is depressed or overwhelmed by stress, or the child is afflicted with a serious mental illness that interferes with bonding (such as autism), growth and development may be compromised. Stress and emotional deprivation may cause developmental problems such as failure-to-thrive syndrome and delayed achievement of milestones.

A Quick Overview of Prenatal Development

First Trimester
This is the period of most dramatic growth and also of vulnerability to external environmental influences (through the influence of *teratogens,* substances that can cause birth defects—see chart Table 9-1). Most major organ systems are fully functional at the end of this trimester, even though the fetus is still very small: three to four inches crown-rump length.

- The period immediately following conception is called the *germinal period*. While traveling down the fallopian tube, the zygote goes through a number of cell divisions but there is no differentiation of cell types and no real increase in size yet. Implantation into the enriched lining of the uterus happens at the end of the first week of pregnancy.
- The *embryonic period* is the next seven weeks during which an incredible differentiation of cell types and the "floor plan" for organ systems is laid down. The fetal environment is formed along with the amniotic sac, which contains the embryo and the placenta, which provides the nourishment and oxygen for the developing baby. The *neural tube* (from which the spinal cord and brain emerge) forms and the central nervous system develops rapidly. The areas of the body become increasingly distinct with trunk, limbs, and sensory organs becoming more and more easily recognizable.
- At 8–12 weeks, we refer to the developing individual as having entered the *fetal period*. The sex organs are formed at this time, and the baby is shown to be male or female depending on whether or not the presence of a Y-chromosome causes a sudden infusion of androgens into the fetal environment. The sex organs develop out of the same structures, and whether you are a male or female is a result of this process. Reflexes and minor movements of limbs become detectable; it is during this period that a parent first hears the fetal heartbeat.

TABLE 9-1
KNOWN CLASSES OF TERATOGENS*

Type	Examples	Possible Effects
CNS depressants	Alcohol, tranquilizers, barbiturates, opiate drugs	Fetal Alcohol Syndrome (#1 and most preventable cause of mental retardation), addiction of fetus to drugs, deformities to face and body.
CNS stimulants	Nicotine, amphetamines, cocaine	Low birth weight, hyperactivity, increased susceptibility to SIDS.
Sexually transmitted diseases	HIV, herpes, syphilis, gonorrhea	Baby born infected, skin and eye problems, central nervous system damage, increased risk of miscarriage.
Other infectious diseases	German measles (rubella), influenza, chicken pox, toxoplasmosis, tuberculosis	Mental retardation, damage to sensory systems, physical deformities, schizophrenia, low birth weight, increased risk of miscarriage.
Environmental toxins/pollutants	Mercury, lead, PCBs, radiation	Mental retardation

*Based on Drinnen & Hall (2001)

Second Trimester

The increase in size of the developing baby is dramatic during this period, increasing to close to twelve to fourteen inches in length and two pounds in weight.

- Brain cells complete their development at this time. Most of the neurons form and migrate to their final destination in the nervous system by month 5 in pregnancy. Formation of nerve connections—synapses—will continue at a high rate to age 6, and even beyond to a lesser extent. A diet with adequate nutrients including fat is also important for young children to promote the formation of glia—those vital maintenance cells in the nervous system that you learned about in Chapter 3.

- Bones will finish hardening during this trimester. The skeletal and muscular systems are fully formed. Mothers can detect the first movements of the baby at about five months.
- Improvements in technology have allowed us to save babies born as early as 24–25 weeks; by 30 weeks survival is almost certain. Prematurity *does* increase the risk of physical and developmental problems later on in life, so despite the technology it is vital to try to provide care and education to at-risk mothers in order to minimize the chance of a premature birth.

Third Trimester

During the last three months, the baby grows to between twenty and twenty-two inches long on average and puts on a lot of vital weight—the average healthy baby is delivered at 6½ to 8½ pounds. It appears that "fattening up" is a primary function of this last trimester. The ninth month is often referred to as the finishing period. The addition of a reasonable amount of fat is a good thing since the fat is important for nerve development, overall growth, and survival. The continued maturing of the fetal nervous system during the third trimester means that self-regulation of vital functions such as breathing, digestion, and temperature will be more easily accomplished after birth—lowering the risk of SIDS (sudden infant death syndrome, which may be related to failure of the brainstem to stabilize and regulate breathing patterns).

General Patterns of Physical Development After Birth

- *Fontanels and sutures.* The infant's head is about one-quarter of its total body size, making birth difficult for mother and baby. Fontanels (spaces) and sutures (seams) make up what are called soft spots on the skull, which, among other things, allow the infant's head to tolerate a certain amount of compression during delivery. Although the fontanels close by 18 to 20 months, the sutures are actually present until adolescence, when physical growth is complete.
- *Appearance of face and eyes.* Facial communication is as vital as verbal communication for humans. From birth, the eyes are the predominant feature of an infant's face. This is probably an evolutionary adaptation which may make a baby look endearing and induce adults to care for him or her. The small size of the infant's nose helps to facilitate breast-feeding by keeping the infant's air supply from being cut off.
- *Functioning of eyes and ears.* Obviously, these are very intimately related to brain development. Problems with sensory functioning can have a detrimental effect on cognitive development unless detected soon after birth. Early screening is essential!
- *Brain growth.* The most dramatic brain growth occurs during the first year of life. Infants sleep a great deal, and they spend more time in REM than at any other time except in utero. Although there is still debate about the relationship between sleep and learning, we suspect that prenatal REM is probably related to central nervous system growth and maturation. Post-natal REM sleep appears to be related to continued CNS maturation and to left hemisphere (language) learning, not only during infancy and

childhood, but also throughout the life cycle. Healthy infants are born with a set of normal *reflexes* (such as the *stepping reflex* and the *tonic neck reflex* in which the infant's head turns in the direction of an extended arm or leg). As the brain matures and the cortical tissue becomes more active, the reflexes are replaced with a variety of voluntary behaviors. If the reflexes are not replaced, it is considered a sign of possible developmental delays. The following brain growth processes are rapid in infancy and childhood:
- Myelination (the laying down of additional myelin sheathing to speed nerve impulses)
- *Synaptogenesis* (the formation of additional synapses, which improves cognitive and motor functioning)
- *Pruning* (the trimming of synapses that are not being used)
- *Lateralization* (the increased specialization in functioning of each cerebral hemisphere)

Because of the intimate connection of motor and cognitive development, Table 9-2 is provided for your reference:

TABLE 9-2
MOTOR MILESTONES DURING THE FIRST TWO YEARS OF LIFE*
Of all infants and toddlers, 90 percent achieve the skill within these limits.

Skill	Age Range
Rolls over	6 weeks to 5 months
Grasps toy	2 to 5 months
Sits alone	4½ to 8½ months
Stands while supporting self	4½ to 10½ months
Standing alone	9½ to 14½ months
Walks	10½ to 15 months
Stacks two cubes	11½ to 21½ months
Climbs stairs by walking	13½ to 23½ months

Cognitive Development

Cognitive development describes the changes in how people think as they grow older. It includes physical development in the first few years of life. Especially in the first three years of life, cognitive development is heavily dependent on physical development.

Language is intimately related to thinking.

How Children Learn

The plan for all development unfolds as each individual matures, but the cognitive achievements of the child are the result of a complex interaction of the biological and genetic blueprint with a dynamic environment. Some milestones are achieved seemingly without effort and intention, and others are the result of deliberate interventions from the environment. It is useful to make the following distinctions:

- *Maturation* is what happens automatically, the simple natural appearance of features and skills at the expected times. The amount of REM sleep that an infant needs is likely a function of maturation and declines steadily throughout the first year of life. An infant's ability to grab an object takes many weeks to appear (between three and six months) and depends heavily on the maturation of the brain, the muscles, and nerves in the spinal cord and arm.
- *Learning* refers to permanent changes in behavior that are the result of experience and may or may not occur "intentionally" (see Chapter 6). It requires a certain level of readiness (dictated in part by the level of maturation). According to some psychologists, language is acquired so effortlessly that learning to speak and understand a language must be primarily a function of maturation. But environmental input must be present; the young child must be surrounded by other individuals who use the language and speak to him or her.
- *Training* involves deliberate change—skills that require teaching and repetition to acquire. Although speech and comprehension of language occur with little training, learning to read a language seems to be mainly the result of training.

The first integrated theory of the development of thinking and reasoning was proposed by Swiss psychologist Jean Piaget (1896–1980). We will now look at his theory as well as some of the recent innovative research on childhood cognitive development.

Piaget was a Swiss psychologist who, while administering intelligence tests to children, became intrigued by the kind of mistakes children made on test questions. He became convinced that children did not necessarily know less than adults do but rather that they think about the world differently. He saw these differences as the result of a complex interaction of the child's biological maturity and the learning and training provided by the environment.

The Basics of Piagetian Development

People of all ages strive to make sense of the world and their experiences. Piaget saw children as active thinkers from almost the moment of birth. He believed that children work to develop *schemas*. Schemas (as you may recall from Chapter 8) are mental frameworks that help us to organize our information and experiences. Children create schemas based on their level of cognitive maturity and the information that they encounter in everyday life. They also periodically revise those schemas based on new information and their own increasing ability to comprehend it. Two processes are involved in the creation and evolution of schemas:

- Individuals assimilate the information—in other words, they change the information to fit what they already know. For example, a 2-year-old child has a pet dog. She sees that the dog is an animal with four legs. For quite some time she may refer to all four-legged animals as "doggies." This is *assimilation*. We change the information to fit our established schemas.
- Eventually, the forces of biological maturation and an increasing amount of new information force us to accommodate—to change a schema to fit with the information. A child learns that there are dozens of types of four-legged animals and they are not all "doggies." She begins to learn the special name of each.

The Four Stages of Piaget's Theory of Cognitive Development

1. Sensorimotor Stage (0–2)

From the moment of birth, a baby must start to understand and integrate sensory input and gain control of motor abilities. A baby probably doesn't even understand that the limbs attached to his body are his. As the baby gains motor ability, everything is handled, touched, and mouthed. The baby practices reaching, grabbing, and sitting—working his way up to the first steps. Motor development takes up a lot of a baby's intellectual energy during the first two years. Piaget assumed that infants during this time think and solve problems in a nonverbal fashion. He developed a step-by-step description of the evolution of an infant's thinking during the sensorimotor period. Over the first two years of life, infants go from reflexes, to cause-and-effect schemas to complex problem solving basically in a nonverbal manner. (See Table 9-3.)

According to Piaget, one of the central cognitive tasks of this stage is the development of a sense of *object permanence*. Before the age of six to eight months, babies appear to lack the idea that a hidden object or person who is out of sight is still present. A toy is hidden and within a second or two, the baby can no longer locate it.

Remember that this is Piaget's inference or interpretation, not a fact. For example, it is unclear that the reason that the baby can no longer locate the object is that he or she "forgets that it exists" or a more simple explanation such as inadequate attention span (which fits with the underdevelopment of the frontal cortex in infants). Whatever it is, the development of object permanence is one of the most cross-culturally uniform events in human cognitive development, emerging between 8 and 10 months in all infants.

TABLE 9-2
SIX STEPS OF SENSORIMOTOR DEVELOPMENT

Step	Age	Description	Behavior
Reflex	0–2 weeks	Simple stimulus-response patterns; reflexes	Baby quiets down to sound of parent's voice.
Primary circular reactions or habits	2 weeks to 4 months	Reflexes used deliberately to explore the world	Baby turns head to look at parent when parent speaks.
Secondary circular reactions or coordinated schemes	4 months to 8 months	Familiar actions lead to new behavior patterns	Baby reaches out to parent when he or she enters the room.
Schemes coordinated ("means") for achievement of ends	8 months to 12 months	Deliberate action leads to new behavior, learning, and goals	Baby points to toy bear that is out of reach when parent enters the room.
Inventing new means	11 months to 18 months	Actions modified or invented to achieve goals	Baby crawls to table to retrieve the toy bear.
Manipulation of mental representations and insight	18 months to 2 years	Actions planned mentally and carried out to achieve goals	Baby puts toy bear into toy car and pushes car along the floor toward parents.

Criticisms of Piaget and New Trends in Infant Cognitive Development. Was Piaget underestimating the intelligence or capabilities of infants? Although Piaget described infants as thinking nonverbally, an infant's receptive vocabulary starts expanding rapidly late in the first year of life. Also, even infants younger than 6 months may actually understand more about the hidden world than Piaget thought. For example, work is being done using the "looking time" (measuring the amount of time that an infant stares at an event as a way to measure surprise) procedure, which suggests that infants may have some limited understanding of gravity and physical laws, and may also have some object permanence as early as four months of age (Baillargeon & DeVos 1991). Infants stare for a long time at unsupported objects that fail to fall or that disappear and reappear seemingly "before their eyes." Other psychologists believe that the staring is simply a result of surprise at a novel event (a perceptual reaction) not evidence of a sophisticated reasoning process (a cognitive event) as Baillargeon proposes (Cashon & Cohen 2000.)

3. Preoperational Stage (2–7)

Preoperational refers to what Piaget described as the child's lack of logical thought processes or "operations." A child in this stage is learning to think symbolically (witness the explosion of language ability at this time) but does not possess the ability to manipulate symbols in order to reason logically. A child in the preoperational stage, for example, is unable to *conserve* mass—to understand that if you put the same amount of a liquid into two different shaped containers, it's the same amount even if the shape is different. Many other versions of the basic conservation task can be used to demonstrate how children in this age group fail to grasp the constant nature of amounts of liquids and solids when the shape of the substance changes.

TABLE 9-4
PROBLEMS OF PREOPERATIONAL THOUGHT

Problem	Description/Example
Egocentrism	Inability to understand other people's perspectives (saying "Look Mommy!" while talking to mother on the telephone)
Centration	Focusing on one, primary physical feature in making assessments (judging the amount of liquid in the beaker by height without taking width of the beaker into account)
Irreversibility	Inability to reason backwards to the starting point (would not understand that subtraction is the reverse of addition)
Classification difficulties	Inability to categorize objects by more than one characteristic (if asked to point out a square blue object, will point to a square object, will point to a blue object, will probably not pick the object with both characteristics)
Seriation difficulties	Inability to put objects in order by size, height, etc. (would have difficulty creating a staircase pattern using blocks of increasing length)
Lack of causal reasoning	Doesn't fully understand cause-and-effect connections, fails to grasp cause and effect (touches a hot iron even though he or she is told not to do so)
Transductive reasoning	Incorrectly connects cause and effect (and so is prone to magical thinking)

Children in this stage also tend to be *egocentric* in thought. They are not self-centered but rather reason as if everyone shares his or her perspective on or view of a situation and are unable to perceive how others might have a different view. They behave as if everyone has the same thoughts, information, and viewpoint. Ask a 4-year-old girl who has a 7-year-old sister whether she has a sister, and she will say "yes." Then ask her if her sister has a sister, and she will most likely be puzzled, unable to see that *she* is her sister's sister.

Theory of Mind. The problem of egocentrism ends when the preoperational period concludes. It is believed that by about age 5 a child overcomes this reasoning problem as he or she develops a sense that others think and see and often do so differently. Since the mind is the intangible product of the brain, we *assume* that others have minds based on their behavior—thus, *theory of mind* (Astington 1994). A 3-year-old is told the following story:

> After making a special birthday cake and telling Johnnie not to touch it while it cools, Mom goes down to the basement to do the laundry. While she is away, Johnnie decides to take a big piece of the cake. He take a big handful and eats it, but before he leaves the kitchen he takes another hunk of cake, and feeds a little of it to the dog as messily as he can, so the dog will have cake all over his face and there is cake on the floor. When Mom comes back up from doing laundry, she sees the half eaten cake and the messy dog. Who will Mom think ate the cake?

He or she will almost always answer that Mom will think that Johnnie ate the cake even while appearing to understand the story. Most 5-year-olds will give the answer "the dog" because they have a theory of mind and know that if Mom did not see Johnnie eat the cake, and the evidence appears to indict the dog, that is what she will believe (at least for awhile).

Theory of mind is an enormous step into the adult cognitive and social world. Without a theory of mind, we could not surprise others, deceive others, or evaluate our own thinking, as well as that of others.

3. Concrete Operations (7–12)

During the *concrete operations* stage, which is the beginning of the age of formal schooling, children can now grasp logical reasoning operations. They can perform simple mathematical operations, conserve, and begin to be able to perform some basic trial-and-error problem-solving strategies. However, they tend to be less able to handle abstract concepts. While preoperational children are comfortable with mental operations that involve fantasy, and formal operations teens are able to imagine possibilities, concrete operational children may be resistant to working with ideas that don't have some basis in the tangible and real. At a magic show, for example, 9-year-old children will likely enjoy explaining the mechanics of the magic tricks almost as much as watching them being performed.

Concrete operational children were thought by Piaget to not be able to do any type of hypothetical problem solving. If the hypothetical scenarios involve real-life situations though, even 7-year-olds may be quite competent.

4. Formal Operations (12–Up)

As children approach the early teen years, they begin to be able to engage in abstract thinking (defining justice, truth, and other terms), to work with *hypothetical* questions (What if?), and to explore ethical dilemmas. Young adolescents are able to imagine future possibilities and can better mentally handle abstract concepts and moral and ethical dilemmas. Most teens are better prepared than school-aged children to discuss scientific theories, speculate about metaphysical concepts, and interpret works of literature and historical events in terms of their larger significance. There are some interesting regressions in the *formal operations* period, though. Developmental psychologist David Elkind has described these regressions.

- The *imaginary audience,* a kind of superficial egocentrism, is prevalent. At this time, teens feel as if others are keenly interested in their appearance, performance, and behavior.
- The *personal fable* ("It won't happen to me.") may explain in part why some teens are so willing to engage in risky behaviors such as reckless driving, drinking, and unprotected sex.

Language Development

Language development begins shortly after birth, explodes in the preoperational stage (2–7 years of age), and continues in some form throughout the lifespan. Language development occurs both *receptively* (the process of comprehension language) and *productively* (making language).

Receptive Language Milestones

1. At around *14 days,* infants should recognize the difference between human voices and other sounds.
2. At *8 weeks,* infants become sensitive to emotional cues in voices and can differentiate between familiar and unfamiliar voices, and male and female voices. (Remember that language is more than words—inflection and tone help us better understand what people actually mean).
3. By *4 months,* most infants recognize their names.
4. At *6 months,* they respond to intonation and vocal rhythm (singing versus spoken language.)
5. By *1 year,* a child can distinguish between the sounds of individual consonant-vowel pairs, or *phonemes*, of their primary language and also can distinguish between pairs of words that differ only slightly, like the consonant difference between the words "cat" and "bat."
6. By *1 year,* a child can also follow simple commands such as "show me the dolly."

We also need to take note of the development of *nonverbal communication*. As early as 3 months, infants will extend their arms to indicate that they'd like to be picked up or held. Pointing to indicate a desired object usually appears during the second six months of life. The use of eye contact also appears at this time and is important for example in the process of *social referencing*, using the caregiver to determine what the nature of the situation might be. If the caregiver smiles, a nervous infant will relax in the presence of strangers.

Productive Language Milestones

1. At *8 weeks* a baby starts *cooing* (making elongated vowel sounds "oooooo" and "aaaaaaaa.")
2. Between *6 and 10 months* the first instances of *babbling* will occur. Babble is made of strings of one syllable utterances beginning with a distinct consonant sound, like "bababa." At first, babies babble the sounds of all human languages and then gradually restrict themselves to the sounds of their native language. Babbling is presumed to be practice in making speech sounds with no symbolic meaning at all.
3. *Jargon*—babbling that sounds like speech—also known as "conversational babbling" is present by around *10 months*. Sometimes the sounds accompany gestures that may indicate a request for an object.
4. The first distinct words may appear anywhere from *10 to 18 months*. The first word is typically the two-phoneme combination "mama," "dada," or perhaps "baba" for a bottle or "nana" for a grandparent. All over the world, although the exact forms vary, these tend to be the first words of infants. *Holographic speech* is the infant or toddler's using one word to convey a whole sentence —"mama" for "I want my mama."
5. This stage is followed at *20 to 24 months* by the first simple *telegraphic sentences,* using two or three-word sentences to convey more complicated meaning. "Play yard?' to mean, "Can I play in the yard?"

What About Vocabulary Size?

Between *18 and 24 months* most infants experience a "vocabulary spurt" involving the rapid acquisition of comprehension and increase in production.

- At *18 months,* vocabulary size for most toddlers is about fifty words.
- At *24 months*, the size of receptive and productive vocabulary is about 300 words.
- The beginning of the vocabulary explosion appears to be between 24 and 36 months; by *age 3 (36 months),* a child should have a vocabulary of at least 900 words. Also by *age 3,* a child should begin to form complex sentences. Shortly after the vocabulary begins to increase, there is a "grammar explosion," which allows the child to do this.
- By *age 4 (48 months),* almost all of a child's speech should be in complex sentences.
- By *age 5,* 2000 words should be mastered, and by *age 6,* they should have a vocabulary of between 8000 and 14,000 words (Templin 1957).

Social Development in Language Learning

Social development is revealed through speech and language learning also. Speech gradually becomes less *egocentric*—there are fewer references to the self and more attempts to engage others in conversation rather than just express needs, actions, and desires. One view of this is that egocentric speech is gradually internalized—this becomes our internal monologue. An increased grasp of *pragmatics* also reveals increasing social sophistication of a child's language use. Pragmatics refers to differences in expression that reflect differences in role and status. A 3-year-old might say "gimme" to a peer but "please more juice" to an adult. A 4- or 5-year-old will start adopting a simpler expression when talking to a toddler but strive to speak clearly to a grown-up.

Piaget and Language Learning

The development of speech tends to reflect some of the cognitive problems of the preoperational stage that were described by Piaget.

- Children often use overextensions. For example, a child might refer to all four-legged animals as dogs or call all cats by the name of the family's pet cat.
- There are misuses of grammar that occur as a child assimilates the rules of speech. While trying to learn the various suffixes that indicate the past tense, a child may engage in *overregularization*—extend the most common rule of "add –ed" to irregular verbs like "to go" saying "goed" to the store instead of "went." This is very similar to what fledgling adult learners do as they take on a second language. It has been argued that this is a very logical way to approach the problem, and this evidence has been presented to bolster the idea that children are prepared innately to learn language (Pinker 1994).

Development of Moral Reasoning

Morals are the standards a culture uses to judge correctness of action or behavior. There are some fairly universal morals (not stealing) and some that are a little more fluid from culture to culture (polygamy). Some that we assume are universal are surprisingly inconsistent (for example, a ban on killing seems obvious to most Westerners, but infanticide, euthanasia, and other practices are acceptable in some world cultures).

Since most adults want to guide children in internalizing a moral code, the development of moral reasoning skills has been of interest to developmental psychologists. It is unclear, however, whether the reasoning skills are actually the most important aspect of learning to be a moral person.

Theories of Moral Development

Piaget's Simple Two-Stage Theory of Moral Development

Ask a preoperational child who is naughtier—the child who accidentally breaks three dishes while helping her mother load the dishwasher, or the child who purposely breaks one dish (pretending it is an accident) and fakes crying so that she will be allowed to stop helping and go watch TV. Because the latter child broke fewer dishes, it is most likely that she will be identified as less naughty, regardless of the lack of intent.

- *Heteronymous morality* is the moral reasoning level of the preoperational child. The child tends to judge on the basis of the action alone without considering intent. The amount of damage is the most important feature to a child in this stage of moral reasoning. A child in this stage will also operate on the principle of *imminent justice*—a kind of magical thinking that accompanies this stage. If the child who broke three dishes then fell down while playing and skinned her knee, a child in the heteronymous stage will see this as punishment.
- *Autonomous morality* begins in the concrete operational period. Children and adults in this stage believe that intentions must be taken into consideration. Thus they know (in considering this scenario) that the child who shirked helping with the dishes after dinner by breaking one dish is the one who is actually naughty. Children at this age also begin to grasp the idea that different contexts and societies may have different moral codes.

Kohlberg's Famous Stage Theory of Moral Development

Lawrence Kohlberg (1927–1987) was interested in how a child reasons in moral terms and uses the way he/she solves a problem like this to classify what stage a child is at in terms of moral development. He was interested in moral decision-making processes rather than the mere internalization of external rules. His stage theory features three levels with two stages each:

Level 1: *Preconventional morality* (moral reasoning based on immediate consequences.)
- Stage 1: *Obedience and punishment*—I do what I am told so I will not be punished.
- Stage 2: *Instrumental morality*—I do what is expected of me in order to gain rewards. (I'll scratch your back if you'll scratch mine.)

Level 2: *Conventional morality* (moral reasoning based on conformity to social rules and expectations)
- Stage 3: *Good boy/girl morality*—I will do what is good. I want to please others.
- Stage 4: *Law and order*—I will obey the law because I wish to do my duty and help maintain social order.

Level 3: *Postconventional morality* (moral reasoning based on principles and ethical ideals)
- Stage 5: *Social contract*—My interest is to achieve the greatest good for the largest number of people and to try to guard the basic rights of all persons.
- Stage 6: *Principles of conscience*—I will try to follow the laws, but in some cases where I believe they are not right I will follow my conscience because laws that violate universal ethical principles are wrong.

Some Criticisms of Kohlberg's Theory. There is almost always a problem with theories that propose the existence of unvarying stages. They don't seem to bear out in real life. Although Kohlberg believed that few people made it past stage 4, it also seems that people can be highly sophisticated morally about some issues (human rights, racial equality, etc.) yet completely comfortable committing small moral infractions of rules regarding property (keeping money when a cashier mistakenly gives them too much change, for example). Moral reasoning is a fascinating intellectual exercise but doesn't tell us very much about how people become moral (or less than moral). More compelling evidence is found in studies of emotional development in young children. Jerome Kagan (2000) proposes that the emergence (as the brain matures and the child interacts with the environment) of complex emotions such as remorse. A child who is exposed to violence and dishonesty may learn not to feel distress over them.

Bandura's Social-Cognitive Learning Theory of Moral Development
As discussed in Chapter 6, Bandura believes that people learn best by watching and imitating other people. He also proposed that they mentally process the consequences that others experience for good and bad behavior.

A child may imitate parents, significant adults (in the community and the media), and high-status peers. The role models for behavior change across the lifespan.

Gilligan's "Ethic of Care"—For Women Only
Gilligan believes that girls and women go through a sequence of stages of moral development, but that these stages involve the individual's perception of herself in relationship to others. Research has born out that some people do base their moral reasoning on relationship considerations, but this is not exclusively a female way of reasoning (Jaffee & Hyde 2000). As is the case with Kohlberg, there does not appear to be any reliable stage sequence.

Level 1—Caring for self (survival). "I have no one but myself."
  • Transition: Self-centeredness to a sense of responsibility
Level 2—Caring for others (goodness)
  • Transition: Conformity based on social expectations to choice (my needs versus those of others).
Level 3—Caring for self and others (balance)

Psychosocial Development

Psychosocial development refers to the emotional and psychological changes across the lifecycle that occur in the context of the individual's changing social environment.

Attachment Theory

The earliest social relationship of interest is the bond of parent and child. *Attachment theory* examines the effects of this bond on psychological development. The earliest studies of attachment come from comparative psychology (using animal behavior as a model for comparison with human behavior).

Arnold Gesell (1880–1961) and Konrad Lorenz (1903–1989), two *ethologists* (scientists who study animal behavior, instinct and species-specific behavioral adaptations) proposed that there was a critical time for bonding of offspring, particularly baby birds and infant mammals, to bond with their mother. They referred to this process as *imprinting*.

There is no evidence for an imprinting process in human babies, but we do have evidence that quality of attachment has substantial biological and psychological impact on the developing person. In viewing the major theories of attachment, we also need to keep in mind the wide variety of cross-cultural variation in what is regarded as healthy attachment. There are many different conceptions of "normal" attachment reflected in child-rearing practices—from Japan, where children sleep in the parental bed until well into school age, to America, where children are expected to sleep in their own beds from early infancy onward.

Major Perspectives on Attachment

- *Freudian.* In his psychosexual stage theory, Sigmund Freud (1856–1939) proposed that developing infants were in the oral stage. He proposed that infants are born expecting instant gratification (the pleasure principle), and that the attachment between mother and child formed as the child learned to delay his or her gratification to the care giver's schedule. If this wasn't accomplished in a satisfactory manner, the baby was on the road to a life of neurosis and distress in the interpersonal realm. Freud's theory is very bound to his time and culture, and there is little empirical support for this view of attachment.
- *Evolutionary.* John Bowlby (1907–1990) took an evolutionary perspective on the development of infant attachment. He saw a long-established pattern of infant signals (all the cute things that infants do, their facial appearance) that encouraged child-tending behaviors in adults (mainly feeding and protectiveness) and helped to ensure the survival of the infant (and therefore the parent's fitness).
- *Harlow.* Harry Harlow (1905–1981) did the famous, or perhaps infamous, experiments where baby rhesus monkeys were separated from their biological mothers and given the choice between surrogate mother dolls made of cloth or wire. The results of his research suggested that there is more to parenting than feeding and tending. Even when only the wire mothers were equipped with a bottle of formula, the baby monkeys preferred the cloth mothers. They only visited the wire mothers to feed. To be comforted, to explore, they preferred the presence of and access to the cloth mothers. Recent research by Tiffany Field (2002) and others, involving human babies born prematurely, have provided further evidence that *contact comfort* is vitally important for infant psychological adjustment and survival.
- *Ainsworth.* Mary Ainsworth (1913–1999) was one of Bowlby's students and was strongly influenced by his work. She devised the famous *Strange Situation* experiments. In these studies, 12- to 15-month-old infants were separated from their mothers for short periods of time in a laboratory made to look like a living room setting. The infants were monitored for the quality and intensity of their reactions. They were classified as secure (considered to be the healthiest), ambivalent, avoidant, and disorganized. Mothers were also observed with their babies at home, and their responsiveness to the baby was evaluated. Ainsworth believed that mother's responsiveness to baby dictated in large part the ultimate state of quality of attachment.

• *Kagan.* Jerome Kagan (1989) (whom we met a little earlier in our discussion of moral development) has raised a significant objection to Ainsworth's analysis. He sees the formation of attachment as a dialog between an inborn *temperament* that the baby has at birth and the way a parent responds *and* is influenced by the baby's disposition. His research suggests that babies arrive in the world with a genetically determined disposition, and that some infants are inhibited or slow to warm up. Baby's temperament influences the response style of the parent; therefore, it is impossible to reliably say whether the parent causes the infant to develop a particular attachment style, or an infant shapes the parent's responsiveness.

Erikson's Eight Stages of Psychosocial Development

Erik Erikson (1902–1990) is an interesting psychological theorist in more ways than one. Erikson never took a doctorate in psychology. He was a would-be artist, a medical student,* an anthropologist, and biographer. He did naturalistic observations of groups and

TABLE 9-5
ERIKSON'S EIGHT STAGES OF PSYCHOLOGICAL DEVELOPMENT

Stage and Age	Conflict	Resolution
Infancy 0 to 1 year	Basic trust versus mistrust	Care givers who reliably meet the infant's needs foster a sense of trust in others.
Toddlerhood 1 to 3 years	Autonomy versus shame and doubt	Reasonable limits by caregivers lead to a basic sense of independence in exploring the world.
Preschool 3 to 6 years	Initiative versus guilt	Child has a sense of purpose and is able to initiate play and reach goals without violating the rights of others.
School age 6 to 12 years	Industry versus inferiority	Child develops a sense of competence and accomplishment.
Adolescence 12 to mid-20s	Identity versus role confusion	Individual achieves a stable sense of identity and makes realistic plans for adult life.
Young adulthood mid-20's to mid-40s	Intimacy versus isolation	Individual establishes meaningful and satisfying close relationships.
Middle adulthood mid-40s to mid 60s	Generativity versus stagnation	Individual attains a sense that he or she is making useful contributions to the world and the future through family and work activities.
Late adulthood mid-60s onward	Ego integrity versus despair	Individual looks at life and decides that on balance it has been meaningful and satisfying.

*Erikson experienced a significant conflict with his stepfather about choosing a career—his stepfather wanted him to be a doctor, and he wanted to be an artist.

individuals and was keenly interested in how some people struggled through adversity to make their contributions—great people like Gandhi and Einstein.

It is interesting to speculate about how Erikson might have been working out his own issues by creating his own stage theory of development, especially reflected in the great emphasis he places upon the formation of a firm sense of identity.

Erikson's theory of psychosocial development in the individual proposes that each stage of life presents a unique set of demands and conflicts in the interpersonal and social realms. Table 9-5 lists eight stages and conflicts of psychosocial development according to Erikson.

Othe Issues in Psychosocial Development

Diane Baumrind's Parenting Styles

Parental discipline style is a topic frequently discussed in examining psychosocial development during childhood and adolescence. Baumrind (1971) developed a model of parenting styles based on levels of two dimensions of parental behavior—control (strictness) and warmth (responsiveness.)

TABLE 9-6

Control→ Warmth ↓	High Control	Low Control
High Warmth	Authoritative style—Parents who make demands but also respect children's rights, provide explanations for rules and consequences, and encourage independent decision making and action.	Permissive style—Permissive parents are very caring but tend to put child's rights before their own, do not enforce rules, set no limits, and give into child's demands without question.
Low Warmth	Authoritarian style—Parents who enforce rules and consequences with no explanations, expect children to conform to adult demands, encourage compliance without question and place little value on child's view or reactions.	Uninvolved or negligent style—Parents who neither enforce rules nor respond to child's views or needs

Baumrind's research showed that children who were raised by the high warmth, high-control authoritative parents tend to become the most independent, well-adjusted adults but there are many potential weaknesses in this research. Because it is correlational, it is inappropriate to conclude that the parenting style actually is responsible for the child's good adjustment. It could be socioeconomic status, genetics, or many other rival explanations. The original sample was small and homogenous (mainly white, middle-class families) and parenting style, like many other concepts examined in developmental psychology, is heavily influenced by culture.

James Marcia's Identity Statuses

Developmental psychologist James Marcia (1980) attempted to refine Erikson's stage 5 (identity versus role confusion) by describing a process of crisis and commitment in identity formation, which is briefly summarized in Table 9-7.

TABLE 9-7
CRISIS AND COMMITMENT IN IDENTITY FORMATION

	Crisis—No	Crisis—Yes
Commitment—No	Identity diffusion	Moratorium
Commitment—Yes	Foreclosure	Identity achievement

- *Identity diffusion.* If asked "Who are you?" the adolescent in identity diffusion would say "I don't know" or "Whatever." This adolescent is doing little in the way of actually investigating life paths. This is normal for very young adolescents (12–15) and more of a sign of possible adjustment problems in older adolescents.
- *Foreclosure.* In answer to the question "Who are you?" an adolescent in foreclosure might say, "I am going to be an insurance agent cause that's what my dad is" or "My plan is to be married by age 22!" This identity status involves making identity decisions without any actual struggle or conflict, in reaction or with reference to other people's interests and not one's own.
- *Moratorium.* This adolescent or young adult is in a period of experimentation and indecision that is actually a prelude to making sound life choices (and is actively struggling, in contrast with the individual who is in identity diffusion). If asked, "Who are you?" the answer might be "I don't know who I am yet" or "There are so many possibilities."
- *Identity achievement.* This young adult experienced moratorium and struggled and, at the end of the process, has made satisfying choices for work and personal life that fit their own experiences and values. When asked "Who are you?" an identity-achieved individual will say, "A future member of the State Bar," "A proud father-to-be," or "A person who has examined the possibilities and made good choices!"

The Psychology of Aging and Death

Physical changes that occur during adulthood often cause anxiety for middle-aged adults. Mainstream American culture tends to view aging as a negative process and generally encourages an attitude of denial toward the processes of aging and dying.

As you may recall from Chapter 7, the cognitive developmental changes faced by healthy older adults are not nearly as dramatic or debilitating as many people fear; however, many of these changes are affected by lifestyle decisions made when we are much younger (and therefore are not thinking about).

Some apparent cognitive changes are the result of what is called behavioral slowing rather than a loss of memory or problem-solving skills. Memory problems can be avoided through a combination of lifestyle decisions and simple mnemonic strategies. Learning helps the brain stay active, so one of the best things one can do is continue to read, write, and get exposure to new ideas and facts (taking classes would be one way to accomplish this.) The brain is a bodily organ, so physical fitness is also important. Regular exercise and good nutrition are crucial, as are avoiding or minimizing the use of all drugs (including alcohol and cigarettes). The time to start thinking about this is not at the retirement party—it is when one is young! As we age, we tend to become more sedentary, so a deliberate commitment to counteract this loss of activity is essential.

Sensory function is affected by aging. In middle age, vision and hearing are mildly affected. Most adults in their 40s start to wear reading glasses, and hearing at the highest frequencies becomes less acute. As we enter our 60s our senses of taste and smell become slightly weaker.

Loss is a theme of old age that causes some psychological distress. As friends and family die, an older person may feel isolated. Loss of functional independence may also contribute to this sense. The grief an elderly person feels in response to these developmental losses is normal and healthy, but probably the best way to counteract this sense of grief is for the older person to remain actively engaged in life and connected with many other people from different ages and backgrounds, rather than to recede into greater isolation as parts of the past are lost.

In summary, according to Rowe and Kahn (1998), the essential aspects of healthy aging are

- Avoiding disease
- Maintaining high cognitive and physical functioning
- Engaging with life

Death and Dying

We spend most of our lives coming to terms with mortality. Recall that Erikson's theory emphasized the importance of feeling that one has made good use of one's allotted time but in fact most of us begin to think about these issues in childhood. It is perhaps one of the most difficult, anxiety provoking aspects of being human. Our grasp of the reality of life and death sets us apart from all other animals.

Over the history of psychological science, attempts have been made to describe a stage-based process of adjustment to one's own impending death (Kubler-Ross 1969). The most recent research has failed to demonstrate any consistent pattern in the mental and emotional processes of the well-adjusted person approaching death. The truth most likely is that dying is an individual and intimately personal process. Some of us do obtain closure on our major life issues, some of us approach death in despair and fear, and some live energetic and busy lives right up to the very last moment.

Connecting Through Chapter Review

WORD-STUDY CONNECTION
Write each of these words on index cards and write their definitions on the opposite side.

assimilation
attachment theory
authoritative
authoritarian
autonomous morality
babbling
central nervous system
cephalocaudal
cognitive
concrete operations
conserve
contact comfort
conventional morality
cooing
critical periods
developmental psychology
differentiation
egocentric
embryonic period
ethologist
fetal period
fontanels
foreclosure
formal operations
germinal period
heteronymous morality
holographic speech
hypothetical

identity achievement
identity diffusion
identity status
imaginary audience
imminent justice
imprinting
jargon
lateralization
learning
maturation
milestones
moral reasoning
moratorium
myelination
neural tube
nonverbal communication
object permanence
oral stage
overextension
overregularization
permissive
personal fable
phonemes
pleasure principle
postconventional morality
pragmatics
preconventional morality
prenatal

preoperational
productive language
  development
proximodistal
psychosocial development
pruning
psychosocial
receptive language
  development
reflexes
schemas
sensorimotor
sensitive/optimal periods
social referencing
stepping reflex
Strange Situation
sutures
synaptogenesis
telegraphic sentences
temperament
teratogens
theory of mind
tonic neck reflex
training
trimester
uninvolved (negligent)

SELF-TEST CONNECTION

PART A. Completion
Write in the word that correctly completes each statement.

1. _____ is the branch of psychology that describes and explains change across the lifespan.
2. The first critical periods for development occur during the _____ period.
3. Studies of children who were initially reared in institutional care suggest that much of infant development is subjected to _____ periods.

4. "Head to tail" development is also called _____ development.

5. During the _____ period, the zygote implants into the enriched lining of the uterus, this usually happens at the end of the first week of pregnancy.

6. Nicotine, amphetamines, and cocaine are examples of _____ , which can lead to low birth weight, hyperactivity, and increased susceptibility to SIDS.

7. Alcohol, tranquilizers, barbiturates, and opiate drugs are examples of _____ , which can lead to fetal alcohol syndrome, addiction of fetus to drugs, and deformities to face and body.

8. _____ and _____ make up what are called "soft spots" on the skull, which, among other things, allow the infant's head to tolerate a certain amount of compression during delivery.

9. The step in sensorimotor development in which the baby's actions are planned mentally and carried out to achieve goals is referred to as _____ .

10. When a child is unable to take another person's perspective, his or her thought is said to be _____ .

11. _____ reflects the idea that others think and see and often do so differently than we do, that others have minds based on their behavior.

12. Children during the _____ stage can grasp logical reasoning operations, perform simple mathematical operations, conserve, and begin to be able to perform some basic trial-and-error problem-solving strategies.

13. _____ occurs when an adolescent feels as if others are watching and evaluating him.

14. _____ is the infant or toddler's using one word to convey a whole sentence, for example "eat" for "I want to eat."

15. By age _____ , almost all of a child's speech should be in complex sentences.

16. The highest level of moral reasoning is the _____ stage in which moral reasoning is based on principles and ethical ideals.

17. _____ believes that girls and women go through a sequence of stages of moral development that are based on herself in relationship to others.

18. In Erikson's conflict of _____ , care givers who reliably meet the infant's needs foster a sense of trust in others.

19. Individuals who establish meaningful and satisfying close relationships by the end of the Intimacy versus Isolation crisis are typically in the _____ period of the lifespan.

20. D. Baumrind developed a model of parenting styles based on two dimensions of parental behavior— _____ and _____ .

21. James Marcia developed a theory of identity development that was based on the work of _____ .

22. Adolescents who have no idea who they want to be and are not actively trying to figure it out are said to be in _____ .

PART B. Multiple Choice
Circle the letter of the item that correctly completes the statement.

1. The two major branches of developmental psychology are cognitive and _____ .
   (a) psychosocial
   (b) memory
   (c) motivation
   (d) clinical

2. The best time for certain events and milestones to be reached occur during _____ .
    (a) critical periods   (b) peak periods
    (c) the prenatal period   (d) None of the above

3. The neurological, skeletal, and muscular development of the organism from the midline outward is referred to as _____ .
    (a) adaptation   (b) proximodistal
    (c) differentiation   (d) cephalocaudal

4. Which of the following is not an environmental factor that influences development?
    (a) Socioeconomic status   (b) Untreated illness
    (c) Culture   (d) Hereditability

5. From what do the spinal cord and brain emerge during prenatal development?
    (a) Neural tube   (b) Hypothalamus
    (c) Fallopian tube   (d) Umbilical cord

6. Which of the following is a sexually transmitted disease that can lead to the baby being born infected, with skin and eye problems and a damaged central nervous system?
    (a) Herpes   (b) HIV
    (c) Gonorrhea   (d) All of the above

7. During which trimester do most of the neurons form and migrate to their final destination in the nervous system?
    (a) First   (b) Second
    (c) Third   (d) Doesn't happen until after the birth

8. How many inches in length is a typical newborn baby?
    (a) 5 to 8 inches   (b) 12 to 15 inches
    (c) 20 to 22 inches   (d) 28 to 30 inches

9. Which of the following brain growth processes, rapid in infancy and childhood, refers to the trimming of synapses that are not being used?
    (a) Myelination   (b) Synaptogenesis
    (c) Pruning   (d) Lateralization

10. Which stage in Piagetian theory reflects the baby's developing motor ability in which everything is handled, touched, and mouthed?
    (a) Sensorimotor   (b) Concrete operations
    (c) Formal operations   (d) Preoperational

11. One problem of preoperational thought that is characterized by focusing on one, primary physical feature in making assessments is _____ .
    (a) centration   (b) egocentric thinking
    (c) irreversibility   (d) lack of causal reasoning

12. The Piagetian stage in which youth can engage in abstract thinking, work with hypothetical questions and ethical dilemmas, imagine future possibilities, and mentally handle abstract concepts is referred to as _____ .
    (a) sensorimotor   (b) concrete operations
    (c) formal operations   (d) preoperational

13. The process of comprehending language is called _____ .
    (a) receptive   (b) responsive
    (c) productive   (d) promotional

14. At what age can most infants recognize their names?
    (a) 2 weeks   (b) 8 weeks
    (c) 4 months   (d) 6 months

15. Piaget would say that a child who tends to judge on the basis of the action alone without considering intent is in the _____ stage of moral development.
    (a) sensorimotor
    (b) concrete operations
    (c) autonomous
    (d) heteronymous

16. Kohlberg's stage of moral development in which moral reasoning is based on conformity to social rules and expectations is referred to as _____ .
    (a) sensorimotor morality
    (b) preconventional morality
    (c) conventional morality
    (d) postconventional morality

17. Arnold Gesell and Konrad Lorenz proposed that there was a critical time for offspring to bond with their mother, which they referred to as _____ .
    (a) suckling
    (b) imprinting
    (c) matching
    (d) posting

18. Who's evolutionary theory of attachment was supported by a long-established pattern of infant signals that encouraged child-tending behaviors in adults and helped to ensure the survival of the infant?
    (a) Freud
    (b) Harlow
    (c) Bowlby
    (d) Ainsworth

19. During which stage of the lifespan do individuals achieve a stable sense of identity and make realistic plans for adult life, according to Erikson?
    (a) Infancy
    (b) Adolescence
    (c) Adulthood
    (d) Late adulthood

20. By resolving the _____ conflict, an individual attains a sense that he or she is making useful contributions to the world and the future through family and work activities.
    (a) ego integrity versus despair
    (b) autonomy versus shame and doubt
    (c) generativity versus stagnation
    (d) industry versus inferiority

21. Authoritative parents are _____ in warmth and _____ control.
    (a) high; high
    (b) high; low
    (c) low; high
    (d) low; low

22. According to Marcia's model, adolescents who have committed to an identity without exploration are said to _____ .
    (a) be in moratorium
    (b) have an achieved identity
    (c) have a diffused identity
    (d) have a foreclosed identity

23. At what approximate age do individuals start to wear glasses and have less acute hearing?
    (a) 20s
    (b) 30s
    (c) 40s
    (d) 50s

24. According to Rowe and Kahn, healthy aging includes _____ .
    (a) avoiding disease
    (b) maintaining high cognitive and physical functioning
    (c) engaging with life
    (d) All of the above

PART C. Modified True-False

If the statement is true, write "T" for the answer. If the statement is incorrect, change the underlined expression to one that will make the statement true.

1. <u>Critical periods</u> are periods of time during which a developing person is maximally sensitive to environmental influences upon development.
2. A <u>deadline</u> is the achievement of a skill or physical characteristic expected within certain timeframes as a part of normal development.
3. The notion that the human organism, from conception to middle childhood, develops from the head is referred to as <u>cephalocaudal</u>.
4. The fetal environment is formed along with the amniotic sac, which contains the embryo and the placenta during the <u>germinal period.</u>
5. <u>Mercury</u> and <u>syphilis</u> are two of the many environmental toxins/pollutants that can lead to the baby being born with mental retardation.
6. Bones of the developing fetus will finish hardening during the <u>third</u> trimester of pregnancy.
7. The first motor milestone that babies are likely to complete is <u>walking.</u>
8. <u>Maturation</u> refers to what happens automatically, the simple natural appearance of features and skills at the expected times.
9. Two processes are involved in the creation and evolution of schemas. One, called <u>accommodation</u>, refers to the way individuals change new information to fit what they already know.
10. In Piagetian theory, <u>object permanence</u> reflects the ability of babies to recognize that a hidden thing or person who is out of sight is still present.
11. The stage in which thinking becomes symbolic, but the child does not possess the ability to manipulate symbols in order to reason logically, is referred to as <u>concrete operations</u>.
12. An example of a <u>personal fable</u> is when an adolescent boy feels as if others are keenly interested in the new pimple that emerged overnight on his face.
13. An infant who extends his/her arms to indicate the wish to be picked up or held is engaging in <u>nonverbal communication</u>.
14. Cooing and babbling are easier forms of <u>receptive language</u>.
15. A child who calls a fire truck a car has engaged in an <u>overextension</u>.
16. <u>Autonomous</u> morality, which begins in the concrete operational period, is characterized by the belief that intentions must be taken into consideration, according to Piaget.
17. <u>Attachment theory</u> attempts to explain the early social relationship created by the bond of parent/caregiver and child and the effects of this bond on psychological development.
18. Recent research by Tiffany Field involving premature babies has provided evidence that <u>contact comfort</u> is vitally important for infant psychological adjustment and survival.
19. Kagan proposed that babies are born with <u>an attachment</u>; in other words, the baby's disposition influences the way a parent responds to the baby.
20. Upon resolving the <u>initiative versus guilt</u> conflict, a child has a sense of purpose and is able to initiate play and reach goals without violating the rights of others.

21. <u>Uninvolved</u> parents tend to be very caring, but put child's rights before their own, do not enforce rules, and set no limits.

22. <u>Authoritative</u> parents enforce rules and consequences with no explanations and expect children to conform to adult demands without question.

23. An adolescent who is experiencing <u>moratorium</u> is in a period of experimentation and indecision that is actually a prelude to making sound life choices.

24. As we age into late adulthood, <u>there is pretty much nothing to be done about cognitive decline</u>.

PART D. Chart Completion

Fill in the missing information in each of the charts. One row is completed in each chart as an example.

PRENATAL DEVELOPMENT

Stage	Time	Changes
First trimester: germinal period	Week 1	Cell divisions and implantation occur at the end of week 1.
First trimester: embryonic period		"Floor plan" for baby, central nervous system develops rapidly, body areas become visible.
First trimester: fetal period	Weeks 8 to 12	
Second trimester		
		All organ systems in place and developed; baby puts on weight and increases in length; maturation of the central nervous system continues.

MAJOR MILESTONES OF CHILDHOOD COGNITIVE DEVELOPMENT

Age	Skill	Description
8 months	Object permanence	Child realizes that a hidden object still exists.
4 to 5 years	Theory of mind	
6 to 7 years		Child understands that changing shape or type of container does not change mass.
12 and older		Child asks "what if?" questions.
12 and older	Abstract reasoning	

LANGUAGE DEVELOPMENT IN THE FIRST TWO YEARS OF LIFE

Age	Ability	Type of Ability (Receptive/Productive)
0 to 1 month	Recognizes difference between human voices and other sounds	Receptive
8 weeks	(1) (2)	(1) Receptive (2) Productive
4 months		Receptive
6 to 10 months	(1) Responds to vocal rhythm and intonation. (2) (3) Jargon or conversational babbling	(1) (2) Productive (3)
1 to 1½ years	(1) (2) One-word holographic or speech	(1) Receptive (2)
1½ to 2 years		Productive

ERIKSON'S STAGES OF PSYCHOSOCIAL DEVELOPMENT

Stage	Age	Conflict	Resolution
Infancy	0 to 1 year	Basic trust versus mistrust	Care givers who reliably meet the infant's needs foster a sense of trust in others.
Toddlerhood			Reasonable limits by care givers lead to a basic sense of independence in exploring the world.
	3 to 6 years	Initiative versus guilt	
		Industry versus inferiority	
Adolescence			
		Intimacy versus isolation	
			Individual attains a sense that he or she is making useful contributions to the world and the future through family and work activities.
	Mid-60s onward		

CONNECTING TO CONCEPTS

Review the chapter and then write down your thoughts about the following questions.

1. Name some of the environmental factors that influence a child's growth and development in the prenatal period and early childhood. Imagine that you are going to design a community program to promote healthy child development. How would you use this information in your program to help parents, care givers, and child care professionals in their child rearing tasks?

2. Define teratogen, and list three to five examples of these and their effects. Name some ways that you believe would allow health and social services professionals to spread the word effectively about teratogens in order to reduce the exposure of children to these substances.

3. Imagine that you were developing a test of cognitive development modeled on Piaget's theory of development. Name each stage and the approximate ages during which a child is in that stage. Give an example of a task for each stage that would test whether or not a child had mastered a skill associated with that stage.

4. Discuss adolescence in terms of any of the theories in this chapter. Try to think of events or situations from your own teen years, or those of a person to whom you are close, that you think you understand better now that you have learned about these developmental theories.

5. Using any theories or concepts from this chapter, discuss how people can prepare early in life for a happy, healthy old age.

CONNECTING TO LIFE/JOB SKILLS

Child Development and Parenting

It is assumed that humans have an "instinct" for parenting and that most of the skills involved are common sense and do not need to be taught. The existence of this instinct is questionable. But the belief that parenting "comes naturally" continues to thrive and be detrimental to many first-time parents. They end up feeling bad about needing help and even worse about admitting to anyone that they do. Family members who are seasoned parents often behave as if it "came naturally" when in fact they learned by trial and error also.

The unacknowledged truth—that most people feel somewhat intimidated and anxious about raising a child—is one reason why child care experts and their books have become so popular over the past century. This is especially true because the extended family model has become less and less common, and families have become more mobile and less connected to a stable community, the articles and books by John Watson (remember him?), Benjamin Spock, Bill and Martha Sears, and many others emerged to fill the void. The internet now also offers an abundance of parenting web sites. The need for support and information persists.

This chapter has provided you with a brief introduction to theory and scientific research that forms the foundation for professions related to child development, including the important work of child-rearing. This chapter was only a brief survey, so you might consider taking a full course in child development or a parenting class if one is available.

You may be planning to raise a family, or you may be unsure about whether or not you will have any biological children. If you decide not to parent, you still may play the role of aunt/uncle, stepparent, coach, mentor or teacher at some time in your life. Almost every adult can benefit from some basic education in the science and art of raising children. You now have some knowledge of healthy prenatal development, expected ranges for milestones in language and motor development (early intervention is crucial if any delay is noticed), and typical issues of childhood and adolescent psychological adjustment. There is much more to know, and (as is the case with psychology in general) the knowledge base is expanding all the time.

Parenting and Child Care Resources on the Web

BABY PLACE

www.baby-place.com/

BRIGHTFUTURES.ORG

www.brightfutures.org/

I AM YOUR CHILD

www.iamyourchild.org/

KIDSHEALTH

www.kidshealth.org

NATIONAL NETWORK FOR CHILD CARE: CHILD DEVELOPMENT WEB SITE

twosocks.ces.ncsu.edu/cyfdb/browse_2pageAnncc.php?subcat=Child+ Development&search=NNCC&search_type=browse

NATIONAL ORGANIZATION FOR FETAL ALCOHOL SYNDROME

www.nofas.org/

NATIONAL PARENT INFORMATION NETWORK

npin.org/

ZERO TO THREE WEB SITE

www.zerotothree.org/

AMERICAN SIDS INSTITUTE

www.sids.org/

WHAT'S HAPPENING!

Geriatric Psychology and Fighting Ageism

The number of people over 60 is rising, but the attitudes toward aging are not changing quickly enough. What are the implications of this dilemma?

The first is that there will be a great demand for clinicians who specialize in the psychological aspects of aging and treating the mental health issues of elderly people—*geropsychologists*. According to one estimate, over 5000 doctoral-level psychologists with intensive training in geriatric psychology will be needed to serve the population adequately in the next decade. New PhDs are not flocking to this specialty, though, despite the need. Cultural biases and personal anxiety over the aging process are perhaps two of the reasons that more new PhDs decide not to specialize in geriatric psychology.

The other effect of our general negative attitude toward aging is that people, as they grow older, tend to neglect the important aspects of their own health care that would raise their chances of having an active and satisfying late adulthood. People's attitudes toward aging determine to some extent how healthy they will be—for concrete, behavior-related reasons. If you have decided when you are 30 that old age is a depressing time of life, when one is isolated and plagued by serious health problems, you may not take care of yourself and thus create a "self-fulfilling prophecy." Remember Erikson's last stage—integrity versus despair. Despair over aging when you are still young can have a lasting negative impact that appears long before the fact.

The information in this section is based on the following web resources—please visit them for more details!

www.apa.org/monitor/may03/fighting.html

This is the web-based version of an article by Melissa Dittman that was published in the May 2003 *Monitor on Psychology*.

www.apa.org/pi/aging/olderadults.pdf

OTHER USEFUL WEB SITES

THE MULTI-DIMENSIONAL HUMAN EMBRYO

embryo.soad.umich.edu/

This is a great site for viewing the steps of early prenatal development.

CHILDSTUDY.NET

childstudy.net/index.html

This site features an interactive tutorial on the major theories of child development and a forum through which questions concerned with child and adolescent developmental and mental health issues can be answered.

THE JEAN PIAGET ARCHIVES

www.unige.ch/piaget/Presentations/presentg.html

This site features biographical and theoretical information about Piaget.

ADULT DEVELOPMENT LINKS

www.hope.edu/academic/psychology/335/webrep2/index.html

Hope College sponsors this site—a collection of links to sites featuring research and theory related to development in all phases of adulthood.

REFERENCES

Astington, J. (1994) *The Child's Discovery of the Mind.* Cambridge, MA: Harvard University Press.

Baillargeon, R. & DeVos, J. (1991) Object permanence in young infants: Further evidence. *Child Development,* 62, 1227–1246.

Baumrind, D. (1971) Current patterns of parental authority. *Developmental Psychology Monographs,* 4(I, Pt. 2).

Cashon, C. H. & Cohen, L. B. (2000) Eight month old infants' perceptions of possible and impossible events, *Infancy* 1(4)

Drinnen B., Hall, W. (2001) *Instructor Manual for Discovering Psychology.* New York: Worth Publishers.

Field, T. (2002) Preterm infant massage studies: An American approach *Seminars in Neonatology* 7(6), 487–494.

Jaffee, S. & Hyde, J. S. (2000) Gender differences in moral orientation: A meta-analysis. *Psychological Bulletin,* 126, 703–726.

Kagan, J. (2000) Library of Congress/National Institute of Mental Health "Decade of the Brain" Project. *Understanding the Effects of Temperament, Anxiety, and Guilt.* *www.loc.gov/loc/brain/emotion/Kagan.html*

Kagan, J. (1989) *Unstable Ideas: Temperament, Cognition and Self.* Cambridge, MA: Harvard University Press.

Marcia, J. E. (1980) Identity in adolescence. In J. Andelson (Ed.), *Handbook of Adolescent Psychology.*

Pinker, S. (1994) *The Language Instinct: The New Science of Language and Mind.* New York: Penguin.

Rowe, J. W. & Kahn R. L. (1998) *Successful Aging.* New York: Pantheon Books.

Templin, M. (1957) Certain language skills in children: Their development and interrelationships. *Institute of Child Welfare Monograph,* Series No. 26. Minneapolis: University of Minnesota Press.

Chapter 10

MOTIVATION

In this chapter you will review the major theories of motivation and the external and internal forces that drive behavior and also explore the origin and functions of human emotion.

What Is Motivation?

Broadly speaking, *motivation* is the internal and external forces that drive our thoughts, moods, and behaviors. The word "motivation" derives from the Latin *movere*—to move. A motive that originates within the organism to meet a basic biological need or satisfies some "higher" need is called *intrinsic*. A motive that stems from influences outside of organism, based on a force or consequence from the environment, is *extrinsic*. The study of motivation is a central part of psychology. In fact, most of the major schools in this science are based on a particular way of viewing human motivation. Trying to describe and explain motivation helps psychologists connect biological states to behavior, identify differences in behavior between individuals (why do some people persist working toward their goals, even in the face of extreme adversity, while others give up rather easily?), and determine the level of responsibility individuals may have for their own actions (vital in the legal sphere).

Major Theories of Motivation

Instinct Theory

Similar to many other late nineteenth-century ideas, instinct as psychological motivation was a fairly direct outgrowth of the research and thinking of Charles Darwin. Evolution proposed that humans, as animals, share many behavioral characteristics with other organisms. *Instinct theory* proposes that organisms are motivated to engage in certain behaviors because of their genetic programming and because these behaviors lead to success in terms of natural selection. Instinct theory casts motivation as essentially intrinsic and biologically based. Migration and mating are examples of instinctually motivated behavior in animals. For example, many animals engage in *fixed action patterns* of behavior (such as mating dances and nest-building sequences in birds). In instinct theory, human behaviors are also viewed as instinctually motivated. Instinct theory in a sense forms the roots of the psychoanalytic school—Sigmund Freud saw humans battling with deeply rooted instincts that motivate destructive behaviors if not kept in check. He saw humans at the mercy of powerful forces that drove survival and gratification needs. This is his idea of the existence of the id, which we will examine in Chapter 13. Freud also originated the idea that behavior could be *unconsciously motivated,* that is, that individuals can be completely unaware of the drives or reasons that are causing them to behave in certain ways.

Although instinct theory is no longer widely regarded as accurate (at least for explaining human behavior), the idea that a limited number of human behaviors may be instinctually driven (mating/reproduction, social dominance) still persists. For example, many of us will refer to a person who is protective of his or her space as "territorial."

Drive Theory

Also known as *drive-reduction* or *homeostatic* theory, this perspective views behavior as motivated by the need to reduce internal tension caused by unmet biological needs. This is the view of motivation held by biological psychologists. Like instinct theory, drive theory has an intrinsic, biological basis. The unmet need "drives" us to behave in a way that causes the intensity of the drive to be reduced. Such drives work by *negative feedback*—one experiences an unpleasant feeling (hunger, thirst) until you meet the need. When the need state/drive arises again, the behavior is repeated. The drives are triggered by an internal mechanism that strives to maintain a state of *homeostasis*—a steady "optimum state." The principle is that the brain monitors and maintains constant levels of internal states (body temperature, fluid levels, energy supplies, need for rest). If any one of these conditions is too far from optimal, the brain (the hypothalamus) triggers the drive for the behavior that will bring conditions back to optimal. Hunger would appear to be a good example of a drive initiated to bring back homeostasis. Though it is based in the negative feedback system of drive, it clearly does not simply respond to signals from an empty stomach. People eat for reasons other than hunger. We will return to this subject shortly.

Certain physiological states are without a doubt homeostatic. The concept of *optimum arousal* extends homeostatic theory to the area of level of alertness and arousal and its effects on task performance. This is sometimes referred to as the *Yerkes-Dodson law*, also known as the inverted-U hypothesis (see Figure 10-1). The graph of the inverted-U shows that, in general, individuals need *some* level of stimulation and *some* anxiety, but we can have too much or too little of either, upsetting our mental homeostasis. If we have too little, we are bored and may not exert ourselves sufficiently, and if we have too much, we are panicked perhaps to the point where we cannot accomplish much. (This would explain a problem like test anxiety.) The level of optimum arousal for situations and activities varies between people and probably between situations—you need a different level of arousal when attending a party and a different one when taking a test. On the way to a party, if you feel as nervous as you do when you are going to take a test, you might not enjoy yourself very much. (This would describe the experience of a person who suffers from *social phobia*.) In general, though, we probably need a moderate level of arousal for the best performance in most circumstances.

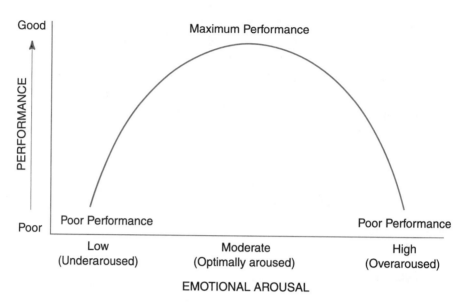

Figure 10.1 The Yerkes-Dodson Law.

Incentive Theory

An incentive is a reward. *Incentive theory* states that behavior is motivated by the pull of external goals, such as rewards. This is an extrinsically based model, based on contingencies, so behaviorists such as B. F. Skinner would have favored this explanation for motivation. In fact, in some ways, incentive theory seems almost indistinguishable from *operant conditioning*. You study hard for your psychology midterm in order to get a good grade; you practice Nineball so you can play with your friends and win a little money; you work out at the gym four times a week to get in shape and get compliments and positive attention.

And yet some behaviors are not well explained by this theory. Curiosity, listening to music, and noncompetitive play would appear to have no reward attached. You might study psychology because you enjoy the subject (right?), practice shooting pool because you enjoy the feeling of being skillful, and work out because you feel great when you do. Even if these things are not necessarily the case, it is almost certainly true that not every human behavior has a direct reward attached to it.

There is also evidence that incentives can work to undermine motivation in some circumstances. The *overjustification effect* occurs when incentives are offered for behaviors that people are already intrinsically motivated to do. In these cases, incentives appear to work to reduce the overall level of motivation. In other words, paying or rewarding people to engage in activities that are intrinsically motivated reduces their overall motivation. If you begin to pay children to play a game that they already enjoy playing, and then you stop paying, they will most likely stop playing.

There has been an ongoing debate about the relative importance of intrinsic versus extrinsic motivation. What is our primary source of motivation? Do we need external incentives? Are we controlled by our own biological or animal natures? Do we have "higher" motives in working toward our goals? Is any one motivation inherently superior to or stronger than the others?

Psychological or Humanistic Theory—
Maslow's Hierarchy

The proposal of this theory coincided with the rise of humanistic psychology. Carl Rogers (whom we will discuss in Chapter 13), Abraham Maslow, and their followers believed that people strive for a positive view of the self to realize their own potentials fully. Maslow and the humanists believed that this need was essentially innate. But without a supportive, nurturing environment, this essential striving for full potential could not take place.

Figure 10.2 represents the Maslow *Hierarchy of Needs*.

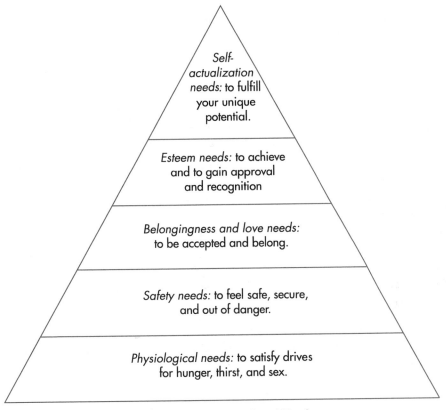

Figure 10.2 The Hierarchy of Needs.

From top to bottom, the needs are:

Self-Actualization. Reaching and using your full potential in your vocational and personal life.
Esteem. The need for respect from others and for a sense of accomplishment.
Social. The need to belong and be connected to other people.
Safety. The need for a personal sense of safety and a reasonable measure of security in future prospects.
Physiological. Basic survival needs—food, water, and air.

This pyramid, called the *hierarchy of needs*, depicts this theory. The person must satisfy the needs at the lower levels before moving on to tackle the ones at the top. There is a certain amount of common sense to this view: If you don't have enough to eat, if you don't feel safe, then striving for personal accomplishments, or worrying about how fulfilled you are will not be possible, or may not seem important.

The bottom (or rather, top) line of this theory is that people strive for self-actualization. That is, they strive to make full use of all their talents, capacities, and potentials, as represented by reaching the top level of the pyramid. These people naturally (according to Maslow) seek to do the best that they can do in all aspects of their lives.

One major flaw of this theory is that it is very difficult to study or support it empirically. The concept of self-actualization is vague and was formulated rather nonscientifically. (Maslow used small samples of people, mostly his own friends or acquaintances. He also worked from the biographies of famous persons with whom he had no contact.) We can certainly question the assumption that because people are famous or accomplished they are necessarily self-actualized. It is possible to find other case studies of people who made full use of their potential without meeting some of the lower levels of needs (Isaac Newton and Ludwig von Beethoven would be just two examples, lonely men who, while not having the affiliation need met, nonetheless made full use of their potentials.) People also have strived to use their talents and creativity even in the face of hardship—beautiful art, poetry and music were created by people living in dire poverty and slavery—probably from the earliest history of our species.

It is reasonable to assume that each of these four theories reflects one part of what contributes to the complex nature of human motivation.

Motivational Theory Applied: Hunger

Hunger seems like a great example of a really straightforward homeostatic drive, but it is far from a simple one. Physiological psychologists are still not sure what exactly triggers the drive of hunger and then the feeling of satiation (fullness) that makes us stop eating.

Let's look at all aspects of motivation for hunger.

The Biology of Hunger

There are short-term and long-term regulatory mechanisms involved in the production of feelings of hunger and satiety (fullness). In the short term, chemicals and hormones in the circulatory and digestive system, the stomach, and the *hypothalamus* all exert influence to produce feelings of emptiness and fullness. This is a complicated process, as you will see. There are two major events that help to trigger hunger:

- A drop in blood glucose occurs
- The hypothalamus responds to the drop in glucose by promoting hunger signals by changing and regulating hormone levels.

Hormones that are secreted in response to hypothalamic activity include:

- *Insulin* is released by the pancreas and metabolizes glucose so that it can be used by body cells for nutrition. It is usually released at the time we begin eating and tapers off when we are done. Excessive amounts of insulin and blood glucose result in increased production and storage of fat.
- *Glucagon* converts stored energy in fat and other body tissues into glucose. It is produced if we need energy and there is no food.
- *Cholecystokinin (CCK)* is a chemical in the body that acts as both a hormone and a neurotransmitter. It is secreted by the small intestine and slows the rate at which the stomach empties. Thus it promotes a feeling of fullness.
- *Orexin* is a hormone produced by the hypothalamus that directly triggers hunger.
- *Leptin* is produced by fat cells in the body and is monitored by the hypothalamus. When leptin levels are high, it works to alert the hypothalamus to stop promoting storage of fat—appetite tends to remain low and organisms tend to be more active.

These are specific areas of the hypothalamus that have been identified in the production of feelings of hunger and fullness (Nisbett 1972):

- The *lateral hypothalamus* appears to be critical for starting the drive to eat (and other drives as well). Damage to this area will cause starvation through lack of interest in food.
- The *ventromedial hypothalamus* is important for regulating the rate at which food is digested. When it is damaged, organisms digest food quickly, eat more, and put on weight.
- The *paraventricular hypothalamus* regulates satiety in the short term, and if this part is damaged, an organism may eat until it is literally about to burst.

What about the obvious part—the stomach? The stomach does have "stretch receptors" that send information to the brain regarding its level of emptiness or fullness, but even people who have had their stomachs removed will report the feeling of "hunger pangs." People who are very hungry (but not starving) tend to refuse food that disgusts them, and people who are forced to consume liquid diets will still complain of hunger after consuming a full portion of the prescribed fare. So there is much more to hunger than how full your stomach is.

Sociocultural Aspects of Hunger

Taste is yet another point at which nature and nurture meet and interact. All healthy humans are born with the four basic taste channels and a distinct preference for salty and sugary flavors. Like other mammals, we also crave the taste of fat (for evolutionary reasons, it's a good source of energy to create reserves for times of famine).

Although these taste tendencies are universal, people from different parts of the world *do* develop various taste preferences. Cuisine (cooking) is an art that reflects cultural preferences. We learn to eat what is familiar to us and what is considered delicious in our culture. Food preferences are *very* culture bound. Members of cultures that live in remote areas eat things that seem more exotic (or even distasteful) to urbanized, affluent humans.

Insects, wood, dog, and rodent, repulsive to us, are standard or even desired fare in other places.

We may also decide, or seem to decide, to eat based on availability of a food or social influence. If you only eat out at expensive restaurants once or twice a year, the dessert cart may be hard to pass up, even if you feel as if you are *beyond* full. We may eat much more than we need to at family gatherings or celebrations, in part because of the expectation that "it is what you do."

Long-Term Regulation of Body Weight

The traditional explanation offered for long-term changes in weight is the *energy balance model*. If the food (calories) we consume matches the amount of energy we expend, our weight will remain stable. Two things are evident about long-term regulation of body weight. In the short term, an individual's weight will appear to fluctuate on a daily basis within a narrow range (less than ten pounds), although it will generally stay within that range within any span of months or even a couple of years. But in the absence of intensive nutrition and fitness monitoring, most people tend to put on weight as they age.

The *set-point theory* of body weight proposes that every person is meant to have an optimal weight, one that the body will be drawn to "stick to" even if we eat too much or too little over any short period of time (Keesey & Powley 1975). This theory is a good explanation in the short term, but not in the long-term (over decades). A new theory, the *settling point theory* states that we have a stable set point from year to year, but that set point "settles" higher and higher as we get older (Pinel et al. 2000). Settling point theory adds the influence of changes in the amount of food we eat, our activity levels, and natural changes to our *basal metabolic rate (BMR)*—our natural energy expenditure rate. About one-third of the body's energy is expended in daily physical activities; the rest is used keeping vital functions going. The rate at which the body uses energy for vital processes is the basal metabolic rate. The BMR slows for all people over the course of the lifespan.

Influence and Problems of Dieting

It is safe to say that most people living in America and some of the wealthier world nations are dieting, or have dieted in the past. Dieting is a multi-billion dollar industry and much of that income comes from "repeat customers." Dieting is at best an inefficient way to lose weight. Dieters often find themselves obsessing about food. Between the thoughts of food and the plentiful advertisements, it is almost impossible to stick to a rigid eating menu and schedule. Also, the typical pattern for the dieter is that a small amount of weight is lost very quickly—as much as five or ten pounds in the first week or two, and then suddenly the weight loss slows or stops. What happens is that caloric restriction has an unintended consequence—it slows the basal metabolic rate. So now the dieter loses weight much more slowly, or not at all, even if he or she is "sticking to the diet." What has happened?

It appears that the modern human in most technologically sophisticated societies is fighting an evolutionary imperative. The body that we have today is the same body that our Ice Age ancestors had tens of thousands of years ago. Two things were very different at this time:

- Food was scarce much of the time—starvation was a constant threat.
- We had to work very hard to obtain the food that was available.

Actually, it was true up until about a century ago, in most parts of the world, that people expended more energy (owing to the absence of labor-saving technologies, such as the now ever-present automobile). There is now much less danger of starvation, but your body doesn't "know" that. The obsessive thoughts of food are also part of the body's survival strategy, motivating the search for food. At the level at which the brain generates the hunger drive, it cannot differentiate between a voluntary diet and a fatal famine. You are starving. These reactions to caloric restriction, which would have helped our ancestors to survive the famine, are an enormous problem for the average dieter. The *plateau* (slowing of weight loss) usually signals the end of the diet. And when the person stops dieting, the metabolic rate stays low long afterwards. This is the cause of the frustrating experience of gaining back even more weight than was lost.

For this reason, it is reasonable to assume that any weight-loss plan that does not include a moderate amount of regular exercise is likely to fail. In fact, it may be true that the exercise regimen is a little more important (and effective) than the caloric restriction in promoting the achievement of a healthy weight. A regular exercise program can help to keep metabolism high, allowing us to eat reasonable amounts of good food, and even indulge occasionally.

Motivational Theory Applied: Sexuality

Early Scientific Work on Human Sexuality: The Kinsey Reports

Throughout history there has been a great deal of interest in and fascination with sexuality. Most world cultures have strong rules and taboos, most of which are known but not consistently obeyed. There has been a great deal of information, misinformation, and misery. Psychology and neuroscience now strive to help us with better ways to understand the complex aspects of sexual behavior and to provide a route to better sexual adjustment for people of all ages and backgrounds.

One of the earliest attempts to study human sexuality scientifically was the landmark survey research done by Alfred Kinsey (1894–1956). Interestingly, Kinsey was a zoologist by training. Although he gathered data between 1938 and 1963, his major surveys were carried out in 1948 (focusing on male sexual behavior) and 1953 (female sexual behavior). Kinsey worked with large samples (over 5000 in the major surveys) and used highly trained interviewers. The sample was not randomly gathered though, and most respondents were middle-class individuals from the Midwestern United States. Still, his work is crucially important to the history of psychology and human sexuality. His results generally indicated that human sexual habits and attitudes are diverse and complicated. His courage in researching the subject paved the way for future scientific investigation by other scientists.

Sexual Arousal and Response

It has been said that the most sexual organ of all is the brain. It is true; the brain does influence people's tastes and preferences in these matters, but it also contains the structures from which the sex drive and ability to respond sexually originate—the hypothalamus and the pituitary gland. These are the parts of the brain that initiate and control the timing of changes associated with puberty. They also control hormonal changes that influence fertility and the strength of the sex drive. Sex is a deeply intrinsically motivated activity. The pleasure associated with sexual activity assures that humans will reproduce (even with recent advances in contraception). Besides reproduction, the pleasure associated with sexual behavior can help motivate couples (of all sexual orientations) to become intimate and stay bonded. So the sex drive contributes to important aspects of human social behavior.

The first studies of human sexual response were carried out by William Masters (1915–2001) and Virginia Johnson (b. 1925), a physician and psychologist (respectively) by training. In the early 1960s, they began laboratory studies of the human sexual response cycle and problems that occurred in this process. In 1966 they published the landmark book *Human Sexual Response* based on their work.

What was groundbreaking in the work of Masters and Johnson was their description of the sexual response cycle in men and women. Their research revealed fundamental similarities (the four stages listed here) and differences (the pattern of *orgasm*, or sexual climax is different for men and women).

The Four Stages of the Human Sexual Response

1. *Excitement* occurs when the physiology of the genitals and the entire body are preparing for sexual activity. The man's penis becomes erect, owing to an increase in blood flow. Women also experience an increased blood flow to the vagina, and this causes swelling and lubrication. Pulse, blood pressure, and respiration rates increase for both sexes.
2. *Plateau* is a constant level of excitement that follows the initial phase of arousal.
3. *Climax,* or *orgasm,* is the sudden and pleasant release of tension that is experienced throughout the body. For males, this is accompanied by ejaculation, which may cause conception and pregnancy. Women's orgasm patterns are more variable; she may have a single orgasm, multiple orgasms, or none. Women's orgasms have no effect (at least none that has been scientifically supported) on conception or pregnancy. Most men can only have one orgasm during any sexual act.
4. *Resolution* is the fourth and final stage, during which the genitals and body return to a nonaroused state. This phase can include a *refractory,* or resting period for the man, during which he cannot become aroused, but after which he can become excited and have another climax.

Patterns of desire, excitement and climax vary from individual to individual. And any person will usually also report that the quality and intensity of excitement and orgasm vary between sexual experiences.

Gender Versus Sexual Orientation

It is important not to confuse the terms "gender" and "sex." *Gender* is primarily a social construction. It refers to aspects of behavior and appearance that identify a person as masculine or feminine, while sex is primarily biological. Sexual orientation refers to a person's preference in sexual partners—same sex (homosexual), opposite sex (heterosexual), or both (bisexual). Twenty-first century humans tend to have a very short view back in history, not realizing that many gender-related customs are completely arbitrary. A good example is "pink" for girls and "blue" for boys; a century ago, it was "energetic" pink for boys and "calm, serene" blue for girls. Over the course of history, and in some world cultures today, the accepted dress for men has included long hair, make-up, jewelry, and colorful clothes. Although many aspects of masculine and feminine behavior are biologically hard-wired (fixed), many conventions of appearance are more flexible and culturally dictated. Attitudes toward sexual orientation have also changed throughout time. In the ancient Western world (the Greek and Roman Empires), homosexuality was accepted as normal sexual behavior, and in many societies, up until a century or so ago, most people did not "declare" a sexual orientation. It was not unusual to have intense friendships or romances with members of either sex and then to settle into heterosexual marriage.

Prenatal Influences on Sex and Gender

Up until about the eighth week of prenatal development, male and female embryos look the same. In fact, each fetus contains structures that form the basis for both male and female genitalia. Depending on the chromosomes (XX or XY) at this point, hormones are secreted that will help to determine whether a fetus will be anatomically male or female. The difference between males and females is determined by the presence or relative scarcity of *testosterone*. If the developing fetus secretes testosterone, the rudimentary genitals will become a *penis* and *scrotum* (the structure that contains the testicles) in males. The very lower levels of testosterone produced by a female fetus cause the structures that become a penis in the male fetus to instead become female genitals—a *vagina, clitoris,* and *labia.* Instead of a scrotum, the fetus develops *ovaries* and *fallopian tubes.* An increase in estrogen in female fetuses also promotes the development of the internal reproductive organs. A small number of fetuses that are genetically XX or XY will develop an "intermediate" anatomical appearance—somewhere between male and female—owing to hormonal conditions in the prenatal environment. These individuals are referred to as *intersexes.* Although attempts have been made in the past to "assign" a sex for them at birth, it is now more common to allow the individual to decide to have sex assignment surgery or remain an intersex.

Sexual Orientation

Among other information to emerge from the Kinsey studies, the idea that sexual preference is more of a continuum than an either/or condition. Some people who identify as "gay" have had some heterosexual experiences, and others who are "straight" have had some homosexual experiences. Although in the twentieth century the Western view came to be that homosexuality was a "sin" or an "illness," scientists and physicians in general now view homosexuality as a normal variety of sexual preference. Researchers are still trying to determine what factors are involved in shaping sexual orientation. Studies of identical twins indicate that if one twin is homosexual, there is higher likelihood that the other will be too. This could be evidence of the effects of genes, prenatal hormones, or both. Other studies have implicated a region on the X-chromosome as possibly linked to homosexuality in males. Studies of brain anatomy have been done, but research on brain differences between homosexual and heterosexual individuals is correlational. This makes it impossible to know whether any differences found are present at birth or result from environmental or lifestyle factors.

The results of research on sexual orientation are still far from conclusive. Most scientists suspect that sexual orientation, like many other aspects of human behavior, is formed by a combination of biology and environment. Based on the evidence, the American Psychological Association and the American Psychiatric Association have strongly rejected the outdated and unsupportable ideas that sexual orientation is a matter of choice and that homosexuality is a mental disorder.

Motivational Theory Applied: Achievement

The online *Dictionary of Vocational Psychology* defines achievement motivation as "a habitual desire to achieve goals through one's individual efforts." Individuals vary quite a bit in this motivation. Managers, coaches, and many types of leaders are keenly interested in how to maximize this type of motivation.

Psychological research on achievement motivation dates back to the mid-1930s when psychologist Henry Murray (1893–1988) was developing the Thematic Apperception Test (TAT), a projective instrument (see Chapter 13) designed to identify the unconscious needs and motives of the test taker. He invented the abbreviation *nAch* to stand for the drive to achieve. Murray's student David McClelland (1918–1998) used nAch in his theory of human behavior, based on three major needs—the need for achievement, the need for power, and the need for affiliation.

Unlike the other two motivations we have discussed (hunger and sex), achievement does not appear to have a clear biological basis. Although strength of appetite and sex drive *does* vary across individuals, they are present to some extent in almost all people. The same is probably not true of achievement motivation. There are also cultural influences (in a collectivistic culture, such as Japan's, a high nAch would not necessarily be considered a good trait, although in many Western societies it clearly would be). There are variations even within individuals, from situation to situation (a person might be very motivated to achieve in the area of becoming a musician but not in athletics or academics). The same person may differently define the words "achievement" and "success" at ages 18, 38, and 68. Achievement motivation might be intrinsic in some situations (if you love to play soccer, your playing aggressively is probably a result of your enjoyment) and extrinsic in others (you may not enjoy studying chemistry very much, but you work hard to get a good grade in order to keep your grade point average up so that you might receive a scholarship).

McClelland (1987) and psychologists who were influenced by his work have developed a list of traits that are found in persons who are high in nAch.

- They prefer tasks that would be described as moderately difficult or challenging.
- They tend to be competitive.
- They prefer to work for clearly defined goals and receive specific and useful feedback.
- They enjoy the feeling of being responsible for the outcome of projects.
- They do not give up easily (they exhibit persistence.)
- They tend to be more accomplished than their peers.

McClelland believed that nAch was learned in childhood, primarily through the role modeling and experiences provided by parents. As is true of the research on parenting style (by Baumrind, see Chapter 9), it is difficult to know whether the behavior, culture, or genes of the parents—or some combination of the three—influence a person's level of achievement motivation.

Connecting Through Chapter Review

WORD-STUDY CONNECTION
Write each of these words on index cards and write their definitions on the opposite side.

achievement
anterior hypothalamus
basal metabolic rate
 (BMR)
cholecystokinin (CCK)
clitoris
drive-reduction
energy balance model
excitement
extrinsic
fallopian tubes
fixed action patterns
gender
genitalia (genitals)
glucagon
glucose
hierarchy of needs
homeostasis
homeostatic

humanistic
hypothalamus
incentive theory
instinct theory
insulin
intersexes
intrinsic
labia
lateral hypothalamus
leptin
motivation
nAch
negative feedback
operant conditioning
optimum arousal
orexin
orgasm (climax)
ovaries
overjustification theory

paraventricular
 hypothalamus
penis
plateau
refractory
resolution
scrotum
self-actualization
set-point theory
settling point theory
sexual orientation
social phobia
testosterone
Thematic Apperception
 Test (TAT)
unconsciously motivated
vagina
ventromedial hypothalamus
Yerkes-Dodson Law

SELF-TEST CONNECTION

PART A. Completion
Write in the word that correctly completes each statement.

1. _____ is the internal and external forces that drive our thoughts, moods, and behaviors.
2. Instinct theory of motivation came out of the theories of evolutionist _____ .
3. _____ reflect species-specific behavior that occurs in a particular order or sequence.
4. _____ occurs when you experience an unpleasant feeling until you meet the need.
5. The _____ tends to reduce motivation as it occurs when incentives are offered for behaviors that people are already intrinsically motivated to do.
6. _____ suggests that behavior is motivated by the pull of external goals, such as rewards.
7. _____ is the highest level of Maslow's hierarchy of needs.
8. _____ is the lowest level of Maslow's hierarchy of needs.
9. The first step by the body to "trigger" the feeling of hunger is _____ .
10. ._____ is released by the pancreas and metabolizes glucose so that it can be used by body cells for nutrition.
11. Food preferences are to a great extent _____ bound.
12. The traditional explanation, called _____ , offered for long-term stability in weight suggests that the food we consume matches the amount of energy we expend.
13. Measured in calories, the _____ is the rate at which we use energy.
14. _____ conducted one of the earliest attempts to study human sexuality scientifically by using survey and interview methods of large numbers of adults in the Midwest.
15. The _____ and the_____ are the two structures in the brain where the ability to regulate the sex drive and the ability to respond sexually originate.
16. _____ is a constant level of excitement that follows the initial phase of arousal in the stages of human sexual response.
17. During the resolution stage of human sexual response, a man may experience _____ during which he cannot become aroused, but after which he can become excited and have another climax.
18. _____ is a social construction that refers to aspects of behavior and appearance that identify a person as masculine or feminine; _____ is primarily biological.
19. Studies of sexual preference have implicated a region on the _____ chromosome as possibly linked to homosexuality in males.
20. Murray developed the _____ , a projective instrument designed to identify the unconscious needs and motives of the test taker.
21. McClelland identified three major needs—the need for achievement, the need for _____ , and the need for affiliation.
22. Henry Murray invented the abbreviation _____ to stand for the drive to achieve.
23. Research has found that achievement as a motive in some countries demonstrates that the need for achievement is influenced by_____ .

PART B. Multiple Choice
Circle the letter of the item that correctly completes the statement.

1. _____ theory of motivation proposes that organisms engage in certain behaviors because of their genetic programming and because these are behaviors that lead to success in terms of natural selection.
   (a) Instinct   (b) Drive
   (c) Extrinsic   (d) None of the above

2. What type of motive originates within the organism to meet a biological need?
   (a) Intrinsic motive   (b) Altruism
   (c) Extrinsic motive   (d) Arousal

3. Freud originated the idea that behavior could be _____ motivated, meaning that individuals can be completely unaware of the drives or reasons that are causing them to behave in certain ways.
   (a) consciously   (b) memory
   (c) unconsciously   (d) intrinsically

4. Drive theory is also known as _____ theory.
   (a) homeostatic   (b) arousal
   (c) drive induction   (d) All of the above

5. According to the Yerkes-Dodson law, people need _____ levels of arousal to create and _____ levels of performance.
   (a) high; high   (b) low; high
   (c) moderate; high   (d) low; moderate

6. An incentive is a _____ .
   (a) condition   (b) punishment
   (c) drive   (d) reward

7. Who developed the hierarchy of needs to explain human behavior?
   (a) Freud   (b) Darwin
   (c) Maslow   (d) Rogers

8. According to the hierarchy of needs, what is the need for respect from others, and for a sense of accomplishment?
   (a) Esteem   (b) Self-actualization
   (c) Social   (d) Safety

9. _____ converts stored energy in fat and other body tissues into glucose.
   (a) Insulin   (b) Cholecystokinin (CCK)
   (c) Orexin   (d) Glucagon

10. What area of the hypothalamus appears to be critical for starting the drive to eat?
    (a) Lateral   (b) Ventromedial
    (c) Paraventricular   (d) None of the above

11. The _____ takes into account that people gain weight as they get older and adjusts for that weight gain.
    (a) setting point theory   (b) energy balance model
    (c) set-point theory   (d) All of the above

12. _____ published the book *Human Sexual Response* based on their laboratory work of sexual behavior.
    (a) Kinsey and Kinsey   (b) Masters and Johnson
    (c) Freud and Jung   (d) Maslow and Rogers

13. According to Masters and Johnson, the first stage of the four stages of the human sexual response is _____ .
   (a) plateau   (b) excitement
   (c) climax   (d) resolution

14. _____ refers to a person's preference in sexual partners.
   (a) Sexual identity   (b) Sexual orientation
   (c) Homosexuality   (d) Transgender

15. Ancient Greeks and Romans were likely to engage in _____ types of sexual relationships.
   (a) heterosexual   (b) homosexual
   (c) neither a nor b   (d) both a and b

16. Up until about the _____ week of prenatal development, male and female embryos look the same.
   (a) first   (b) eighth
   (c) fifteenth   (d) twenty-sixth

17. The hormone that will help to determine whether a fetus will be anatomically male or female is _____ .
   (a) estrogen   (b) testosterone
   (c) androgen   (d) gonad

18. The term used to describe the small number of fetuses that are genetically XX or XY, but develop an "intermediate" anatomical appearance resulting from hormonal conditions in the prenatal environment is _____ .
   (a) transgender   (b) intersex
   (c) homosexual   (d) androgynous

19. Male chromosomes are _____ and female chromosomes are _____ .
   (a) XX; XY   (b) XX; XX
   (c) XY; XX   (d) XY; XY

20. Studies of sexual preference of identical twins indicate that if one twin is homosexual, there is _____ likelihood that the other will be too.
   (a) higher   (b) lower
   (c) equal   (d) This has never been examined.

21. Most scientists believe that sexual orientation is _____ .
   (a) biological only   (b) both biological and environmental in nature
   (c) a matter of choice   (d) environmental in nature

22. _____ motivation is "a habitual desire to achieve goals through one's individual efforts."
   (a) Achievement   (b) Sexual
   (c) Hunger   (d) Instinct

23. _____ developed a theory of human behavior based on three major needs—the need for achievement, the need for power, and the need for affiliation.
   (a) Maslow   (b) Murray
   (c) McClelland   (d) Piaget

24. Which motive is the least likely to have a biological basis?
   (a) Hunger   (b) Sex
   (c) Achievement   (d) Affiliation

25. Researchers have found that persons who are high in nAch are also likely to be _____ .
   (a) intelligent   (b) easy-going
   (c) extroverted   (d) competitive

PART C. Modified True-False
If the statement is true, write "T" for the answer. If the statement is incorrect, change the underlined expression to one that will make the statement true.

1. <u>Cognition</u> is the external and internal forces that drive behavior.
2. A motive that originates within the organism to meet a basic biological need or to satisfy some higher need, is called <u>extrinsic</u>.
3. Doing well in school because your parents paid you for each "A" earned is an example of an <u>intrinsic</u> reward.
4. According to instinct theory, motivation is essentially <u>extrinsic</u>.
5. Drives are triggered by an internal mechanism that strives to maintain a state of <u>homeostasis</u>.
6. <u>Negative feedback</u> extends homeostatic theory to the area or level of alertness and arousal and its effects on task performance.
7. <u>Intrinsic</u> theory is an extrinsically based model, based on contingencies.
8. The <u>homeostasis</u> law demonstrates that in general people need some arousal—just not too much.
9. Maslow's hierarchy of needs coincided with the rise of <u>behavioral</u> psychology.
10. According to Maslow's hierarchy of needs, <u>social</u> needs must be met before <u>safety</u> needs are met.
11. <u>Esteem</u> needs are reaching and making use of your full potential in your vocational and personal life, according to Maslow's hierarchy of needs.
12. One criticism of Maslow's hierarchy of needs is that lower needs <u>must always be met</u> before the higher needs are met.
13. When triggering hunger, the <u>pituitary gland</u> responds to the drop in glucose by changing and regulating hormone levels.
14. In experimenting on rats, damaging the <u>paraventricular hypothalamus</u> may cause the rat to eat until it is literally about to burst.
15. The <u>energy balance model</u> of body weight proposes that every person is meant to have an optimal weight, one that the body will stay at even if we eat too much or too little over any short period of time.
16. The BMR <u>speeds up</u> for all people over the course of the lifespan.
17. Research on hunger has demonstrated that it is both <u>physiological</u> and <u>sociocultural</u> in nature.
18. Male and female social roles reflect <u>gender.</u>
19. <u>Climax</u> refers to the fourth and final stage of the human sexual response, during which the genitals and body return to a non-aroused state.
20. People who are <u>homosexual</u> have sexual preferences for both men and women.
21. If a developing fetus secretes testosterone, the rudimentary genitals will become a penis and <u>ovaries</u> in males.
22. The Kinsey studies suggested that sexual preference is more of a <u>continuum</u> than an <u>either/or condition</u>.
23. McClelland's three major needs included the need for <u>achievement</u>, the need for <u>power</u>, and the need for <u>sex</u>.
24. Unlike the motivations of hunger and sex, achievement does not appear to have a clear <u>biological</u> basis.

PART D. Chart Completion

Complete the charts with the correct information. The first row is completed for demonstration.

GENERAL THEORIES OF MOTIVATION

Theory	Description	Influenced Which School of Psychology
Instinct	Motivation is comprised of innate, biologically based drives for survival.	Psychoanalytic
Drive (homeostatic)		Biological/neuroscience
Incentive		Behaviorism
Psychological/Humanistic		

INFLUENCES ON HUNGER MOTIVATION

Type of Influence	Examples	Action
Hormonal	Insulin, glucagon, orexin, CCK, leptin	Work in digestive tract and bloodstream to influence levels of hunger in the short and long term.
Hypothalamic	Lateral, paraventricular and ventromedial regions	
Sociocultural		
Metabolic	Set-point or settling point; BMR	
Dieting		Lowering calorie intake in the absence of increased exercise can disrupt BMR in the long term
Evolutionary	Labor-saving technology combined with plentiful food in most wealthy world cultures	

CONNECTING TO CONCEPTS

Review the chapter and then write down your thoughts about the following questions.

1. Choose one general theory of motivation to define and describe. Give two examples of behaviors that you believe can be explained by this theory, and explain why you think they can be explained in this manner.
2. Define and describe the Yerkes-Dodson law, and describe a situation in which you think you perform better with moderate to high levels of anxiety, and one in which you think you do better when you have a low level of arousal or anxiety.
3. Given the action of various influences on hunger motivation, describe how you believe people in this society can effectively strive to keep weight in a healthy range.
4. Define and distinguish between gender and sex and describe the various influences on each of these aspects of human behavior.
5. What are the qualities of a high-achieving person, according to McClelland? Do you think that these qualities would promote achievement across all situations, or only specific ones? In which situations do you think these qualities are most helpful?

CONNECTING TO LIFE/JOB SKILLS

Industrial-Organizational Psychology

As you might have guessed, maximizing achievement motivation is important in the world of business. Motivation theory plays a prominent role in *Industrial-Organizational* or *I/O* psychology. This is a popular branch of applied psychology, combining aspects of social, counseling and personality theory (among others) to explain individual and group behavior in the work place and to improve productivity, morale, and performance.

Many individuals who were originally trained in traditional psychology graduate programs teach and do research in I/O psychology. It is also possible to apply directly to master's and doctoral programs in industrial-organizational psychology. At many schools, these programs are housed in the business school rather than the psychology department. I/O psychologists also frequently work as consultants to all kinds of businesses.

To find out more about advanced study in industrial organizational psychology, visit the following web sites:

SIOP: THE SOCIETY FOR INDUSTRIAL AND ORGANIZATIONAL PSYCHOLOGY

siop.org/

ASSORTED LINKS ON INDUSTRIAL-ORGANIZATIONAL PSYCHOLOGY

psych.athabascau.ca/html/aupr/industrial.shtml

ABOUT—INDUSTRIAL-ORGANIZATIONAL PSYCHOLOGY

psychology.about.com/library/weekly/aa043000a.htm

WHAT'S HAPPENING!

Self-Determination Theory

Self-determination theory is a new, comprehensive perspective on human motivation. It is similar to humanistic theory in that it assumes that people strive to achieve personal growth and use their full potential. In contrast to traditional humanistic theory, it focuses on the degree of volition or choice that people exercise in achieving their goals. It also assumes a greater role of the social context, examining the extent to which the environment helps or hinders the choices that people make.

Current applications of self-determination theory include:

- Examining the overjustification effect in applied settings such as schools and businesses—to what extent do rewards undermine intrinsic motivation?
- The possible negative effects of widespread, state-mandated testing programs in American schools, especially when school funding and resources will depend on the overall scores of the students ("high-stakes testing").

Self-determination researchers hypothesize that testing and incentives may, in fact, work against a natural inclination that people have to achieve and strive to find alternative ways to encourage the innate drive to "choose" to grow and achieve.

To learn more about self-determination theory, visit this web site:

SELF-DETERMINATION THEORY: AN APPROACH TO HUMAN MOTIVATION AND PERSONALITY

www.psych.rochester.edu/SDT/index.html

OTHER USEFUL WEB SITES

ENCYCLOPEDIA OF PSYCHOLOGY: MOTIVATION ENTRY

www.psychology.org/links/Environment_Behavior_Relationships/Motivation/

This site presents general information on theories of motivation related to education and organizational psychology.

REFERENCES ON MOTIVATION

www.ping.be/jvwit/motivationwork.html

This site provides links embedded in an essay motivation theory and its various applications.

ABRAHAM MASLOW BIOGRAPHY

/www.ship.edu/~cgboeree/maslow.html

This site presents an account of Maslow's life and how he developed his theory of motivation.

MEDLINE PLUS PAGE ON OBESITY

www.nlm.nih.gov/medlineplus/obesity.html

This web site on weight and health is sponsored by the National Institutes of Health.

THE NEW YORK OBESITY RESEARCH CENTER

cpmcnet.columbia.edu/dept/obesectr/NYORC/links.html

This very active and innovative center does research on obesity with great information and resources for both professionals and the general public.

UNDERSTANDING ADULT OBESITY

www.niddk.nih.gov/health/nutrit/pubs/unders.htm#distribution

This web site is sponsored by the National Institute of Diabetes and Digestive Diseases of the National Institute of Health.

THE KINSEY INSTITUTE

www.indiana.edu/~kinsey

This web site is a great source of information on the famous researcher and his work. The site also has recent research, publications, and related links.

SEXUALHEALTH.COM

www.sexualhealth.com/

This is a great comprehensive resource on all aspects of sexual behavior and health.

SIECUS WEB SITE

www.siecus.org/

SIECUS is an acronym for Sexuality Information and Education Council of the United States. SIECUS is a clearinghouse for research on sexual behavior and health.

REFERENCES

The *Dictionary of Vocational Psychology* (VocationalPsychology.com web site). *www.vocationalpsychology.com/term_nAch.htm*

Keesey, R. E. & Powley, T. L. (1975) Hypothalamic regulation of body weight. *American Scientist*, 63, 558–565.

McClelland, D. C. (1987) Characteristics of successful entrepreneurs. *Journal of Creative Behavior*, 3, 219–233.

Nisbett, R. E. (1972) Hunger, obesity, and the ventromedial hypothalamus. *Psychological Review*, 79, 435–453.

Pinel, J. P. J., Assanand, S. & Lehman, D. R. (2000) Hunger, eating and ill health. *American Psychologist*, 55, 1105–1116.

Chapter 11

EMOTIONS, STRESS, AND COPING

In this chapter you will review the latest scientific information on emotions and their functions in human communication and adjustment. You will learn about stress and its potential influence on mental and physical health. You will also learn about how psychology assists us in learning to manage stress more effectively.

Emotions: Purpose and Process

Emotions are a vital form of information and communication. Emotions can help us understand our own motivations, attitudes, and needs as well as those of others. People who experience damage to the emotion centers of the brain not only have difficulty expressing and controlling emotions but also may behave impulsively, may be unable to interpret the emotions of others, and may not be able to make decisions or problem-solve. Emotions are not the opposite of thought and reason; they are a vital part of our internal system for understanding and managing our own lives and relating to others.

The Biological Basis of Emotion: Autonomic Nervous System Function

The *autonomic nervous system* regulates the functioning of internal organs and vital bodily processes. The sympathetic and parasympathetic nervous systems, the subdivisions of the autonomic system, work in opposition to each other. The *sympathetic* nervous system is an "activation system." It prepares the body for "fight" or "flight" when we experience feelings of fear or anger. In response to an environmental stimulus, it promotes the release of adrenaline into the bloodstream and nervous system, which increases the pulse, the breathing rate, and sweating. If the sympathetic nervous system promotes energy expenditure, the *parasympathetic* nervous system promotes energy conservation and restoration by lowering heart rate and breathing rates and promoting digestion and restorative other functions. This happens when we feel relaxed and at times of day when we rest (such as late in the evening). Both systems are working to some degree all the time. When we are in homeostasis (see preceding discussion), the balance between their functioning in response to the environment is just right. It is thought that the two systems work in a complimentary fashion. This is the *opponent process* principle, which states that the end of a stimulus that excites the sympathetic nervous system causes an upsurge in the functioning of the parasympathetic nervous system. For example, a reporter who is covering a guerilla battle spends twenty minutes hearing bullets whizzing by within inches of his head, and he is in a continuous state of terror. In the moments after the fighting subsides, when he realizes that he is alive and safe, he experiences a feeling of tremendous happiness and peace.

Emotion, the Autonomic System, and the Effects of Perception and Cognition

The autonomic nervous system is not "acting alone" in creating our level of arousal and emotional reaction to stimuli. It is responding to signals from the command center—the central nervous system. The brain, in which our perception and interpretation of events in the environment takes place, has a crucial role. There have been three different theories offered over the past century to explain the interaction of the environment, the brain, and the autonomic nervous system.

- *Cannon-Bard theory.* The parts of the brain that process sensory information—such as the thalamus, send out two messages: one to the autonomic nervous system (to dictate the level of activation) and another set to the limbic system and cerebral cortex, so that the sensory message can be interpreted and the stimulus is responded to appropriately.
- *James-Lange theory.* This theory states that the emotional reaction begins in the cerebral cortex. We perceive and interpret a stimulus and an autonomic nervous system reaction is elicited. Our emotional reaction is based on our interpretation of our physical response (I am crying so I must be sad).
- *Schachter and Singer's two-factor theory.* This theory separates the physiological state from the emotion. The intensity is the degree of the sympathetic system arousal, but this does not determine the type of emotion we experience (you can be very excited because you are scared or because you are happy). The cerebral cortex makes the determination of which emotion we are feeling, by assessing the situation. The assessment of the situation comes before the autonomic response.

The Biological Basis of Emotion: The Face and the Limbic System

Recent research has linked the production and interpretation of powerful emotions such as fear or disgust to the *amygdala*. The amygdala appears to process information relative to several kinds of strong emotion intrapersonally (with the person who is experiencing them). If the amygdala is damaged, a person's ability to experience these feelings may be impaired. Damage to the amygdala also diminishes the ability to recognize the signs of these feelings in other people. There is evidence of a complex interaction between the *limbic system* and faces. Facial expression is a very old, very powerful, and constant form of human communication. If an individual has difficulty reacting to or interpreting facial expression, the result can be major social and psychological difficulty (Adolphs et al. 2002). Congenital (from before birth) damage to the amygdala has been linked to the development of the *autism spectrum disorders* (see Chapter 14).

Universal Basic Emotions

Psychologists believe there are six or more *basic emotions* that are innate and found across cultures, but there is still some disagreement about which emotions are the basic ones.
What is the evidence for the existence of basic emotions?

- *Facial Expressions.* Certain expressions are found in every culture (smiles, frowns, crying, etc.). These facial expressions are even produced by blind infants, so evidently the amount of imitation needed to produce them is minimal. In evolutionary time, as primates and hominids spent more time in an upright position, facial expression became a vital channel for communication of emotions. All people become more facially expressive in the presence of others. Facial expression is a more accurate way to gauge a person's feelings than what they say. With a little bit of training, anyone can learn to tell the difference between a "forced smile" (you make this smile for an obligatory school or social photograph—"say cheese!") and the natural smile of true delight, the *Duchenne smile* or D-smile, which involves much more pronounced action of the eye muscles. You would not produce a D-smile for a photographer unless you were being photographed in a moment of pure joy.
- *Cross-cultural Agreement.* Members of all world cultures readily and correctly identify basic emotions. People of different world cultures do not always agree on what an emotion is, but they *do* recognize the facial expressions associated with feelings with an amazing consistency.

What makes an emotion a basic emotion?

- It must be found in all world cultures.
- The biological processes that produce the emotion must be unique—occurring only for that particular emotion.
- The way it is expressed must be the same across all cultures—it must be communicated with the same unique facial expression by people in Minnesota or Mozambique.
- It must be present at birth or very shortly thereafter.

Representative Theories of Basic Emotion

Based on these criteria and their own evidence and hypotheses, several psychological scientists have proposed theories of basic emotion. Here are the emotions thought to be basic by two leading researchers in the field.

Paul Ekman (1992) has proposed the existence of six basic emotions:

Happiness
Sadness
Anger
Fear
Disgust
Surprise

Robert Plutchik (1997) proposed that there are eight basic emotions:

Acceptance
Anticipation
Anger
Disgust
Fear
Joy
Sadness
Surprise

These emotions are found across cultures. According to Plutchik, there are other emotions that result from blends of these eight, that are more complex and culture-specific. For example, disappointment would involve a combination of anticipation, sadness, and surprise.

Other Ways to Express Emotions

The face is a vital channel of emotional communication, but it is not the only one: Gestures, changes in vocal tone, and social context are all involved in the process of perception and interpretation of emotion. One reason that computers are far from mastering human speech has to do with the importance of gestures and vocal intonations. They are as important as the words we use because they add the colors of emotion to our meaning.

Theories of Stress

Before we discuss the two major theories of stress, let's clarify what we mean by the word "stress." *Stress* is a reaction that is caused by *stressors*. The stress response is the mental and physical response to challenges that we face in everyday life. Often the first sign that we are experiencing stress is the fight-or-flight reaction generated by the sympathetic division of the autonomic nervous system (recall Chapter 3). A stressor is anything that brings on the reaction of stress—a person, place, or event. If you have a psychology test tomorrow, and you are feeling uneasy, the test would correctly be labeled a stressor. Stress can be good (eustress), bad (distress), or "mixed"—an event can produce both types of stress. For example, the birth of a baby is often a joyous occasion for a family, but it may create new financial and practical difficulties that need to be managed as well.

Walter Cannon (1871–1945), the same psychologist who helped to create the Cannon-Bard theory of emotion (mentioned earlier) first formally described the fight-or-flight response. The reaction occurs in the sympathetic division of the autonomic nervous system. It mobilizes the body for action, usually in the face of stress.

This response was originally highly adaptive in the ancestral environment. Most stressors that we faced were of the short-term variety—they were *acute*. A predator, or a fight with another group of humans were stressors that would be over in a matter of minutes; either we escaped or we were eaten, we won or we were defeated and possibly killed. Although many of us have at some time in our lives found ourselves being drawn into a fight or followed by a person who intends to harm us, most modern stressors are very different. Many of the stressors we face are not life threatening, but they tend to go on indefinitely or occur on a regular basis (traffic jams, noise, financial difficulties). They are *chronic stressors*. Whether or not a modern stressor poses a threat to our life or health, our body produces the same fight or flight response. This may have some damaging consequences for us.

The General Adaptation Syndrome

Hans Selye (1907–1982) was an Austrian physician who developed a model for the possible effects of chronic stress on the body. He characterized stress as "the nonspecific response of the body to any demand made upon it" (Seyle 1979). The activation of the sympathetic nervous system has some predictable effects on the body. Activated by the hypothalamus and the pituitary gland, the adrenal glands secrete the hormone *adrenaline,* which functions both in body tissues and in the brain (as the neurotransmitter *epinephrine*) to promote increases in respiration, circulation, and other body functions that enhance strength and alertness. The body can recover easily from short activations of this powerful defense system.

Seyle's model is the general adaptation syndrome. The syndrome occurs in three stages: alarm, resistance, and exhaustion.

- The *alarm stage* is triggered when the individual encounters a threatening stimulus or situation. The alarm stage is a relatively short period of activation of the fight-or-flight response. If the threat is avoided, the stage ends, and the body returns to a more relaxed state.
- If the threat does not end, and the initial reaction turns into a prolonged state of stress, the *resistance stage* begins. This is a chronic, moderate state of activation. It cannot be kept up indefinitely.
- The *exhaustion stage* starts when the individual's energy and strength are used up as a result of maintaining a prolonged state of resistance. Seyle believed that vital resources were drained from the immune system, leaving the organism vulnerable to illness, fatigue, and injury.

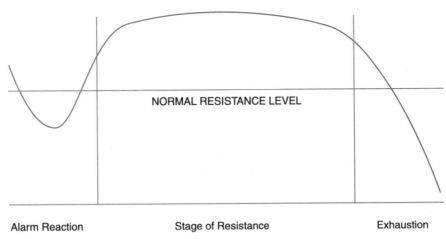

Figure 11.1 The General Adaptation Syndrome.

Change and Stress

Selye believed that changes in our lives lead to stress. One current widely used stress assessment, the Holmes and Rahe Life Change Stress Scale (Holmes and Rahe 1967), is based on this idea. This view has been criticized as limited, not recognizing that circumstances surrounding an event may dictate the level of stress it generates. A change can be for the better or the worse. Also, the effects of chronic conditions such as illness and poverty are not taken into account. One psychologist, Arnold Lazarus (b. 1922) challenged the change = stress model and presented an alternative perspective.

Lazarus' View of Stress

Arnold Lazarus and his son Clifford (Lazarus and Lazarus 1999) have written books for the general public about maintaining good mental health and techniques of stress management. In their view, the degree of stressfulness of any event depends upon:

- Our *appraisal* of the event—how relevant the event is to our well-being.
- The *resources* we have available for managing the stressor. If the impact of the event exceeds the psychological, physical, and material resources we possess, we may experience a great deal of stress in response to it.
- The nature of the other events in our lives—the other stressors that we are managing at the time.

Lazarus notes that the appraisal of stress is subjective (depends on the individual), so, outside of some extreme events and conditions that all would agree represent enormous sources of stress, the amount of stress that a person experiences, or even whether or not the person will experience stress in response to an event, depends on the individual. Lazarus has been influenced by the cognitive-behavioral school of psychotherapy, and his view reflects this. He believes that people can learn to reframe (change the way they think about events) and manage some stressors actively instead of shutting down and passively reacting to a threat.

The Stress-Illness Connection

Stress is an everyday part of life. If we had no stress at all, we would probably "die of boredom." Stress may have some benefits (see discussion that follows). So the question is then, how much is too much? It may depend on the context and the tasks we face (recall the Yerkes-Dodson law, reviewed in Chapter 10). It is not news that high levels of stress have some potential negative effects on performance and behavior. Research over the past decades has indicated that when people are highly stressed, their ability to remain focused—to keep fixed and steady attention—suffers.

Burnout is a phenomenon well known to stress researchers. Burnout is a syndrome (not considered to be a mental illness) that depresses mental and physical functioning and is usually the result of chronic work-related stress. Human services and medical professionals are most likely to report burnout, but it can happen to workers in any field.

Stress-Related Psychological Disorders

Traumatic stress is usually the result of exposure to events that are well beyond the usual levels of daily stress—such as witnessing a fatal car accident or surviving a violent crime. *Acute stress disorder (ASD)* and *posttraumatic stress disorder (PTSD)* are disorders that may follow such an experience. Acute stress disorder is diagnosed only in the first month after such an event, if a person manifests symptoms of depression or anxiety. If these symptoms persist or worsen beyond a month the individual is usually diagnosed with posttraumatic stress disorder. Commonly reported symptoms include: *flashbacks* (vivid memories of the traumatic event), overwhelming panic and other strong emotional outbursts, chronic tension, guilt (for survivors of mass tragedies—"why did I survive while others died?"), and nightmares. Although the symptoms of ASD and PTSD (in the wake of war and other mass tragedy) have been recorded in history and literature for centuries, PTSD began to receive greater attention from psychologists and physicians in the mid-twentieth century when Vietnam War veterans and rape survivors came forward to report their symptoms and seek treatment. Not everyone who survives a traumatic event develops ASD or PTSD, so there are still questions about the causes of these disorders. Having a history of mental health disorders or previous life trauma appears to raise an individual's vulnerability, so it may be a matter of having one's psychological resources already too severely taxed.

Psychosomatic Illness

People often become confused when trying to understand what a psychosomatic illness is. It is neither an imaginary nor a faked illness. When a person pretends to have an illness to avoid consequences if they were healthy, or to get money, it is referred to as *malingering*. If they fake the illness just to get attention, it is called a *factitious disorder*. *Psychosomatic illnesses* are real physical illnesses caused by psychological or emotional distress.

If no other cause can be found, and malingering and factitious disorders have been ruled out, the person is said to be suffering from a psychosomatic illness. Certain disorders appear to be more likely to be psychosomatic—skin diseases, ulcers, and allergies are examples. Evidence suggests that some people may have a family history (therefore a genetic predisposition) to psychosomatic illness. If untreated, some psychosomatic disorders can lead to serious, chronic, life-threatening conditions—cardiovascular disease, asthma, stroke, and many others may possibly develop or worsen.

How Does Stress Cause Illness?

It is not clear that stress is actually capable of "causing" illness, although evidence of a connection between the nervous system and the immune system has been growing. *Psychoneuroimmunology* is the term for the study of this connection (see "What's Happening" at the end of the chapter). In some ways, the connection is probably an indirect one. Psychologists have recently identified the "nocebo" effect. When people have negative beliefs—whether they have adopted a pessimistic attitude, or have had a "curse" placed on them—often their behavior is subtly affected. They don't take care of themselves and their own negative expectations lead to deterioration in occupational performance, interpersonal relationships, and self-care. Sometimes when people are under a great deal of stress, they start to make destructive lifestyle choices—lousy nutrition, drug abuse, poor sleep, and lack of exercise. These are all established contributors to poor health in the short term and premature death in the long term. Lack of attentiveness to one's health maintenance is another possible contributor. If you develop a serious illness—cancer, for example—the sooner you are diagnosed, the better. Ignoring the symptoms, failing to perform self-examinations, and putting off doctor's visits may be additional ways that a person's life stress ends up further compromising health—lowering the chances of effective treatment and a good prognosis.

The Type A—Heart Disease Connection

In the late 1950s and early 1960s, two cardiologists (Meyer Friedman and Raymond Rosenman) performed correlational research comparing men who developed heart disease and those who did not (Friedman and Rosenman, 1974). They hypothesized a link between personality type and likelihood of developing heart disease. *Type A personality* describes a very competitive, hard driving, success-oriented person. *Type B personality* designates those who are easygoing, mellow, and not entirely focused on work and success. In the decades since, the link between high-intensity disposition and heart disease has not consistently been borne out, with one exception. When the Type A person also has a hostile attitude, the risk of heart disease does appear to increase significantly. Still it is important not to overstate the relationship, especially because the research is correlational and therefore inappropriate for determination of cause. Lifestyle factors and genetics are far more important in raising or lowering one's risk of cardiovascular illness. It is not even clear that any person is a consistent Type A or Type B—a common criticism of personality trait theory, which we will explore in Chapter 13.

Stress and Coping Strategies

Stress is evitable, so strategies are necessary for managing it. We refer to various tactics for managing, eliminating, or tolerating stress under the general term *coping*. There are many coping strategies, some very effective, and some less so. In this section, we will try to categorize them broadly and to discuss the strengths and weaknesses of each general type.

It helps in developing any stress management program to remember that stress is necessary and may even be good for us, in small to moderate doses. The only time our lives are truly stress-free is when they are over. As we saw in Chapter 10, a certain level of arousal is needed for good performance on a wide variety of tasks. When we feel mildly stressed by the prospect of a test, we may be motivated to study more, and do better. When we are faced with mild to moderate stressors, and can master them, we increase our own feelings of competence—in other words, the mastery of stress can be good for our self-esteem.

Some people appear to be better at managing their stress than others. What qualities and circumstances can help us to become better at the art of coping?

- *Attitude.* Individuals who tolerate stress well tend to keep a positive attitude and work actively to achieve the most desirable outcome. They are not blindly optimistic, but they do tend to try to find ways to "make the best of the situation." Stress researchers refer to *hardiness* (Maddi & Kobasa 1984) as a trait that is associated with good coping and stress resistance. A person who has this trait feels challenged, rather than threatened, by most stressors. As a result, he or she may make more positive appraisals, which, according to Lazarus (see previous discussion), does have an impact on the level of stress experienced.
- *Social support.* Some relationships may be sources of stress, but overall, people who tolerate stress well tend to have networks of friends and family to provide assistance, advice, and comfort.

The following strategies are considered to be *constructive coping methods*. Constructive coping is considered to be adaptive, meaning that it not only relieves stress to some extent but also improves the psychological adjustment of the person who is dealing with a stressor. In constructive coping, the individual

- Evaluates the stressor realistically.
- Confronts the stressor directly.
- Manages strong emotional reactions to the situation.
- Controls or changes any potentially harmful behavioral reactions.

Constructive Coping Strategies

Some active, constructive coping methods follow:

- *Taking effective action* when the stressor or problem has a clear solution. If you have a test next week, you don't need to hire a PhD to tell you to hit the books.
- *Systematic problem solving* when the solution is not clear. Problem solving usually includes the following steps:
  - Defining the problem.
  - Brainstorming—think of as many possible strategies as possible, without worrying about how effective or realistic they might be.
  - Assessing each strategy and choosing the one that seems best.
  - Trying the strategy out, remaining open to revising the strategy if necessary.
- *Seeking social support* can provide great relief. Make time to talk to a friend, a trusted family member, or a counselor. Support groups are often available that address specific chronic stressors—illness, death in the family, and so on.
- *Reframing the problem* is a skill that is associated with hardiness (see previous discussion). Learning to see the problem a different way, or to see possible positive aspects of what seemed to be a negative situation, can be very helpful in overcoming stressors. "When one door closes, another opens."

Active strategies may be less than constructive. Lashing out or blaming others, for example, has long had an undeserved reputation for being a stress reliever (based on Freud's notion of *catharsis* or venting painful emotions, thoughts, and experiences.) But evidence suggests that allowing one's self to express anger just leads to increased anger, rather than relief (Tavris 1983). And an apparent connection between hostile attitudes and cardiovascular illness (see earlier discussion) makes this an even less desirable stress management tactic.

Some methods are less active but are still considered constructive. When would such methods be adaptive? When there truly is nothing you can do—if you are traveling cross country and your connecting flight is canceled, besides making arrangements to spend the night in a motel at the airline's expense, there is little you can do. Buy a pizza, turn on the TV, and try to enjoy the free lodging.

The following are constructive methods of coping for such nonnegotiable problems. You can see that they involve distraction from the problem rather than direct engagement.

- *Relaxation*—meditation techniques (see Chapter 5) or simply spending some quiet, alone time listening to music or writing in a journal to clarify one's thoughts.
- *Exercise*—physical activity not only provides a channel for focusing one's attention away from a problem but also has health benefits that can improve stress tolerance.
- *Hobbies/other pursuits*—anything from going to the movies or going fishing to coaching a children's sports team to take the focus off of one's own problems and create positive emotions.
- *Humor*—unless there are severe, life-and-death consequences (and sometimes even if there are) trying to find something to laugh at is a very good way to alleviate stress.

As is the case with the active strategies, more passive, distraction-oriented strategies are not necessarily effective. Distracting one's self with a huge shopping spree or a drinking binge can have more stress-inducing consequences later on. Simply giving up, used as a consistent strategy (sometimes called *learned helplessness* by psychologists), can lead to despair and clinical depression (Seligman 1992). Self-blame in mild doses may lead to greater understanding of how one's actions may have made a stressful situation worse, but in large doses it can lead to a feeling of hopelessness or be used as an excuse simply to give up.

Connecting Through Chapter Review

WORD-STUDY CONNECTION

Write each of these words on index cards and write their definitions on the opposite side.

acute stress disorder (ASD)
acute stressors
adrenaline
alarm stage
amygdala
appraisal
autism spectrum disorders
autonomic nervous system
basic emotions
burnout
Cannon-Bard theory
catharsis
chronic stressors
constructive coping methods

coping
Duchenne smile
emotions
epinephrine
exhaustion stage
factitious disorder
fight-or-flight reaction
flashbacks
general adaptation syndrome
hardiness
James-Lange theory
learned helplessness
limbic system
malingering
opponent process

parasympathetic
posttraumatic stress disorder (PTSD)
psychoneuroimmunology
psychosomatic illnesses
reframing
resistance stage
resources
social support
stress
stressor
sympathetic
two-factor theory
Type A personality
Type B personality

SELF-TEST CONNECTION

PART A. Completion
Write in the word that correctly completes each statement.

1. _____ is a physiological change and conscious feelings of pleasantness or unpleasantness.
2. The _____ nervous system regulates the functioning of internal organs and vital bodily processes.
3. After a fight-or-flight response, the _____ promotes energy conservation and restoration by lowering heart rate and breathing rates.

4. The _____ states that the end of a stimulus that excites the sympathetic nervous system causes an upsurge in the functioning of the parasympathetic nervous system.

5. The _____ theory of emotion suggests that we feel emotion after we notice our physiological arousal.

6. _____ and _____ believe that the cognitive labels that individuals put on their arousal is essential to the emotional experience.

7. An emotion is a(n) _____ emotion if it is found in all world cultures.

8. Stress that tends to be good is referred to as _____ .

9. _____ developed the general adaptation syndrome.

10. In the general adaptation syndrome, if the threat does not end and the initial reaction turns into a prolonged state of stress, the _____ stage begins.

11. Selye believed that _____ in our lives lead to stress, or _____ = stress.

12. Lazarus and Lazarus believe that the degree of stressfulness of any event depends upon the _____ of the event, the _____ we have available for managing the stressor, and the _____ in our lives.

13. Burnout is usually the result of _____ .

14. If symptoms of depression or anxiety persist or worsen beyond a month after experiencing traumatic stress, the individual is usually diagnosed with _____ .

15. To be diagnosed with _____ , malingering and factitious disorders have to be ruled out first.

16. _____ personality describes a very competitive, hard-driving, success-oriented person.

17. _____ is considered to be adaptive and also improves the psychological adjustment of the person who is dealing with a stressor.

18. _____ is one means of constructive coping in which an individual talks to a friend, trusted family member, or a counselor.

19. Learning to see the problem a different way, or to see possible positive aspects of what seemed to be a negative situation, is referred to as _____ .

20. _____ developed the notion of catharsis.

21. More recent evidence suggests that allowing one's self to express anger leads to _____ anger, rather than relief.

22. One technique for nonnegotiable problems is _____ , which can involve meditation, quiet or alone time, or writing in a journal.

PART B. Multiple Choice
Circle the letter of the item that correctly completes the statement.

1. The _____ nervous system and _____ nervous system are the two subdivisions of the autonomic system and work in opposition to each other.
   - (a) brain; spinal
   - (b) sympathetic; parasympathetic
   - (c) skeletal; somatic
   - (d) central; peripheral

2. The _____ nervous system is an "activation system."
   - (a) sympathetic
   - (b) parasympathetic
   - (c) autonomic
   - (d) limbic

3. Which of the following is *not* one of the three theories offered over the past century to explain the interaction of the environment, the brain, and the autonomic nervous system on emotion?
   - (a) James-Lange theory
   - (b) Schachter and Singer's two-factor theory
   - (c) Cannon-Bard theory
   - (d) Maslow's one-trait theory

4. The _____ processes information relative to several kinds of strong intrapersonal emotion.
   - (a) prefrontal cortex
   - (b) amygdala
   - (c) pituitary gland
   - (d) thalamus

5. Which of the following is *not* a basic emotion, according to Ekman?
   - (a) Disgust
   - (b) Annoyance
   - (c) Surprise
   - (d) Anger

6. Which of the following is *not* a potential stressor?
   - (a) Person
   - (b) Event
   - (c) Place
   - (d) All are potential stressors.

7. Who first formally described the fight-or-flight response, which occurs in the sympathetic division of the autonomic nervous system?
   - (a) Lange
   - (b) Cannon
   - (c) James
   - (d) Bard

8. Why was the fight-or-flight response originally highly adaptive in the ancestral environment?
   - (a) Stress was acute.
   - (b) Our ancestors did not understand stress.
   - (c) Stress was chronic.
   - (d) Our ancestors had no stress.

9. Which of the following is *not* one of the three stages of the general adaptation syndrome?
   - (a) Alarm
   - (b) Panic
   - (c) Resistance
   - (d) Exhaustion

10. When an individual's energy and strength are used up as a result of maintaining a prolonged state of resistance, the person enters the _____ stage of the general adaptation model in which the organism is vulnerable to illness, fatigue, and injury.
    - (a) Alarm
    - (b) Panic
    - (c) Resistance
    - (d) Exhaustion

11. According to Lazarus and Lazarus, which of the following will effect stressfulness of an event?
    - (a) Appraisal
    - (b) Time of day when the event occurs
    - (c) Change
    - (d) Season of when the event occurs

12. Lazarus believes that people can learn to _____ (change the way they think about events) and manage some stressors actively instead of shutting down and passively reacting to a threat.
    - (a) reselect
    - (b) reframe
    - (c) return
    - (d) remove

13. _____ is diagnosed in the first month after such a traumatic event, if a person manifests symptoms of depression or anxiety.
    - (a) Chronic stress disorder
    - (b) Posttraumatic stress disorder
    - (c) Stress-induced illness
    - (d) Acute stress disorder

14. Which of the following is *not* a commonly reported symptom of PTSD?
    (a) Overeating   (b) Guilt
    (c) Flashback   (d) Panic
15. When a healthy person pretends to have an illness to avoid consequences or to get money, it is referred to as _____ .
    (a) factitious   (b) psychosomatic
    (c) malingering   (d) None of the above
16. Which of the following is more likely to be psychosomatic?
    (a) cancer   (b) HIV
    (c) stroke   (d) skin diseases
17. _____ personality designates those who are easygoing, mellow, and not entirely focused on work and success.
    (a) Type A   (b) Type B
    (c) Type C   (d) Type D
18. When the Type A person also has _____ , the risk of heart disease does appear to increase significantly.
    (a) a hostile attitude   (b) high blood pressure
    (c) bipolar disorder   (d) a Type B personality
19. Which of the following is generally associated with better coping?
    (a) Positive attitude   (b) Social support
    (c) Low stress   (d) Both a and b
20. Which of the following is *not* a characteristic of constructive coping of a stressor?
    (a) Direct confrontation (b) Realistic evaluation
    (c) Managed emotions   (d) All of the above are characteristics.
21. What is the first step in systematic problem solving?
    (a) Defining the problem (b) Trying out new strategies
    (c) Brainstorming   (d) Assessing strategies
22. Which is an example of social support seeking?
    (a) Going for a long walk (b) Talking to a friend
    (c) Taking a nap   (d) All of the above
23. With what trait is reframing the problem associated?
    (a) Hardiness   (b) Problem solving
    (c) Kindness   (d) Changing your attitude
24. Which of the following is constructive for non-negotiable problems?
    (a) Relaxation   (b) Problem solving
    (c) Reframing   (d) Taking effective action
25. Which of the following is *not* constructive for nonnegotiable problems?
    (a) Humor   (b) Exercise
    (c) Hobbies   (d) Catharsis

PART C. Modified True-False

If the statement is true, write "T" for the answer. If the statement is incorrect, change the underlined expression to one that will make the statement true.

1. Emotions <u>are</u> the opposite of thought and reason.
2. <u>Sympathetic nervous system</u> prepares the body for "fight" or "flight" when we experience feelings of fear or anger.

3. The <u>Cannon-Bard theory</u> of emotion suggests that we feel emotions at the same time that we experience physiological arousal.

4. Certain <u>spoken</u> expressions are found in every culture.

5. Anticipation and <u>anger</u> are two emotions that Plutchik believes are basic emotions, but Ekman does not.

6. The <u>stress response</u> is the physical and mental response to challenges that we face in everyday life.

7. Stress that is considered "bad" is also referred to as <u>eustress</u>.

8. The fight-or-flight response, which mobilizes the body for action, occurs in the <u>parasympathetic</u> division of the autonomic nervous system.

9. Many of the stressors we face are considered to be <u>acute</u> stressors, as they are not life threatening, but they tend to go on indefinitely or occur on a regular basis.

10. The <u>resistance</u> stage of the general adaptation syndrome model is triggered when the individual encounters a threatening stimulus or situation.

11. The <u>resources we have for an event</u> refers to how relevant the event is to our well-being.

12. <u>Burnout</u> is a syndrome that depresses mental and physical functioning and is usually the result of chronic work-related stress.

13. Someone who has been held up at gunpoint is likely to experience <u>chronic</u> stress.

14. PTSD began to receive greater attention from psychologists and physicians in the twentieth century following the <u>Korean War</u>.

15. A <u>psychosomatic</u> illness occurs when someone fakes being sick to get attention.

16. The <u>placebo</u> effect can occur when people have adopted a pessimistic attitude and they don't take care of themselves, which leads to deterioration in occupational performance, interpersonal relationships, and self-care.

17. <u>Friedman</u> and <u>Rosenman</u>, two cardiologists, compared men who developed heart disease with those who did not and hypothesized a link between personality type and likelihood of developing heart disease.

18. <u>Coping</u> refers to the various tactics for managing, eliminating, or tolerating stress.

19. <u>Resistance</u> refers to a trait that is associated with good coping and stress resistance and is characterized by feeling challenged, rather than threatened, by most stressors.

20. In <u>destructive</u> coping, the individual controls or changes any potentially harmful behavioral reactions.

21. <u>Brainstorming</u>, an aspect of systematic problem solving, involves thinking of as many possible strategies as possible, without worrying about how effective or realistic they might be.

22. When the stressor or problem has a clear solution, it is a good idea to <u>take effective action</u>.

23. Freud's notion of the <u>unconscious</u> refers to venting painful emotions, thoughts, and experiences.

24. For nonnegotiable problems, <u>attention to</u> the problem is more constructive than direct engagement.

25. <u>Engaging in a distracting hobby</u> is a constructive form of coping for nonnegotiable problems, except when there are severe, life and death consequences.

PART D. Matching

Place the name of the concept related to thinking next to correct example of that concept.

Biological Basis of Emotions and Stress

autonomic nervous system   adrenaline   cerebral cortex
opponent process theory   thalamus   amygdala
sympathetic nervous system   limbic system   homeostasis
parasympathetic nervous system

1. This system regulates internal organs and bodily systems. _____
2. This peripheral nervous system subdivision activates the body during strong emotion and stress. _____
3. In this state, the body's response to the environment is balanced. _____
4. This hormone is released into the bloodstream in response to stress. _____
5. The peripheral nervous system subdivision that relaxes the body and conserves energy. _____
6. The principle that certain bodily systems work together in a complimentary fashion. _____
7. The inner part of the brain that generates drives and emotions. _____
8. Damage to this part of the limbic system may interfere with the ability to recognize facial expressions and emotions of others. _____
9. This part of the brain determines which emotion we are experiencing by assessing the situation, according to the two-factor theory of emotion. _____
10. The part of the brain that processes sensory information. _____

Theories of Emotions and Stress

Cannon-Bard theory   Nocebo effect   James-Lange theory
two-factor theory   Ekman's theory   Lazarus's theory
fight-or-flight theory   Type A/Type B   Plutchik's theory
general adaptation syndrome

1. Our emotional reaction is determined by our brain's interpretation of our physical response. _____
2. There are six basic universal emotions: Happiness, sadness, anger, fear, disgust, and surprise. _____
3. The intensity of a stressor is determined in part by the individual's appraisal of its significance. _____
4. The major aspects of emotion are its intensity and our assessment of which one is being experienced. _____
5. Stress originates in the sympathetic nervous system, which prepares the body for action. _____
6. There are eight basic emotions and many others that are a combination of the blending of these. _____
7. The parts of the brain that process sensory information activate the autonomic nervous system, the limbic system, and the cerebral cortex. _____
8. Personality traits dictate reaction to stress; one style may lead to heart disease. _____

9. There are three stages of reaction to chronic stress: alarm, resistance, and exhaustion. _____

10. Negative beliefs can influence behavior and worsen the effects of stress. _____

Which Type of Coping Is It?

humor   relaxation   reframing
hobby   giving up   social support
hardiness   effective action   exercise
systematic problem solving

1. Sam held a brainstorming session to find solutions with his co-workers when his department's profit margin appeared to be dropping. _____

2. Jane spends more time at the women's club when she is not at the hospital with her mom who is being treated for cancer. _____

3. Albert tries to see the funny side, even when things are going badly for him. _____

4. Meg tends to see obstacles as challenges. _____

5. Yuki goes for long walks in a quiet park when she feels stressed out. _____

6. John is taking the medical school admissions test in three months and he has started studying for it at least one hour per day. _____

7. Letisha realizes that getting laid off from her job allows her more time to find a new and better one. _____

8. Instead of blowing up at his annoying office mate, Gerald goes to the gym for an hour. _____

9. While he is waiting for his standardized test results, John joins a club that builds and races remote-controlled cars. _____

10. After being rejected by four different girls for a prom date, Murray just quits trying. _____

CONNECTING TO CONCEPTS

Review the chapter and then write down your thoughts about the following questions.

1. List and describe the different theories that explain how the brain and body generate emotion. Which theory do you believe is most accurate in explaining the processes of emotion?

2. Compare and contrast Ekman and Plutchik's theories of emotion. Discuss the ways in which culture influences the rules for emotional expression.

3. Describe the stages of the general adaptation theory. Give an example of an incident in which your fight-or-flight response was a help to you, and another incident in which it made it more difficult for you to function.

4. To what extent do you think change creates stress? To what extent do you believe that a person's appraisal of a stressor matters in determining the level of stress experienced?

5. List the major coping strategies reviewed in this section. Which ones do you tend to use? Why?

CONNECTING TO LIFE/JOB SKILLS

Emotional Intelligence

Dr. Daniel Goleman, though not the originator of the idea of "EQ" or emotional intelligence, has been traveling the world over the past decade, promoting the concept of a separate form of intelligence—emotional intelligence, which is the ability to detect and understand one's own emotions, as well as those of others. (It is similar to a combination of Gardner's interpersonal and intrapersonal types from the multiple intelligences theory.)

Having read the chapter, you are now aware that emotions are important information. They only interfere with our ability to think and act rationally when they are strong and uncontrolled. An understanding of emotional reactions may be useful in many situations for effective social functioning, good leadership, and adequate performance in a variety of group tasks. Some level of emotional awareness appears to be necessary for good decision making. For these reasons, emotional intelligence training is growing in popularity in the world of business. In some companies, it is a trait more valued by management than traditional "cognitive" intelligence. At one of the web sites listed here, you can find information about tests that are being developed to determine a person's EQ level. How valid are these assessments? It is probably too early to tell.

Besides the business applications, training for parents, teachers, and students is becoming popular also. You can find a great deal of information about EQ on the internet. Here are some starting points:

EMOTIONS AND EMOTIONAL INTELLIGENCE

trochim.human.cornell.edu/gallery/young/emotion.htm#what%20is%20EI

EQ INTERNATIONAL SITE

eqi.org/

CONSORTION FOR RESEARCH ON EMOTIONAL INTELLIGENCE

www.eiconsortium.org/

6 SECONDS EMOTIONAL INTELLIGENCE NETWORK

www.6seconds.org/

WHAT'S HAPPENING!

Psychoneuroimmunology

The new multidisciplinary field of psychoneuroimmunology was mentioned briefly in the chapter. Because stress appears to lead to illness in people, a link has been suspected for a long time. But there was no evidence for any direct somatic connection, and at first psychoneuroimmunology was greeted with an understandable skepticism. The link was thought to be behavioral (that is, a lifestyle issue rather than a biological one).

Through improved medical technology and research, there now is a growing body of evidence that the central nervous system and the immune system are linked. They communicate with and influence each other. If this is true, then stress and other nervous system reactions may have a direct impact on immune system functioning. Nothing about the connection defies known principles of biopsychology. It is thought that the two systems communicate through the flow of neurotransmitters and hormones.

Here are some web sites to introduce you to this relatively new field of investigation. In the next few years, we should know how direct and powerful the connection between stress, the brain, and health actually are, and perhaps this will yield some very useful information in combating the negative health effects of chronic stress.

PSYCHONEUROIMMUNOLOGY RESEARCH SOCIETY

www.pnirs.org/

PSYCHONEUROIMMUNOLOGY RESOURCES ON THE INTERNET

www.msu.edu/user/chenhao/pniweb.htm

PSYCHNET-UK: PSYCHONEUROIMMUNOLOGY

www.psychnet-uk.com/pni/pni.htm

OTHER USEFUL WEB SITES

BASIC EMOTIONS

www.personalityresearch.org/basicemotions.html

The basic emotions theories are reviewed at this web site.

FACIAL ANALYSIS

mambo.ucsc.edu/psl/fanl.html

This web site includes historical and current information and links related to the various perspectives on studying facial expressions.

THE AMERICAN INSTITUTE OF STRESS

www.stress.org/

This useful information is provided by a nonprofit organization dedicated to studying and reducing the negative effects of stress in our lives.

FACT SHEET ON STRESS

www.nmha.org/infoctr/factsheets/41.cfm

This wonderful fact sheet provided by National Mental Health Association.

THE MEDICAL BASIS OF STRESS

www.teachhealth.com/

This is a commercial site, but it does include accurate and useful information on stress and health in a very easy-to-read format.

STRESS AT WORK

www.cdc.gov/niosh/stresswk.html

This web site provides information about work stress and wellness courtesy of the CDC and the National Institute for Occupational Safety and Health.

REFERENCES

Adolphs, R., Baron-Cohen, S. & Tranel, D. (2002) Impaired recognition of social emotions following amygdala damage. *Journal of Cognitive Neuroscience,* 14(8), 1264–1274.

Friedman, M. & Rosenman, R. F. (1974) *Type A Behavior and Your Heart.* New York: Knopf.

Ekman, P. (1992) An argument for basic emotions. *Cognition and Emotion,* 6, 169–200.

Holmes, T. K. & Rahe, R. H. (1967). Holmes-Rahe life changes scale. *Journal of Psychosomatic Research,* 11, 213–218.

Lazarus, A. & Lazarus, C. (1999) *The 60-Second Shrink.* New York: Barnes and Noble Books.

Maddi, S. R. & Kobasa, S. C. (1984) *The Hardy Executive: Health Under Stress.* Homewood, IL: Dow Jones-Irwin.

Plutchik, R. (1997) *Psychology and Biology of Emotion.* Boston: Addison-Wesley.

Seligman, M. (1992) *Helplessness.* New York: Freeman.

Seyle, H. (1979) Stress, cancer and the mind. In J. Tache, H. Seyle & S. B. Day (Eds.), *Stress, Cancer and Death* (11–27) New York: Plenum.

Tavris, C. (1983) *Anger: The Misunderstood Emotion.* New York: Simon and Schuster.

Chapter 12

SOCIAL PSYCHOLOGY

In this chapter you will review the influence that individuals have upon each other's attitudes, thoughts, and behaviors in the context of relationships and groups.

A Note About the Role of Culture

In all social and personality psychology research, it is important to be aware of cultural differences. Although there are more similarities than differences between humans across all cultures, the differences that exist should not be dismissed as trivial. The discrepancies between values and attitudes in cultures often affect the way people interpret their own feelings, motives, and behaviors as well as those of others.

One difference to note is orientation to individual or collective values. People who are brought up in Western cultures or cultures heavily influenced by Western values (the United States is a good example) often view behavior as generated by the individual, arising from the individual's feelings, needs, character, and abilities. A young adult in America is more likely to attribute her accomplishments to the need to be successful for her own sake and to attribute her success to "talent." A young adult in a more collectivistic culture (such as Japan) is more likely to be concerned about how his success reflects on his family, co-workers, and the company for which he works and to acknowledge the contributions of these groups to his success. It is most likely true that any person's behavior is influenced by a combination of individual and external influences; we are simply noting a fundamental difference in perspective that will come up from time to time in the next two chapters and should be kept in mind.

Attributions, Attitudes, and Persuasion

As soon as we are old enough to have a theory of mind, we begin trying to explain why other people do what they do. *Attribution theory* is a framework for understanding how people explain the others' behavior as well as their own. It emerged in the mid-twentieth century out of the work of several social psychologists working independently (see "Other Useful Web Sites" at the end of this section).

An *attribution*, in social psychology, is an explanation for the cause of behavior. Attributions are either stable or unstable (making reference to a permanent or temporary condition) and internal or external (related to the person or the situation). So if you say,

He's dishonest	You've made a stable, internal attribution
He's in a bad mood	You've made an unstable, internal attribution
He lives in a rough neighborhood	You've made a stable, external attribution
He is having a bad day	You've made an unstable, external attribution

Some social psychologists call internal attributions *dispositional* and external attributions *situational*. According to one of the founders of attribution theory (Kelley 1967), in order to make an attribution, we compare people's behavior to that of other individuals (Kelley called this *consensus*), evaluate how *consistent* their behavior is over time, and how similar it is to their behavior in other situations—in other words, how *distinctive* it is. Often we (in individualistic cultures) tend to prefer to use dispositional attributions to situational ones in explaining the behavior of others, ignoring the power the situation can have to influence action. This tendency is referred to as the *fundamental attribution error*. At the same time, we are more likely to use situational attributions, or unstable internal attributions, to explain our own behavior—especially to relieve ourselves of responsibility—a form of social cognitive bias called the *actor-observer effect*. Consider the following examples:

- I won the racquetball match because I am a talented player and practice hard.
- He lost the racquetball match because he was too lazy and arrogant to practice.
- I lost the club championship because the floors had just been waxed and I couldn't settle into a decent stance.

These are examples of *self-serving biases* or self-enhancement strategies that will help us understand common tendencies in attributional style, especially in individualistic cultures. We usually need to see our performance and behavior in the best possible light. We will frame our relationship to other people and groups according to this tendency also. We *bask in reflected glory* (BIRG) when our home team wins. (*We* won!) And we *cut off reflected failure* (CORF) when the same team loses (*They* lost.) We tend to overestimate how accurate our judgments and beliefs are, how many people agree with our opinions, and how many people would behave the same way as we do, especially when we violate moral standards ("everyone lies about their kids' ages to save money at the movies). Finally, most people adhere to the *just world hypothesis*. This is the belief that "what goes around comes around." If we could sit and systematically tally the good and bad deeds that each person has committed, and the good fortune and misfortune that befell each person, we would soon see that (besides the logical consequences of some behaviors) there is no "just world." It gives us a feeling a control to think that there is a connection, and also helps us feel safe when we encounter reports of crime, accidents, and other frightening possibilities.

Attitudes and Persuasion

Everyone knows what an *attitude* is—it is your feeling toward a person, thing, or issue. One of the most interesting and widely applied areas of social psychology theory concerns how people develop attitudes and how methods of *persuasion* are used to alter them. In business (especially marketing), political science, and many other areas, this knowledge is especially useful and important.

How We Change Our Own Attitudes

We tend to assume that our attitudes dictate our behaviors, but a clever series of experiments done in the 1950s and 1960s showed that this may not always be the case; in fact, our behaviors are equally capable of influencing our attitudes. In 1959, Leon Festinger and his associate James Carlsmith were able to induce a majority of college students in his study sample to change their attitudes toward a boring task simply by underpaying them to do it. When the students received a generous payment ($20.00), they remained fixed in their opinion that the task was boring, but if they received only a small payment ($1.00) they were more likely to say the task was "fun" and "interesting." Festinger and Carlsmith inferred that the students would have a hard time admitting to themselves that they had spent close to an hour doing something so tedious for so little money (placing them in a state that he referred to as *cognitive dissonance*). To relieve their own dissonance, they changed their attitudes toward the task—the more we have to suffer for something, the more we are inclined to like it. A number of interesting replications of the original experiment suggest that cognitive dissonance occurs frequently in everyday life and is managed through changes in attitude. Cognitive dissonance does not operate uniformly across cultures (Iyengar & Brockner 2001). The fact that individualistic cultures tend to value the power of choice or control makes it more likely to occur in this cultural context (in the Festinger and Carlsmith experiment—"I chose to do this because it was fun").

How Others Change Our Attitudes

Social psychologist Robert Cialdini (1993) is one of the foremost experts on types of persuasion and how to resist them. Generally, persuasion goes in one of two directions.

- If you do change your mind or comply with a request, the results will be good. Most commercial products are advertised as tools to help you improve your life—think of ads for diets and fitness equipment.
- If you change your mind, or comply with a request, you will prevent something bad from happening. (Consider "scare tactics"—a good example would be ads for home protection systems. Chain letters—in the mail or on the internet—also use this strategy.)

Cialdini has identified six common dynamics that can be effectively used in the art of persuasion.

- *Reciprocity, or reciprocation.* If you give something to a person you are trying to influence, they will be more willing to give something back to you. (Think of the free samples of food that are distributed at supermarkets and bulk stores.)

- *Social proof.* Think of this as a kind of peer pressure. If we look around and see those whom we perceive as similar to us doing something, we are more likely to do the same. (Laugh tracks are employed during the taping of comedy shows to influence us to laugh.)
- *Liking or attractiveness.* Those people we find likeable or attractive are more likely to influence us. (Just think about all the attractive models of both sexes used to sell products.)
- *Scarcity.* Products become more desirable when they appear to be in short supply. (Many advertisements end with the statement "for a limited time only!")
- *Authority.* We are more likely to be influenced by those we perceive as being powerful or knowledgeable. (Many celebrities appear in advertisements, right?)
- *Consistency.* We tend to act in a manner consistent with our previously expressed opinions and actions. (If you buy a particular brand of computer, you may find yourself telling your friends why it is the best brand on the market.)

Here are some other common techniques of persuasion described by Cialdini and others:

- *The foot-in-the-door technique.* First, a small or reasonable request is made, followed by a larger one.
- *The door-in-the-face technique.* First, a completely inappropriate or outrageous request is made, so that the less outrageous one that follows seems very small indeed.
- *The that's-not-all technique.* Additional goods or services are added to the offer before we agree to buy or sign the contract.
- *The bait-and-switch technique.* First, a very attractive offer is made, but before the deal is closed, additional demands are made in order to secure the price or goods.

Persuasive messages sometimes work directly and immediately, and sometimes have an effect later on. The *sleeper effect* occurs when a message is rejected, at first, but later works to change the attitude of the person who hears it. Similarly, the few who hold a minority opinion in a social setting may move on long before their opinion actually begins to influence the majority, but it may very well do this over the long term. (This is called *minority influence.*)

One weakness of research on the manipulation of attitudes and methods of persuasion stems from the fact that the data are usually collected by survey methods. As we saw in Chapter 1, surveys can be very weak sources of information. People don't always answer truthfully or carefully, or may not even know how they actually feel about an issue.

Interpersonal Attraction

Our most important set of attitudes concerns those people whom we like and care about. What draws us to the people who become our friends and intimate companions? Social psychology research has identified the following factors as important in the process of creating interpersonal attraction:

- *Similarity.* We like people who are like us, similar in culture/socioeconomic background, values, and interests.
- *Reciprocity of feeling.* We like people who like us.

- *Nearness or proximity.* As we grow more familiar, we tend to eventually become friends with people who live nearby, work with us, or go to school with us.
- *The mere exposure effect.* Given that our initial reaction is neutral or positive, the more often we interact with another person, the more we will start to like him or her. If we dislike or hate the person, the feeling will not change with further exposure. This effect is called the *primacy effect*—a strong first impression is hard to change.
- *Social exchange theory.* We seek people with whom we can establish a roughly equal interpersonal exchange—each person giving something to the relationship as well as taking.

The Role of Physical Attraction

People tend to downplay their interest in and admiration for attractive people, but it appears to be true that both men and women value physical attractiveness in intimate partners and, to a lesser extent, friends. Attractive people have more social influence (see earlier discussion) and tend to be treated better in almost all situations. Evolutionary psychologists have proposed, based on biological theory and cross-cultural research, that attractiveness may be taken as a signal that an individual is healthy and has good genes. Although some details of attractiveness vary across cultures and may have some relationship to affluence (for example, larger bodied women tend to be considered more appealing than very thin women in cultures where resources are more scarce, while the opposite is true in affluent societies), the relationship to health and fertility is probably real. Research on physical attractiveness is based on surveys and can be highly speculative. Its results should be interpreted with caution.

Stereotypes, Prejudice, and Discrimination

What Is a Sterotype?

In Chapter 8, we learned about concepts and prototypes, the most typical example of a concept or category. *Stereotypes* are social prototypes—pictures in our heads—made up of a set of related beliefs about how members of social groups (ethnic/racial groups, occupations, age groups or members of either sex) behave. Like prototypes, stereotypes are cognitive (thought-based) and serve an information processing function. Like concepts in general, they are one device to help us organize information about the world.

Stereotypes are inaccurate to a large extent because they are broad generalizations about members of groups—qualities are attributed to all members of a given group, without regard to variations that may exist among group members. They can be described as overgeneralizations, and as such are always somewhat distorted. Many have some valid basis or a "kernel of truth," but stereotypes cannot be accurately used to describe or fully understand a whole person or all members of a group.

Prejudice and Discrimination

Prejudice is an emotional state, an attitude toward members of a group. Usually prejudice is negative; sometimes it is unrealistically positive. Often members of groups that hold negative stereotypes and are prejudiced against members of minority groups (such as the Nazis held in the early twentieth century) also believe that they are special, entitled, and superior to others. If you believe that all members of your own group are good, kind, loyal, smart, and virtuous, then you are prejudiced *toward* them. This forms the basis of the *In-group/Out-group phenomenon*. This is an "us versus them" way of seeing others, especially those against whom we hold prejudices. A person may not hold any prejudices based on personal qualities, but if she is a rabid sports fan, she might see all the fans of her team as the in-group and all the fans of the rival team as the out-group.

The following behaviors are associated with the in-group/out-group phenomenon:

- Members of the in-group will be perceived as being quite varied as individuals (in-group heterogeneity).
- Members of the out-group will be seen as being all the same in terms of personal characteristics (out-group homogeneity).
- Differential interpretation of the qualities that members of two groups possess—positive interpretation when exhibited by the in-group, negative interpretation when exhibited by the out-group. (We are thrifty, but they are stingy; we are fun loving, but they are irresponsible, etc.)

Racism and *ethnocentrism* are the most damaging forms of in-group/out-group bias.

Discrimination is the behavioral manifestation of prejudice. Discrimination occurs when one acts on one's prejudices, denying rights to one group and promoting the interests of another. The history of many groups of Americans in the latter part of the nineteenth century—former slaves and immigrants from most parts of Europe and Asia—is full of examples of outright discrimination. (No Blacks/Irish/Chinese/fill in the name of the ethnic group need apply!) *Scapegoating* is an another example of a discriminatory behavior. When members of a group are frustrated or oppressed, they may turn against another (usually less powerful) group, blaming them and venting their rage. Discrimination is not always expressed overtly; sometimes the effects are quite subtle and insidious (see next section).

Other Implications of Prejudice and Discrimination

Social psychology researchers have created interesting studies that suggest that our expectations of others, based on stereotypes and prejudiced attitudes, may have a real impact on their behavior. Here are some classic studies that illustrate these consequences.

- *The "blue-eyes/brown-eyes" experiments.* In 1968, a third-grade teacher, Jane Elliott, was able to duplicate quickly (and frighteningly realistically) the dynamics of societal prejudice and segregation in her classroom simply by telling her students that it had been scientifically demonstrated that people of one type of eye color were superior to those with the other.

- *Pygmalion in the classroom.* In 1968, a Harvard psychologist (Robert Rosenthal) and a Boston public school principal (Leonora Jacobson) administered an IQ test and selected random students as having achieved scores indicative of "academic blooming" potential. They told the teachers but not the students. Several months later, the selected children's IQ scores had improved, in some cases substantially.
- *Psychology of Rumor Experiments.* Gordon Allport (1887–1967) and his colleague Leo Postman did a series of experiments originally designed to describe the process and progress of rumors (1947). One of the experiments involved showing people a picture of a white man holding a knife or razor in front of a black man and asking them to relate the story in the picture to others who had not seen it. In most cases, the stories told were about a black man threatening a white man with a razor. Allport went on to write the Nature of Prejudice (1954.) He was a major contributor in many areas of psychology during the mid-twentieth century.

Group Dynamics, Conformity, and Obedience

In social settings, others influence us in important ways. They are a source of crucial information about situations (informational social influence). They communicate the rules regarding expected behavior by which we conduct ourselves in situations, called *norms* (this is referred to as *normative social influence*.)

Group Influences on Behavior

Task Performance

The presence of more than one person during an event or a task is sometimes helpful, sometimes less so. If you have the lead in a school play, and are well rehearsed, the audience will probably have a beneficial effect on your acting. This is called *social facilitation*—any improvement in performance that results from the presence of other people. If you are more nervous than usual, did not rehearse, or are feeling sick, the effect of being watched may be more detrimental. The results of studies from the field of sports psychology (Guerin 1986) suggest that athletes benefit from the presence of a crowd and other athletes.

When being with others has the opposite effect, it is called *social loafing*. This is the tendency we have to do less work when we are with other people. It reflects the same sense of "diffused responsibility" that may explain some bystander dynamics (see discussion that follows). Social loafing is not inevitable among work groups and appears to be more likely in very large groups or groups in which there will be no clear way to separate any one individual's contribution apart from those of others (Karau & Williams 1995.) It appears to be far more likely to occur in work groups with individualistic cultural values.

Group Decision Making

Although groups can be a source of ideas and insight, groups engaged in problem-solving or decision-making efforts can fall into some serious traps. When most members of a group already hold an extreme opinion on an issue, further discussion only serves to reinforce their views. Members who hold strong opinions actively discourage those who do not agree from voicing their opinions, and sometimes the dissenting minority remains silent. The group appears to have reached a consensus when in fact it has not. This is called *group-think*. One of the most famous historical examples of groupthink was the discussion that resulted in the Bay of Pigs invasion plan during the Kennedy administration.

Conformity

Conformity to rules that benefit the members of society in general is necessary for our survival as a species. *Conformity* is the maintenance or the alteration of one's behavior to match the behavior and expectations of others. At first it was believed that people were most likely to conform in ambiguous situations where it is common to be unsure of one's own judgment. Solomon Asch's classic experiment (1955) demonstrated that conformity was also likely even when individuals could be fairly confident in their judgments. He conducted research that demonstrated the power of the group to influence behavior. Asch recruited volunteers for a "visual judgment" study. Each volunteer reported to the laboratory where he was instructed to join a group of five other students. The other five students were research confederates, who were working for Asch. For each experimental task, the confederates gave their answers first. Their answers were frequently wrong. The real experimental participant would give his answer last. One-third of the time, he would also give a wrong answer. The results of this study have been replicated several times. It has been done in other cultures. The participants behave in a similar manner no matter where the study is done. The most interesting difference occurs when participants are *debriefed* or questioned about their feelings after the study. In individualistic cultures, people are more surprised by their own behavior; in more collectivistic ones, for example, Asian cultures, people will acknowledge their own desire not to make others uncomfortable by disagreeing.

Asch found in later studies that the tendency to conform can be manipulated by changing certain situational factors.

- The size of the group can be changed (the larger the group, the greater the tendency to conform—think groupthink).
- The group is viewed as high status (think of college fraternities and sororities.)
- The group has tended to be unanimous in its opinions, without dissenters (groupthink, again).
- The person entering the group feels insecure about his or her status, or uncertain of his or her opinions.
- Members of the group actively monitor each other's behavior (this is how twelve-step groups use their influence to encourage sobriety).
- The group's culture of origin is collectivistic or highly oriented toward societal standards.

Leadership and Authority

Many social psychologists were inspired by the disturbing events of World War II and especially the Nazi genocide. Kurt Lewin and his associates (1939) were able to demonstrate that leadership style influenced worker personality and behavior through a clever study. He arranged for three groups of boys in an after-school program to work in turn with each of his three assistants. Each assistant used one particular leadership style: authoritarian, permissive, and authoritative. The bossy, tyrannical *authoritarian* leader's style motivated the boys to work very hard—when he watched them, and to abuse each other when he did not. The *permissive* leader's style resulted in almost no work being done. The *authoritative* leader provided a mix of structure and discipline along with encouragement for the boys to participate in group decision making. This last style produced the most consistent level of good effort and quality work.

One of the most well-known research studies in social psychology, perhaps in psychology in general, is Stanley Milgram's 1963 study of obedience to authority (Milgram 1974). He sought to determine how common obedience to authority, even an authority giving immoral orders, was.

Working out of a storefront in Bridgeport, Connecticut, he invented a cover story to bring in research participants. He claimed to be studying learning processes and punishment. He had two main confederates: an "experimenter" who wore a standard white lab coat and gave the orders and a "subject," a learner, who was to be shocked every time he gave a wrong answer to the questions that the "teacher" (the research participant) asked. The teacher was to administer the shocks. He could not see the subject, so he could not see that after the subject was seated behind a wall, a tape recorder was turned on, from which the answers and the screams of pain actually originated. The shocks were to be increased in strength each time the learner gave a wrong answer, and were shown on the teacher's console to go right up to the lethal level.

What was shocking (so to speak) about Milgram's results was how many of the teachers followed the order to continue administering the shocks. Almost two-thirds of those in the original study administered shocks up to the lethal level.

In subsequent studies, Milgram found that obedience was enhanced or diminished by the following factors:

- Distance from the learner—the more contact the teacher had with the learner, the more human the learner seemed, the less likely the teacher was to give him strong shocks.
- The presence of "trappings of authority" (teachers were more likely to obey the experimenter when he wore the lab coat) or known affiliation to institutions with legitimacy and prestige (study done by Yale as opposed to by a private researcher).
- Seeing other teachers refuse to do the task encouraged others to rebel and quit the study.

And, notably:

- Age, sex, religion, and other personal characteristics of the teachers had no effect on compliance rate.

Role, Situation, and Behavior

Several other famous and controversial studies in social psychology have led to disturbing conclusions about the influence of the other people, and the situation, on human behavior.

- *The situation and behavior—The Stanford prison experiment.* When twenty (basically average, well-adjusted) male college student volunteers were randomly assigned to play either guards or prisoners in a two-week prison simulation at Stanford University, their behavior became so real and the situation became so intense that the experiment had to be called off on the sixth day. The guards were at times extraordinarily brutal. Most of the prisoners became deeply depressed and apathetic, although a couple of them were energetically rebellious. But the research team (Haney, Banks, and Zimbardo, 1973) was amazed at the realism of the "simulation."

- *Responsibility towards others—bystander effects and altruism.* Americans were stunned by the 1964 murder of Kitty Genovese, in which dozens of people were apparently awake and aware that she was being repeatedly attacked outside their windows, but none intervened or even summoned the police. She might have survived the attack if someone had done something. A series of studies done by Latane and Darley (1970) suggested that the presence of other people may make it *less* likely that help will be offered. They referred to this as the *diffusion of responsibility* effect. Bystanders are likely to say or to think, "Someone else surely will help, so I don't have to do anything." *Pluralistic ignorance* is a variant of this effect. If there is a problem that needs to be addressed within a group of people (family, organization, or society), we often assume that others know better than we do. So we end up saying or doing nothing.

On a more positive note, a few studies that illustrate the positive effects of the situation on behavior should be cited (so you don't become too discouraged about the effect that people have on each other!). The situation can be a powerful positive influence on behavior. We saw this with the Pygmalion in the classroom study. Here are two more encouraging examples.

- *Reducing hostility and prejudice—the Robber's Cave studies.* Working with boys at a summer camp, Muzafer Sherif (1966) and his associates were able to separate and manipulate two groups of campers into feeling an intense rivalry and group loyalty. After the groups were strongly prejudiced against each other, he introduced a series of threats to both groups that required cooperative efforts to overcome. The result was a marked reduction in intergroup hostility and an increase in good feelings between the members of the formerly hostile groups.

- *Cooperation for academic success—the jigsaw classroom.* Another study done in response to a real-life social crisis (in this case the desegregation of school systems in the 1960s) showed that setting up classroom activities that force students to cooperate, help, and teach each other reduces hostility and anxiety among the students and promotes learning. Elliot Aronson and several of his colleagues (1987) created classroom activities in which students were first separated into task groups to learn one part of the daily lesson. Then, each task group was separated and the members were placed in *jigsaw groups*—made up of one representative from each task group. The members of the jigsaw groups helped each other learn the lesson, allowing all the students to learn from each other and feel more competent and calmer than in the traditional classroom setup.

Connecting Through Chapter Review

WORD-STUDY CONNECTION
Write each of these words on index cards, and write their definitions on the opposite side.

actor-observer effect	diffusion of responsibility	persuasion
attitude	discrimination	pluralistic ignorance
attraction	dispositional	prejudice
attribution	distinctive	primacy effect
attribution theory	door-in-the-face technique	proximity (nearness)
authoritarian	ethnocentrism	reciprocity
authoritative	foot-in-the-door technique	reciprocity of feeling
authority	fundamental attribution	scapegoating
bait-and-switch technique	error	scarcity
basking in reflected glory	groupthink	self-serving bias
(BIRG)	in-group/out-group	similarity
bystander effects	phenomenon	situational
cognitive dissonance	internal/external	sleeper effect
conformity	jigsaw groups	social exchange theory
consensus	just world hypothesis	social facilitation
consistency	leadership	social loafing
consistent	mere exposure effect	social proof
culture	minority influence	social role
cutting off reflected failure	norms	stable/unstable
(CORF)	obedience	stereotype
debriefed	permissive	that's-not-all technique

SELF-TEST CONNECTION

PART A. Completion
Write in the word that correctly completes each statement.

1. _____ is the branch of psychology that describes and explains the causes, types, and consequences of human interaction.
2. A person from a(n) _____ culture is focused on independence, self-reliance and self-responsibility.
3. An attribution that is considered to be _____ means that it refers to a relatively permanent condition.
4. People who tend to prefer to use dispositional attributions to situational ones in explaining the behavior of others, ignoring the power the situation can have to influence action, often make a(n) _____ .

5. The tendency to frame our relationship to other people and groups so that we see our performance and behavior in the best possible light occurs in the form of _____ and _____ .
6. A(n) _____ is your feeling toward a person, thing, or issue.
7. _____ involves first making a small or reasonable request followed by a larger one.
8. The _____ occurs when a message is rejected, at first, but later works to change the attitude of the person who hears it.
9. The _____ suggest that given that our initial reaction is neutral or positive, the more often we interact with another person, the more we will start to like him or her.
10. According to _____ psychologists, attractiveness may be taken as a signal that an individual is healthy and has good genes.
11. _____ is an emotional state, an attitude toward members of a group, usually negative.
12. The behavioral manifestation of prejudice is _____ .
13. In the _____ experiments, a teacher was able to duplicate the dynamics of societal prejudice and segregation in her classroom simply by telling her students that it had been scientifically demonstrated that people of one type of eye color were superior to those with the other.
14. The process by which others communicate the rules regarding expected behavior by which we conduct ourselves in situations is referred to as _____ .
15. _____ occurs when some group members actively discourage those who do not agree from voicing their opinions and the group appears to have reached a consensus when in fact it has not.
16. In _____ classic experiment on conformity using the pretense of a "visual judgment" study, he demonstrated that conformity was likely even when individuals could be fairly confident in their judgments.
17. _____ was able to demonstrate that leadership style influenced worker personality and behavior through a study on leadership style.
18. _____ conducted one of the most famous studies in psychology on obedience to authority.
19. The Stanford prison experiment had to be cut short (after six days) as the behavior of the guards become extraordinarily _____ and most of the prisoners became _____ .
20. The 1964 murder of _____ ignited much research on bystander effects and diffusion of responsibility.
21. The Robber's Cave studies demonstrated that _____ behavior can reduce _____ between groups of boys at a summer camp.
22. In the studies that involve deception (Asch's conformity study, for example), the participants were _____ after the study in which they were told the true nature of the experiment.

PART B. Multiple Choice
Circle the letter of the item that correctly completes the statement.

1. _____ theory is a framework for understanding how people explain the others' behavior as well as their own.
   (a) Conformity   (b) Social norm
   (c) Motivational   (d) Attribution
2. Which of the following is *not* a possible characteristic of an attribution?
   (a) Stable   (b) Internal
   (c) Accurate   (d) External
3. What are other ways of describing internal attributions and external attributions?
   (a) Both dispositional
   (b) Dispositional and situational
   (c) Situational and dispositional
   (d) Both situational
4. The belief that "what goes around comes around" is known as _____ .
   (a) Cut off reflected failure   (b) Self-enhancing bias
   (c) The actor-observer effect   (d) The just world hypothesis
5. _____ occurs when two beliefs or one's belief and behavior are at odds.
   (a) Cognitive dissonance   (b) Self-enhancing bias
   (c) Social loafing   (d) Altruism
6. In what type of culture is cognitive dissonance most likely to occur?
   (a) Individualistic   (b) Collectivist
   (c) Horizontal   (d) Vertical
7. Which of the following is *not* one the identified six common dynamics that can be effectively used in the art of persuasion?
   (a) Reciprocity   (b) Social loafing
   (c) Attractiveness   (d) Scarcity
8. One technique in which a very attractive offer is made first, but before the deal is closed, additional demands are made in order to secure the price or goods is referred to as _____ .
   (a) foot-in-the-door   (b) that's-not-all
   (c) door-in-the-face   (d) bait-and-switch
9. Which of the following reflects the idea that we like people who like us?
   (a) Similarity   (b) Reciprocity of feeling
   (c) Proximity   (d) Social exchange theory
10. _____ are social prototypes made of a set of related beliefs about members of social groups.
    (a) Stereotypes   (b) Prejudices
    (c) Social norms   (d) Discriminations
11. One characteristic of the in-group/out-group phenomenon is that members of the out-group will be seen as being all the same in terms of personal characteristics. This is called _____ .
    (a) stereotypes   (b) prejudices
    (c) out-group homogeneity (d) in-group heterogeneity

12. When members of a group are frustrated or oppressed, they may turn against another (usually less powerful) group, blaming them and venting their rage resulting in _____ .
    (a) scapegoating
    (b) reciprocity of feeling
    (c) prejudice
    (d) downward social comparison

13. Allport and Postman conducted a series of experiments originally designed to describe the process and progress of _____ . The studies had additional implications on the nature of prejudice.
    (a) stereotypes
    (b) rumors
    (c) discrimination
    (d) malingering

14. The rules regarding expected behavior by which we conduct ourselves in situations are called _____ .
    (a) social influence
    (b) bias
    (c) norms
    (d) obedience

15. Any improvement in performance that results from the presence of other people is _____ .
    (a) social loafing
    (b) group norms
    (c) social facilitation
    (d) None of the above

16. The tendency we have to do less work when we are with other people is referred to as _____ .
    (a) social loafing
    (b) diminished capacity
    (c) social facilitation
    (d) All of the above

17. Which factor influences the occurrence of social loafing?
    (a) Group size
    (b) Gender of the participants
    (c) Obedience
    (d) All of the above

18. _____ is/are the maintenance or the alteration of one's behavior to match the behavior and expectations of others.
    (a) Social norms
    (b) Obedience
    (c) Social loafing
    (d) Conformity

19. Which of the following is *not* a factor that influences the likelihood of conformity occurring?
    (a) Social loafing
    (b) Group norms
    (c) Collectivist culture
    (d) All of the above

20. In Milgram's classic study on obedience, approximately how many of the participant "teachers" shocked the "learners" to the maximum amount?
    (a) One-fifth
    (b) One-third
    (c) One-half
    (d) Two-thirds

21. Which of the following conditions lead to an *increase* in the obedience to authority?
    (a) Closer distance of the learner to the teacher
    (b) Professional attire of the experimenter
    (c) Experimenter wearing casual clothes
    (d) All of the above

22. Which experiment assigned participants to play either guards or prisoners in a two-week prison simulation that examined the importance of roles, behavior, and context?
    (a) Asch's conformity study
    (b) Milgram's obedience study
    (c) Lewin's leadership study
    (d) The Stanford Prison experiment

23. _____ is a variant of the bystander effect, which suggests that if there is a problem that needs to be addressed within a group of people (family, organization, or society), we often assume that others know better than we do.
    (a) Pluralistic ignorance   (b) Altruism
    (c) Social loafing   (d) None of the above
24. Who conducted the Robber's Cave studies in which boys at a summer camp demonstrated that cooperative behavior can reduce hostility between groups?
    (a) Genovese   (b) Milgram
    (c) Zimbardo   (d) Sherif
25. In response to _____ , Aronson conducted the jigsaw classroom study which showed that setting up classroom activities that force students to work together reduces hostility and anxiety among the students and promotes learning.
    (a) housing integration   (b) outlawing same-sex schools
    (c) school desegregation   (d) Title IX

PART C. Modified True-False

If the statement is true, write "T" for the answer. If the statement is incorrect, change the underlined expression to one that will make the statement true.

1. A person from a collectivist culture is likely to be concerned about how his behavior reflects on his family.
2. An attribution, in social psychology, is an explanation for the cause of behavior.
3. An attribution that is considered to be external means that it is related to the person.
4. If you say, "she's a liar," you have made a stable, external attribution.
5. The likelihood that we use situational attributions, or unstable internal attributions, to explain our own behavior is called the actor-observer effect.
6. You are basking in reflected glory if you say "we won" when your candidate won the election.
7. People are more likely to use self-serving biases in individualistic cultures.
8. When someone is experiencing cognitive dissonance, they are most likely to change their belief.
9. According to Cialdini, persuasion goes in one of two directions: if you do change your mind or comply with a request, the results will be good or the results will be bad.
10. One of the common dynamics that can be effectively used in the art of persuasion is reciprocity, in which we are more likely to be influenced by those we perceive as being powerful or knowledgeable.
11. The technique known as the door-in-the-face technique occurs when a completely inappropriate or outrageous request is made first so that the smaller one that follows seems very small indeed.
12. According to the notion of reciprocity of feeling, we seek people with whom we can establish a roughly equal interpersonal exchange—each person giving something to the relationship as well as taking.
13. Prejudices are cognitively based and are generally inaccurate because they are broad generalizations about members of groups.
14. In-group heterogeneity, associated with the in-group/out-group phenomena refers to the idea that members of the in-group will be perceived as being quite varied as individuals.

15. Stereotypes occur when one acts on one's prejudices, denying rights to one group and promoting the interests of another.
16. In the Pygmalion in the classroom study, researchers demonstrated the influence of teacher expectations on student achievement.
17. Informational social influence is the process by which others are a source of crucial information about situations.
18. Research that demonstrates that athletes benefit from the presence of an audience or other athletes supports the concept of social loafing.
19. In the debriefing of participants in studies of conformity, people from collectivist cultures are more surprised by their own behavior, while people from individualistic cultures more readily acknowledge their own desire not to make others uncomfortable by disagreeing.
20. If a member of a group feels secure in his or her opinions, he or she will be more influenced to conform.
21. Making the size of the group larger will decrease the tendency to conform.
22. Demographic characteristics (age, sex, religion) of the teacher (participant) had a strong effect on compliance rate in the Milgram studies of obedience.
23. Asch conducted the Stanford prison experiment, which examined the importance of roles and behavior.
24. The notion that the presence of other people may make it less likely that help will be offered is referred to as the diffusion of responsibility effect.
25. Altruism refers to the idea that people help others without personal gain.

PART D. Matching

Place the name of the concept related to thinking next to the correct example of that concept.

Social Cognition

CORFing   just world hypothesis   internal, stable attribution
BIRGing   external, stable attribution cognitive dissonance
external, unstable attribution   self-serving bias
out-group homogeneity   internal, unstable attribution

Your friend says,

1. "What goes around comes around." _____
2. "You got up on the wrong side of the bed this morning." _____
3. "Most of the people who failed the midterm are just not very bright—but I did not do well because I did not sleep well the night before the test." _____
4. "Our school won the championship!" _____
5. "She cheated on the exam because she was just born dishonest, that's all." _____
6. "He cheated on the exam because his family is poor and he desperately needed to win the scholarship for college." _____
7. "I cheated on the exam because the answers were just lying there on the teacher's desk for everyone to see." _____
8. "They blew the game in the final seconds." _____

9. "Of course he cheated on the exam. His kind, you know, they're all like that." _____

10. "I am joining the triple-Omega sorority this year. It's really hard to get into so it must be the best one on campus!" _____

Social Cognition

"good results"	reciprocity	scarcity
foot-in-the-door	door-in-the-face	authority
that's not all	scare tactics	
consistency	social proof	

The advertisement says,

1. All your hippest friends are buying Old Army sac pants this fall! _____
2. If you've bought the other 250 Henry Spotter mysteries, you won't want to miss installment 251 of this classic series—*Henry Spotter and the Enchanted Omelet Pan.* _____
3. In a less than safe world, shouldn't you have the Armor Plate Home Protection system for true peace of mind? _____
4. Join our DVD of the month club and receive twelve free DVDs for a mere commitment to buy six more over the next year. _____
5. Miss America buys only genuine "Cover Face" cosmetics. Shouldn't you? _____
6. The Ab-buster machine is only $1299.99—and if you call in the next ten minutes you'll receive, for free, a year's supply of Quackremedy's ultra fat-burning crème. _____
7. If you don't feel ready to buy the official Ab-buster for $1299.99, enjoy our special fat burning crème for only $39.99 a jar.
8. Buy a carton of Quackremedy fat-burning crème for only $99.99, and receive a special offer to buy the amazing Ab-buster for only $1099.99 plus shipping and handling. _____
9. If you don't at least try our amazing Ab-buster, don't be surprised if you never have another date for the rest of your miserable, lonely life! _____
10. Only while supplies last! _____

Attraction and Person Perception

scapegoating	mere exposure	prejudice
in-group/out-group	social exchange	similarity
proximity (nearness)	reciprocity of feeling	discrimination
stereotyping		

1. Your co-workers begin to grow on you after a month or so. _____
2. Most of your friends belong to the same political party as you do and support the same causes. _____
3. Your friend thinks that all people from New York are pushy and stressed-out. _____
4. You were indifferent to your friend's older brother or sister at first, but now you find him/her kind of attractive. _____

5. You take turns with your friends buying lunch or movie tickets for the whole crowd. _____

6. You became good friends with a classmate who admires your taste in clothing and your career ambitions. _____

7. You despise all people who go to the same school as the person who broke up your steady relationship. _____

8. Your uncle won't hire anyone who doesn't belong to the same church as he does. _____

9. You learned in history class that the Nazis blamed Jews for their economic problems in the 1920s and 1930s. _____

10. You and your fellow juniors are fun, diverse, and down to earth, but the seniors are a bunch of stuck-up snobs. _____

Classic Social Psychology Studies
Match the name of the study and researcher to the subject of the research study.

obedience   conformity   reducing intergroup prejudice
cooperation   prejudice   power of the situation
leadership style diffusion of
prejudice and perception   responsibility
influence of expectations on performance

1. Zimbardo et al.'s Stanford Prison experiment _____
2. Elliot's brown-eyes/blue-eyes _____
3. Asch's visual judgment study _____
4. Rosenthal and Jacobson's Pygmalion in the classroom _____
5. Allport and Postman's psychology of rumor study_____
6. Milgram's Shock-the-learner study _____
7. Sherif's Robber's Cave experiment _____
8. Lewin's After-school groups _____
9. Latane and Darley's bystander effects _____
10. Aronson's jigsaw classroom _____

CONNECTING TO CONCEPTS
Review the chapter and then write down your thoughts about the following questions.

1. Choose one area of social psychology covered in this chapter, and discuss what you have learned about the possible influence of culture on human social behavior in this area.
2. Define the different types of attributions listed in this chapter. What types of attributions do you usually make about your own behavior? How about the behavior of your friends, and that of people you do not know or like?
3. Define the major types of persuasion and influence that you learned about in this chapter. Find two or three advertisements that are examples of persuasive techniques with which you are now familiar.
4. Think about the people with whom you spend the most time (who are not members of your family). Which processes of interpersonal attraction worked to bring you together with your friends or your crowd?

5. Choose one of the classic studies in social psychology, and summarize its findings. See if you can find one example of similar behavior and events from "outside the social psychology laboratory."

CONNECTING TO LIFE/JOB SKILLS

Cooperative Learning and Team Building

The jigsaw classroom study was one of the first of many cooperative learning interventions that have been used in academic settings both to reduce competition and hostility and to promote *active learning* on the part of the students. When students feel empowered and confident, they learn more and are more creative in their use of the learning—they feel more as if they "own" the knowledge. More and more frequently teachers are mixing traditional lecture activities with group activities that rely on students to teach each other the material.

A knowledge of group dynamics is a tool with applications outside of the classroom as well. Coaches, athletes, and business owners or managers can improve performance and morale using these principles.

Visit these web sites for more information:

JIGSAW CLASSROOM

www.jigsaw.org/

COOPERATIVE LEARNING NETWORK

home.att.net/~clnetwork/

COLLABORATIVE LEARNING

id-www.ucsb.edu/IC/Resources/Collab-L/CL_Index.html

COOPERATIVE LEARNING TECHNIQUES

www.mathgoodies.com/articles/coop_learning.shtm

GROUP DYNAMICS FOR ATHLETES AND COACHES

www.iusb.edu/~edp647/Group_Dynamics/Group_Dynamics.htm

TEAM BUILDING

www.mapnp.org/library/grp_skll/teams/teams.htm

TEAM BUILDING CONSULTANTS (COMMERICAL SITE)

www.accel-team.com/

WHAT'S HAPPENING!

Conflict Resolution

Lately we have all been more concerned about the possibility of violence and conflict touching our lives. Geopolitical turmoil has been a fact of life practically since the dawn of history, but we have recently become more conscious of such problems, it seems. One area in which social psychological concepts can be applied to improve life for all people is in the area of *conflict resolution*. Social psychologists believe that if their work is to have any lasting influence, it will be in applications that promote peace and justice and reduce the chance of war, terrorism, and civil conflict—all of which we have witnessed in the past two decades. These are the "big issues" in social psychology today (P. Zimbardo, personal communication, May 2003).

In this chapter, you have learned about some of the basic principles of reducing prejudice and conflict and the factors that contribute to prosocial and antisocial behaviors within and between groups. There is much more to this area. In small human groups, couples, and families, how conflict is handled is crucial to the healthy functioning of relationships. In business, such skills are necessary to help different departments and levels (management versus support and production staff) get along and be productive. Conflict resolution courses are taught in business schools and consultants work with businesses to teach these skills to staff in all divisions.

Conflict resolution is of interest to all of us because conflict is a fact of life. Visit some web sites related to academic and applied research on conflict resolution:

INCORE INSTITUTE

www.incore.ulst.ac.uk/

CONFLICT RESEARCH CONSORTIUM

www.colorado.edu/conflict/

CONFLICT RESOLUTION CENTER INTERNATIONAL

www.conflictres.org/

THE SOLOMON ASCH CENTER

www.psych.upenn.edu/sacsec/about/solomon.htm

OTHER USEFUL WEB SITES

NATIONAL INSTITUTE OF MENTAL HEALTH:
BASIC BEHAVIORAL SCIENCE RESEARCH

www.nimh.nih.gov/publicat/baschap5.cfm
www.nimh.nih.gov/publicat/baschap7.cfm

These are NIMH's web sites on social cognition and the influence of culture on social adjustment.

INFLUENCE AT WORK

www.influenceatwork.com/

This is a business-oriented web site on using influence to improve employee morale, productivity, and, of course, the bottom line.

THE STANFORD PRISON EXPERIMENT

www.prisonexp.org/

This web site has a fascinating slide show of the experiment from beginning to end.

STANLEY MILGRAM

www.stanleymilgram.com/

This web site describes Milgram's work and recognizes its importance to humanity.

MUZAFER SHERIF

www.disinfo.com/pages/dossier/id383/pg1/

This site includes a biography and discussion of Sherif's work and also features many links to other social psychology web sites.

REFERENCES

Allport, G. W. (1954) *The Nature of Prejudice.* Cambridge, MA: Addison-Wesley.

Allport, G. W. & Postman, L. F. (1947) The basic psychology of rumor. In *Readings in Social Psychology* (160–171). New York: Holt.

Aronson, E. (1987) Teaching students what they think they already know about prejudice and desegregation. In V. P. Makosky (Ed.), *G. Stanley Hall Lecture Series* (Vol. 7). Washington, DC: American Psychological Association.

Asch, S. (1956) Studies of independence and conformity: A minority of one against a unanimous majority. *Psychological Monographs: General and Applied* 70(9), No. 416.

Cialdini, R. B. (1993) *Influence—The Power of Persuasion.* New York: Morrow.

Festinger, L. & Carlsmith, J. M. (1959) Cognitive consequences of forced compliance. *Journal of Abnormal and Social Psychology, 58,* 203–210.

Guerin, B. (1986) Mere presence effects in humans: A review. *Journal of Experimental and Social Psychology,* 22(volume), 38–77.

Haney, C., Banks, W. C. & Zimbardo, P. G. (1973) A study of prisoners and guards in a simulated prison. *Naval Research Review* 3, 4–17.

Iyengar, S. S. & Brockner, J. (2001) Cultural differences in self and the impact of personal and social influences. In B. Cialdini, (Ed.), *The Practice of Social Influence in Multiple Cultures* (13–32). Mahwah, NJ: Lawrence Erlbaum Associates.

Karau, S. J., & Williams, K. D. (1995) Social loafing: Research findings, implications, and future directions. *Current Directions,* 4, 134–139.

Kelley, H. H. (1967). Attribution in social psychology. *Nebraska Symposium on Motivation,* 15, 192–238.

Latane, B. & Darley, J. M. (1970) *The Unresponsive Bystander: Why Doesn't He Help.* New York: Appleton-Century-Crofts.

Lewin, K., Lippett R. & White R. K. (1939) Patterns of aggressive behavior in experimentally created social climates. *Journal of Social Psychology* 17(9), 271–301.

Milgram, S. (1974). *Obedience to Authority: An Experimental View.* New York: Harper & Row.

Rosenthal, R., and Jacobson, L. (1968) *Pygmalion in the Classroom.* New York: Rinehart and Winston.

Sherif, M. (1966) *In Common Predicament: Social Psychology of Intergroup Conflict and Cooperation,* Boston: Houghton-Mifflin.

Chapter 13

PERSONALITY THEORY AND TESTING

In this chapter you will review the history of personality as a concept and the major theories of personality. You will examine the process and problems of attempting to describe and test it also.

The History of Personality as a Concept

Personality is the relatively stable way a person thinks, feels, and behaves in all situations. Culture must be considered in examining the degree to which the construct "personality" influences people's behavior. The first mention of personality comes from ancient Greek philosophy and medicine. In fact, the ancient Greeks originated the first personality theory, relating a person's disposition to the relative quantity of a certain "humor" or fluid in his or her body. Thus, a person with a relatively high proportion of blood was *sanguine* or cheerful; a person with a lot of yellow bile was angry or *choleric*; too much black bile would make a person sad or cause *melancholy*; and a person who had a greater proportion of phlegm was *phlegmatic*—slow and unenergetic. In a way, we have come full circle—we have improved our technology to allow us to begin to explore the biological basis of temperament and behavior, though we are certainly much more sophisticated and accurate in our understanding than describing the influence of the "four humors."

It is important to note the early origins of personality theory also because it comes from the same roots as much of the Western perspective. It is not an accident that the idea of an individual personality arose from this framework and not from a more collectivistic view. Those of us raised in the Western tradition prefer to view the individual as having the most influence on his or her own behavior. Yet as you have seen (in Chapter 12), the situation can have a considerable influence on how people behave, and that influence is also relatively consistent across many different and unique individuals.

We will cover five major perspectives on modern personality theory in the first sections of this chapter.

- *The psychoanalytic view,* introduced by Freud and modified to some degree by his followers, is founded on the idea that human behavior is shaped by early childhood experiences and driven by powerful unconscious forces. This is the most dated of personality theories currently in use and has been criticized for its lack of empirical support.
- *Trait theory* developed over the course of several generations of psychologists and is based upon an ever-decreasing number of essential traits. This view purports that a cluster of essential characteristics can summarize any individual's personality, or traits, which occur in varying degrees in each person.
- *The humanistic view,* shaped by Maslow and Rogers, is based on the notion that people have an innate desire to be good and make the most of their own potential. This view has also been criticized recently for its relatively unscientific basis, although it remains popular.
- *The social-cognitive view,* developed by Albert Bandura, combines observational learning, cognitive factors, and social factors to explain human behavior. According to this view, personality is the result of a continuous dialog between behavior, internal processes, and environmental feedback.
- *Biological perspectives* combine recent advances in genetic research, developmental psychology, and neuroscience, which are helping us to better understand the influence of biology on thought, feeling, and action and describe a biological basis of personality. (See "What's Happening!" at the end of the chapter.)

Personality is an elusive concept, partly because the influence of the situation cannot be easily dismissed. There are psychologists (Mischel 1990) who have argued in a compelling manner that the situation is a better predictor of behavior than the construct "personality" (the *person-situation* debate). Also, to a greater degree than some other branches of psychological research and theory, personality psychology has been haunted by a certain pseudoscientific taint. One of the earliest personality theories (nineteenth century) was based on the idea that personal characteristics could be detected by feeling the shape and lumps on a person's head (phrenology). Charges of pseudoscience made against psychoanalytic theory are not lightly dismissed—Freud's theories do not stand up to empirical examination. Other low points in personality theory include Sheldon's personality categories based on body type (somatotyping), which was merely a re-working of some tired stereotypes about thin, fat, and muscular people. Currently, the field of personality assessment is also struggling with charges that long-favored instruments (the Rorschach and the Myers-Briggs Type Indicator are two examples) are similar to horoscopes and tealeaf reading in scientific basis and utility. We will visit this debate at the end of the chapter.

Sigmund Freud and the Psychoanalytic School

Freud was a major influence in shaping psychology in the early twentieth century. Part of the reason for this power is simply that he was good at promoting his own ideas. He gained a large following in the city of Vienna (a center of intellectual and cultural activity at this time).

We now understand that the basis on which Freud founded many of his ideas was shaky at best. As a psychiatrist he treated about 500 patients, yet he based his theories on fewer than twenty case studies plus his understanding of his own development and psychological life. As you learned in Chapter 1, case study methodology is appropriate for rare and unusual disorders, but it is not appropriate for generalizing to a large number of other individuals. Certainly there are cross-cultural issues. For example, we probably can't use theories based on the lives and experiences of a small number of affluent Viennese people to understand the experiences of poor farmers living in Guatemala—not beyond some broad and obvious truths about what motivates people, at any rate.

Some of Freud's more lasting contributions include:

- The idea of the *unconscious* and its role in driving human behavior. Unfortunately, the unconscious is a construct that cannot be effectively empirically observed or measured. (This is one reason why strict behaviorists, and others, have traditionally discounted or rejected it.)
- The role of early childhood experiences in shaping the person during the first few years of life.
- The idea that development was a sequence of stages and that each stage involves resolving some type of conflict (the developmental "crisis"). Freud's stages are *psychosexual*. This idea was expanded and arguably made more useful in Erikson's eight psychosocial stages (see Chapter 9) and some more recent theories of child and adult lifespan development.
- The idea that sexual adjustment has an impact on overall psychological health.
- Freud expanded on the ancient idea that dreams provide some type of information that may be important in understanding a person's issues and current functioning.

To his credit, Freud was reported to have said that he expected that his theories would eventually be borne out by the scientific study of brain biology. He was certainly aware that the study of human behavior was hampered by the lack of understanding of the brain, and probably would have enjoyed and promoted the advances that are now coming from neuroscience technology and research. Although his theory of id, ego, superego, and the five stages of psychosexual development may seem dated now, these seem to explain some aspects of human behavior. They help to form a foundation for modern clinical and developmental psychology. Freud's theories are constantly alluded to in the imagery of writing, television, movies, and even cartoons of the twentieth century. It can also be argued that given the current rate of progress in the scientific study of the brain and human behavior, Freud's most lasting contributions will be cultural and not scientific.

The Components of Personality, According to Freud

Id (The Latin word for "it.")—This is the most primitive part of the personality, functioning entirely at an unconscious level. It is the only part that is present at birth. It is immune to logic, values, morality, danger, and demands of the outside world. This inner "demon" is ruled by the *pleasure principle*—a relentless drive toward satisfaction of basic urges. According to Freud, a helpless little newborn is completely ruled by his or her id. Id is gradually "sealed off" in the human mind. Freud referred to the emergence or overt influence of the id on a person's behavior as psychosis.

Ego (or "I")—As the child grows and experiences the world, his or her caretakers can't or won't always immediately satisfy his or her needs. The ego begins to form as the "middle person" between basic needs that require fulfillment and the restrictions of the outer world. This is the *reality principle,* which refers to the understanding that one must sometimes defer gratification until the appropriate times and circumstances dictated by the environment.

For example, a little girl learns to say "Please" to get a cookie as a snack; a little boy learns to wait his turn for a ride on the swing. According to Freud, the little girl who steals the cookie when her caretaker isn't looking and the little boy who punches or yells at the child who is on the swing in order to hasten his turn are still responding indiscriminately to the urges of the id or have insufficient ego strength.

Ego may have to invest a lot of energy thwarting urges that cannot be satisfied in a socially acceptable way. Internalization plays a much bigger and more important role in the theories of Freud than in other personality theories. This thwarting forms the basis of the defense mechanisms (see discussion that follow).

Superego ("over I")—The last part of the personality structure to form. The superego is the internalized values system of the culture/society in which a person is raised. It is roughly equivalent to the "conscience." The way that values are taught to a child plays a big part in how the superego operates. It is the internalized voice of the parent and other figures that provided discipline during the child's early life. Superego can be an effective monitor or a punitive creator of unnecessary anxiety or guilt (which Freud called *neurosis*).

Defense mechanisms—According to Freud, if a conflict cannot be resolved between these three components in an appropriate manner, a person may use one or more defense mechanisms. All defense mechanisms are not equal. Some (such as rationalization and sublimation) are fairly healthy, while others (such as displacement and projection) might not be troublesome if used once in a while, but Freud considered it a sign of psychological distress if used as a preferred strategy.

The Process of Lifespan Development, According to Freud

Freud's Psychosexual Stages

Freud believed that lifespan development involved the gradual sublimation of inappropriate and asocial urges originating in the libido (the sexual energy that drives a person to seek gratification without regard to the rules and taboos of society) into socially acceptable drives to find and remain with a stable, heterosexual love object.

- Ages 0–1, *Oral stage.* During this stage the focus of gratification is the mouth. The infant experiences the world through sucking, biting, and mouthing things. The infant must accept the control over feeding and other avenues of oral satisfaction as this stage progresses. People who suffer from drug dependence—especially those that involve mouth contact (smoking and drinking alcohol) are thought to be fixated in the oral stage, as a result of frustration or overindulgence, according to a strict Freudian interpretation.

TABLE 13-1
DEFENSE MECHANISMS

Defense Mechanism	Description	Example
Rationalization	Making up reasons why an event that is distressing or disappointing is actually for the best	Joe did not get the high-paying job in New York City, but he "didn't really want to move there anyway."
Sublimation	Spending more time engaged in work or other activities to distract attention from an unpleasant event or circumstance	Shareice broke up with her boyfriend last month and is now spending 55–60 hours a week working, including weekends.
Projection	Accusing others of having the same motives, feelings or intentions as you have	Susie, who hates calculus class, says, "The math professor hates me—I just know he does!"
Displacement	"Taking it out on someone else"; venting anger or another unpleasant emotion provoked by one source at another	Henry was turned down for a date by a girl he really likes. He spends the weekend yelling at his little brother.
Reaction formation	Stating strongly that one's feelings are completely opposite from what they actually are	Henry told everyone that the girl who turned him down was really annoying, stupid, and not pretty.
Undoing	Performing acts that are believed to "undo" an immoral or unacceptable act	Lisa gives $5.00 of the $10.00 that she received for writing a phony excuse note for another student to a homeless person.
Denial	Refusing to admit that a problem is real or significant	After three DUI arrests, Sam states adamantly that he does not have a drinking problem.
Repression	"Forgetting" a past event, future obligation, or any other information because it is disturbing or unpleasant	A teacher who smokes a pack of cigarettes a day forgets to include nicotine as an addictive substance in his lecture on drug dependence.
Suppression	Deliberately putting something unpleasant out of your mind	Yuki counts to 20 whenever she thinks about how embarrassed she was when she forgot her lines in the school play.
Regression	Acting younger than your age in response to stress	Don doesn't think about his boring job much now that he has a remote control car.
Daydreaming	Retreating into fantasy life in response to stress	Sara (who has never sung in public) is failing college but she has been spending a lot of time planning her new career as a rock singer, so it's cool.

- Ages 1–3 *Anal stage*. Freud noted that toilet training takes place during this span of time. He hypothesized that gratification comes from the child's attaining control or lack of control of elimination. The child must gain control over this function. In nonpsychotic adults, the same effect is obtained by the controlling or the spreading around of one's money or possessions. Thus, you may have an *anal-retentive* (overcontrolled) friend who won't let you touch anything on his or her desk for fear that you will "mess it up" or an *anal-expulsive* (under-controlled) friend whose apartment floor and countertops are covered with papers, dirty dishes, laundry, and all manner of used and messy stuff.
- Ages 3–6 *Phallic stage*. Freud believed that this is the first time in life when pleasure is obtained from manipulation of the genitals. He theorized that a child develops sexual attraction to the opposite sex parent and homicidal rage at the same sex parent—the *Oedipal* or *Electra complex*. The child becomes fearful that the same sex parent will sense the threat and harm him or her. Boys see their sisters who do not have penises and fear that she *did* have one—she had been a boy—and father cut it off (*castration anxiety*). Girls see that boys have a penis while they do not, and they develop *penis envy*. The child must resolve this crisis by overcoming the attraction to the opposite sex parent and identifying with the same sex parent. Boys and girls in this age group are certainly curious about anatomical differences and are rapidly internalizing the schemas for gender roles. However, these theories are some of the most empirically questionable that Freud generated. Freud is probably guilty of misinterpreting the Oedipus myth, which is really about the power of *fate*—a frequent theme of ancient Greek literature. Oedipus is a foundling—sent away from his biological parents as an infant after the oracle predicts that he will kill his father and marry his mother. When he kills his father and marries his mother, he has no idea who they are. Many psychologists have presented a plausible alternate interpretation of penis envy—that what women actually envy is the status and power that maleness confers in most societies.
- Ages 6 to puberty, *Latency stage*. Allegedly at this age sexual tension subsides and children focus on mastery of tasks related to later competency in the world of work. This is debatable (as are many other Freudian concepts based on inference and speculation). There are a few alternative interpretations of the sex-segregated world of middle childhood. The social gulf between boys and girls at this time could reflect the impact of pressure of socialization, or in-group/out-group tendencies (see Chapter 12) that may accompany the gradual, complex process of identity formation.
- Adolescence and adulthood, *Genital stage*. Freud believed that, in this period, "mature" sexuality develops. Strong sexual interest does emerge in this stage. According to Freud, to resolve the crisis of this stage, one must find an appropriate, permanent heterosexual love interest and sublimate interest in other partners into work ("love and work"). Freud's opinion about what constitutes mature sexuality was somewhat more restrictive than is currently the case for psychologists who research and work in the area of human sexuality. For example, Freud viewed homosexuality as a form of "psychosis"—most (though not all) modern psychologists see it as a normal variant. As mentioned in Chapter 10, the major professional organizations of the mental health professions have officially rejected this view.

Followers of Freud

Carl G. Jung

Carl Gustave Jung (1875–1961) was a follower of Freud who fell out with him over several important theoretical points. Although Jung subscribed to the notion of powerful unconscious forces, his theory puts less emphasis the destructive qualities of those forces. His notion of libido has both positive and negative aspects. Jung's theory is as lacking in empirical basis as Freud's—it is often referred to as *transpersonal*. Jung proposed the existence of humanity's *collective unconscious*. Jung would use this to explain why people are much more frightened of spiders, snakes, and heights than cars and other everyday, more common dangers. He believed that people carry other information related to personality in the collective unconscious—*archetypes*, which are figures and images passed from generation to generation and found in all world cultures, and the male and female traits that he believed make up every individual's personality (*animus* and *anima*).

Alfred Adler

Alfred Adler (1870–1937) believed that events of childhood shape adult personality but rejected the psychoanalytic view that behavior is driven by unconscious forces. Instead, he proposed that most children developed *inferiority complexes* in early childhood. In response to this complex, a healthy child forms a *will-to-power* and begins to *strive for superiority*. Healthy adjustment is achieved when the child overcomes the inferiority complex and grows into an adult who has good self-esteem, and feelings of autonomy and power in his or her life.

Karen Horney

Karen Horney (1885–1952) challenged Freud's views of women as being biased and inaccurate. She introduced the idea that penis envy was more about power than anatomy (see preceding discussion). She proposed that children's development is impacted by parental nurturance. If a child does not feel loved and protected, he or she will be hampered by a sense of *basic anxiety* as an adult. She believed that as an adult, a person searches for a sense of connection to others in one of three ways: moving *toward* others by connecting positively and seeking acceptance; moving *against* others by trying to dominate and control them; or moving *away* from others by seeking to be self-sufficient and independent. Healthy adjustment reflects a balance of all three of these "directions" in interpersonal relationships.

Anna Freud

Freud's youngest child (1895–1982) and the one who most closely "followed in his footsteps," Anna Freud continued to promote his theories and the work of psychoanalysis. She is considered the founder of child psychology and had a special interest in the psychological development of adolescents. She also expanded on her father's theories regarding defense mechanisms. Her best-known work is the book *The Ego and the Mechanisms of Defense*.

Trait Theories

The idea behind trait theory is fairly simple: Personality results from the interaction of a specific number of basic characteristics or traits. This theory was first conceived of by Gordon Allport, although some of Carl Jung's work lays a foundation for the idea of traits. Looking at the number of trait-related words in the dictionary, and interesting characters from world literature, he developed a relatively complex trait theory that was somewhat impractical for use in describing and predicting individual behavior. Other psychologists attempted to develop their own versions. Raymond Cattell (see Chapter 8) worked out a theory based on sixteen fundamental characteristics or *source traits* and developed a test based on it—the Sixteen Personality Factor Questionnaire. Hans Eysenck (also mentioned in Chapter 8) and his wife Sybil used a complex statistical technique developed by Spearman, *factor analysis*, to distill out the broadest sets of related traits (thus revealing underlying factors). It measures the strength of associations between every possible combination of them. Factor analysis detects the pattern of relationships within any group of traits (or other constructs), so it is very useful in the study of intelligence and personality. The Eysencks reduced the number of traits to three dimensions: emotional stability (level of neuroticism); extraversion, and psychoticism (propensity for aggression and loss of touch with reality). The Eysenck Personality Questionnaire (EPQ) is used to measure these traits. It appears to be fairly valid cross culturally, according to research by one of the authors (Eysenck 1990).

Five Personality Factors

As is the case with many new ideas in science, more than one set of researchers has contributed independently to the notion of five specific personality dimensions. McCrae and Costa (1990) developed the *five-factor model (FFM)*, and Goldberg (1993) presented the *Big Five theory*, which was comprised of the same personality dimensions. The psychologists who proposed the five dimensions built upon the work of many other psychologists, from their own contemporaries all the way back to Allport. The acronym OCEAN makes it easy to remember these factors, which are presented in Table 13-2.

The Big Five/five-factor model has been criticized for having a relatively unscientific, nonempirical basis (given it roots in Allport's working from dictionaries rather than in actual observations or assessments). Researchers have identified other possible trait dimensions not accounted for in the model (Paunonen & Jackson 2000) such as masculinity-femininity. Cross-cultural support for the model is mixed. Overall, the model provides a reasonably good way to organize and describe personality. It appears to have little predictive power (compared to situational factors, as pointed out by Mischel; see preceding discussion) and tells us nothing about how people develop these traits (Matsumoto 2000.)

TABLE 13-2
THE "BIG FIVE" PERSONAL TRAITS

Dimension	A person is relatively...	Or tends to be more...
Openness	Receptive to new ideas, creative, broad in interests, interested in variety HIGH IN OPENNESS	Conventional, practical, narrow in interests, comfortable with what's familiar LOW IN OPENNESS
Conscientiousness	Responsible, organized, disciplined, achievement-oriented HIGH IN CONSCIENTIOUSNESS	Careless, disorganized, impulsive, lazy LOW IN CONSCIENTIOUSNESS
Extraversion	Outgoing, fun-loving, assertive, talkative HIGH IN EXTRAVERSION	Shy, serious, passive, quiet LOW IN EXTRAVERSION
Agreeableness	Warm, trusting, helpful, easy-going HIGH IN AGREEABLENESS	Cold, suspicious, uncooperative, argumentative LOW IN AGREEABLENESS
Neuroticism	Emotionally unstable, insecure, anxious, moody HIGH IN NEUROTICISM	Emotionally stable, confident, calm, even-tempered LOW IN NEUROTICISM

Humanistic Theories of Personality

Humanistic theories were generated partially in response to the view that some psychologists held that psychoanalytic and behavioral views of human personality and motivation were too negative and mechanical, respectively. These theories are founded on the idea that people are born good, that behavior is driven by the motivation to be good, and that a person's subjective view of the world must be understood in order to describe personality fully (and to change behavior, as we will see in Chapter 15).

We have already encountered one of the two humanistic personality theories in Chapter 10, Maslow's theory. Recall that Maslow proposed that people are innately (from birth) driven to *self-actualize*—to completely achieve their own full potentials. Self-actualization is a process, not a state. A person who is self-actualized views problems as challenges, and maintains a high degree of self-respect and self-acceptance in the face of setbacks and obstacles. He or she respects others and makes positive contributions to society.

The other major humanistic personality theory was developed by Carl Rogers (1902–1987). Similar to psychoanalytic theory, childhood was viewed as a critical time in humanistic theory—although it was critical in a different way. Based on experiences in the home and school environment, a child develops a first *self-concept*—an internalized view of his or her qualities, behaviors, and beliefs. At the same time, the child develops a notion of an ideal self. When the child's self-concept does not match the view of ideal self, distress and maladaptive behavior result. Rogers believed that parents played an important part in this. Parents may give a child only *conditional* love and positive regard. An example of conditional love would be a parent who rejects a child who yells or aggressively expresses anger at a sibling or at the adult. Rogers theorized that *unconditional positive regard* from a parent was more likely to produce a child with high self-esteem, and *congruence* (a match) between self-concept and ideal self. In expressing unconditional positive regard, the parent would help the angry child to express his or her feelings appropriately and explore whether or not there was anything to be angry about, rather than simply rejecting the child. The idea is fairly similar to the notion of "love the sinner, hate the sin." The parent should separate the behavior from esteem for the child.

Similar to psychoanalytic theory, humanism has been criticized for being weak from an empirical viewpoint. Although the humanistic view has had a large impact on the practice of psychotherapy (see Chapter 15), it is hard to validate its usefulness in a scientific manner. Rogers and Maslow "made up" their theories using their own clinical and personal experience, in much the same way that Freud created his. Maslow based the idea of self-actualization on case studies, which he picked specifically because he believed they demonstrated his preformulated notion. Humanistic personality theorists have been labeled as unrealistic or overly optimistic by those who wish to explain more disturbing aspects of human behavior—mass murder, corruption, and other violence.

The Social Cognitive View

Behaviorism had a brief fling as a personality theory, but it was rejected as too narrow and mechanistic by most psychologists. As useful as classical and operant conditioning may be for describing and manipulating behavior in specific contexts, they do not account for the large number of influences that shape personality more broadly. Learning theory has continued to influence personality psychology, though, through the work of Albert Bandura and Julian Rotter (b. 1916).

Albert Bandura: Social Cognitive Perspective

As you recall, Albert Bandura helped to develop and promote *observational learning* as an important way that experience changes human behavior. The fact that people can watch, think about, and learn from their own behaviors is a key part of Bandura's personality theory (Bandura 1986). A person does something—acts or behaves. That individual then observes what kind of impact his or her behavior has had on the environment. Do good or bad things happen? Are they rewarded, punished, or does it not matter much? Do people encourage or discourage the behavior? The person then thinks and feels in reaction to the environment. Did the individual like the result? Or would he or she rather have a different outcome? Through this interaction of behavior, environmental reaction, and internal processing, which Bandura called *reciprocal determinism*, a person will make changes to some aspect of behavior (therefore changing his or her behavior) and remain the same in others. Bandura believes that the most well-adjusted people have a strong sense of *self-efficacy*, a sense of competence in managing one's life and mastery in achieving one's personal goals.

Julian Rotter: Locus of Control

Julian Rotter's theory is more narrowly focused—behavior and emotion are shaped by thought or *expectancy*. Rotter believes that we frame the world in one of two ways:

- We believe that we have a great deal of influence over events in our lives (called an *internal locus of control*).
- We believe that we have very little influence over events in our lives (an *external locus of control*.)

Rotter developed a simple checklist that can be used to determine which cognitive style a person prefers to use. Overall, those who obtain a high internal locus score appear to be better adjusted. They are more achievement-oriented, healthier, and less likely to be depressed. It is hard to know whether this is a result of the locus of control or environmental factors (poverty, discrimination, or unemployment might create legitimate external constraints on a person's ability to influence or control his or her life). When people believe they cannot influence their environments or control their own lives, they may succumb to a sense of *learned helplessness* (Seligman 1972), which has been linked to depression and other negative mental health outcomes.

Social cognitive theories are appealing because they address Mischel's complaint about personality theory—they take the situation into account. The development of the Rotter scales and Bandura's ongoing research lend scientific credibility to this view (which humanism and psychoanalytic theory lack). Social cognitive theorists have yet to address the effects of early childhood development to the satisfaction of many contemporary psychologists who were raised on the psychoanalytic and humanistic traditions. Even though the evidence for early childhood and unconscious origins of some behavior is hard to measure, it may be premature to dismiss them from personality theory entirely.

Personality Testing

Recall from the material on intelligence and intelligence testing in Chapter 8, that assessing intelligence, which might seem straightforward, is actually not so simple. Personality, a construct that is arguably more vague and harder to define, presents the same challenges in a greater degree.

Often personality assessment is done through interview and observation. Some clinicians feel that these methods are too subjective and open to interpretation (and are therefore unreliable). Observations can be performed using carefully constructed checklists that specify the behaviors to record. Interviews can be structured using a protocol for questioning. Both of these techniques may reduce this risk of erroneous or biased recording and interpretation, but they do not guarantee accuracy.

Personality *assessments* or tests can also be administered. There are two broad categories of personality assessments,

- *Objective tests*. These are relatively straightforward *self-report* instruments—in other words, the person who is assessed answers questions about him or herself. The best known of these tests are standardized and normed in a way similar to IQ tests. They usually have a *forced choice* or true-false format. A forced choice presents two options from which a person must pick one. Some valid criticisms of this method have been made—referring back to the person-situation debate, what if the choice would depend on the situation? Objective tests are subject to deliberate deception on the part of the test taker.

It is not difficult to present one's self as much better, or much worse, than one actually is. The first versions of some personality tests (such as the MMPI, see following discussion) were standardized on samples of people who were *not* representative of a culturally diverse underlying population. Cultural bias in objective personality testing has been addressed in updated versions of the most widely used tests, but problems continue to arise in interpretation related to the influence of culture on behavior.

• *Projective tests.* These tests are less straightforward than the objective tests because they are designed to help reveal unconscious processes. The usual format involves the presentation of a stimulus that is ambiguous or "open to interpretation" by the test taker. The psychologist who gives the test analyzes the responses, usually (but not always) according to a scoring protocol. These methods have come under a lot of scrutiny and criticism in the past decade for being unscientific, unreliable, and invalid (Lilienfeld et al. 2001). Even the creation of standardized scoring methods (such as the Exner system for the Rorschach) for these tests has not increased their reliability nor removed the danger of subjective interpretation and bias. Finally, projective tests appear to tell us nothing more than would be revealed from observation or a well-conducted interview. For example, when a mentally ill person is having distorted thoughts or hallucinations, these symptoms are usually clearly evident in conversation—the use of a test to reveal such psychotic processes is superfluous.

Table 13-3 lists the most commonly used personality assessments.

TABLE 13-3
COMMONLY USED PERSONALITY TESTS

Test Name	Type	Brief Description
Minnesota Multiphasic Personality Inventory—2 (MMPI-2)	Objective	Adult and adolescent versions, both very long (over 300 questions). True-false format. Scoring by computer, provides many subscales for traits and symptoms, and includes subscales to detect faking and inconsistent answering patterns.
Myers-Briggs Type Indicator	Objective	Loosely based on Jung's personality theory, forced-choice format. Identifies four dimensions of personality style.
Rorschach Inkblot Test	Projective	Ten ambiguous blots are presented; subject is asked, "What might this be?" Responses are recorded word for word. Scoring systems are available; these do little to improve reliability and validity.
Thematic Apperception Test (TAT)	Projective	Between 5 and 22 stimulus cards with images drawn from magazine art of the mid-twentieth century. Subject is asked to tell a story about the card. Clinician subjectively analyzes story.
Rotter Incomplete Sentences Blank	Projective	Child, adolescent, and adult versions available. Subject completes 20–25 statements. Clinician subjectively analyzes responses.
Human Figure Drawings/ House-Person-Tree	Projective	Person is asked to make drawing. Some scoring systems are available, but usually the responses are analyzed subjectively.

Connecting Through Chapter Review

WORD-STUDY CONNECTION
Write each of these words on index cards, and write their definitions on the opposite side.

anal stage	id	psychotic processes
animus/anima	inferiority complex	reality principle
archetypes	internal locus of control	reciprocal determinism
assessments	latency	sanguine
basic anxiety	latency stage	self-actualize
Big Five theory	learned helplessness	self-concept
biological	melancholy	self-efficacy
castration anxiety	neurosis	self-report
choleric	observational learning	social cognitive
collective unconscious	objective tests	social-cognitive view
conditional positive regard	OCEAN	source traits
congruence	Oedipal complex	strive for superiority
crisis	oral stage	superego
defense mechanisms	penis envy	trait theory
ego	person-situation debate	traits
Electra complex	personality	transpersonal
expectancy	phallic stage	unconditional positive
external locus of control	phlegmatic	regard
factor analysis	pleasure principle	unconscious
five-factor model (FFM)	projective tests	will-to-power
forced choice	psychoanalytic view	16PF
genital stage	psychosexual	
humanistic view	psychosis	

SELF-TEST CONNECTION

PART A. Completion
Write in the word that correctly completes each statement.

1. _____ is the relatively stable way a person thinks, feels, and behaves in all situations.
2. In the _____ view of personality, human behavior is shaped by early childhood experiences and driven by powerful unconscious forces.
3. The person-situation debate reflects the opposition of the differing predictors of person versus the situation in the explanation of _____ .
4. The role of early childhood experiences in shaping the person during the first few years of life was a key characteristic of _____ personality theory.

5. The _____ depicts a relentless drive toward satisfaction of basic urges, according to Freud.

6. Freud would call the internalized values system of the culture/society in which a person is raised the _____ .

7. When the superego becomes the creator of unnecessary anxiety or guilt _____ develops.

8. Deliberately putting something unpleasant out of your mind is the _____ defense mechanism.

9. The defense mechanism of _____ occurs when one retreats into fantasy life in response to stress.

10. Freud believed that _____ involved the gradual sublimation of inappropriate and asocial urges originating in the libido into socially acceptable drives.

11. Someone who is _____ tends to be overcontrolled, and someone who is _____ tends to be undercontrolled, according to the Freudian theory of development.

12. Boys, who see that their sisters do not have penises and who fear that they did have one once but that it was cut off, are likely to develop _____ , according to Freud.

13. _____ developed the notion of the collective unconscious, which described the aspect of the unconscious that is shared by all people.

14. Adler believed that events of childhood shape adult personality and suggested that most children developed _____ in early childhood.

15. According to trait theory, personality results from the interaction of a specific number of basic characteristics or _____ .

16. _____ and _____ developed theories of personality based on five factors.

17. According to the five-factor model, someone who is careless, disorganized, impulsive, and lazy is _____ .

18. Bandura and Rotter supported the _____ view of personality.

19. According to Rotter, if we believe that we have a great deal of influence over events in our lives, we have a(n) _____ locus of control.

20. The two types of personality assessments, or tests, are _____ and _____ .

21. The _____ is an objective test that has both adult and adolescent versions, comes in a true-false format, and provides many subscales for traits and symptoms, including subscales to detect faking and inconsistent answering patterns.

22. The _____ , a projective test that has child, adolescent, and adult versions available, has the participant fill in the end of twenty to twenty-five incomplete statements.

PART B. Multiple Choice
Circle the letter of the item that correctly completes the statement.

1. The first mention of personality comes from ancient _____ philosophy and medicine.
   (a) Egyptian (b) Greek
   (c) Roman (d) Chinese

2. The humanistic view of personality, shaped by _____ , is based on the notion that people have an innate desire to be good and make the most of their own potential.
   (a) Maslow and Rogers (b) Bandura
   (c) Freud (d) Piaget and Erikson

3. According to the _____ view, personality is the result of a continuous dialog between behavior, internal processes, and environmental feedback.
   (a) humanistic   (b) biological
   (c) trait   (d) social-cognitive

4. Freud suggested the notion that sexual adjustment has an impact on overall _____ .
   (a) physical health   (b) psychological health
   (c) personality   (d) long-term relationships

5. _____ is the most primitive part of the personality, functioning entirely at an unconscious level.
   (a) Ego   (b) Id
   (c) Superego   (d) Oedipal complex

6. The _____ refers to the understanding that one must sometimes defer gratification until the appropriate times and circumstances dictated by the environment.
   (a) pleasure principal   (b) id
   (c) reality principal   (d) superego

7. Which defense mechanism reflects spending more time engaged in work or other activities to distract attention from an unpleasant event or circumstance.
   (a) Rationalization   (b) Reaction formation
   (c) Projection   (d) Sublimation

8. Kicking the dog when you are mad at your boss is an example of what type of defense mechanism?
   (a) Displacement   (b) Repression
   (c) Projection   (d) Denial

9. Eating an entire box of cookies while refusing to believe that the behavior might be problematic reflects what defense mechanism?
   (a) Undoing   (b) Denial
   (c) Projection   (d) Displacement

10. During which stage of development did Freud theorize that a child develops sexual attraction to the opposite sex parent and homicidal rage at the same sex parent, known as the Oedipal or Electra complex.
    (a) Latency   (b) Anal
    (c) Oral   (d) Phallic

11. According to Freud, girls see that boys have a penis while they do not; they will then develop _____ .
    (a) castration anxiety   (b) penis envy
    (c) Electra complex   (d) phallic

12. At which stage in development, according to Freud, does sexual tension subside and children focus on mastery of tasks related to the world of work.
    (a) Latency   (b) Anal
    (c) Genital   (d) Phallic

13. According to Jung, the unconscious ideas and images that are inherited and are components of the collective unconscious are referred to as _____ .
    (a) transpersonal   (b) personality characteristics
    (c) archetypes   (d) animus

14. Who challenged Freud's views of women as being biased and inaccurate and introduced the idea that penis envy was more about power than anatomy?
    (a) Erikson   (b) Adler
    (c) Jung   (d) Horney

15. Anna Freud, Freud's youngest child, continued to promote his theories and the work of psychoanalysis and is considered the founder of _____ psychology.
    (a) infant
    (b) toddler
    (c) child
    (d) young adult

16. Who developed a theory based on sixteen fundamental characteristics or source traits, and also developed the Sixteen Personality Factor Questionnaire?
    (a) Eysenck
    (b) Cattell
    (c) Jung
    (d) Spearman

17. A person who is shy, serious, passive, and quiet is low in _____ , according to the five-factor model.
    (a) agreeableness
    (b) neuroticism
    (c) extraversion
    (d) openness

18. Carl Rogers developed a humanistic theory of personality in which a child develops a _____ , which is an internalized view of his or her qualities, behaviors, and beliefs.
    (a) self-concept
    (b) self-actualization
    (c) internal working model
    (d) none of the above

19. A match between self-concept and ideal self is considered to be _____ , according to Rogers.
    (a) conditional
    (b) unlikely
    (c) congruent
    (d) All of the above

20. Bandura believes that the most well-adjusted people have a strong sense of _____ , a sense of competence in managing one's life, and mastery in achieving one's personal goals.
    (a) self-esteem
    (b) self-efficacy
    (c) self-loathing
    (d) self-importance

21. If we believe that we have very little influence over events in our lives, we have _____ .
    (a) low self-esteem
    (b) an internal locus of control
    (c) low self-efficacy
    (d) an external locus of control

22. Seligman developed the idea that when people believe they cannot influence their environments or control their own lives, they may succumb to a sense of _____ .
    (a) learned helplessness
    (b) imaginary audience
    (c) insecurity
    (d) fear of failure

23. _____ tests of personality are generally straightforward self-report instruments, which are standardized and normed in a way similar to IQ tests.
    (a) Subjective
    (b) Projective
    (c) Objective
    (d) None of the above

24. The _____ is a projective test in which between five and twenty-two stimulus cards with images drawn from magazine art of the mid-twentieth century are shown to a participant and the participant is asked to tell a story about the card.
    (a) TAT
    (b) MMPI-2
    (c) FCC
    (d) Myers-Briggs

25. The objective test that is loosely based on Jung's personality theory and identifies four dimensions of personality style is the _____ .
    (a) Myers-Briggs Type Indicator
    (b) Minnesota Multiphasic Personality Inventory—2
    (c) Rorschach Inkblot Test
    (d) Human Figure Drawings Test

PART C. Modified True-False

If the statement is true, write "T" for the answer. If the statement is incorrect, change the underlined expression to one that will make the statement true.

1. According to ancient Greek notions of personality, personality was influenced by underlined unconscious forces.
2. The humanistic theory of personality purports that a cluster of essential characteristics can summarize any individual's personality, or traits, which occur in varying degrees in each person.
3. Phrenology is one of the earliest personality theories and was based on the idea that personal characteristics could be detected by feeling the shape and lumps on a person's head.
4. Freud's psychosocial stages reflected the developmental "crisis" notion.
5. When the id has an overt influence on a person's behavior, it is called psychosis.
6. The superego acts as a "middle person" between basic needs that require fulfillment and the restrictions of the outer world.
7. When a conflict between the ego, id, and superego cannot be resolved, a person may use one or more defense mechanisms.
8. Acting younger than your age in response to stress reflects the projection defense mechanism.
9. The defense mechanism of reaction formation occurs when someone states strongly that one's feelings are completely opposite from what they actually are.
10. The libido is the sexual energy that drives a person to seek gratification without regard to the rules and taboos of society.
11. The endpoint of lifespan development is to find and remain with a stable, heterosexual love object.
12. People who are addicted to drugs, especially those that involve mouth contact, are thought to be fixated in the anal stage, owing to frustration or over-indulgence.
13. Freud believed that in the latency period, people develop strong, mature sexual interest which requires finding an appropriate, permanent heterosexual love interest and sublimating interest in other partners into work.
14. The male traits that make up every individual's personality are called anima, and the female traits that make up every individual's personality are called animus, according to Jung.
15. Horney proposed that children's development is impacted by parental nurturance, such that if a child does not feel loved and protected, he or she will develop a sense of depression as an adult.
16. The Eysencks advocated for three dimensions of personality—emotional stability, neurosis, and well-being.
17. A person who is high in extraversion will be receptive to new ideas, creative, and have broad interests, according to the five-factor model.
18. A person who is low in neuroticism is emotionally unstable, insecure, anxious, and moody, according to the five-factor model.
19. Humanistic theories were generated partially in response to the view that some psychologists held that psychoanalytic and behavioral views of human personality and motivation were too negative and mechanical, respectively.

20. Rogers theorized that <u>unconditional positive regard</u> from a parent was more likely to produce a child with high self-esteem and a match between self-concept and ideal self.
21. Bandura examined the interaction of behavior, environmental reaction, and internal processing and called it <u>reciprocal determinism</u>.
22. A high locus of control is <u>negatively</u> associated with good pyschological adjustment.
23. <u>Objective</u> tests are designed to help reveal unconscious processes.
24. <u>Adler</u> Inkblot Test is a projective test that consists of ten ambiguous blots, in which the subject is asked to state what the inkblots appear to be.
25. Projective tests are likely to be scored by <u>clinical analysis</u>, while objective tests are likely have a <u>numerical scoring system</u>.

PART D. Chart Completion

Fill in the missing information in each of the charts. One row is completed in each chart as an example.

PERSONALITY THEORY

Personality Theory	Basic Principles	Psychologist(s) Associated with Theory
Psychoanalytic/ psychodynamic	Personality shaped by early childhood experiences and unconscious forces.	Freud, Jung, Adler, A. Freud, Horney
Trait theories		Allport, _____, _____ , _____
Humanistic		_____, _____
		Bandura, Rotter

PART E. Matching

Match the description to the defense mechanism it represents.

Defense Mechanisms

denial	projection	undoing
sublimation	displacement	reaction formation
repression	regression	daydreaming
rationalization		

1. Holly keeps "forgetting" to call her ex-boyfriend to ask him to pick up his CDs at her apartment. _____
2. Jerry tells you that he is over Holly, even though he still has pictures of her on his desk at work and in his bedroom. _____
3. Serena lies about almost everything, but she always thinks people are lying to her. _____

4. Tyrone had a terrible day at work, and he made his roommates' lives miserable all evening. _____

5. Ever since Boris was turned down for the promotion for which he applied, he's been spending a lot more time sailing competitively. _____

6. Jessica's parents are getting divorced after twenty-eight years of marriage. She tells her friends "It's for the best, and it's none of my business anyway." _____

7. After barely making a C average in his first semester of law school, Dan quit and moved to Hawaii to surf in amateur competition. _____

8. After telling her best friend's most embarrassing secrets to a new boyfriend, Sara offers to spend the weekend pet sitting for that friend at no charge. _____

9. Whenever his dad starts yelling at him, Carl thinks about his plans for a future career as a professional baseball player. _____

10. Jerry says that he is no longer hung up on Holly. He says it a lot. He says it to his friends almost everyday, whether or not they bring up the subject. _____

Personality Theories

Match the concept to the personality theory or theorist with which it is associated (answers may be used more than once).

Adler	Freud	trait theory
Jung	Horney	Rotter
Bandura	humanistic theory/Rogers	

1. Id, ego, and superego _____
2. Collective unconscious _____
3. OCEAN _____
4. Locus of control _____
5. Unconditional positive regard and congruence _____
6. Striving for superiority _____
7. Defense mechanism _____
8. Reciprocal determinism _____
9. Oral stage and fixation _____
10. Basic anxiety _____

CONNECTING TO CONCEPTS

Review the chapter and then write down your thoughts about the following questions.

1. List and briefly describe the different psychoanalytic personality theories. If you had to choose one, which would you say helps you to understand human behavior. If more than one does, or none do, please explain why.

2. Think of a time when you were faced with an unpleasant situation or feeling and you used a defense mechanism. Which one was it, and how did it help you? Do you prefer one defense mechanism to the others, or do you use more than one depending on the situation?

3. Pick a celebrity or other well-known person and describe his or her personality using the five-factor model (OCEAN). How good is the model for describing this person's temperament and behavior? Do you think the person has any traits that are not accounted for by the modes?

4. Compare and contrast the humanistic, psychoanalytic, and social-cognitive views of personality. Which one do you think is most accurate?

5. Define objective and projective in relation to personality testing. What are some of the problems that psychologists face in trying to assess personality?

CONNECTING TO LIFE/JOB SKILLS

Personality and Career Testing

To what extent does the career you choose need to fit your personality? People often make statements such as "he has an engineer's personality" or "she would make a great actress," but these are statements based on overly simple stereotypical ideas about careers and people. Often career counselors give assessment batteries that feature both personality and career interest inventories, so one might assume that there is a close relationship between personality and career interest and satisfaction. Like everything else that influences human behavior, though, it is probably not so simple and clear-cut. There is much more to what makes a career work for you than any inventory of personality style, traits or temperaments, and interests can detect. The process of finding a career is a long, complex evolution. There is good reason, as you have seen, to anticipate that your interests and your personality will change across time and situations. Tests and counselors are only one set of tools. It is in your best interest to educate yourself about these instruments so that you can use them wisely, so please visit the following web sites:

THE JOB HUNTERS BIBLE

www.jobhuntersbible.com/counseling/counseling.shtml

ASSESSMENTS WITH CAREER COUNSELING

www.careers-by-design.com/assessments_online.htm

CAREERDOWELL.COM

careerdowell.com/Counseling/Counseling.htm

YOUR CAREER PLANNING GUIDE

www.career-counseling-help.com/

WHAT'S HAPPENING!

Biological Basis of Personality

In Chapter 2 "What's Happening!" we learned about one relatively new field of psychology, *behavioral genetics*. Behavioral geneticists try to determine the extent to which genes influence individual differences in personality. They also design studies to determine the relative proportion of the contributions to personality that come from genes and the environment, using twin studies, family studies, and, most recently, the direct study of the human genome. Without a doubt, personality is determined to some extent by genes, but it is also, without a doubt, determined by the environment. What complicates matters is that it is very hard to tease apart the genetic from the environmental when examining research subjects who share a family environment as well as genes. Most of the research has been done by self-report surveys, another source of concern due to reporting biases (recall from Chapter 1). Behavioral genetics has generated a great deal of debate over the importance of the family environment, including claims that the actions of parents are relatively unimportant in shaping personality in children (relative to the influence of genes and the peer group). In 1998, Judith R. Harris published the book *The Nurture Assumption*, which presented this argument. She based her claims in part on the recent findings of behavioral genetics. A link to the web site associated with the book is provided here.

Advances in neuroscience permit us to study the brain's relationship to mood and behavior in ways that further illuminate the biological basis of personality. As early as 1848, we had evidence that the brain generated temperament when a railroad foreman, Phineas Gage, survived an accident in which a metal rod passed through his skull and destroyed a large part of his frontal lobe. A man who was a controlled, modest, and polite individual became impulsive, insensitive, and foul-mouthed. We can now study (through brain imaging instead of damage) the contributions of the limbic system and cortex to character and temperament, including recent research in the role of the frontal lobes and limbic system (see Chapter 11) in helping us to understand our own emotions and those of others.

THE NURTURE ASSUMPTION

home.att.net/~xchar/tna/

ANNUAL REVIEW OF PSYCHOLOGY: BIOLOGICAL THEORIES OF PERSONALITY

www.findarticles.com/cf_0/m0961/2001_Annual/73232708/p9/article.jhtml?term=

THE PHINEAS GAGE INFORMATION PAGE

www.deakin.edu.au/hbs/GAGEPAGE/

LIFE AFTER BRAIN INJURIES: ARE WE STILL THE SAME PEOPLE?

serendip.brynmawr.edu/bb/neuro/neuro02/web2/adymkowski.html

THE NEUROBIOLOGY OF MORALS

www.nature.com/nsu/991021/991021-6.html

OTHER USEFUL WEB SITES

PERSONALITY THEORIES

www.ship.edu/~cgboeree/perscontents.html

Dr. C. George Boeree of Shippensburg University provides a comprehensive catalog of personality theories and theorists, with additional links to other sites.

THE CG JUNG PAGE

www.cgjungpage.org/

This web site is devoted fully to the work of Freud's former student.

THE FREUD MUSEUM

www.freud.org.uk/

Although Freud is gradually receding in importance to the science of psychology, he will always remain an important part of its history. Visiting this site is a great way to learn about his works.

PERSONALITY TESTS

www.yorku.ca/psycentr/tests/per.html

York University's psychology department has assembled an impressive list of personality tests. Click on the name of any test to learn more about it.

REFERENCES

Bandura, A. (1986) *Social Foundations of Thought and Action: A Social-Cognitive Theory.* Englewood Cliffs, NJ: Prentice-Hall.

Eysenck, H. J. (1990) An improvement on personality inventories. *Current Contents: Social and Behavior Sciences,* 22(18), 20.

Goldberg, L. R. (1933) The structure of phenotypic personality traits. *American Psychologist,* 48, 26–34.

Lilienfeld, Wood, J. M. & Garb, H. N. (2001) What's wrong with this picture? *Scientific American,* May, 81–89.

McCrae, R. R. & Costa, P. T. (1990) *Personality in Adulthood.* New York: Guilford Press.

Matsumoto, D. (2000) *Culture and Psychology.* Belmont CA: Wadsworth.

Mischel, W. (1990) Personality dispositions revisited and revised: A view after three decades. In L. Pervin (Ed.), *Handbook of Personality: Theory and Research,* 21–65. New York: Guilford Press.

Paunonen, S. P. & Jackson, D. N. (1992) Personality structure across cultures: A multimodal evaluation. *Journal of Personality and Social Psychology,* 62, 447–456.

Seligman, M. E. P. (1972) "Learned helplessness." Annual Review of Medicine, 23, 407–412.

Chapter 14

PSYCHOPATHOLOGY

Psychopathology refers to mental illness. In this chapter you will review the history of mental illness as a concept, the current system for diagnosing and classifying mental illnesses, and the controversies surrounding such disorders arising in the medical and legal fields.

Normal and Abnormal

Mental illness is a general term for a wide variety of disorders that manifest through disturbed mood, behavior, and thought. *Disturbed* means that by some clear and well-defined standard the person is not functioning "normally." The person's mood, thinking, or actions are abnormal. This invites the question: What *is* normal? It is very difficult to define normal without considering the context in which the person is situated. Dancing at a party is considered normal; under most circumstances, dancing on a crowded city street is not. A person who is crying in public might be viewed as acting strangely; unless we are told that that person just received a call on his or her cell phone that a close relative or friend had died, we might think the person has an emotional problem.

One of the major criticisms of the idea of mental illness is based on the subjectivity involved in the business of determining what is normal versus what is not.

Consider also the viewpoint of Thomas Szasz MD (b. 1920), a psychiatrist who wrote a classic book (1961), *The Myth of Mental Illness*. He offers the reader a complex attack on psychiatry. Here are some of his major points:

- There is a distinction between the branch of medicine that treats problems of the brain, called *neurology,* and the branch of medicine that treats problems of living, which is called *psychiatry*. Psychiatry is far less scientific than neurology and walks the fine line between medical practice and social control (controlling people by diagnosing them, and subjecting them to psychotherapy and biomedical treatments, not infrequently against their wills).
- Diagnostic labels used in psychiatry are not scientific. They are assigned as a way to say that these people annoy us, make our lives inconvenient, or make us uncomfortable.
- The definition of mental illness/abnormality has changed over the course of history and is not standard across cultures. The sixteenth century had witches and witchcraft, and the twenty-first century has patients and mental illness. This is simply another label for

behaviors that are not considered normal. Not being normal does not necessarily mean that one is ill (or that one is a witch for that matter).

Szasz's views are extreme. (He doesn't support the idea that schizophrenia is a mental illness, for example.) But the extremity of his views is not sufficient grounds on which to reject them. During the twentieth century, people in America and the Soviet Union were sometimes treated against their wills in psychiatric hospitals for what would be accurately described as socially or politically deviant behavior. Part of the justification for placing actress Frances Farmer (1914–1970) in a mental hospital was that she was very sexually active; homosexuals were considered to be mentally ill, and homosexuality was included in the first versions of the Diagnostic and Statistical Manual (see discussion later in this chapter). Szasz would point out, rightly, that engaging in behavior that a number of people find morally objectionable is not grounds for declaring them mentally ill. In the former USSR (Soviet Union), institutionalization was used to control people who did not agree with the communist government. Clearly the potential for abuse exists. Regarding the evolution of mental illness as a label for generic abnormal behavior, consider the diagnosis of attention deficit/hyperactivity disorder (ADHD). This disorder is relatively common now, especially in school-age (5 to 12) boys. A century ago it was almost unheard of—boys were rarely labeled this way. Does the disorder exist apart from social context? Is it biologically based? Probably, we know that from birth children vary in temperament. There may be children who are "too active" and "too distractible" due to brain-based problems. A century ago most children spent fewer than four hours a day in school; now they spend eight to ten. After school, children worked for their families at home or on a farm, helped out in the family trade, or played outdoors most of the rest of the time. If there is an underlying neurological problem that causes ADHD, the changes in technology and society have caused its effects to be much more noticeable. There are psychological disorders that are culture-specific, such as Koro, a complaint of Malaysian men. It is a mass delusion in which they fear that their genitals are shrinking and receding into their bodies. Koro does not occur in other cultures. Why does Koro only occur in this region of Southeast Asia? All of these facts suggest that notions of normality and abnormality are subject to complex sociocultural influences.

As you read through the chapter keep in mind that "not normal" is not necessarily the same as "mentally ill." If something is wrong with a person's brain, it is technically a physical illness. Brain-based illnesses are shown through behavioral, mood, and thought problems. We usually do not stigmatize cancer sufferers, but we do stigmatize people who suffer from schizophrenia. Though many of the diagnoses included in the DSM-IV-TR (the current version of the Diagnostic and Statistical Manual) have an identified biological basis, some do not. Finally, the disorders listed in the DSM are voted in and out of the manual by a consensus of mental health professionals and organizations. Disorders have come and gone. The argument that Szasz and others make about the unscientific nature of diagnostic labels is hard to dismiss given this fact.

There are many different ways to conceptualize mental illness. The disorders that are currently considered to be mental disorders cause the following three problems for the individual who is suffering from such a disorder (Holmes 2000):

- *Distress.* The person reports that he or she is suffering from psychological discomfort.
- *Disability.* The individual feels unable to perform typical activities of daily life.
- *Deviance.* By any reasonable objective criteria, the person's mood, thought, or behavior is not normal or typical for his or her situation.

Mental Illness and Its Treatment in History

Prehistoric humans most likely identified the cause of disturbed behavior as "evil spirits." There are techniques that were developed before the start of recorded history. One was *trephination*, the drilling of holes in the skull. It is believed that this was done to allow evil spirits to escape. The other was *exorcism*, a ritual (usually religious) to drive an evil spirit out of the body. This ritual is still practiced in some cultures. The ancient Greeks (and later Romans) had a system for explaining mental illnesses based on their limited understanding of physiology—the four humors described at the beginning of Chapter 13. A person with the symptoms of a mental illness was thought to be suffering from an imbalance of humors. The treatments Greek and Roman doctors used were relatively humane—rest, exercise, and dietary changes. The period of Western history referred to as the Middle Ages (also called the Dark Ages) saw a return of belief in evil spirits, demonic possession, and witchcraft—abnormal behaviors for which the "treatment" sometimes was execution. In the eighteenth century, medical doctors gradually began to take over supervision of the treatment of mental illness—at least in the case of the wealthier social classes. Many poor mentally ill persons ended up in asylums. These institutions were charged to protect the mentally ill, but often they were quite unpleasant places where patients were chained, abused, and neglected. It was common for rich Londoners to visit the Hospital of St. Mary of Bethlehem (called Bedlam) and pay to be allowed to walk around staring at the patients, simply for amusement. During the same period of history, the moral philosophy of treatment (based on Protestant philosophies of protection and compassion) began to be promoted, finally taking hold in nineteenth century America and Europe through the work of Benjamin Rush, Dorothea Dix, and Jane Addams. At first "moral treatments" varied in quality and scientific basis. Clean, safe living arrangements were provided, but some patients were bled and drugged, often with bad consequences. In other cases, the patients were placed in restraining devices to "calm" them or put to work to help them learn to control themselves. Hypnotism was introduced at this time as a treatment (see Chapter 5).

At the end of the nineteenth century, Freud and other physicians and psychologists began to explore mental illness and its treatment in more organized and scientific ways. The twentieth century saw great advances in understanding the brain's role in these disorders, and improvements in many forms of treatment. Mental institutions began to be monitored by independent and government-based organizations charged to protect patient's rights—more than a few were closed when they failed to provide humane care. (One tragic example was Willowbrook State Hospital in Staten Island, New York, which was closed in 1970.) See the last section of this chapter for more information on the legal rights of persons receiving inpatient treatment.

The Classification of Mental Illnesses: DSM-IV-TR

Classification of mental disorders was a lot simpler in Freud's time—people were simply classified as either *neurotic* (a vague term that refers to experiencing symptoms of emotional distress, immaturity, or instability) or *psychotic* (out-of-touch with reality—having delusions, hallucinations, and severe behavioral problems).

As time passed, the classification scheme gradually become much more complicated, leading to the creation of the six successive versions of the *Diagnostic and Statistical Manual of Mental Disorders* (DSM I, II, III, IIIR, IV, and IV-TR.)*

The first version (I) of the DSM was published in the early 1950s. This manual describes the specific symptoms and diagnostic guidelines for different psychological disorders. There are some important advantages to using this system. It provides mental health professions with the following:

- A common language with which to label mental disorders, allowing effective communication between the disciplines that may serve these patients—human/social services, medical, educational, or psychological.
- A full set of guidelines to use in diagnosing mental disorders.

Of course, it has always been far from perfect and has gone through many revisions. As further evidence of both the sociocultural aspects of mental illness and the arbitrary nature of these classification systems, one can track the history of homosexuality in the DSM.

- First, it was a full-blown diagnosable mental disorder (DSM).
- Then it was considered an illness only when it was "ego-dystonic"—meaning that the homosexual person was unhappy about being homosexual (DSM-III).
- Then, it was not diagnosable at all (DSM-IIIR).

Usually the last sections of the DSM contain disorders "under consideration"—perhaps to be included in the next edition, or phased out after being included in earlier editions. One example of the latter is passive-aggressive personality disorder. "Passive-aggressive" is a term for hurting people by *not* doing things—a sin of omission—forgetting birthdays, being chronically late, and the like. Is it a personality disorder or merely an annoying personal characteristic?

The chief drawback of the DSM system, as Szasz and others have suggested, is that it is easy to confuse the diagnosis with the person to whom the diagnostic label is attached. The label may influence how we see the person. If we are told ahead of time that a person has a certain personality disorder, we will "see" the characteristics when we actually meet him or her. The labels may elicit the self-fulfilling prophecy. After the diagnosis is known, a clinician or other person working with the patient will treat him or her in ways that elicit the behavior. An interesting research study, done by Robert Rosenhan (1973), produced evidence that diagnostic labels may encourage biased preconceptions. In the study, eight people faked symptoms such as auditory (sound) hallucinations long enough to be admitted to several inpatient mental hospitals. Once they were admitted, they began to act normally. In all cases, several days elapsed before any staff member detected the deception. Some of the "pseudopatients" went undetected for several weeks. Ironically, the real patients were more likely to identify the imposters than the unit staff members were.

The latest version of the DSM reflects the movement toward a *biopsychosocial* view of mental illness. This perspective attempts to factor in all the major components that might contribute to mental illness. The five axes of the DSM are designed in part with reference to this model:

*I, II, III, IV, and V are the roman numerals for 1, 2, 3, 4 and 5, respectively. R stands for revision, TR for text revision.

- *The biological component*—problems with the brain, nervous system, or endocrine system that might have an effect on behavior, mood, and thought.
- *The psychological component*—the person's life events, belief system, and values that might shape the way he or she experiences the world.
- *The social component*—stressors based in the environment, economic conditions, and cultural influences that would have an impact on the person's ability to function.

The Five-Axis DSM-IV System

Axis I—Clinical/Functional Disorders

Clinical/functional disorders are said to involve a deterioration from a point in time in which functioning was better or normal. The large majority of disorders appearing in the DSM are diagnosed on Axis I, including:

- All mental disorders beginning in childhood/adolescence, such as *autism*, *conduct disorder*, and *attention deficit hyperactivity disorder*.
- *Delirium/dementia, amnesia,* and other cognitive disorders usually involve damage to the central nervous system owing to disease process, stroke, or injury to the brain. An example is *Alzheimer's disease*.
- Disorders related to misuse or continuous use of psychoactive substances include substance-related dependence, abuse, withdrawal, intoxication, mood, and psychotic disorders.
- *Schizophrenia, delusional disorders,* and other disorders that feature psychotic symptoms (thought and sensory disturbances).
- *Mood disorders* have primary symptoms that involve disturbance of emotions and include m*ajor depression, dysthymia,* and *bipolar illnesses*.
- *Anxiety* d*isorders* include the various *phobias, panic disorder,* and *generalized anxiety disorder* in which anxiety is experienced to a debilitating degree.
- *Somatoform disorders* are mental health problems that are experienced through physical symptoms. *Hypochondria* and *conversion disorders* are examples.
- *Factitious disorders* are mental health symptoms faked for attention or sympathy. Such fakery is called *malingering* when there is a clear gain to be had (insurance benefits or lawsuit award).
- *Dissociative disorders* feature disruptions in memory, consciousness, or integrity of identity. Some of these are very controversial partly because these disorders can be easily faked—one example is *dissociative identity* (multiple personality) *disorder*.
- *Sexual* and *gender identity disorders* are disorders of attraction, arousal, desire, and gender identification. These are only identified as disorders if no clear physical cause can be found.
- *Eating* and *sleep disorders* involve disturbances in patterns of food consumption, sleep, interruptions, lack of sleep or too much sleep. *Narcolepsy, bulimia,* and *anorexia* are examples.
- *Impulse-control disorders* involve an inability to resist physical and behavioral impulses. *Kleptomania* (compulsion to steal), *trichotillomania* (inability to resist pulling out one's hair), and *Tourette's syndrome* (vocal and physical tics) are examples.

• *Adjustment disorders* relate to the occurrence of what is deemed to be an "abnormal" level of distress related to an identifiable life stressor or event (such as a severe depressive reaction to a death in the family). This category has been criticized for being somewhat arbitrary and culture bound. Adjustment disorders are classified according to the mood of the individual—adjustment disorder with depressed mood, with anxious mood, etc.

Axis II—Personality (Character) Disorders and Mental Retardation

There are only two broad types of mental illness diagnosed on Axis II.

• *Personality disorders* are pervasive, rigid patterns of maladaptive behavior and mood. There are ten specific personality disorders organized into three related "clusters":
  • Cluster A (odd or eccentric behavior): *paranoid, schizoid,* and *schizotypal* personality disorders.
  • Cluster B (erratic or emotional behavior): *borderline, narcissistic, histrionic,* and *antisocial* personality disorders.
  • Cluster C (anxious or fearful behavior): *avoidant, dependent, obsessive compulsive* personality disorders. (This last one is not to be confused with *obsessive-compulsive Anxiety* disorder (OCD), an Axis I diagnosis.)
• *Mental retardation* is characterized by an IQ score of less than 70 and relative inability to manage one's own daily functioning (get to appointments for example). The most common and preventable cause of mental retardation is *fetal alcohol syndrome* (effects of exposure to alcohol through mother's drinking before birth) followed by various genetically based disorders such as *Down's syndrome*.

Axis III—General Medical Conditions

Axis III disorders are medical problems that influence the mental disorder or are relevant to understanding or managing the mental disorder. Conditions like asthma, diabetes, and lupus among others would be highly relevant. A diagnosis of cancer might influence an Axis I diagnosis of adjustment disorder with depressed mood or major depression.

Axis IV—Psychosocial and Environmental Problems

Because Axis IV illnesses do not arise "in a vacuum," stressors in the person's environment may be affecting the individual's overall level of functioning—things like legal, educational and marital problems. There are eight broad categories, such as family problems, school problems, involvement with the legal system, and the like.

Someone who can manage quite well with a latent or underlying Axis I or II disorder may deteriorate quite markedly in response to problems like these. And, of course, the mental health problem may worsen the environmental stressor in turn.

Axis V—Global Assessment of Functioning (GAF)

The global assessment of functioning (GAF) is a number that is used to represent the overall mental health of the individual being diagnosed. As is usual, high is good, and low is not so good. The range is from 0 to 100. 0–10 is in need of hospitalization, 80–100 is functioning well with no or minor symptoms.

Some Axis I Disorders in Depth*

Anxiety Disorders

Anxiety is normal under many circumstances. It helps us to prepare to meet the challenges of everyday life. Anxiety disorders involve levels of fear and nervousness that are out of proportion given the level and nature of threat or the challenge(s) faced by the individual—to the point where the person feels distress and inability to function in day-to-day life. Table 14-1 lists the major anxiety disorders.

TABLE 14-1
ANXIETY DISORDERS

Disorder: Phobias

Primary Symptoms: Extreme fear of a situation or thing. Typical phobias include open spaces (agoraphobia), closed spaces (claustrophobia) and specific fears of heights, social events, animals, etc. Panic attacks are present sometimes.

Prevalence: About 10–11% of the population will suffer from a phobia at some time.

Possible Cause(s): May be learned through conditioning. Some phobias are more easily acquired than others, suggesting an evolutionary basis (fear of spiders, for example).

Treatment(s): Exposure therapies such as systematic desensitization (see Chapter 15). Drug therapies using minor tranquilizers are used for short-term symptom management.

Disorder: General anxiety disorder (GAD)

Primary Symptoms: Persistent and pervasive state of worry and concern. Irritability, fatigue and mild depressive symptoms are common also.

Prevalence: About 5% of the population is diagnosed with GAD.

Possible Cause(s): Genetic tendency; exposure to extreme stressors; unconscious conflicts. May be present with another mood disorder ("co-morbid").

Treatment(s): Combination of drug therapy (with antidepressants) and psychotherapy.

Disorder: Panic disorder

Primary Symptoms: Sudden onset of increased heart and breathing rates, sweating, chest pains and faintness; usually (but not always) brief in duration.

Prevalence: Between 5 and 10% of the general population will experience panic attacks. About 2% of the population qualifies for the diagnosis.

Possible Cause(s): Genetics and life stress are thought to play a role. Caffeine consumption is suspected also. Once a person begins to breath rapidly, he or she may hyperventilate and make the symptoms worse.

Treatment(s): Cognitive and supportive psychotherapy (advice and comfort); antidepressant drugs

Disorder: Obsessive-compulsive disorder

Primary Symptoms: Obsessions (recurrent uncontrollable thoughts) and compulsions (irresistible behaviors). Thoughts of germs and cleaning (hand washing) is a common OCD combination.

Prevalence: About 2–3% of the population suffers from OCD at any time.

Possible Cause(s): Has been linked to high levels of activity in the frontal lobes and low serotonin levels.

Treatment(s): Exposure, cognitive therapy, and drug therapy (antidepressants.)

*Information drawn from the DSM-IV-TR and the National Institutes of Mental Health web site.

Mood Disorders

Sadness and joy are normal emotional responses to events in our lives, and fatigue sneaks up on all of us from time to time. When these emotional states are extreme, it may be a sign of an *affective* or mood disorder. Table 14-2 lists common mood disorders.

TABLE 14-2
MOOD DISORDERS

Disorder: Major depression

Primary Symptoms: Persistent extreme sadness and negative emotion; lack of energy; loss of interest in enjoyment of life, sleep disturbances; possible suicide risk.

Prevalence: About 15% of the general population will experience major depression. Estimates of lifetime risk are as high as 25% for some segments of the population (women and college-educated persons).

Possible Cause(s): Genetic vulnerability, environmental stress; association with low levels of certain neurotransmitters (serotonin, norepinephrine, and dopamine); hormone imbalances (postpartum depression); negative attributional style.

Treatment(s): Drug therapy (antidepressants); cognitive therapy; transmagnetic cranial stimulation; electroconvulsive shock therapy (for extreme cases only), inpatient treatment

---

Disorder: Seasonal affective disorder (SAD)

Primary Symptoms: Symptoms same as major depression but occur only in autumn and winter.

Prevalence: About 3% of the general population will suffer from SAD.

Possible Cause(s): Lack of adequate light appears to have an effect on neurotransmitter levels.

Treatment(s): Light therapy—extended exposure to bright therapeutic lights on a regular basis.

Disorder: Dysthymia

Primary Symptoms: Mild but chronic version of major depression

Prevalence: 3% of the general population suffers from dysthymia.

Possible Cause(s): Same as major depression; co-morbidity is common.

Treatment(s): Cognitive therapy; antidepressant medication.

Disorder: Bipolar illness: Type 1 (mania and depression); Type 2 (low-grade mania and depression)

Primary Symptoms: Swings of emotional state from highly energetic and agitated ("manic") to extremely sad and hopeless (depressed).

Prevalence: 1% of the general population suffers from some form of bipolar disorder.

Possible Cause(s): Strong, consistent evidence of genetic basis; stress may contribute to onset of symptoms; imbalance of neurotransmitters and brain malformations.

Treatment(s): Drug therapy is mandatory (anticonvulsants; antidepressants, and antipsychotics are all used); ECT and TCM; supportive psychotherapy and psychoeducational support for patient and family.

Psychotic Disorders

Disorders that are referred to as "psychotic" or psychoses involve a "break with reality." The major symptoms are classified into two types: *positive* (as in an unusual behavior that is added or appears) symptoms such as *delusions* (distorted thoughts and beliefs) and *hallucinations* (false sensory experiences) and *negative* (as in an expected or normal behavior that

does not occur or is lost) symptoms such as lack of emotional expression and poverty of speech or language. The most well-known psychotic disorder is *schizophrenia*. People commonly confuse schizophrenia with multiple personality disorder (dissociative identity disorder) but it has nothing to do with split personality. The confusion originates from the word "schizophrenia" which means split mind. At first, some clinicians interpreted the presentation and behavior of some patients with schizophrenia as a "split" of emotions from cognitive functioning. Table 14-3 lists the four subtypes of schizophrenia, which may actually be four separate illnesses, along with the milder schizoaffective and delusional disorders.

TABLE 14-3
PSYCHOTIC DISORDERS

Disorder: Schizophrenia (paranoid type)

Primary Symptoms: Complex hallucinations; delusions of persecution (being spied on) or grandeur (I am God.)

Prevalence: About 1–2% of the general population is afflicted with some type of schizophrenia.

Possible Cause(s): Leading theory combines strong evidence for genetic basis with brain damage due to prenatal complications or other postnatal brain injury; neurotransmitter imbalance; stress may contribute.

Treatment(s): Drug therapy is mandatory (anti-psychotic drugs); supportive psychotherapy, social skills training; psychoeducation for patient and family; inpatient treatment may be necessary during course of illness.

Disorder: Schizophrenia (catatonic type)

Primary Symptoms: Shifts from excessive activity to rigid inactivity and lack of response to outside stimuli

Prevalence: See above

Possible Cause(s): See above

Treatment(s): See above

Disorder: Schizophrenia (disorganized type)

Primary Symptoms: Incoherent speech/language; social isolation; odd and disorganized behavior

Prevalence: See above

Possible Cause(s): See above

Treatment(s): See above

Disorder: Schizophrenia (undifferentiated type)

Primary Symptoms: Hallucinations, deficits in daily functioning, delusions, inappropriate emotional responses (laughing at sad news, for example.)

Prevalence: See above

Possible Cause(s): See above

Treatment(s): See above

Disorder: Schizoaffective disorder

Primary Symptoms: Depressed mood and presence of at least two symptoms associated with schizophrenia.

Prevalence: 0.5–1% of the population suffers from schizoaffective disorder.

Possible Cause(s): Same as schizophrenia.

Treatment(s): Drug therapy; supportive psychotherapy; social skills training

TABLE 14-3 (Continued)
PSYCHOTIC DISORDERS

Disorder: Delusional disorders

Primary Symptoms: One or more major nonbizarre delusions; usually one of the following: erotomanic (someone is in love with me), grandiose (I am important), persecutory, jealous; overall behavior is well organized (compared to other psychotic disorders).

Prevalence: About 0.5% in the general population affected

Possible Cause(s): Abnormalities of brain structure or function (neurotransmitters); may result from prolonged substance abuse (if this is revealed, may be rediagnosed as substance-related disorder)

Treatment(s): Drug therapy (anti-psychotic drugs); supportive psychotherapy

Mental Illness and the Criminal Justice System

Many lay (nonlegal and nonmental-health) people hold mistaken notions regarding mental illness and crime. Here are some of these "myths" of mental illness.

- Mentally ill people are more dangerous than other segments of the population. *With the single exception of those diagnosed with antisocial personality disorder, this is not true.*
- "Insanity" is a diagnostic term. *It is a strictly a legal term. The most commonly used definition of insanity is based on the M'Naghten rule, from nineteenth-century British law. It refers to being in a state in which one cannot understand right from wrong owing to a mental defect or illness. One is considered to be so disordered that one cannot have understood his or her own behavior. Most states use some modified version of the M'Naghten Rule in determining whether a defendant meets the criteria for the condition of insanity.*
- The insanity defense is used frequently. *According to the American Psychiatric Association (1996), it is used in less than 1 percent of criminal cases nationwide.*
- A successful insanity defense is easily obtained. *Of the above-mentioned 1 percent, the defense is successful only about one-quarter of the time. Media attention and a general tendency to be outraged by criminals and crime have given the public a distorted view of this process.*
- A successful insanity defense is an "easy out" from conviction. *Whether a person is found "incompetent to stand trial" or "not guilty by reason of insanity" or "guilty but mentally ill" this is far from true. In all three of these scenarios, the defendant is committed to a mental hospital. He or she stands a very good chance of remaining there longer than if actually convicted of the crime. Using this defense may save the defendant from the death penalty, but unlike a convict who can count on eventual parole hearings, the "insane" person may face an indefinite confinement.*

Connecting Through Chapter Review

WORD-STUDY CONNECTION

Write each of these words on index cards, and write their definitions on the opposite side.

adjustment disorders
affective
Alzheimer's disease
amnesia
anorexia
antisocial
anxiety disorder
attention deficit
  hyperactivity disorder
  (ADHD)
autism
avoidant
axis
bipolar illness
biopsychosocial
borderline
bulimia
conduct disorder
conversion disorder
delirium/dementia
delusional disorder
delusions
dependent
deviance
disability

dissociative disorder
dissociative identity
  disorder
distress
disturbed
Down's syndrome
dysthymia
eating/sleep disorder
exorcism
factitious disorder
fetal alcohol syndrome
gender identity disorder
generalized anxiety
  disorder
global assessment of
  functioning (GAF)
hallucinations
histrionic
hypochondira
impulse-control disorder
insanity
kleptomania
M'Naghten rule
major depression
malingering

mental illness
mental retardation
mood disorder
narcissistic
narcolepsy
negative symptoms
neurology
neurotic
obsessive compulsive
panic disorder
paranoid
personality disorders
phobia
positive symptoms
psychiatry
psychotic
somatoform disorder
schizoid
schizophrenia
schizotypal
sexual disorder
trephination
trichotillomania
Tourette's syndrome

SELF-TEST CONNECTION

PART A. Completion

Write in the word that correctly completes each statement.

1. _____ is a general term for a wide variety of disorders that manifest through disturbed mood, behavior, and thought.
2. According to Szasz, _____ treats problems of the brain, and _____ is the branch of medicine that treats problems of living.
3. An ancient, religious ritual, known as _____ , was used to drive an evil spirit out of the body and is still practiced in some cultures.
4. The _____ component of the DSM accounts for the person's life events, belief system, and values that might shape the way he or she experiences the world.

5. The DSM-IV-TR system has _____ (number) axes.
6. Personality disorders are listed on Axis _____ .
7. _____ are found on Axis IV.
8. _____ disorders are mental health problems that are experienced through physical symptoms.
9. _____ are pervasive, rigid patterns of maladaptive behavior and mood.
10. Phobias are a type of _____ disorder.
11. _____ is characterized by recurrent uncontrollable thoughts and irresistible behaviors.
12. Mental retardation is characterized by an IQ score of less than _____ and a relative inability to manage one's own daily functioning
13. The primary symptoms of _____ are persistent, extreme sadness and negative emotions; lack of energy; loss of interest in enjoyment of life, sleep disturbances; and possible suicide risk.
14. Tourette's syndrome, characterized by vocal and physical tics, is a type of _____ disorder
15. Disorders that are referred to as _____ or psychoses involve a "break with reality."
16. The major symptoms of psychotic disorders are classified into two types: _____ and _____ .
17. _____ is treated by drug therapy (antipsychotic drugs), supportive psychotherapy, social skills training, psychoeducation for patient and family, and possibly inpatient treatment.
18. _____ schizophrenia is characterized by incoherent speech/language, social isolation, and odd and disorganized behavior.
19. The primary difference between schizophrenia and schizoaffective disorder is that schizoaffective disorders also has the symptom of _____ .
20. Delusional disorders are generally treated by _____ and _____ .
21. The most commonly used definition of insanity is based on the _____ rule from nineteenth century British law.
22. Insanity refers to being in a state in which one cannot understand _____ owing to a mental defect or illness. One is considered to be so disordered that one cannot have understood his or her own behavior.
23. The insanity defense is attempted in about _____ of cases nationwide.

PART B. Multiple Choice

Circle the letter of the item that correctly completes the statement.

1. _____ refers to mental illness.
   (a) Physiology   (b) Psychology
   (c) Pharmacology   (d) Psychopathology
2. How are the disorders listed in the DSM?
   (a) Voted in by experts   (b) Randomly
   (c) Legislature   (d) None of the above
3. What kind of problem does a disorder that is considered to be a mental disorder cause for the individual:
   (a) Distress   (b) Disability
   (c) Deviance   (d) All of the above

4. What does DSM stand for?
   (a) Diagnosis Services for Mental Health
   (b) Diagnostic and Statistical Manual of Mental Disorders
   (c) Diagnostic and Service Manual for Mental Disorders
   (d) None of the above

5. Axis I of the DMS-IV TR consists of _____ .
   (a) personality disorders
   (b) mental retardation
   (c) clinical and functional disorders
   (d) general medical conditions

6. A number that is used to represent the overall mental health of the individual being diagnosed is called a _____ .
   (a) GAF   (b) DSM
   (c) FDR   (d) PDF

7. All mental disorders beginning in childhood/adolescence, such as autism, conduct disorder, and attention deficit hyperactivity disorder, would be found on which axis?
   (a) I   (b) II
   (c) III   (d) IV

8. If someone has cardiovascular (heart) disease, it will be classified on which axis?
   (a) I   (b) II
   (c) III   (d) IV

9. What category of disorders has been criticized for being somewhat arbitrary and culture bound?
   (a) Personality disorders (b) Adjustment disorders
   (c) Mental retardation   (d) Mood disorders

10. What disorder characterized by extreme fear of a situation or thing do approximately 10 to 11 percent of the population experience?
   (a) Personality disorder   (b) Phobia
   (c) Mania   (d) Mental retardation

11. Borderline, narcissistic, and antisocial are all types of what kind of disorder?
   (a) Anxiety   (b) Depressive
   (c) Psychotic   (d) Personality

12. This anxiety disorder is characterized by sudden onset of increased heart and breathing rates, sweating, chest pains, and faintness and is usually treated by cognitive and supportive psychotherapy and antidepressant drugs.
   (a) Phobia   (b) Obsessive-compulsive disorder
   (c) Panic disorder   (d) Generalized anxiety disorder

13. About what percentage of the general population will experience major depression?
   (a) 1–2 percent   (b) 5 percent
   (c) 7–8 percent   (d) 15 percent

14. What is a mild but chronic version of major depression?
   (a) Minor depression   (b) Dysthymia
   (c) Chronic depression   (d) Bipolar disorder

15. Who of the following is at greater risk for major depressive disorder?
   (a) College graduates   (b) Men
   (c) Children   (d) The middle class

16. Delusions and hallucinations are what type of psychotic symptom?
    (a) Positive   (b) Negative
    (c) Active   (d) Passive

17. Poor hygiene is an example of a _____ psychotic symptom?
    (a) positive   (b) negative
    (c) active   (d) passive

18. Someone who thinks that God is talking to him or her through the television is likely experiencing _____ .
    (a) a delusion   (b) a manic episode
    (c) a hallucination   (d) a depressive episode

19. Which type of schizophrenia is characterized by shifts from excessive activity to rigid inactivity and lack of response to outside stimuli?
    (a) Paranoid   (b) Disorganized
    (c) Catatonic   (d) Undifferentiated

20. The leading theory for the cause of _____ combines strong evidence for a genetic basis with brain damage due to prenatal complications or other postnatal brain injury.
    (a) bipolar disorder   (b) schizophrenia
    (c) phobias   (d) somatoform disorder

21. What type of schizophrenia is characterized by hallucinations, deficits in daily functioning, delusions, and inappropriate emotional responses?
    (a) Paranoid   (b) Disorganized
    (c) Catatonic   (d) Undifferentiated

22. The only exception to the fact that mentally ill people are not more dangerous than other segments of the population are people with _____ .
    (a) bipolar disorder   (b) dissociative identity disorder
    (c) schizophrenia   (d) antisocial personality disorder

23. If someone is legally _____ , he or she is considered to be so disordered that he or she cannot have understood his or her own behavior.
    (a) delusiona   (b) insane
    (c) criminal   (d) mentally ill

24. According to the American Psychiatric Association, an insanity plea is successful about _____ of the time when it is used.
    (a) 100%   (b) 50%
    (c) 25%   (d) 10%

25. One of the standards used to determine insanity is the _____ rule.
    (a) Freudian   (b) M'Naghten
    (c) Szasz   (d) DSM

PART C. Modified True-False

If the statement is true, write "T" for the answer. If the statement is incorrect, change the underlined expression to one that will make the statement true.

1. All psychological disorders are universal; none are culture-specific.
2. In ancient times, people used trephination, the practice of drilling holes in the skull to allow evil spirits to escape.

3. The philosophy of moral treatment, which was based on the Protestant philosophies of <u>protection and punishment</u>, began to take hold in nineteenth-century America and Europe through the work of Benjamin Rush, Dorothea Dix, and Jane Addams.

4. The latest version of the DSM reflects the movement towards a <u>biopsychosocial</u> view of mental illness in which the components of a person's biological, internal, and social experience are taken into account.

5. The <u>biological</u> component of the DSM accounts for stressors based in the environment, economic conditions, and cultural influences that would have an impact on the person's functioning.

6. <u>Dissociative disorders</u> are disorders that feature disruptions in memory, consciousness, or integrity of identity.

7. Sexual and gender identity disorders are only identified as disorders if no clear <u>psychological</u> cause can be found.

8. <u>Depressive</u> disorders involve levels of fear and nervousness that are out of proportion with the level and nature of threat faced by the individual. This is experienced to the point where the person feels distress and inability to function in day-to-day life.

9. <u>Phobia</u> is characterized by a persistent and pervasive state of worry and concern, irritability, fatigue, and mild depressive symptoms.

10. Obsessive compulsive personality disorder and obsessive-compulsive anxiety disorder <u>are related</u> illnesses.

11. <u>Obsessions</u>, characterized by recurrent uncontrollable thoughts, and <u>compulsions</u>, characterized by irresistible behaviors, are the two primary features of <u>OCD</u>.

12. The most likely cause of <u>major depression</u> is lack of adequate light, which appears to have an effect on neurotransmitter levels.

13. A person who suffers from <u>dysthymia</u> will have dramatic changes in mood.

14. The difference between Bipolar I and Bipolar II is that <u>Bipolar I</u> has both mania and depression while <u>Bipolar II</u> has low grade mania and depression.

15. <u>Delusions</u> are distorted thoughts and beliefs, and <u>hallucinations</u> are false sensory experiences.

16. Lack of emotional expression and poverty of speech or language are examples of <u>positive</u> symptoms of psychotic disorders.

17. An easy (and accurate) way to describe <u>schizophrenia</u> is to say "split personality."

18. About <u>9 to 10 percent</u> of the general population is afflicted with some type of schizophrenia.

19. Delusions of persecution (being spied on) or grandeur (I am God.) are often experienced by people with <u>catatonic</u> schizophrenia.

20. Schizophrenia is <u>less</u> common in the general population than schizoaffective disorder is.

21. The behavior of those who suffer from delusional disorders is generally <u>more well organized</u> than that of those who suffer from other psychotic disorders.

22. <u>Paranoid schizophrenia</u> is characterized by one or more major non-bizarre delusions—usually one of the following: erotomanic, grandiose, persecutory, or jealousy.

23. It is generally <u>not true</u> that mentally ill people are more dangerous than other segments of the population.

24. Insanity is not a <u>diagnostic</u> term but rather strictly a <u>legal</u> term.

25. A person who is found "incompetent to stand trial" is likely to <u>be set free</u>.

PART D. Chart Completion
Complete the tables with the correct information. The first row is completed for demonstration.

HISTORY OF MENTAL HEALTH TREATMENT

Historical Period	Treatment Methods
Prehistory	Trephination, exorcism
Ancient Greece and Rome	
	Exorcism, persecution, execution
Eighteenth and early nineteenth centuries	
Late nineteenth century	
Twentieth century to present time	

DIAGNOSTIC AND STATISTICAL MANUAL-IV-TR

Axis #	Disorders/Information	Specific Examples of Disorders or Information
I	Clinical/functional disorders	Mood, psychotic, impulse control, anxiety etc.
	Personality disorders, mental retardation	
III		
	Psychosocial stressors	
		75 (marginally well); 15 (in need of intensive mental health care)

AXIS I DISORDERS

Group	Example(s)	Major Symptoms
Mood disorders	Major depression, bipolar disorder, dysthymia.	Irritability, mood swings, extreme sadness, periods of intense activity
Psychotic disorders		Delusions, hallucinations, lack of or inappropriate emotional expression.
Anxiety disorders		
	ADHD, autism	Hyperactivity and inability to concentrate in school, social withdrawal, impulse control problems, aggression
		Stealing, pulling out hair, outbursts of aggression.
Eating and sleep disorders		
Adjustment disorders		

AXIS II DISORDERS

Group	Example(s)	Major Symptoms
Cluster A personality disorders	Paranoid, schizoid, and schizotypal personality disorders	Odd or eccentric behavior
Cluster B personality disorders		Erratic or highly emotional behavior
Cluster C personality disorders		
	Fetal alcohol syndrome, Down's syndrome	

CONNECTING TO CONCEPTS

Review the chapter and then write down your thoughts about the following questions.

1. Describe Thomas Szasz's criticism of psychiatry. What are the strengths of his argument? What are its weaknesses?
2. What do we learn about mental illness from studying the history of abnormal behavior and its treatment?
3. What does DSM-IV-TR stand for? What is its intended purpose? Outline the five axes of the DSM, and discuss the strengths and weaknesses of using this system to diagnose and classify.

4. Choose any group of mental disorders. Identify the axis on which it would be classified; name some examples from the group and major symptoms of such disorders.

5. Discuss the prevalence and relative success of the "insanity plea" in the American criminal justice system. Be sure to separate fact from fiction.

CONNECTING TO LIFE/JOB SKILLS

Suicide: Information and Prevention Strategies

Given the prevalence of mood disorders and stress, it is possible that you will have some contact with a person who is seriously considering suicide. There are over eighty suicides a day in the United States, according to the American Academy of Suicidology. Most people who are planning to commit suicide talk about it before they attempt it. Taking a psychology course in no way qualifies you to "cure" a depressed or suicidal friend, but a little bit of information can help you to help that person get the professional support that he or she may need.

What are the factors that raise a person's chance of attempting suicide?

- Previous history or family history of suicide
- Recent major stressor or loss
- Social isolation
- Substance abuse or dependence
- Unemployment/dismissal from school

Suicide in teenagers and young adults has been on the rise up until recently, but the age group with the greatest risk of suicide is the elderly, especially elderly men. Women attempt suicide more often than men, but complete it far less frequently. Men tend to use more lethal means than women do; although they attempt suicide less frequently, men are likely to succeed.

So what are some appropriate steps you can take if you believe a person you know is seriously contemplating suicide?

- Listen and ask questions. You will not, as the mistaken belief suggests, "put any ideas in his or her head." You will be able to get a better idea of how real the danger is—generally, the more well-defined the plan, the more real the risk.
- Be reassuring. Unless your friend is suffering from a terminal illness, suicide is generally a permanent solution to a temporary problem. See if you can help him or her think of other, non-destructive ways to solve problems.
- Suggest that the person seek professional help.

A person may ask that you "keep it a secret." Although this may be an issue of respect, it is also a life and death matter. One advantage of not being a therapist is that you have no legal obligation to worry about. If you are really concerned about the person's welfare, call a suicide or crisis hotline, or tell a counselor or other trusted professional.

FACTS AND MYTHS ABOUT SUICIDE

www.counseling.tcu.edu/documents/facts_myths_suicide.doc

KIDSHEALTH.ORG

kidshealth.org/teen/your_mind/problems/talking_about_suicide.html

SUICIDE MYTHS AND FACTS

www.yellowribbon-pa.org/myths&facts.html

LIFE FORCE (Australian Web Site, Very Helpful Information)

www.wesleymission.org.au/centres/lifeforce/about.asp

WHAT'S HAPPENING!

Early Intervention for Schizophrenia: Pros and Cons

As our understanding of the biological basis of serious mental disorders such as schizophrenia and bipolar disorder has improved, the prospect of early intervention has become more real. We know that the majority of cases of schizophrenia emerge in mid to late adolescence, and that the psychosocial difficulties and stress experienced before the diagnosis is made can cause long-term problems (job loss, dropping out or expulsion from school, disrupted family relationships, and other serious problems that emerge making recovery even more difficult).

The National Institute of Mental Health has been examining the benefits and possible problems involved in following young people who have a family history of developing schizophrenia in order to begin treatment and support services as early as possible. Prodromal (early warning signs) of schizophrenia almost never occur in children before puberty—even if a child has thinking or sensory problems at this age, not enough is known about the nature of the disorder in childhood to make a diagnosis. Young teenagers with signs of the disorder are being followed and provided with support services at this time. Drug treatment for schizophrenia involves the use of powerful antipsychotic medications with potentially serious side effects (tremors and other motor problems) so the use of drugs at this age poses serious ethical questions. Drug treatment (along with other services) remains the treatment of choice for schizophrenia so these issues must be addressed.

To read more about the research on early detection of schizophrenia, visit this web site:

NIMH EXPLORATORY REPORT ON EARLY RECOGNITION AND INTERVENTION

www.nimh.nih.gov/events/earlyrecognition.cfm

OTHER USEFUL WEB SITES

THE THOMAS SZASZ CENTER

www.szasz.com/

This is a clearinghouse for information about Dr. Szasz.

NATIONAL MENTAL HEALTH ASSOCIATION

www.nmha.org/

This is the official web site of NMHA, a nonprofit advocacy organization addressing societal issues related to mental health and mental illness.

PSYCHIATRY 24X7

www.psychiatry24x7.com/home.jhtml;jsessionid=IA2E4OEHN4U4DQFIBYHSF3Q

Although this is a commercial site, it has abundant information about diagnostic classifications and treatments for mental illness.

NATIONAL ALLIANCE FOR THE MENTALLY ILL

www.nami.org/

This is the web site of a grass-roots organization involved in education and advocacy on behalf of those who suffer from mental illnesses.

Sites Addressing Specific Mental Illnesses

PERSONALITY DISORDERS

mentalhelp.net/poc/center_index.php?id=8

AUTISM

www.autism-society.org/

SCHIZOPHRENIA

www.schizophrenia.com/

PANIC DISORDER

www.apa.org/pubinfo/panic.html

OBSESSIVE-COMPULSIVE DISORDER

www.ocfoundation.org/

DEPRESSION

www.depressionalliance.org/

BIPOLAR DISORDER PORTAL

www.pendulum.org/

DISSOCIATIVE DISORDERS

www.religioustolerance.org/mpd_did.htm

REFERENCES

American Psychiatric Association (2002) *Diagnostic and Statistical Manual of Mental Disorders-IV-TR.* Washington, DC: Author

Holmes, D. (2000) *Abnormal Psychology.* Boston: Allyn and Bacon.

National Institute of Mental Health Web Site
www.nimh.nih.gov/home.cfm

American Psychiatric Association—Public Information on the Insanity Defense (1996)
www.psych.org/public_info/insanity.cfm

Rosenhan, D. L. (1973) On being sane in insane places. *Science* 179, 250–258.

Szasz, T. (1961) *The Myth of Mental Illness.* New York: HarperCollins.

Chapter 15

MENTAL HEALTH TREATMENT

In this chapter you will be introduced to methods for treatment of psychological disorders including different types of psychotherapy and the biomedical treatments and psychoeducational interventions. Prevention, community psychology, and legal issues related to mental health treatment will also be summarized.

Types of Psychotherapy

Psychotherapy refers to a broad range of techniques designed to address problems of psychological functioning and improve an individual's personal and social adjustment. Many different types of professionals provide these services:

- Psychologists
- Medical personnel (psychiatrists and psychiatric nurses)
- Clinical social workers
- Counselors (marriage and family therapists; chemical dependency counselors, and others)
- Clergy members (priests and ministers)

The schools of therapy are methods that are based on different theories of learning, motivation, and personality with which you are now acquainted. Very few therapists use methods from one school exclusively although they may prefer one perspective for *conceptualizing* (making sense of or understanding) a client's issues. Many therapists are called *eclectic* because they use a combination of approaches.

Psychoanalysis/Psychodynamic Therapy

The theories of Sigmund Freud form the basis of *psychoanalysis* and *psychodynamic psychotherapy*. Freud believed that personality and psychological problems are both products of the interaction of conscious and unconscious forces. To treat mental health problems and promote self-understanding, treatment is designed to help the patient bring unconscious material to awareness.

Psychoanalysis is the original version of Freudian psychotherapy. True psychoanalysis is not commonly practiced (although there are institutes in the United States and Europe that offer the Freudian, Jungian, and Adlerian versions of this treatment). True psychoanalytic treatment requires the patient to work with the therapist (called an analyst) four to five times a week for two years or more, making analysis costly and impractical for most patients. In fact, the people who are most likely to have been in analysis are analysts themselves, as it is almost always required as part of their training. The classic setup for psychoanalysis (patient lying on a couch, not looking at the analyst) promotes what is called *free association* by encouraging the patient to talk without focusing on the analyst's reactions. Early in the treatment, an analyst usually says almost nothing to the patient. While associating, the patient begins talking about any issue or problem that comes to mind without any direction or comment from the analyst. In the course of free association, unconscious or repressed feelings, thoughts, and memories should surface. The opening up of these hidden internal processes and release of feelings may be a powerful experience, a *catharsis*. The patient also may begin reacting to the analyst in a manner similar to the other important figures in his or her life. This process is called *transference,* and (when the analyst points it out) it can provide valuable information for the patient's self-understanding. Psychoanalysts interpret the patient's statements, dreams, and transference. If the patient does not accept the analyst's interpretations, he or she is being *resistant* to psychoanalysis. It is part of the analyst's job to overcome the patient's resistance.

Because psychoanalysis is neither affordable nor practical for most therapy clients, many professionals offer a version of analysis—psychodynamic psychotherapy—in once or twice a week sessions. The psychodynamic therapist may not use the "couch" and will probably be more interactive than a traditional analyst. He or she will make all the same interpretations of conversation, dreams, and transference.

Behavioral Therapies

Behavioral therapies are based on principles from classical and operant conditioning. Behavioral therapies (unlike the psychoanalytically based ones discussed earlier) never refer to unconscious processes and repressed material—they only address behaviors and symptoms that cause distress or disability. The goals in a behavior therapy treatment plan are usually specific, concrete, and measurable changes in behaviors or reduction of symptoms such as

- Enabling the patient to overcome a fear and engage in a specified activity. (Reduce the fear of flying so the patient can take a vacation trip to Hawaii.)
- Reducing and eliminating fighting with classmates during recess.

Classical-Conditioning-Based Therapies

Classical conditioning is the learning of associations. When an association between a stimulus and response (a phobia of spiders—the stimulus—leading to the maladaptive response of inability to relax in one's own home) is causing problems for an individual, a classical-conditioning-based therapy provides a way to unlearn the troublesome association and replace it with a different reaction associated with the stimulus (indifference to spiders leading to more comfort and rest at home). There are two categories of these therapies.

- *Exposure therapies.* These treatments use the principle that avoidance prevents extinction, in reverse. The patient is not allowed to avoid the stimulus so that gradually he or she becomes desensitized to it. A person with a fear of spiders must spend time near spiders, perhaps even handling spiders. The most gradual form of exposure therapy is called *systematic desensitization.* Sometimes the exposure occurs very rapidly—a technique called *flooding.* Exposure therapy for some fear-causing conditions used to be expensive, time-consuming, and downright impractical (as in the case of fear of flying), but recent innovations in virtual reality technologies have made many of these treatments easier, cheaper, and quicker.
- *Aversion therapies.* In exposure therapies, an old fear is unlearned. In aversion therapies, a new fear is created in order to discourage a specific behavior. *Antabuse* is a drug therapy for people who suffer from serious chronic alcoholism—taking the drugs causes nausea if the person consumes alcohol. Mild electric shocks are used in some facilities that treat seriously developmentally disabled persons to prevent them from engaging in serious self-injurious behaviors. Each time a patient bangs his head or tries to chew off a finger, a counselor administers a mild but attention-getting shock. Even though the point is not to hurt the patients but to keep them from hurting themselves seriously and permanently, this is a highly controversial therapeutic technique.

Operant-Conditioning-Based Therapies

Operant conditioning is used to shape and create voluntary behaviors. Treatments based on operant conditioning aim to encourage patients to voluntarily reduce their maladaptive behaviors and replace them with more constructive and healthy ones.

- *Behavior Modification.* A simple behavior modification program can be implemented without the assistance of a therapist, but a good behavior therapist can provide expertise along with feedback and encouragement. Behavior modification involves identifying one or more specific target behaviors that need to be increased or eliminating and providing reinforcers accordingly. So, if the target behavior is a daily thirty-minute workout, every time the patient works out for the stated thirty minutes, her husband agrees to put $5 in an account designated for the purchase of a special gift or vacation trip. Eventually, as the behavior becomes habitual, the reinforcers are decreased in frequency. There are many possible versions of a behavior modification program.
- *Token Economy.* This is a group behavior modification arrangement. In a classroom, students receive tokens or scrip for engaging in certain behaviors (sitting quietly, raising their hands, working on their lessons) or not engaging in them (fighting or talking during the lesson). Usually the tokens can be exchanged for treats. These methods are frequently used in inpatient treatment centers for children and adolescents. One shortcoming of this treatment is that incentives in "real-world" settings often occur on a far less frequent schedule, so it is unclear whether the power of a token economy to shape behavior results in permanent changes.

Social Learning and Psychotherapy

Many cognitive and behavioral therapists include *participant modeling* in addition to the interventions associated with their typical treatment plan. Participant modeling is a therapeutic strategy based on principles of observational learning. For example, a therapist carrying out a systematic desensitization program with a patient who has arachnophobia (fear of spiders) might bring a tarantula to a therapy session and hold it and handle it in front of the patient, so that the patient observes this and feels motivated to imitate the behavior.

Cognitive Therapies

Cognition is thinking, and *cognitive therapies* are designed to change the patient's thoughts. The underlying theory is that it is the way a person thinks about the situation, not the actual situation, that is the main cause of poor adjustment and distress. There are two major types of cognitive therapies.

• *Rational-emotive therapy (RET)*. This treatment was developed in the mid-twentieth century by Albert Ellis. Ellis (1961) proposed that irrational thoughts lead to negative emotions and that controlling and changing such thoughts is the key to better mental health. So, a young man who was stood up might say (before RET) "What an *awful* thing to have happened to me. I must be a total loser for my date to have stood me up." After RET, such an event would be reframed and he might say instead "That was disappointing. But it's not the end of the world. Maybe she had an emergency. Even if she did not, I will meet someone else who won't stand me up next time."

• *Cognitive-behavior therapy (CBT)*. Aaron Beck (1976) believes that depression and other mood disorders result primarily from negative self-talk and the distorted perceptions of self that result from it. As in RET, the therapist puts more emphasis on changing the person's interpretation of thoughts and events. CBT often includes homework assignments. For example, CBT often starts with the therapist asking the patient to keep a journal of thoughts during the day. The journal is reviewed for common errors of thought such as exaggerating bad events, minimizing good ones, and introducing other problems. The therapist may later ask the patient to do something outside of therapy that directly challenges or tests his or her beliefs. For example, if a patient is convinced that a co-worker does not like her, the therapist may assign her to sit with the co-worker at lunch. Even if the patient's worst fears are confirmed, "surviving" the experience (or seeing that she actually doesn't care what the co-worker thinks) can often result in improved self-perception and less negative emotion for the patient.

Humanistic Therapy

Humanistic therapy is based on the personality and motivational theories of Carl Rogers and Abraham Maslow. Recall that these psychologists believed that humans are born with the need to strive toward making use of their full potentials and continuing personal growth. During childhood an individual develops a self-concept and an image of the *ideal self* he or she would like to be. When the patient perceives a large difference between the ideal and the real, emotional distress results.

- *Person-centered therapy*. Carl Rogers (1961) is credited with developing the most common humanistic treatment—*person-centered therapy*. The most important element of treatment is the *unconditional positive regard* provided for the patient (usually called a *client* in humanistic treatment) by the therapist. The client should be able to disclose anything to the therapist without fear of judgment or rejection. The therapist tries to be empathetic—to understand how the client experiences the world and appreciate his or her feelings. She does not direct the client's behavior, give advice, or try to interpret the client's thoughts, dreams, or behaviors. The experience is intended to lead the client to greater self-acceptance and behavior change based on improved self-esteem. A depressed client comes to therapy saying, "I am fat. I hate myself. Why would anyone care about me?" At the end of successful therapy, he says, "I will lose weight because I respect myself and want to look my best and be healthy. I care about me."
- *Existential humanistic therapy (EHT)*. This treatment is founded on the same belief in the natural human potential for psychological growth as person-centered therapy, but it also includes important elements from existentialism, a philosophical movement of the mid-twentieth century (Bugental 1978). In existentialism, the individual is responsible for creating a meaningful life despite the apparent randomness and lack of meaning that can dominate day-to-day existence. Psychological distress results when a person feels unable to make choices and create meaning. EHT is a therapy that provides a safe place for the client to explore his or her situation without judgment, and be challenged by the therapist to take responsibility to make important decisions and create a meaningful life.

Other Psychotherapy Techniques

Psychotherapy does not have to occur in a one-on-one format. *Group therapy* is offered by one or two therapists to a small group of patients (usually no more than eight to twelve). The group members listen to each other's problems and discuss them. A group setting for treatment can lower the cost, is usually time-limited, and provides the additional help and feedback of other group participants. Some drawbacks are the lack of individual attention and the reduced level of confidentiality. (The therapists are bound by professional ethics, but other members, though encouraged not to reveal others' personal information may do so anyway. Unlike the therapist, they cannot be sued for doing so.) Whole families receive treatment in *family systems therapy*. Often a family enters therapy because one member appears to have a problem. From the family systems perspective, since the individual's problems arise in a family setting, the family's dynamics and issues should be discussed. The goal is to improve family functioning by encouraging clear and honest communication about issues and problems between its members. *Inpatient psychiatric treatment* is reserved for those who are suffering severe disruptions in functioning. Many people voluntarily enter treatment, but sometimes people are committed without consent, which creates some ethical concerns (see discussion later in this chapter). Inpatient treatment usually combines biomedical treatments with a structured daytime schedule including individual therapy, group therapy, and innovative therapeutic interventions such as art, music and play/recreation therapy which provide creative ways to express feelings and thoughts.

Evaluating Psychotherapy

Psychotherapeutic treatment can be costly in terms of time and money. So is reasonable to ask whether or not the results justify the cost. Some psychologists have pointed out that placebo effects and the simple passage of time may be responsible for at least some of the successes achieved by psychotherapy, regardless of technique (Kalat 2001). In the early 1990s, a leading professional organization, the American Psychological Association (1994) reviewed a number of *meta-analytic* studies of psychotherapy and concluded that psychotherapy is effective for most people. A weakness of meta-analyses is that they tend to include only published studies, meaning that many unpublished studies in which psychotherapy did not appear to be helpful were left in the "file drawer." If included, these studies may have contributed to a different conclusion. In 1995, an interesting study was done by a magazine with no connection to the profession—*Consumer Reports*. Its findings lent support to APA's conclusions. Professional treatment by a trained and licensed clinician can be very helpful. The method used is not particularly important, nor is the provider's discipline (social worker, MD, PhD, etc.). Professionalism *is* important though— the overall level of training, experience, licensing, and ability to provide linkage (connections) to other providers (medical doctors, substance abuse treatment programs, and other resources) do seem to matter in promoting a good treatment outcome.

Biomedical Treatments for Mental Illnesses

Advances in medical technology have allowed us to identify the likely biological causes for many mental illnesses. Using this knowledge, three categories of biomedical treatment have been developed over the past two generations. The three categories of biomedical treatment are drug therapy, psychosurgery, and electrical therapies.

Pharmacotherapy (Drug Therapy)

The discovery of the many neurotransmitters and evidence that some mental illnesses are associated with imbalances has inspired the creation of several generations of psychiatric drugs. There are six major classes of these drugs, which are summarized in the Table 15-1.

Psychosurgery

Surgery on the brain earned a bad reputation in the mid-twentieth century. The *lobotomy* was devised to control the symptoms of schizophrenia by disconnecting the frontal lobes from the rest of the brain. The problem was that, before the technology existed to fully understand how the lobes of the brain worked, this surgery was based on a mere speculation. Lobotomies did make some schizophrenia sufferers more docile, but the procedure did not fully control the symptoms. As was the case with so many other treatments, the surgery was often used abusively to control patients whether or not it was medically necessary.

TABLE 15-1
COMMON PSYCHIATRIC MEDICATIONS

Drug Class	Typical Brand Names	Neurotransmitters/ Brain Structures Acted On	Symptoms Controlled	Some Possible Side Effects
Antipsychotic	Haldol, Mellaril, Risperidal, Thorazine	Dopamine (reduced); serotonin (increased).	Decrease positive and negative symptoms of psychosis (delusions, hallucinations, lack of emotion)	Sleepiness, anxiety, appetite changes, motor problems (tremors and tics)
Mood stabilizer	Eskalith (lithium)	Glutamate (reduced); increases volume of gray matter in cerebral cortex.	Reduces or eliminates episodes of mania	Lithium is a toxic metal and blood levels must be monitored to prevent damage to internal organs.
Anticonvulsant	Tegritol, Phenobarbital	Reduce firing of cortical neurons	Reduces seizures	Constipation, nausea, mild dizziness
Antidepressant	Prozac, Elavil, Imipramine	Serotonin (increased); epinephrine/norepinephrine (increased)	Increases energy, improves sleep and mood.	Appetite problems, weight gain/loss, dry mouth, nausea
Antianxiety	Valium, Librium, Xanax	GABA (reduced); sympathetic nervous system activity (reduced)	Decreases nervousness, promotes sleepiness	Dependence, sleep disturbances
Stimulant	Ritalin, Cylert	Increase dopamine levels	Increases attention and ability to focus	Appetite suppression, sleep disturbances, slows growth in children

Psychosurgery is now used more cautiously, and often with much more success. Epilepsy is successfully controlled with various forms of psychosurgery—from relatively minor procedures involving the removal of small pieces of cortical tissue to the more radical severing of the *corpus callosum* (the bundle of axons that allows the two hemispheres of the brain to communicate; see Chapter 3), which surprisingly makes very little difference in day-to-day functioning, to the removal of a full hemisphere (*hemispherectomy*; see Chapter 3) which can be done to children with serious degenerative brain illnesses. Because of the relative *plasticity* of the brain early in life, most functions can be recovered as the remaining cortical neurons "rewire" the brain, forming new synapses.

Electrical Therapies

Electroconvulsive therapy (ECT) also gained a bad reputation in the last century because of its abusive use by doctors, hospital staff, and occasionally families of patients (who would consent on the patient's "behalf"). This treatment used electrical currents passed through the brain to induce seizures. It remains, in more limited use, with voluntary consent of the *patient* only, an undeniably effective treatment for serious, intractable depression—depression that does not respond to any other standard therapy (especially if suicide is a risk for the depressed patient). For many patients, ECT brings about a relatively long reduction of depressive symptoms. Weighing some of the serious side effects (memory loss, seizures) against the danger of suicide, some patients are willing to undergo ECT.

A newer and less dangerous electrical treatment is *transmagnetic cranial stimulation (TMS)*. In this therapy, electromagnets are used to disrupt briefly the firing of cortical neurons. It is painless and induces no serious side effects. It appears to be as effective as ECT in causing remission of depressive symptoms.

Prevention and Community Mental Health

Another way to "treat" mental illness is to try to stop it from occurring in the first place. Outside of the more remote promise of genetic screening and gene therapy, early intervention to reduce some of the environmental factors that contribute to mental illness can be effective. The *community psychology perspective* is that psychologists should be present in the community to provide services toward educating the public and preventing mental illness. There are three types of prevention strategies.

- *Primary prevention methods* are those that seek to "stop mental illness before it starts" by providing stress management education, human factors analyses and social interventions, and various types of health care services that relate to psychological adjustment. For example, good prenatal care lowers the chance that a baby will be born with organic brain damage.
- *Secondary prevention* involves identifying a disorder in its early stages and treating it before it becomes serious. Some neurologists have begun to monitor children in families with histories of serious mental disorders (schizophrenia and bipolar disorders) so that if symptoms begin to emerge, treatments can be offered before the individual's life becomes too badly disrupted.
- *Tertiary prevention* is "relapse prevention." It includes offering both transitional services to help people recovering from serious mental illness return to the work force and develop social networks, and psychoeducational and support services (such as respite care—a break from caring for a mentally ill loved one) for the families of those who suffer from mental illness.

Self-help groups and *paraprofessional counselors* can be used for primary, secondary, and tertiary prevention efforts. Paraprofessional counselors are unlicensed but trained and are often peers in the community in which they service (recovering substances abusers, for example.) Groups are highly effective for starting informal support networks and spreading helpful information; involving community members in prevention efforts can be very empowering.

Legal Aspects of Mental Health Treatment

Confidentiality and Consent to Treatment

Earlier in the chapter the issue of *confidentiality* (nondisclosure of private information) was mentioned (the lack of legal obligation for group members to protect each other's confidentiality). Therapists *are* obligated to protect patient confidentiality whether the treatment is provided in an individual, group, or inpatient setting. Only under a limited set of circumstances may a therapist break this obligation.

- The patient's actions pose a threat to an identifiable, foreseeable victim—as in the (1976) California case *Tarasoff v. the Regents of University of California.* A psychologist at the university knew that his patient had the intention to kill a specific university student and had the means to do so. He warned the police but not the family of the threatened student. The case established that a counselor or psychologist is required to warn the victim of the patient's intent.
- The patient's behavior, through evidence of suicidal intent, or gross inability to care for him- or herself, means that it is likely that the patient will come to serious harm. In this case, the mental health provider may notify the police or local hospital to have the patient evaluated for involuntary commitment to inpatient care. This is referred to as a "duty to warn."

Consent to treatment is desirable but may not be necessary (as mentioned earlier). Minors under the age of 12 may not give consent for mental health treatment under any circumstances; from age 12 on, the therapist has some discretion to accept the minor's consent under certain circumstances (for example, if the minor desires treatment for substance abuse or dependence). Parents may demand information about treatment under such circumstances (they have a right to do so until the minor patient turns 18). If a therapist can convince the parents to respect a minor's confidentiality it is usually a better situation in terms of promoting effective treatment.*

Involuntary Commitment and Treatment

As already mentioned, if an individual's mental condition means that his presence in the community poses a danger to self or others or the individual is completely unable to care for him- or herself, psychologists and other social services professionals can take steps to compel the person to receive treatment, usually by committing that person to inpatient care. The call can be tough for just one person to make, so most social welfare systems provide for the licensing of multidisciplinary *psychiatric evaluation teams* (PET) to visit the patient in the community or meet the patient at the hospital and make a decision as to

---

*Consent and confidentiality rules applying to parents and minors may vary somewhat from state to state.

whether inpatient care is mandated. Typically, several trained professionals are on the PET team. The relative difficulty involved in committing a person against his or her will is a legacy of the time when people were committed as a social control tactic rather than for therapeutic purposes.

Deinstitutionalization

Just as persons with mental illnesses cannot be "locked away" without sufficient evaluation and consideration of alternatives, they should not be discharged into the community after their illnesses have been made manageable without long-term treatment plans and adequate support. This was the hard lesson of the deinstitutionalization movement. For economic reasons, in the late twentieth century many long-term inpatients were released from care—discharged without any support or follow-up arrangements. Many remained on the streets, homeless and ill. Some died. Others were arrested and thrown in jail. Treatment teams in inpatient settings must work with the social welfare system to develop specific and thoughtful transition plans for maintaining the adequate functioning of those with chronic mental illnesses, and those who are recovering. To discharge a patient without support and supervision is as unethical and lacking in compassion as involuntary commitment without adequate cause.

Connecting Through Chapter Review

WORD-STUDY CONNECTION
Write each of these words on index cards, and write their definitions on the opposite side.

Antabuse
aversion therapy
behavior modification
behavioral therapy
catharsis
cognition
cognitive-behavior therapy
   (CBT)
cognitive therapy
commitment
community psychology
   perspective
conceptualizing
conditional
confidentiality
consent to treatment
corpus callosum
deinstitutionalization

drug therapy
duty to warn
eclectic
electroconvulsive therapy
   (ECT)
existential humanistic
   therapy
exposure therapy
family systems therapy
flooding
free association
group therapy
hemispherectomy
humanistic therapy
ideal self
inpatient psychiatric
   treatment
lobotomy

meta-analytic
paraprofessional counselors
participant modeling
person-centered therapy
pharmacotherapy
plasticity
primary prevention
   methods
psychoanalysis
psychodynamic
   psychotherapy
psychosurgery
psychotherapy
rational-emotive therapy
   (RET)
resistant
secondary prevention
self-help groups

systematic desensitization
Tarasoff v. the Regents of
University of California
tertiary prevention

token economy
transference
transmagnetic cranial
 stimulation (TCS)

unconditional positive
 regard

SELF-TEST CONNECTION

PART A. *Completion*
Write in the word that correctly completes each statement.

1. _____ is a term that refers to a broad range of techniques designed to improve psychological functioning and personal or social adjustment.
2. _____ such as priests and ministers sometimes provide psychotherapy services.
3. Therapists who use a variety of psychotherapy techniques are called _____ .
4. Psychodynamic psychotherapy is based on the theories of _____ .
5. In psychoanalysis the patient may react to the therapist in a way that resembles his or her reaction to a parent or other important person. This is a process called _____ .
6. The goals of a(n) _____ treatment plan are usually specific, concrete, and measurable.
7. Exposure therapies are based on principles of _____ .
8. The use of the drug Antabuse is a type of _____ therapy.
9. Some behavior therapists include in their treatment plan a strategy based on social learning theory called _____ .
10. Cognitive therapies attempt to change a person's _____ about themselves or their situation.
11. _____ is the creator of CBT or cognitive-behavioral therapy.
12. The most important element of Rogers' person-centered therapy is the therapist's _____ positive regard for the patient.
13. One element of group therapy about which each patient must be aware is the fact that the level of _____ is somewhat less than in individual therapy.
14. _____ is reserved for those who are experiencing extreme distress and disruption of their everyday functioning.
15. A weakness of meta-analyses is that they tend to include only _____ studies of a subject.
16. Haldol and Thorazine are examples of _____ drugs used to treat schizophrenia.
17. Anticonvulsant drugs are used to reduce the number of _____ a person with epilepsy may have.
18. Psychosurgery has a bad reputation in part because of the number of unnecessary _____ that were done.
19. _____ is an electrically based therapy that is as effective as ECT and appears to have fewer side effects.
20. _____ involves identifying mental disorders in their early stages and taking steps to reduce the severity of the symptoms as they emerge.

21. _____ are trained, unlicensed counselors who provide prevention and support services in the community.

22. Therapists are obligated to protect a patient's _____ unless there is reason to believe that the patient's behavior represents a danger to self or others.

23. _____ are multidisciplinary teams that make assessments regarding the possible need for involuntary commitment.

24. In the 1980s many inpatients were _____ from state hospitals without outpatient treatment plans, follow-up, or support of any kind.

PART B. *Multiple Choice*

Circle the letter of the item that correctly completes the statement.

1. Which of the following professions would *not* typically be a provider of psychotherapy services?
   - (a) Psychiatrists
   - (b) Clinical social workers
   - (c) Lawyers
   - (d) Counselors

2. The release of powerful, hidden emotions in the course of psychoanalysis is called _____ .
   - (a) transference
   - (b) catharsis
   - (c) resistance
   - (d) free association

3. "Decrease the number of times patient starts fights with classmates to zero times per week" would be a typical goal in a _____ treatment plan.
   - (a) psychoanalytic
   - (b) behavior therapy
   - (c) humanistic
   - (d) family systems

4. Rapid and intense exposure to a stimulus with the goal of desensitization is a therapeutic technique called _____ .
   - (a) flooding
   - (b) aversive therapy
   - (c) group therapy
   - (d) systematic desensitization

5. Using mild electric shocks to prevent developmentally disabled inpatients from self-mutilating is a technique called _____ .
   - (a) flooding
   - (b) aversive therapy
   - (c) group therapy
   - (d) systematic desensitization

6. A person who rewards herself with a trip to the nail salon every three times she goes to the gym and works out is engaging in her own program of _____ .
   - (a) humanistic therapy
   - (b) flooding
   - (c) token reinforcement
   - (d) behavior modification

7. Rational-emotive therapy is a cognitive technique developed by _____ .
   - (a) Carl Rogers
   - (b) Aaron Beck
   - (c) Albert Ellis
   - (d) Albert Bandura

8. A person who has been given an assignment to keep a journal of her thoughts during the day is probably receiving _____ therapy.
   - (a) exposure
   - (b) aversive
   - (c) cognitive-behavioral
   - (d) systematic desensitization

9. A therapist believes that the patient is suffering from depression owing to the incongruence of his ideal self with his current self-concept. The therapist is probably providing _____ treatment.
   - (a) rational-emotive
   - (b) humanistic
   - (c) psychoanalytic
   - (d) family systems

10. What form of therapy has its roots in a school of philosophy?
    - (a) Rational-emotive
    - (b) Psychoanalytic
    - (c) Existential-humanistic
    - (d) Group

11. _____ is the magazine that featured a review of the quality of psychotherapy in 1995.
    - (a) *Newsweek*
    - (b) *Journal of Counseling*
    - (c) *Psychotherapy News*
    - (d) *Consumer Reports*

12. Pharmacotherapy is another term for _____ .
    - (a) drug therapy
    - (b) brain surgery
    - (c) TCM
    - (d) behavior therapy

13. Which of the following is *not* an antipsychotic drug?
    - (a) Mellaril
    - (b) Haldol
    - (c) Tegritol
    - (d) Thorazine

14. A person who suffers from major depression might be prescribed _____ to relieve his or her symptoms.
    - (a) Valium
    - (b) Haldol
    - (c) Elavil
    - (d) Cylert

15. What part of the brain may be severed in order to control seizures?
    - (a) Frontal lobes
    - (b) Brainstem
    - (c) Hippocampus
    - (d) Corpus callosum

16. _____ can still be administered with the patient's consent in cases of severe depression.
    - (a) Lobotomy
    - (b) Haldol
    - (c) ECT
    - (d) Trephination

17. _____ is a key element of the community psychology perspective.
    - (a) Inpatient treatment
    - (b) Drug therapy
    - (c) Family systems therapy
    - (d) Prevention

18. Another term for tertiary prevention is _____ prevention.
    - (a) primary
    - (b) relapse
    - (c) drug
    - (d) confidentiality

19. The *Tarasoff* case established that a person who provides psychotherapy also has a _____ intended victims of a patient's violence.
    - (a) duty to warn
    - (b) confidentiality obligation toward
    - (c) right to treat
    - (d) consent decree for

20. In the 1980s _____ resulted in the imprisonment and deaths of many mental patients.
    - (a) lobotomy
    - (b) ECT
    - (c) deinstitutionalization
    - (d) Thorazine use

PART C. Modified True-False

If the statement is true, write "T" for the answer. If the statement is incorrect, change the underlined expression to one that will make the statement true.

1. Some <u>medical personnel</u> may provide psychotherapy services.
2. <u>Freud, Jung, and Adler</u> developed different forms of psychoanalysis.
3. <u>Transference</u> is the process by which the psychoanalytic patient talks about whatever comes to his or her mind during the treatment session.
4. Behavior therapy is based on the idea that <u>unconscious conflicts</u> cause psychological distress.
5. <u>Avoidance prevents extinction</u> is the principle that underlies the exposure therapies.
6. Behavior modification uses <u>electric shocks</u> to increase or reduce a target behavior.
7. Participant modeling is a type of therapy strategy based on <u>humanistic psychology</u>.
8. <u>Cognitive therapy</u> tries to change a person's destructive unconscious processes.
9. <u>Rational-emotive therapy</u> is an example of a cognitively based treatment.
10. <u>Abraham Maslow</u> developed cognitive-behavioral therapy.
11. A person-centered psychotherapist helps to relieve a patient's psychological distress by providing <u>conditional positive regard.</u>
12. <u>Family systems therapy</u> helps to relieve distress by encouraging a patient to make meaning out of a seemingly random and chaotic existence.
13. The type of professional who provides therapy <u>makes a great difference</u> in how successful the outcome of therapy will be.
14. Motor tics and tremors are a common side effect of some of the <u>antipsychotic</u> medications.
15. <u>Prozac</u> is an example of an anticonvulsant medication used to treat seizure disorders.
16. <u>Valium</u> is an example of an antianxiety drug with addictive potential.
17. <u>Lobotomies</u> are performed on the brains of children in order to control serious seizures that do not respond to medication.
18. <u>ECT</u> involves the use of electromagnets to disrupt briefly the firing of cortical neurons.
19. The goal of <u>primary prevention</u> is to stop mental illness before it starts.
20. Paraprofessional counselors and persons who run self-help groups are usually <u>licensed therapists</u>.
21. <u>Under no circumstances</u> may a therapist violate the confidentiality of his or her patients.
22. A patient may be committed to inpatient treatment if it is determined that his or her behavior poses a <u>danger to self or others</u>.
23. A psychiatric evaluation team is composed of <u>only medical personnel</u>.
24. It is <u>relatively difficult</u> to commit a person to psychiatric treatment against his or her will.
25. Deinstitutionalization <u>was a successful movement</u> to release hospitalized mental patients back into the community.

PART D. Matching

Match the correct term to the information provided.

Which Type of Therapist Would Say This?

Answers can be used more than once.

> behavior therapist
> psychoanalytic or psychodynamic therapist
> rational-emotive therapist
> existential humanist therapist
> cognitive-behavioral therapist
> person-centered therapist

1. You are reacting to me the way you did when your mother would lie to you. _____
2. Here are five pieces of scrip earned for staying in your seat all during algebra class today. _____
3. Was that *really* such an awful thing? You act as if not getting that promotion was the *most* awful thing that ever could have happened to you. Was it really? _____
4. I want you to watch as I take the spider out of his tank and hold him in my hand. The spider really feels soft. _____
5. When you are ready, I want you to move closer to me and take the spider in your hand, very slowly. _____
6. Whether or not you fail mathematics this semester, I know you are a worthy person. We will figure out why you are having such difficulty with this subject, in due time. _____
7. Next week at work, your assignment is to write down every compliment you receive from your co-workers and superiors. _____
8. I want you to lie down and just say whatever comes into your mind for the next fifty minutes. _____
9. Your second goal for therapy is to reduce the number of times you yell at your brother from 3 to 1 over the next three months. _____
10. You are having a hard time seeing any meaning in life since your brother passed away. We will work together to see if we can create a new meaning for you. _____

Which Therapy Concept Is It?

> participant modeling
> unconditional positive regard
> free association
> behavioral treatment plan
>
> transference
> token economy
> exposure
>
> homework
> reframing
> making meaning

1. You are reacting to me the way you did when your mother would lie to you. _____
2. Here are five pieces of scrip earned for staying in your seat all during algebra class today. _____
3. Was that *really* such an awful thing? You act as if not getting that promotion was the *most* awful thing that ever could have happened to you. Was it really? _____
4. I want you to watch as I take the spider out of his tank and hold him in my hand. The spider really feels soft. _____

5. When you are ready, I want you to move closer to me and take the spider in your hand, very slowly. _____

6. Whether or not you fail mathematics this semester, I know you are a worthy person. We will figure out why you are having such difficulty with this subject, in due time. _____

7. Next week at work, your assignment is to write down every compliment you receive from your co-workers and superiors. _____

8. I want you to lie down and just say whatever comes into your mind for the next fifty minutes. _____

9. Your second goal for therapy is to reduce the number of times you yell at your brother from 3 to 1 over the next three months. _____

10. You are having a hard time seeing any order or use in life since your brother passed away. We will work together to see if we can find some kind of sense it in for you. _____

PART E. Chart Completion

PHARMACOTHERAPY (DRUG THERAPY)

Drug Class	Typical Brand Names	Neurotransmitters/ Brain Structures Acted On	Illnesses for Which It Might Be Prescribed
Antipsychotic	Haldol, Mellaril, Risperidal, Thorazine	Dopamine (reduced); Serotonin (increased)	Schizophrenia, schizo-affective disorder, delusional disorder
Mood stabilizer		Glutamate (reduced); increases volume of gray matter in cerebral cortex.	
	Tegritol, Phenobarbital	Reduce firing of cortical neurons.	
Antidepressant			
		GABA (reduced), sympathetic nervous system activity (reduced)	

CONNECTING TO CONCEPTS

Review the chapter and then write down your thoughts about the following questions.

1. If you were shopping for a therapist, which type of therapy would you find most comfortable? Describe the features that you believe would fit for you? Do you think the type of therapy that would be most comfortable for you would also be the most helpful? If not, which one do you think would be most helpful? Why?

2. Given that most health insurance plans now only allow a set number of therapy sessions, which type of therapy would be best for a time-limited plan? Explain your choice.

3. Compare and contrast any of two types of therapy in terms of how change is achieved in the course of treatment.

4. Discuss the positive and negative aspects of drug treatment for mental illnesses.

5. Describe the philosophy behind community psychology. Imagine that you are a community psychologist assigned to work in an inner city neighborhood. What services and plans would you offer to promote primary, secondary, and tertiary prevention?

6. Identify and discuss some of the ethical issues faced by professionals who provide mental health treatment services.

CONNECTING TO LIFE/JOB SKILLS

Peer and Crisis Counseling

Students who are considering advanced study in psychology often find it helpful to spend time as peer or volunteer crisis counselors. Peer counseling programs almost always provide a basic training in listening skills used by psychotherapists at all professional levels. Additionally, they give you a chance to try out work similar to that done by clinicians, and can be enormously rewarding (if occasionally draining). Finally, graduate programs in psychology and related disciplines look favorably on such experience.

If your school does not use peer counselors, you may be able to find a local community agency that does. Rape crisis, hospice, substance abuse suicide and other groups that deal with specific issues may periodically recruit and train volunteers to provide counseling and support. Spend some time browsing at the library, on the internet, or through the community pages of your local phone book to find local agencies that might be able to use your services.

To find out more information about what it's like to be a peer counselor check out these sites:

CARNEGIE MELLON PEER COUNSELING GUIDELINES

www.studentaffairs.cmu.edu/student-life/ra-virtual/roles/peercoun/peercoun.html

WHAT IS CRISIS COUNSELING?

www.crisiscounseling.com/Handouts/WhatIsCrisisCounseling.htm

ASSISTING A STUDENT WHO HAS BEEN SEXUALLY ASSAULTED

www.bu.edu/counseling/assisting1.htm

WHAT'S HAPPENING!

Positive Psychology

> Modern psychology has been co-opted by the disease model. We've become too preoccupied with repairing damage when our focus should be on building strength and resilience, especially in children.
>
> — Martin E. P. Seligman, Ph.D

Positive psychology is a recent outgrowth of the humanistic psychology school that seeks to emphasize human strengths, talents, and potential. As psychological science has sought to identify the causes of weakness, disease, and suffering, those scientists who identify with the positive psychology movement seek to identify the causes of giftedness and resilience and adaptive behaviors. Positive psychology's goal is to discover what is good and excellent in humans and to figure out how to cultivate these qualities throughout society.

In psychotherapy, positive psychologists work with the client to build strengths. In fact, a positive psychologist will focus on this rather than emphasize the repair of emotional damage or the management of disease. The goal of therapy is to empower the client by emphasizing and building on the strengths the client already has and to instill a sense of hope and faith in self. According to the positive psychology framework, these are things that competent therapists do all the time, but they are downplayed in favor of the more scientific-sounding practices that go along with cognitive-behavioral, behavior, and psychodynamic techniques.

To learn more about positive psychology, visit the following web sites:

MARTIN SELIGMAN RESEARCH ALLIANCE

www.positivepsychology.org/index.htm

THE PURSUIT OF HAPPINESS

www.davidmyers.org/happiness/positive.html

INTERNATIONAL NETWORK ON PERSONAL MEANING:
POSITIVE PSYCHOLOGY LINKS

www.meaning.ca/links/positive_psychology_links.html

OTHER USEFUL WEB SITES

Finding a Therapist

AMERICAN PSYCHOLOGICAL ASSOCIATION
CONSUMER INFORMATION CENTER

helping.apa.org/

AMERICAN ASSOCIATION OF MARRIAGE AND FAMILY THERAPISTS

www.aamft.org/TherapistLocator/index.htm

AMERICAN COUNSELING ASSOCIATION CONSUMER/MEDIA INFORMATION

www.counseling.org/consumers.htm

AMERICAN PSYCHIATRIC ASSOCIATION: CHOOSING A PSYCHIATRIST

www.psych.org/public_info/choose_a_psy.cfm

AMERICAN PSYCHOANALYTIC ASSOCIATION: ABOUT PSYCHOANALYSIS

www.apsa-co.org/ctf/pubinfo/about.htm

FINDING THE RIGHT THERAPIST (CHILD PSYCHOLOGY)

kidshealth.org/parent/emotions/feelings/finding_therapist_p3.html

NATIONAL ASSOCIATION OF CLINICAL SOCIAL WORKERS REGISTER

www.socialworkers.org/register/default.asp

THE ALBERT ELLIS INSTITUTE

www.rebt.org/

This web site describes the basics of Rational-Emotive therapy.

AMERICAN PSYCHOANALYTIC ASSOCIATION

www.apsa.org/index.htm

This is the homepage of the American Psychoanalytic Association and features information about the therapy as well as the life and work of Freud.

THE CBT WEB SITE

www.cognitivetherapy.com/

This web site is a good introduction to cognitive-behavioral therapy.

THE CENTER FOR STUDIES OF THE PERSON

www.centerfortheperson.org/

This site is intended as a training resource for humanistic and client-centered psychotherapists and has a lot of information.

REFERENCES

APA Practice Directorate (1994)
www.apa.org/practice/peff.html

Beck (1976) *Cognitive Therapy and the Emotional Disorders.* New York: The New American Library.

Bugental, J. F. T. (1978). *Psychotherapy and Process: The Fundamentals of an Existential-Humanistic Approach.* Reading, MA: Addison-Wesley.

Ellis, A. (1961) *A Guide to Rational Living.* Englewood Cliffs, NJ: Prentice-Hall.

Kalat, J. W. (2001) *Introduction to Psychology.* Belmont, CA: Wadsworth/ITP.

Rogers (1961) *On Becoming a Person.* Boston: Houghton Mifflin

Seligman, M. (1995) The effectiveness of psychotherapy: The *Consumer Reports* study. *American Psychologist,* 50, 965–974. Online at *www.apa.org/journals/seligman.html*

HAIM WEINBERG'S GROUP PSYCHOTHERAPY WEB SITE
www.group-psychotherapy.com/index.htm

GLOSSARY

Absolute threshold—The minimum detectable strength or level of a sensory stimulus under conditions that are deemed ideal for detection.

Accommodation—From Piaget's theory of cognitive development, when the child changes his or her schema in response to new knowledge or experience.

Acetylcholine—A neurotransmitter thought to be important for muscle function and memory.

Action potential—The electrochemical signal or "firing" of a neuron that includes the brief depolarization of the neuron and allows a neurotransmitter to be released into the synapse.

Activation-synthesis hypothesis—An explanation for dreaming—it proposes that random nerve firings occur during REM sleep and that the cerebral cortex attempts to make sense out of this activity, thus producing story-like dreams.

Actor-observer effect—The tendency to attribute one's own behavior mainly to situational causes while explaining the behavior of others as a result of character or disposition.

Acute—Any state or condition that is relatively short in duration but also relatively intense.

Addiction—Also called *dependence*; a persistent and harmful pattern of substance use resulting in increasing tolerance for a drug and withdrawal symptoms when it is not ingested in sufficient quantities.

ADHD (Attention Deficit Hyperactivity Disorder)—A commonly diagnosed disorder featuring symptoms such as distractibility, short attention span, fidgeting, and similar symptoms. Usually diagnosed in childhood.

Adjustment disorder—Behavioral or emotional symptoms developed by an individual in response to a specific, recent life stressor.

Adrenaline—A hormone secreted from glands on the kidneys, usually in response to activation of the sympathetic nervous system (stress). Chemical identical to the neurotransmitter epinephrine.

Affective—Related to or pertaining to emotions.

Afferent—Referring to nerve tracts that carry information toward the brain—sensory nerve tracts.

Algorithm—A procedure composed of clear, specific steps that, if followed, guarantees a solution to a problem.

All-or-none law—Refers to the fact that nerve cells either fire or do not fire when stimulated.

Alpha waves—Brain waves that are produced typically when a person is drowsy or passing into Stage 1 NREM sleep.

Altruism—Behaviors that appear to benefit other individuals but not the person performing the actions.

Alzheimer's disease—A severe degenerative brain condition arising in mid to late life that results in loss of memory, loss of self-care abilities, and eventual death.

Amacrine cells—One of the three types of cells that make up the second layer of the retina.

Amino acids—A group of essential organic compounds with two carbon bonds. These are building blocks for the chemicals in the nervous and endocrine systems.

Amnesia—Refers to several types of temporary or permanent memory loss. Can be a symptom of another disorder (i.e., Alzheimer's disease) or a condition caused by brain damage. *Anterograde* amnesia refers to an inability to make new memories; *retrograde* is the loss of memories that were already stored.

Amplitude—The size (or height) of sound waves; this corresponds with the loudness of the sound.

Amygdala—An almond-shaped structure in the limbic system, involved in memory and emotional processing.

Animus (anima)—In Jung's psychoanalytic theory, the hidden male or female elements of an individual's personality.

Anxiety—A physiological and emotional reaction to a perceived threat.

Applied research—Scientific investigation done in order to address or improve a real-world problem.

Aqueous humor—A watery fluid in the space between the cornea and the iris.

Archetypes—In Jung's psychoanalytic theory, figures, events, or symbols that are universally held in the collective unconscious.

Assessment—Any technique for measuring a psychological construct.

Assimilation—In Piagetian theory, a process by which new information is changed to fit in with established mental frameworks or schemas.

Association areas—Parts of the cerebral cortex where sensory information is blended in higher level processing activities.

Attribution—A causal explanation for an individual's behavior.

Attribution theory—A framework for explaining the cognitive and social processes by which we formulate our explanations for our own and others' behaviors.

Auditory nerve—The major pathway for auditory signals traveling from the inner ear to the brain.

Autism—A range of complex developmental disorders, most likely organic in origin, involving varying degrees of social, emotional, and intellectual impairment.

Autonomic nervous system—The division of the peripheral nervous system that controls involuntary motor responses and many of the life-sustaining processes that depend upon them.

Aversion therapy—A type of therapy, based on classical conditioning, in which a response to a desirable stimulus is paired with an unpleasant stimulus in hopes of eliminating that response.

Axon—A long arm of the neuron through which nerve signals travel—through the axon a neuron sends the signal on to neighboring neurons.

Basal ganglia—A cluster of neurons, located at the base of the forebrain, that are crucial for motor function.

Basic research—Research done primarily for the purpose of gaining new knowledge.

Basilar membrane—A thin layer of cells that vibrate in response to sound waves and create motion in the hair cells in the cochlea.

Behavioral genetics—The scientific study of the genetic basis of human experience.

Behaviorism—A framework for the scientific study of psychology that depends on the description and measurement of observable behavior.

Behavior modification—Also called *behavior therapy*; the use of principles of learning theory to change behavior (create or increase desired behaviors and decrease or eliminate undesirable behaviors).

Beta waves—Also called *sawtooth waves*; low-voltage, rapid brain waves that are present during the waking state and also during REM.

Binocular cue—Cues for depth perception that require the use of both eyes.

Biopsychosocial model—A model for viewing health and illness that depends on the interaction of elements from physiology, emotion, and the environment.

Bipolar cells—One of the three types of cells that make up the second layer of the retina.

Bipolar illness—Formerly known as *manic-depressive illness*, bipolar illness has several versions. The major symptom of the bipolar illnesses is a cycling between periods of depression and periods of normal or extremely elevated mood (mania.)

Blind spot—The place in the retina where the axons of the ganglion cells exit the eye, creating a small spot with no photoreceptors and therefore no visual information.

Blocking—One of the seven sins of memory, in which one is unable to recall information even when one "knows that one knows it."

Blood-brain barrier—A system of tissue layers around the brain that help to filter from the blood potentially toxic substances that might cause damage.

Body senses—A collective term for the senses of touch, pain, proprioception, and balance, the sense systems that keep the brain informed of the position and condition of the body.

Bone conduction hearing—Translation of sound waves into auditory nerve signals through the action of the three small bones in the middle ear.

Brain—The central and most important part of the nervous system, comprised of interconnected layers and smaller components that control almost all aspects of human behavior.

Brainstem—The lowest part of the brain (actually the very top of the spinal cord), this structure contains components that regulate vital life processes.

Bruxism—This is excessive grinding of the teeth, which may be related to central nervous system malfunction.

Burnout—This is a loss of energy and interest in work or life due to excessive demands of stressors.

Bystander effects—The impact that different numbers of observers (bystanders) have on the behavior of other individuals in a social context, especially with reference to the scene of an accident or crime.

Cannabinoids—A family of plants containing the psychoactive ingredient THC.

Case study—A research method involving intensive study of a single individual, group, or event.

Catharsis—The expression of very strong but hidden or repressed emotion, assumed to have some therapeutic value in psychoanalytic literature.

Cell body—The part of any cell that contains the nucleus and other life-sustaining organelles.

Central nervous system (CNS)—The parts of the nervous system that control all of its functions (specifically the brain and the spinal cord).

Cephalocaudal—A term describing the progress of physical development in early life, literally from the head down.

Cerebellum—The second largest discrete structure in the brain. It is attached to the brainstem and controls body movements, coordination, and balance.

Cerebral cortex—The top layer of the cerebrum.

Cerebrum—The uppermost region of the brain containing tissues in charge of higher cognitive processes (thinking, perception, declarative memory).

Chemical senses—Collective term for the senses of smell and taste.

Chromosome—Composed of DNA, these structures are usually found in the nucleus of a cell and contain the genes.

Chronic—Any condition or illness that is long lasting.

Circadian rhythms—Daily cycles of bodily activities and levels of alertness, controlled by processes in the limbic system and brainstem.

Classical conditioning—A type of learning in which an organism forms associations between neutral stimuli and involuntary or reflex response.

Clinical—Pertaining to the treatment of physical or mental disorders.

Closure—The Gestalt law that states that perception acts to "close" gaps in figures and make them unbroken or whole.

Cochlea—The major structure of the inner ear; it contains the specialized receptor cells that act to turn sound waves into nerve impulses.

Cognition/cognitive—Pertaining to mental processes such as thought and memory.

Cognitive behavioral therapy—A therapy that blends elements of cognitive therapy (changing thinking) and behavior therapy (changing behavior using conditioning techniques).

Cognitive dissonance—Psychological tension that we experience when two thoughts, or our thoughts and actions, do not coincide.

Cognitive maps—Mental representations that usually describe places or procedures in our external environment.

Cognitive therapy—Any psychotherapy that attempts to help people change the way they think, in order to improve the quality of their emotional life and behavior.

Collective unconscious—From Jungian psychoanalytic theory, a shared store of knowledge passed down to us from our ancestors through the history of humanity.

Colliculi—Structures in the midbrain that control reflex reactions to auditory and visual stimuli.

Common fate—The Gestalt law stating that we perceive objects that are moving together as also belonging together as a unified whole or group.

Concepts—Any mental grouping of people, things, events, or ideas that hold certain key features in common.

Conceptualization—Referring to psychotherapy, the process of defining the issues and themes in a case history and treatment plan.

Conditioned response—An involuntary or reflex response that has been associated with a conditioned (formerly neutral) stimulus.

Conditioned stimulus—A formerly neutral stimulus that has been successfully linked to an unconditioned stimulus and therefore to an involuntary or reflex response.

Confidentiality—A therapist's obligation to protect the privacy of a client's information except in certain carefully defined circumstances.

Consciousness—Our awareness of our own inner states and external environment.

Conduction deafness—Deafness caused by damage to parts of the middle ear.

Cones—The receptors in the retina that are sensitive to color, detail, and other features of daytime vision.

Consent—Also called *informed consent*; in research or psychotherapeutic treatment, the principle that patients and participants should be given full information about the activity to which they are consenting before they agree to begin participating.

Conservation—In Piagetian theory, the understanding that changing the shape of a mass of material or the container into which a liquid has been poured does not change the amount of matter or liquid. This skill develops in children at the beginning of the concrete operational stage.

Consolidation—The process of formation of long-term memories.

Construct—An abstract psychological concept that we attempt to describe and measure accurately.

Control group—In experimental and quasi-experimental research, the group that does not get the treatment or the active condition of the independent variable.

Coping—The act of actively managing one's stress levels by dealing appropriately with life stressors.

Cornea—The very thin but tough protective outer layer of the eyeball.

Corpus callosum—The thick bundle of axons that allows the two hemispheres of the cerebral cortex to communicate with each other.

Correlation—Research and research analysis techniques that are used when the investigator has no control over the variables of interest.

Counterconditioning—Various techniques, based on classical conditioning, which are used to try to eliminate links between stimuli and responses.

Cranial nerve—A set of twelve nerves in the central nervous system that take sensory information to the brain and send motor information to various regions of the body with the help of peripheral pathways.

Culture—A collection of rules, information, and behaviors learned and held in common in any particular society.

Cutaneous receptor—Receptors for various types of touch information located in the skin.

Day residue—Information and experiences from our fully conscious activities of the day that may become incorporated in our dreaming.

Decay theory—The "use it or lose it" theory of memory—simply stating that if information is not accessed, used, or linked to new information, it is eventually lost.

Decibel—A unit of measure used to describe the loudness of sounds.

Declarative memory—The types of explicit, long-term memories that involve conscious knowledge and deliberate recall—semantic (informational) and episodic (experiences) are the two major types of declarative memory.

Defense mechanism—In Freudian psychoanalytic theory, any one of a number of cognitive and behavioral strategies used to defend the ego against unacceptable emotions and impulses.

Deinstitutionalization—The mass release of patients who had been committed to long-term care in inpatient mental health facilities.

Delirium—A state of extreme cognitive and sensory confusion caused by organic factors.

Delta waves—The low-voltage, large brain waves produced during slow-wave sleep (Stages III and IV NREM).

Delusion—A relatively fixed belief in something that is false or nonexistent—a false thought that is believed in spite of evidence to the contrary.

Dementia—Loss of memory and personality/behavior changes resulting from degeneration of various brain systems. The most well-known form of dementia is Alzheimer's disease.

Dendrite—Branches of the neuron that contain receptor sites; thus they receive incoming nerve signals.

Dependent variable—In an experiment or quasi experiment, the variable that measures changes caused by the independent variable (also known as the response variable).

Depolarization—A change in the internal change of a neuron—from opposite to the same as outside the neuron—that enables the action potential to travel through the cell and on to the neighboring neurons.

Depressants—Also called *CNS depressants*; any one of a number of drugs that act to slow the functioning of processes directed by the central nervous system.

Depression—A mood disorder involving persistent sadness, lack of energy and motivation, negative thoughts, and many other symptoms leading to poor functioning and adjustment in everyday life.

Descriptive—In research, a type of investigation that seeks only to discover information about a phenomenon or problem. No attempt to control or manipulate any variable is made.

Desensitization—Growing used to a stimulus, or gradually losing the response to it.

Determinism—The idea that all behavior is determined (fixed) and predictable because of certain conditions or forces (i.e., God, genes).

Developmental psychology—The study of psychological changes across the lifespan.

Difference threshold—The smallest difference in the strength of a stimulus (weakening or increasing) that can be detected as a change by an organism at least 50 percent of the time.

Diffusion of responsibility—A bystander effect which states that as the number of people present at a crime or accident increases, the chances that any one of them will try to intervene or help decreases.

Diploid—A characteristic of body cells, which possess the full number of chromosomes typical for the species.

Discrimination—A behavior in which one either favors or acts against a person or group of persons based on prejudice and stereotypes.

Dissociation—A failure of the personality or self to integrate fully. Some psychologists believe that this can lead to amnesia and multiple personalities in certain instances.

Dizygotic—Twins that form from two simultaneous but separate fertilizations (also called *fraternal twins*).

DNA—The chemicals that make up the genes and chromosomes of every living organism; they contain the instructions for each particular organism.

Dominant gene—A gene that will manifest its associated traits under most conditions, whether paired with another dominant or a recessive gene.

Drug abuse—A pattern of drug misuse that leads to negative consequences in the interpersonal, legal, or occupational realms. There is typically no compulsive need to use.

Dualism—The idea that the mind is separate from the brain rather than a product of it.

Dura mater—A thick layer of tissue that helps to protect the brain from the skull (literally "tough mother").

Duty to warn—Refers to a therapist's obligation to break a client's confidentiality under a limited set of circumstances (e.g., if he or she has reason to believe that the client has plans to harm a known person or group of people).

Dysthymia—A low-grade but chronic form of depression.

Eating disorder—Disorders involving disturbed eating habits such as anorexia (deliberate self-starvation) and bulimia (binging, usually followed by purging).

Eclectic—An approach to psychotherapy that involves blending and applying aspects of various types of treatment.

Efferent—Referring to nerve tracts that carry motor information from the brain to the muscles and joints.

Ego—In psychoanalytic theory, the part of the personality that represents the self and its needs and interests in the interpersonal world.

Egocentrism—In Piagetian theory, this refers to a preschooler's inability to view a situation from someone else's perspective.

Electrochemical—Describing the activity of neural transmission, which involves electrical charges and chemical messengers (neurotransmitters).

Electroconvulsive therapy—Also known as *ECT*; a last resort treatment for intractable depression that involves passing a strong electric current through the brain.

Embryo—A term for a developing human in utero during the first trimester between weeks 2 and 8.

Emotion—A reaction that includes a recognizable pattern of physiological, cognitive, and behavioral changes usually made in response to an external or internal event.

Empirical—Another term for scientific evidence or evidence based upon processes that can be directly observed and measured.

Encoding—The formation of a memory or mental representation.

Encoding failure—A term for a type of forgetting that occurs when information does not pass completely from short-term to long-term memory.

Endocrine gland—Any gland that produces and releases hormones into the bloodstream and tissues of the body.

Endorphins—Also called *endogenous opiates*; a type of neurotransmitter that appears to reduce pain and relieve some of the negative effects of stress.

Engram—A term for the hypothetical location of a discrete stored memory in the brain.

Epinephrine—A neurotransmitter that activates the central nervous system; chemically identical to the hormone adrenaline.

Episodic memory—Also called *autobiographical memory*; memory for our own life events.

Ethnocentrism—Related to prejudice, the belief that one's own national, racial, or ethnic group is superior to others and entitled to special treatment.

Evolutionary—Related to the theory of evolution, that life has changed and adapted to maximize survival and reproduction over the course of time.

Evolutionary theory of sleep—The theory that sleep patterns are dictated by adaptations suited to an animal's typical habitat and maximize an organism's survival.

Excitatory—A term that refers to any nerve transmission that encourages the firing of the neighboring neurons.

Existential-humanistic therapy—A psychotherapy based on humanistic personality theory (founded on the idea that humans strive for growth and self-actualization) and existential philosophy (which deals with personal choice and responsibility for the self).

Expectancy—In various social and interpersonal situations, when other individuals communicate in various ways their expectations for our performance or behavior, they help to create the reaction that they anticipated.

Experiment—A research study in which the investigator is able to control or manipulate directly at least one variable of interest.

Explicit memory—Any long-term memory of which we have direct knowledge (we know that we know the information).

Exposure therapy—Psychotherapy interventions based on classical conditioning, usually involving the direct exposure of an individual to a stimulus that provokes an unpleasant reaction (e.g., fear) until he or she gets used to the stimulus (becomes desensitized).

Extinction—In classical conditioning, extinction is the loss of a response to a stimulus; in operant conditioning it is the cessation of a behavior.

Factitious—Any symptom generated for a psychological benefit (e.g., attention or sympathy).

Factor analysis—A complex statistical technique that is used to estimate the strength of relationships between a set of variables.

Family systems therapy—Any therapy based on the idea that family relationships affect behavior and functioning; it almost always involves bringing all members of the family into therapy sessions.

Feature detectors—Cells in the visual cortex that appear to fire only when they encounter specific aspects of an object being viewed (e.g., shape or angle).

Fetus—The developing human in utero from week 9 until birth.

Field study—Any research study done outside a laboratory setting, in an environment to which the results might be applied.

Firing—Also called an *action potential*; the activity of neurons that allows information to be transmitted between them.

Five-factor model—A personality theory that is based on the idea that there are five fundamental traits, and that a person's behavior and disposition can be described and predicted by examining the degree and nature of these traits within him or her.

Flashbacks—Vivid and intrusive recollections of traumatic events, a typical symptom of PTSD (posttraumatic stress disorder).

Flashbulb memory—A vivid memory of the moment of a dramatic event; it may or may not be very accurate.

Flooding—A therapeutic intervention for phobia or anxiety based on classical conditioning, in which the patient is exposed to a fear-inducing stimulus for a prolonged time, at intense levels, in order to be desensitized.

Fontanels—The soft spots in a newborn's skull that allow compression to take place during birth without brain damage.

Forced choice—Any item on an assessment that requires that one of two answers be selected. (There is no "neither" or "n/a" type option.)

Forebrain—The limbic system and cerebrum of the brain.

Fovea—The area of the retina in which the most cones are located, therefore the area in which daytime vision is most acute.

Free association—In psychoanalysis, the patient discusses whatever comes to mind without any prodding or interruption by the analyst.

Free will—The idea that all human behavior is the product of individual choice, without any influence from deterministic underlying forces.

Frequency principle—A theory of pitch perception stating that the rate of vibration of a sound in the basilar membrane produces a particular frequency in the rate of the firing of neurons in the auditory system, which is interpreted by the brain as a sound's pitch.

Functionalism—An early perspective of psychology that examined the purpose (or function) of an organism's behavior within the environment.

Fundamental attribution error—The tendency of those in individualistic cultures to overestimate the contribution of a person's character traits or dispositional factors and to underestimate the influence of situational factors in shaping behavior.

Fungiform papillae—Clusters of taste buds found on the tongue.

g—According to Spearman, the factor that underlies intelligence in general, held in common by all the cognitive skills.

GAF—The Global Assessment of Functioning, a rating scale on Axis V (5) of the DSM-IV-TR.

Ganglion cells—The third layer of cells in the retina. The axons of the ganglion cells exit the back of the eyeball, forming the beginning of the optic nerve.

Gate control theory—A theory of pain that proposes that our experience of pain is influenced by the activity of "gates" in the spinal cord.

General adaptation syndrome—According to Hans Seyle, the three stages (alarm, resistance, exhaustion) experienced by an organism that is exposed to a stressor over the long term.

Genes—Units of DNA that make up the chromosomes.

Genetic—Related to or carried by genes.

Genotype—The specific genetic instructions for an organism (whether or not these traits or characteristics manifest as the organism develops.)

Gestalt—A school of psychology that proposes the idea that perception acts to put information into a unified, whole image or experience.

Glia/glial cell—Small fatty nerve cells that do not transmit information but do perform many important support functions in the nervous system.

Gray matter—The top layer of tissue in the cerebral cortex of the brain.

Group therapy—A form of psychotherapy in which several patients agree to work together with at least one trained therapist.

Groupthink—A false unity of opinion arising in groups because no dissenters will voice their opinions.

Gustation—A technical term for the sense of taste.

Hallucination—A false sensory experience in any sense channel.

Hallucinogens—Psychoactive drugs that promote hallucinations.

Haploid—A characteristic of sex cells or gametes—they only have half the number of chromosomes typical for that organism.

Hardiness—A characteristic that promotes good stress tolerance by cultivating an attitude of viewing stressors as challenges rather than setbacks.

Hemisphere—One half of the cerebrum/cerebral cortex (right/left). Each hemisphere is specialized for certain vital cognitive functions, but the two hemispheres work for the most part in unison.

Hemispherectomy—A surgical procedure performed in young children to control intractable seizures.

Hereditability—Given that the environment is held constant, the degree to which differences between individuals are the sole result of genetic factors.

Heredity—The source of an individual organism's genetic make-up.

Hertz—A measurement of sound wave frequency.

Heuristic—A problem-solving strategy that may provide a quicker solution but that does not necessarily provide the right one.

Hippocampus—A structure in the limbic system that appears to be vital for the consolidation and storage of long-term declarative or explicit memories.

Horizontal cells—One of the three types of cells that make up the second layer of the retina.

Hormone—Slow-acting chemicals secreted by the endocrine glands; can cause temporary or relatively permanent changes in body structure, mood, or behavior.

Humanism—Also called *humanistic psychology*; the perspective that emphasizes human potential for psychological growth and positive behaviors/experience.

Hyperpolarized—The state of the neuron immediately after firing, when the charge inside the neuron is very much opposite of the charge outside, and the neuron is unable to fire. See *refractory period*.

Hypnosis—A mildly altered state of consciousness, involving an increased degree of suggestibility, brought on through the voluntary, cooperative interaction of a hypnotist and subject or by self-induced concentration and focus.

Hypothalamus—A structure in the limbic system that directs the activity of the endocrine glands and basic drive such as hunger, thirst, and sexual desire.

Hypothesis—A testable proposition regarding the relationship between two variables.

Id—In Freud's psychoanalytic theory, the most primitive layer or aspect of personality, containing all the physical and aggressive drives of the individual.

Implicit memory—Type of long-term memory that is usually always available for use but not deliberately or consciously recalled.

Imprinting—In ethology, the organism's original connection or bond to the parent.

Impulse control disorder (kleptomania, trichotillomania, Tourette's)—A disorder in which an urge is acted on because it is experienced as impossible to control.

Incus (anvil)—One of the three bones in the middle ear that help to transduce sound into nerve impulses.

Independent variable—In a true experiment, any variable that is under the direct control of the researcher.

Induced motion—A visual illusion in which a stationary object appears to move and the background does not, when in fact the opposite is occurring (the background is moving but the object is not).

Inhalants—Psychoactive substances that must be inhaled ("breathed in").

Inhibitory—Any nerve signal that acts to reduce the likelihood of firing by the receiving neuron.

Inpatient—Referring to any psychotherapeutic treatment offered in a full-time, residential setting.

Insanity—A legal term referring to the defendant's proposed inability to distinguish between right and wrong as a result of mental incapacity.

Insight—A sudden realization related to a problem's solution, usually occurring after some deep thought or effort to solve it.

Insomnia—Inability to go to sleep or stay asleep, perhaps as a result of stress or as a symptom of a psychological disorder such as depression.

Intelligence—A general term for the range of cognitive abilities possessed by an individual.

Interference—Memories getting in the way of other memories being accessed. Usually a problem with similar types of information (e.g., phone numbers). When we cannot remember new information because of the interference from the old, it is proactive; when we can't remember old information because we have learned new information, it is retroactive interference.

Interneuron—One of the three broad categories of neuron. Interneurons transmit information between neurons of all types. Most neurons are interneurons.

Involuntary commitment—Confinement against one's will to an inpatient mental health treatment facility. Permissible under a narrow set of circumstances (danger to self, danger to others, gross inability to meet one's own basic daily needs).

Ions—Atoms that possess an electrical charge because they have too many or too few electrons.

IQ—Intelligence quotient; a score on a test designed to measure cognitive abilities.

Iris—The muscle that surrounds the pupil and acts to make it smaller (constriction) or wider (dilation) depending on lighting conditions of the environment and physiological conditions of the organism. The iris also gives the eye its color.

Just noticeable difference—Also called the *JND*; the difference that must occur in a stimulus already in progress (increase or decrease) in order for an organism to notice the change.

Just World hypothesis—The sometimes comforting notion that "what goes around comes around." In reality, there is probably little reason to believe in a "just world."

K-complexes—Bursts of brain activity, typically occurring during Stage 2 NREM sleep. They appear to have a "K" shape on the polysomnograph readout.

Kinesthetic—Related to the body sense; also known as *proprioception*—the information about the position of our limbs in space and the amount of muscle strain we are experiencing.

Korsakoff's syndrome—A type of dementia that usually occurs as a result of chronic alcoholism.

Latent—A trait that is not manifested but is present.

Lateral geniculate nucleus—Part of the optic tract; a cluster of neurons in the thalamus that receives and helps to integrate visual information.

Lateral inhibition—A phenomenon that causes objects to look brighter when seen against a dark background than they do when seen against a light background; the result of specialized cells in adjacent regions of the retina preventing each other's firing.

Lateralization—The gradual assignment of different functions to each of the two hemispheres, typically occurring in early childhood.

Law of effect—The basis of operant conditioning, which states that behavior is influenced to continue or end based on its consequences.

Learned helplessness—Prolonged exposure to adverse conditions without any hope of escape leads to passivity and giving up as a preferred strategy.

Learning—Any relatively permanent change in behavior (or mental processes, according to cognitive psychologists) that results from experience.

Lens—The flexible structure in the eye, located behind the pupil, which functions to direct the light to the retina in the back of the eye.

Limbic system—A cluster of structures under the cerebral cortex that help to generate physical drives, emotional responses, and memory. These include the hypothalamus, hippocampus, and amygdala among others.

Lobotomy—A variety of surgical procedures that prevent the frontal lobes from communicating with the rest of the brain. Used as a treatment before the functions of the frontal lobe were well understood, and rarely if ever done currently.

Locus of control—A theory of motivation and personality that proposes that behavior and attitudes are influenced by a person's notion of the degree of control that he or she actually has over the course of life—tending toward the belief in a great degree (internal) or very small amount (external) of control.

Long-term memory—Any type of memory that is successfully stored and available for retrieval later.

Malingering—The faking of psychological or physical symptoms in order to obtain financial or other material gain.

Malleus (hammer)—One of the three bones in the middle ear that helps to transduce sound into nerve impulses.

Maturation—Naturally occurring changes in the behavior and functioning of an organism over the course of development, mostly influenced by the genetic make-up of the species.

MDMA—The acronym for the chemicals that comprise the popular stimulant/hallucinogen usually called *ecstasy*.

Mean—The sum of all scores divided by the number of scores (a type of average).

Mechanoreceptors—One of the types of receptor cells in the muscles and joints. It transduces sensory information about limb position and strain.

Medulla (medulla oblongata)—The part of the brainstem that is responsible for regulating basic life functions such as respiration and circulation.

Melatonin—A hormone generated in response to levels of sunlight by the pineal gland and important for regulating sleep and wakeful states.

Memes—A hypothetical unit for transmitting culture and knowledge between people and over generations.

Mental retardation—Limited cognitive functioning, operationally defined as an IQ lower than 70–75 and severe deficits in ability to perform activities of routine daily self-care.

Mere exposure—The gradual effect of starting to like people with whom you interact on a regular basis.

Meta-analysis—A research method in which the results of a number of studies are combined and analyzed.

Midbrain—A small region, located deep in the brain, containing structures that process auditory and visual sensory inputs.

Milestones—Behavioral, biological, or functional markers of development, signaling a healthy progression of the course of maturation.

Mitosis—Cell division that creates new body cells—forty-six chromosomes split and become two identical sets of the same chromosomes.

Modules—A term from evolutionary psychology; a term for cognitive or behavioral patterns that have value in promoting an individual's fitness.

Monocular cue—Any cue for depth perception that can be processed with input from one eye only.

Monozygotic—A term that refers to twins who share the same genetic make-up—identical twins.

Moon illusion—The visual illusion that causes the moon to look bigger when it is down at the horizon than it does when it is higher up in the sky, probably as a result of the presence of visual cues for nearness when the moon is low.

Motor neuron—Nerve cells that relay information from the central nervous system to the muscles and joints; they make up the efferent tracts of the nervous system.

Multiple sclerosis—A chronic degenerative nervous system disorder in which the myelin is lost from the neurons in the motor tracts.

Myelin—A substance in the nervous system made of and by the glial cells; it aids and speeds up the transmission of the actions potentials.

Myelination—The formation and addition of myelin to the nerve tracts, usually most rapid and dramatic in the early years of life.

Narcotics—A type of psychoactive drug that depresses the functioning of the central nervous system.

Nativism—The view that the brain is specially preprepared for language learning.

Natural selection—The evolutionary process by which characteristics are "selected" as a result of their contribution to successful survival and reproduction of members of a species.

Negative—In learning theory, the removal of a stimulus or consequence. In psychopathology, symptoms of absence (e.g., lack of emotional expression).

Nerve deafness—Impairment of hearing caused by damage to any part of the auditory nerve.

Neural tube—The beginnings of the spinal cord found in a developing embryo.

Neurocognitive theory—The theory that dreaming is mainly a form of thinking.

Neurology—The medical specialty that studies and treats problems of the nervous system.

Neuron—The cell that is specialized for sending and receiving information within the body.

Neuroscience—The study of the chemistry and physiology of the nervous system as it relates to human behavior and emotion.

Neurosis—From psychoanalysis, a general term for the presence of unpleasant emotion (anxiety, depression) and thoughts or behaviors that promote it.

Neurotransmitters—Chemicals produced by the cells of the nervous system that help to transmit information within that system.

Neutral stimulus—In classical conditioning, a stimulus that originally elicits no reaction is paired with an unconditioned stimulus and thus becomes capable of eliciting an unconditioned response.

Nocioreceptors—The free nerve endings in body tissues that detect and transduce painful stimuli.

Nodes of Ranvier—Gaps in the myelin sheathing on the axons of some types of neurons.

Nontaster—Persons who have fewer than average taste receptors and therefore do not experience taste stimuli as intensely as other individuals.

Normal curve—A theoretical symmetrical curve that represents the distribution of scores on various attributes found in the general population.

Norms (social psychology)—Rules of behavior for various social situations that are not necessarily written or directly expressed.

Norms (statistics)—Comparison standards based on measurements of a representative group of people on any given trait.

NREM—Also known as *quiet sleep*; the four stages of sleep in which there are no detectable rapid eye movements.

Nucleotides—Chemical building blocks (molecules) that make up RNA and DNA in organisms.

Nucleus ruber (red nucleus)—A midbrain structure that is involved in the integration of voluntary motor functions.

Observational learning—Learning by watching the behavior of others or the consequences of that behavior.

OCEAN—The acronym that represents the trait dimensions that make up the "Big Five."

Occipital lobes—The areas at the rear of the cerebral cortex that are entirely dedicated to visual processing.

Olfaction—Another term for the sense of smell.

Olfactory bulb—The small structure toward the front of the brain that processes input from smell receptors.

Olfactory epithelium—The surface of the interior of the nose, which is covered with smell receptors.

Operant conditioning—The learning and shaping of voluntary behavior through the use of rewards and punishments.

Operational definition—A definition of a variable that makes it observable and measurable.

Opponent process theory—In color vision theory, the idea that color arises from the receptors cells' sensitivity to various opposing pairs of colors; in a more general sense in psychology, the idea that many behavioral and physiological functions involve the interaction of opposite processes (e.g., arousal and relaxation).

Optic chiasm—The point in the brain at which the nerves from each eye meet and "cross over" to the other side of the brain.

Optic nerve—The axons of the ganglion cells that exit the eyeball at the back and carry information to the brain structures that process visual information.

Organelles—Small parts of body cells that perform various functions related to nutrition, metabolism, and reproduction.

Organ of Corti—A structure in the inner ear, one of the subdivisions of the cochlea involved in the transduction of sound waves.

Ossicles—The general term for the three bones (incus, malleus, and stapes) in the middle ear that are involved in the conduction of sound waves.

Otoliths (otolith organs)—The organs in the ear that contain hair cells—receptors for the sense of balance.

Oval window—The opening from the middle ear that connects it to the inner ear.

Panic—A term for an acute and severe episode of anxiety.

Paraprofessional—A lay person with basic training, who sometimes assists in the support and care of patients in health care or community mental health settings.

Parasomnia—"Strange occurrences during sleep"—sleep walking, night terrors, and other unusual behaviors associated with sleep.

Parasympathetic nervous system—The division of the autonomic nervous system that includes various restorative, maintenance, and energy conservation functions.

Parietal lobes—The sections of the cerebral cortex that process and interpret bodily sensations, among other functions.

Participant modeling—A form of behavior therapy in which the therapist performs certain activities in hopes of encouraging the patient to imitate them.

PCP—The acronym for a drug of abuse with strong stimulant and hallucinogenic properties.

Perception—The processing and interpretation of sensory inputs occurring at the cortical level.

Perceptual set—One's "frame of mind" that often influences how sensory inputs may be interpreted.

Peripheral nervous system—The division of the nervous system that relays sensory information into the central nervous system and motor information out of the CNS to the extremities.

Personality—A person's usual or characteristic way of thinking, feeling, or acting.

Personality disorder—A pervasive, long-term mental disorder involving inflexible patterns of thought, mood, and behavior that are maladaptive by the standards of culture and society.

Persuasion—Techniques used to change the attitudes and behaviors of others.

Phantom limb—The experience of sensations in a missing limb, owing to the fact that the brain still has areas devoted to feeling and movement in that limb.

Pharmacotherapy—Also called *drug therapy*; treatment of mental illness using drugs to alter nervous system chemistry and function.

Phenotype—The degree to which a genetically influenced trait actually is manifested, usually because of environmental influences on the organism.

Phobia—A condition in which an individual fears a particular object or event to a degree that is out of proportion to the threat that it actually represents.

Photopigments—The chemicals found in the photoreceptors.

Photoreceptors—The technical term for the rods and cones, the cells that transduce light information.

Pia mater—Literally the "soft mother"—one of the protective layers of tissue that surrounds the brain.

Pineal gland—A small structure in the limbic system that produces melatonin in response to information from the visual system related to levels of sunlight.

Pinna—The outermost part of the ear; in humans and other animals shaped in a way that promotes sound gathering.

Pitch—The lowness or highness of sound as determined by the frequency of sound waves.

PKU—A genetic disorder that results in inability to metabolize an enzyme. Usually if untreated, PKU results in mental retardation. This can be effectively controlled or avoided through dietary restrictions.

Placebo—An inert pill or sham treatment administered to a group of experimental subjects to account for the effects of the participants' expectations—changes that result from such expectations are referred to as the placebo effect.

Place coding or place principle—The theory that the frequency of sound waves determine where on the basilar membrane the receptor cells will vibrate. The location of the vibration in turn determines the sound's pitch.

Plasticity—A quality of brain tissue that allows it (especially in early childhood) to "rewire" and move functions to other parts of the brain in response to disease or damage through the formation of new synaptic connections.

Polarization—The state of having opposite electrical charges, as in the state of resting potential in a neuron.

Polysomnograph—A type of enhanced EEG machine that includes various physiological monitors, usually used in research on the sleep cycle.

Pons—A structure in the brainstem that acts to relay information to and from the cortex to the cerebellum and other parts of the lower brain.

Positive—In learning theory, the application of a stimulus as a consequence. In psychopathology, symptoms that appear as a result of a disorder such as hallucinations and emotional outbursts.

Posttraumatic stress disorder (PTSD)—A severe, chronic anxiety disorder that usually appears after exposure to a catastrophic or life-threatening event.

Pragmatics—Informal rules for using language that refer to social status and other interpersonal variables.

Prägnanz—The Gestalt law that states that the mind seeks the simplest interpretation of a stimulus.

Prefrontal cortex—The foremost section of the frontal lobes of the human brain.

Prejudice—An attitude, unduly negative or positive, toward the members of a particular group, usually based on stereotypes or preconceptions.

Primary reinforcer—A reinforcer that directly gratifies a physical need (e.g., food or warmth).

Procedural—Long-term memories for associative processes (e.g., motor activities), generally requiring little conscious or deliberate recall. Typing or bicycle riding would be examples of activities that rely primarily on procedural memory.

Projective—A type of personality test that relies on a trained interpretation of responses to ambiguous stimuli.

Proprioceptors—Receptors in the joints and muscles that transduce information about strain and position.

Prospective memory—The type of memory that allows one to project oneself forward into the future.

Prototype—Referring to concepts, the most typical or representative example of a concept or category.

Proximodistal—A trend of organismal development referring to growth and maturation/control proceeding from the midline out to the extremities.

Pruning—A gradual process of loss of synapses that tend to accelerate in adolescence and adulthood.

Psychiatry—The branch of medical practice that diagnoses and treats mental disorders.

Psychoactive—A term that refers to drugs that alter mood, thought, and behavior.

Psychoanalytic—The school of psychology founded by Sigmund Freud and his associates.

Psychodynamic—Another term for psychoanalytic treatment practices and the theory that underlies it.

Psychometric approach—A view of human cognitive abilities that presupposes that these abilities can be identified and quantified or measured.

Psychosomatic—Disorders that are thought to have a psychological cause but that also produce real symptoms and physical damage.

Psychosurgery—Any surgical procedure done on the brain.

Psychotherapy—A wide variety of psychological techniques used to treat emotional, behavioral, and interpersonal problems.

Punishment—In operant conditioning, any consequence intended to reduce or eliminate a behavior.

Pupil—The opening in the eye behind the cornea that allows light to enter the eye and that can expand and contract through the action of the iris.

Quasi-experimental—A research design that compares two conditions of a variable that cannot actually be manipulated.

Random assignment—In research design, the placement of participants into one of two or more conditions by means of random selection from the participant pool.

Random selection—Any method of choosing research participants in which all members have an equal chance of being chosen.

Rebound—"Making-up" a particular stage of sleep (usually stage 4 NREM or REM) after having been deprived of it during the previous night.

Receptors—The openings on the surface of a dendrite that receive the molecules of neurotransmitters sent across the synapse from a neighboring neuron.

Recessive gene—A gene that will not be able to manifest its associated trait or behavior unless paired with another recessive gene.

Reciprocal determinism—A social-cognitive model of personality development and functioning that proposes that personality is shaped by the reciprocal interaction of a person's behavior, thought, and social environment.

Reflex—An automatic behavior that requires no cognitive processing and that usually is controlled from the spinal cord.

Refractory period—In physiological psychology, the period during which a neuron is hyperpolarized and cannot fire. In the human sexual response cycle, the period right after orgasm during which the male cannot achieve an erection.

Reinforcement—In operant conditioning, any consequence that is intended to promote or increase a certain behavior.

Reliability—In psychological assessment, the quality of a test in which it produces consistent scores over the course of two or more administrations.

REM—Rapid eye movement sleep; the stage during which the eyes dart back and forth behind the eyelids and physiological and brain wave monitors have readouts virtually identical to the awake state.

Representative—In research design, the fact that a sample of research participants resembles the population to which the investigator wishes to generalize study results.

Resting potential—The state of a neuron in which it is not producing an action potential (not "firing").

Restorative theory—The theory of sleep that proposes that its main purpose is to provide a time for the body to restore and repair itself.

Reticular activating system—Also called the *reticular formation* or the *RAS*; a structure in the brainstem that appears to "activate" the higher regions of the brain periodically.

Retina—Located at the back of the eyeball, structure that contains all the photoreceptors (the rods and cones).

Retrieval cues—Any piece of information, hint, or prompt that is capable of promoting recall of other related information stored in long-term memory.

Reuptake—After the action potential releases neurotransmitters into the synapse, the molecules of the neurotransmitter are drawn back into the vesicles at the axon terminal.

RNA—Genetic instructions for the production of protein at the cellular level.

Rods—The cells in the retina that function to enable vision in conditions of dim light.

Schema—A type of mental "script" or sketch for a situation, event, or problem.

Schizophrenia—A pervasive mental disorder that causes severe distortions in thought and disruptions of mood and behavior and that usually results in chronic inability to care for oneself and relate to others.

Sclera—The relatively tough outer layer of the eyeball.

Secondary reinforcer—A reinforcer that acquires its power to condition through its association with primary reinforcers (e.g., money).

Self-actualization—A state described by Maslow and the humanistic psychology in which one is using all one's potentials and living life to the fullest.

Self-concept—One's set of beliefs and perceptions about one's self; a self-schema.

Self-efficacy—A belief in one's ability to meet challenges and manage one's life stressors with effective behaviors and confidence.

Self-report—Any survey or other research instrument in which measurement occurs through the participants' reports on their own experiences or opinions.

Self-serving bias—Any tendency to make attributions that cast one's own behaviors in the best light, especially the idea that one's failures are the result of external causes and one's successes are the result of internal qualities such as virtue or talent.

Semantic memory—The type of long-term memory that involves knowledge, usually verbal or symbolic.

Semicircular canal—Fluid-filled chambers in the inner ear that contain the receptor cells for the sense of balance.

Sensation—The detection of physical stimuli and the translation (transduction) of those stimuli into action potentials.

Sensory adaptation—Casually known as "getting used to it"—an adjustment in perceptual processes that appears to lower the strength or priority of a sensory input.

Sensory memory—Also called the *sensory register*; the first stage of memory in which all incoming information and sensations are detected or experienced.

Sensory neuron—A neuron that detects and tranduces physical stimuli into action potentials.

Serial order effect—The primacy and recency effects—the fact that it is usually easier to remember the beginning and end of a list.

Sex cells—Also called *gametes*; the cells that fuse in sexual reproduction to create a new individual.

Sexual disorder—Any disorder, physiological or psychological in nature, that involves disruption of sexual drive or response.

Shaping—The gradual creation of complex voluntary behaviors through the use of operant conditioning techniques.

Short-term memory—The stage of memory in which information is held for about 30–45 seconds before being either processed and stored or forgotten.

Sleep spindles—Bursts of brain wave activity typically seen during stage 2 NREM sleep. The significance of these bursts is still not well understood.

Sleep thinking—The mental activity that probably characterizes most of our dreaming, a kind of ordinary dwelling on daily concerns.

Social-cognitive—A theory of personality, proposed by Bandura, that attributes personality development and functioning to a variety of influences inside (thoughts and beliefs) and outside (experience and observation of others' behavior) of the individual.

Social facilitation—The idea that the presence of other people enhances an individual's performance.

Social learning—Learning that occurs by observation and imitation.

Social loafing—The idea that when people work in groups, the amount of effort put in by most individuals will decline.

Sociobiology—The theory that social organization and group behavior are shaped by processes that influence natural selection; thus social behavior that leads to reproductive success will be selected in evolutionary processes.

Soma—The part of a neuron that contains the nucleus and other organelles that perform basic maintenance functions.

Somatic nervous system—The division of the peripheral nervous system that controls voluntary motor activity (also called the *skeletal* or *voluntary nervous system*).

Spinal cord—The central nervous system structure that relays information back and forth from the brain and appears to control many reflex responses.

Spontaneous recovery—The sudden reappearance of a conditioned response after its apparent extinction.

Standard deviation—In statistics and assessment, an average or typical deviation of scores from the mean.

Standardization—A process by which norms are established through administration of an assessment to a very large and representative group of individuals.

Stapes (stirrup)—One of the three bones in the middle ear that help to transduce sound into nerve impulses.

Stereotype—A mental image of a person; a social prototype.

Steroid—A class of drugs that increase the hormones that influence muscle building and other androgenic (related to male sex hormones) tendencies.

Stimulants—A class of drugs that increases central nervous system activity.

Stimulus generalization—After a stimulus has been conditioned, the organism has the conditioned response in the presence of similar stimuli as well as the original conditioned stimulus.

Stimulus threshold—A minimum level at which a stimulus can be detected usually defined by a 50 percent detection rate.

Stress—The physiological and psychological reaction that occurs when an organism experiences events that are perceived as threatening.

Stressor—Any event or situation that is perceived as potentially threatening.

Structuralism—Early school of psychology that attempted to describe the components (structure) of human mental processes, emotions, and experiences.

Subject variable—A variable based on a quality or construct that cannot be manipulated or altered by the researcher (e.g., age, sex, SES).

Subliminal—A term that describes any stimulus that falls below sensory or absolute thresholds.

Substance P—The neurotransmitter that is thought to be involved primarily in the generation and transmission of pain messages.

Substantia nigra—A midbrain structure that is heavily involved in the production of the neurotransmitter dopamine.

Superego—According to Freud, the component of personality that evaluates behavior and attempts to impose moral standards; roughly equivalent to "conscience."

Supertaster—A person who possesses elevated taste sensitivity most likely because of a surplus number of taste receptors.

Suprachiasmic nucleus—A group of neurons in the hypothalamus that appear to generate circadian rhythms.

Sutures—The ridges in the human skull that are not quite closed at birth (allowing the infant's head to be compressed during birth). They slowly close up over the course of early childhood.

Sympathetic nervous system—The activating division of the autonomic nervous system that produces an arousal response that helps the organism to escape from or respond to stressors.

Synapse—Gaps between the axons and the dendrites of neurons, across which nerve signals travel via the action of neurotransmitters.

Synaptogenesis—The process of formation, branching and growth of synapses, which occurs at a high rate during infancy and early childhood.

Syntax—Referring to language, all the rules for putting words or symbols together to create meaningful statements.

Taste bud—The small groupings of taste receptors found on the mouth and tongue.

Tectum—A structure in the midbrain involved in the control of auditory and visual responses.

Temperament—A predisposition, thought to be inborn, toward a certain level of activity, quality of mood, and way of responding to the environment.

Temporal lobes—The areas on each side of the cerebral cortex, involved in auditory processing, some aspects of visual processing, and memory.

Teratogen—Any substance capable of creating physical defects in a developing embryo or fetus if mother is exposed to it.

Thalamus—The major sensory relay and integration structure in the brain thought to process all types of sense information except smell.

Theory of mind—The idea that others' minds are separate from one's own. This skill emerges for most children before or around age 5.

Theta waves—A type of synchronized wave that appears in the EEG readout at the beginning of the NREM sleep stages.

Timbre—A term that refers to the complexity of a sound wave and therefore that of the sound.

Token economy—A form of psychotherapeutic treatment based on behaviorist principles in which points or other "tokens" are used to reinforce desired behavior. These tokens are secondary reinforcers that can be exchanged for other rewards.

TOT—The acronym for "tip of the tongue" phenomenon; when a person knows the information but cannot bring it to the level of conscious recall.

Trait—An enduring predisposition or quality of a person thought to influence personality in a relatively predictable way.

Transduction—The translation of sensory stimuli into action potentials by specialized receptor cells.

Transference—In psychoanalysis, the unconscious projection of thoughts and feelings about a person on to one's analyst or other authority figure.

Transmagnetic cranial stimulation—A newer and milder (than ECT) form of electrically based therapy for depression.

Transpersonal—A term used to refer to Jungian psychoanalysis and other forms of psychotherapy that deal with spiritual as well as psychological and social elements of a person's life.

Trichromatic theory—A theory of color vision based on the interaction of three primary types of cones—those that detect red, green, and blue light (long-, medium-, and short-wave length light, respectively).

Tympanic membrane—A technical term for the eardrum.

Umami—A proposed fifth type of taste receptor that is sensitive to a distinct meaty flavor found in some Asian cuisines.

Unconditional positive regard—Esteem and value to people regardless of their failings or strengths and successes. Humanistic psychotherapists believe that this is the most helpful attitude with which to address the therapy patient.

Unconditioned response—A natural, unlearned, automatic, or reflexive response to a stimulus.

Unconditioned stimulus—A stimulus that elicits an unconditioned (automatic or reflexive) response.

Unconscious—In psychoanalytic theory, the part of the mind or personality that holds thoughts, feelings, and motives of which the person is unaware.

Validity—The ability of an assessment to measure what it is actually designed to measure.

Vesicles—The small sacs in the axon terminal that hold and release neurotransmitters during an action potential.

Vestibular sense—A term for the sense of balance or equilibrium, which gives the brain information about the position of the head relative to the ground.

Vicarious conditioning—The shaping of behavior through the observation of the consequences that result from others' actions.

Vitreous humor—The jellylike substance in the eyeball that fills the space behind the pupil and in front to the retina.

Voluntary—A term that refers to behaviors that are guided by conscious and deliberate choices.

Weber's law—A law of sensation and perception that proposes that detection of a difference in the intensity of a stimulus is proportional to the original strength of that stimulus.

White matter—The heavily myelinated axons that comprise the lower layers of the cerebral cortex and allow the different areas of the cortex to communicate with each other.

Withdrawal—The unpleasant symptoms that occur when a person who is dependent on any addictive psychoactive substances ceases to use it. The body is reacting to the temporary depletion of that chemical.

Working memory—A form of processing intimately related to short-term memory—the simultaneous processing of new information and that which is already stored in long-term memory.

ANSWERS TO THE SELF-TEST CONNECTION

Chapter 1

PART A
1. psychology
2. construct
3. dualism
4. determinism
5. Ebbinghaus
6. Binet, Simon
7. Functionalism
8. Gestalt
9. biological
10. unconscious
11. cognitive
12. industrial-organizational psychologists
13. 16
14. scientific method
15. applied
16. hypothesis
17. descriptive
18. experiment
19. case study
20. independent

PART B
1. b
2. d
3. c
4. c
5. d
6. a
7. b
8. b
9. a
10. d
11. c
12. b
13. d
14. b
15. a
16. b
17. d
18. c
19. c
20. b

PART C
1. T
2. F; independent variable

3. F; clinical psychology
4. F; hypothesis
5. T
6. F; biological or neuroscience
7. T
8. F; Pavlov
9. T
10. T

PART D
1. yes
2. no
3. yes
4. no
5. yes
6. yes
7. no
8. yes
9. yes
10. no
11. yes
12. yes

Chapter 2

PART A
1. genetically based (inherited)
2. Heredity
3. nucleotides; DNA
4. RNA
5. 46
6. recessive
7. genotype; phenotype
8. Behavioral genetics
9. Monozygotic
10. genetic (inherited)
11. Hereditability
12. modules
13. genes; offspring
14. Evolutionary psychologists
15. meme
16. nature (or genes); nurture (or environment)

PART B
1. b
2. a
3. c

4. a
5. b
6. d
7. b
8. c
9. d
10. d
11. c
12. c
13. c
14. b
15. a
16. c

PART C
1. F; hard to separate
2. T
3. F; RNA
4. F; Recessive
5. T
6. F; Monozygotic twins
7. F; heredity
8. T
9. T
10. F; complimentary
11. F; reproductive success
12. T
13. F; meme theory
14. F; combined
15. T; genes and environment

Chapter 3

PART A
1. Glia (or glial cells); neurons
2. brain; spinal cord
3. blood-brain barrier
4. skull
5. reflexes
6. afferent
7. efferent
8. autonomic
9. parasympathetic
10. endocrine
11. peptides
12. Adrenaline
13. Motor
14. Interneurons
15. organelles

16. myelin
17. vesicles; action potential
18. ions; resting potential
19. depolarize
20. stimulus threshold
21. inhibitory
22. GABA
23. CAT scan
24. pons
25. cerebellum
26. hypothalamus
27. smell
28. hippocampus
29. basal ganglia
30. white matter
31. occipital
32. primary somatosensory cortex
33. frontal lobes
34. association areas
35. left hemisphere
36. recognize faces

PART B
1. b
2. b
3. c
4. a
5. d
6. b

7. c
8. d
9. b
10. a
11. b
12. c
13. a
14. b
15. d
16. a
17. c
18. d
19. c
20. d
21. b
22. d
23. b
24. d
25. c

PART C
1. T
2. F; the central and the peripheral nervous systems
3. F; the central nervous system
4. F; the skull
5. T
6. F; sympathetic nervous system
7. T

8. F; thyroid
9. T
10. F; Motor neurons
11. F; glial cells outnumber neurons
12. F; synapses
13. T
14. T
15. F; the axon of the sending neuron from the dendrite of the receiving neuron
16. T
17. F; neuron either fire or they don't fire
18. F; neurotransmitters
19. T
20. T
21. F; limbic system
22. T
23. F; The midbrain is
24. T
25. T
26. F; White matter
27. T
28. F; face and hands
29. F; frontal lobes
30. F; use both hemispheres in an integrated fashion

PART D

PARTS AND SUBDIVISIONS OF THE NERVOUS SYSTEM

Structure or Subdivision	Located in	Function
Spinal Cord	Central nervous system	Controls reflex functions and conduit to the brain
Brain	Central nervous system	Controls all divisions and functions of the nervous system
Autonomic Nervous System	Peripheral nervous system	Controls involuntary processes such as respiration and digestion
Somatic Nervous System	Peripheral nervous system	Controls most voluntary movements
Sympathetic Nervous System	Autonomic nervous system	Controls "crisis management"—fight-or-flight functions
Parasympathetic Nervous System	Autonomic nervous system	Controls long-term, life-sustaining bodily functions

PARTS AND FUNCTIONS OF THE NEURON

Part	Function
Cell body	Contains nucleus and organelles
Dendrite	Receives action potentials from neighboring neurons
Axon	Sends information to neighboring neurons
Myelin	Speeds transmission of messages from neuron to neuron
Vesicles	Contains and releases neurotransmitters
Synapse	Gap between neurons over which electrochemical message of the action potential travels
Neurotransmitter	Chemical messenger contained in the neuron

NEUROTRANSMITTER OR HORMONE?

Chemical Name	Classification	Function
GABA	Neurotransmitter	Lowers brain activity; visual processing
Thyroxin	Hormone	Regulates metabolic processes
FSH/LH	Hormone	Produces sex cells
Dopamine	Neurotransmitter	Movement, sensory function, thought
Endorphins	Neurotransmitter	Inhibits pain, promotes good feelings
Oxytocin	Hormone	Muscle contractions—labor, milk let-down
Serotonin	Neurotransmitter	Sleep and mood regulation
Melatonin	Hormone	Maintains sleep cycles
Insulin	Hormone	Regulates blood sugar levels and appetite
Substance P	Neurotransmitter	Transmits sensations of pain
Acetylcholine	Neurotransmitter	Muscle function and memory
Adrenaline/ Norephinephrine	Neurotransmitter/hormone	Memory, learning, enables stress reaction

BRAIN ANATOMY

Structure	Location	Function
Amygdala	Forebrain/limbic system	Enhances memory for emotional stimuli; generates aggressive impulses
Pons	Hindbrain/brainstem	"Bridge" from cerebral cortex to hindbrain
Red nucleus	Midbrain/brainstem	Integrates voluntary movements
Occipital lobes	Forebrain/cerebral cortex	Location of the primary visual cortex
Reticular Formation	Hindbrain/brainstem	Regulates brain arousal for different states of consciousness
Hippocampus	Forebrain/limbic system	Formation and storage of new memories
Cerebellum	Hindbrain/brainstem	Coordination of motor functions and juggling multiple sensory stimuli
Frontal lobes	Forebrain/cerebral cortex	Planning and exercising voluntary movement
Thalamus	Forebrain/limbic system	Attention, sensory processing and integration
Medulla	Hindbrain/brainstem	Controls basic autonomic functions
Temporal lobes	Forebrain/cerebral cortex	Location of primary auditory cortex
Basal ganglia	Forebrain/limbic system	Planning and producing movement

Chapter 4

PART A

1. The kinesthetic sense
2. Smell; taste
3. transduction
4. sensory or absolute threshold
5. subliminal
6. sensory adaptation
7. Perception
8. Vision
9. cornea
10. lens
11. vitreous humor
12. retina
13. rods
14. Photopigments
15. amacrine cells; horizontal cells
16. primary visual cortex
17. feature detectors
18. integrated theory
19. frequency (pitch)
20. pinna
21. ossicles; bone conduction
22. cochlea
23. place coding/place principle
24. olfactory
25. limbic system
26. fungiform papilla
27. Pacinian/Meissner
28. hands
29. Substance P
30. semicircular
31. Muscle spindles
32. perceptual set
33. shape
34. figure and ground relationship
35. induced motion
36. binocular
37. Müller-Lyer illusion

PART B

1. a
2. c
3. a
4. b
5. d
6. c
7. b
8. d
9. b
10. c
11. b
12. d
13. c
14. b
15. a
16. c
17. a
18. b
19. b
20. c
21. d
22. b
23. c
24. c
25. a
26. d
27. c
28. a
29. c
30. a

PART C

1. F; smell and taste
2. T
3. F; detection of changes in stimulus strength
4. F; Transduction
5. F; Aqueous humor
6. T
7. T
8. F; Rods outnumber cones
9. F; bipolar, amacrine, and horizontal
10. T
11. T
12. T
13. F; The basilar membrane and the cochlea
14. F; The temporal lobes
15. T
16. F; the frontal lobes
17. T
18. F, Compared to smell, taste
19. T
20. T
21. F; hands and face
22. T
23. F; Endorphin
24. T
25. T
26. F; the visual and balance systems
27. T
28. F; Muscle spindles (or joint receptors) and Golgi tendon organs
29. T
30. T
31. F; shape
32. T
33. F; induced motion
34. F; (use any of the monocular cues listed in Table 4-3)
35. T

PART D

THE EIGHT SENSES

Sense	Physical Stimulus/Stimuli	Receptor(s)
Vision	Light waves	Rods and cones
Hearing	Sound waves	Cochlea: basilar membrane, organ of corti and hair cells contained within
Smell	Chemical molecules	Olfactory receptors
Taste	Chemical molecules	Fungiform papillae/microvilli
Touch	Pressure, vibration, temperature, etc.	Cutaneous receptors such as Merkel discs and Meissner corpuscles
Pain	Tissue damage	Free nerve endings
Balance	Position and speed of head	Hair cells in semicircular canals and otolith organs
Kinesthetic	Muscle strain and position of limbs	Proprioreceptors: Golgi tendon organs, muscle spindles, joint receptors

THE VISUAL SYSTEM

Structure	Location	Function
Cornea	Outer layer of eyeball	Protects eye and gathers light waves
Pupil	Under aqueous humor and cornea	Controls amount of light entering eye
Iris	Center of eye, surrounds pupil	Muscles that causes pupil to dilate and constrict
Lens	Behind pupil	Focuses light on the retina
Retina	Back of eyeball	Contains photoreceptors to transduce light into action potentials, sends messages to brain
Optic nerve	Exits eyeball at the blind spot	Takes visual information to optic chiasm and thalamus for initial processing
Lateral geniculate nucleus	Part of thalamus	Begins processing and integration of visual information
Occipital lobes	Back portion of cerebral cortex	Primary sight for processing of visual information
Temporal lobes	Both sides of cerebral cortex	Additional visual processing areas

THE AUDITORY SYSTEM

Structure	Location	Function
Pinna	Outside of head	Gathers sound waves
Tympanic membrane	Middle ear	Contains the ossicles that vibrate in response to sound waves
Cochlea	Inner ear	Contains receptors for transduction of sound waves
Hair cells	Inner ear	Transduction of sound waves
Primary auditory cortex	Temporal lobes	Auditory processing and perception of sound

THE CHEMICAL SENSES

Structure	Location	Function
Olfactory epithelium	Inside of nasal cavity	Contains olfactory receptors
Olfactory bulb	Right below the frontal cortex	Initial processing of smell information; sends signals on to limbic system and cerebrum
Tongue	Inside of mouth	Holds most of the taste receptors
Fungiform papillae (taste buds)	On the surface of the tongue, in the cheeks, and in roof of the mouth	Detects and transduces information about the flavor of substances
Thalamus	Forebrain (top of brainstem)	Begins processing and integration of taste information
Limbic system and cerebral cortex	Forebrain	Processing and perception of taste and smell

THE BODY SENSES

Structure	Location	Function
Skin	Covers entire body	Contains various types of cutaneous receptors
Primary somatosensory cortex	Parietal lobes	Processing and perception of touch information
Free nerve endings (nocioreceptors)	Skin and other body tissues	Transduces information related to pain and other unpleasant sensations
Substance P	In neurons of peripheral nervous system	Neurotransmitter that sends pain messages to CNS
Semicircular canals	Inner ear	Contains hair cells that transduce balance information
Otolith organs	Inner ear	Contain otoliths
Cerebellum	Hindbrain/brainstem	Integrates information about balance and motion
Mechanoreceptors (or proprioreceptors)	Joints, muscles and tendons	Transduces information about limb position and muscle strain

Chapter 5

PART A

1. Consciousness
2. Circadian rhythms
3. brainstem; limbic system
4. limbic
5. reticular activating system (RAS)
6. Melatonin
7. restorative
8. graveyard
9. Sleep apnea
10. parasomnias
11. REM sleep behavior disorder
12. REM
13. four (4)
14. Stage 4
15. neurocognitive
16. Hypnosis
17. pain
18. meditation
19. tolerance; withdrawal
20. Type 2
21. Alcohol/barbiturates
22. stimulant
23. cannabinoid

PART B

1. d
2. a
3. c
4. c
5. b
6. d
7. c
8. b
9. b
10. d
11. b
12. a
13. a
14. b
15. d
16. c
17. b
18. a
19. d
20. a

PART C

1. T
2. F; circadian rhythm
3. F; pineal gland
4. T
5. T
6. F; restorative theory
7. F; brainstem
8. F; polysomnograph
9. T
10. T
11. F; Stage 4 NREM and REM
12. T
13. F; neurocognitive
14. T
15. T
16. T
17. F; an opposite reaction to
18. T
19. T
20. T

PART D

1. Although research suggests that some stages of sleep are important for consolidation of learning during the day, it is highly unlikely that he would be able to learn new material based only on exposure during sleep. Your friend should take a good course in Spanish while he is awake.
2. Hypnosis is an altered state of consciousness that occurs in the course of a voluntary social interaction. The "chickens" are doing what they want to do, most likely to receive attention. Hypnosis is not a reliable method for recovering memories of this life or "past lives"—anyone who has seen movies or read books about past historical periods can produce "memories" of these times.
3. Unfortunately, almost all products that promise quick and effortless weight loss are scams.
A product that contains ephedrine is a stimulant medication that carries all the risks associated with that class of drugs.

Chapter 6

PART A

1. Learning
2. behaviorist
3. classical
4. Pavlov
5. neutral
6. before
7. unconditioned
8. unconditioned
9. neutral; conditioned
10. extinction
11. voluntary
12. Thorndike
13. shaped
14. reinforcement
15. "positive"
16. secondary
17. negative
18. punishment
19. schedules
20. fixed
21. cognition
22. Tolman
23. cognitive map
24. Bandura

PART B

1. b
2. a
3. c
4. c
5. d
6. d
7. a
8. a
9. b
10. c
11. a
12. c
13. a
14. c
15. c
16. d
17. d
18. c
19. d
20. b
21. a
22. d
23. c
24. a
25. d

PART C
1. T
2. F; behaviorist/behaviorism
3. F; Pavlov
4. F; classical conditioning
5. T
6. T
7. T
8. F; Extinction
9. T
10. F; prevents
11. T
12. T
13. F; Thorndike
14. T
15. F; subtract or remove
16. T
17. T
18. F; negatively punished
19. T
20. F; fixed interval
21. T
22. F; Tolman
23. T
24. F; do learn aggression
25. T

PART D
1. a. A parent might use positive reinforcement of good manners, and social learning in being a role model by using good manners. b. A teacher could use positive reinforcement (incentives) for performance and could encourage peers to be role models for each other. c. An animal trainer could use classical conditioning to prime a dog to expect a certain sequence of actions that lead to a reward (positive reinforcement). d. An athletic coach could use positive reinforcement with rewards, or negative reinforcement (more training unless performance improves). He or she could have the team members role model for each other. e. A manager could use incentives (positive reinforcement) and employee of the month (positive reinforcement and role modeling). *There are other examples of good answers for each of these items; these are*

just possible correct answers.
2. *This answer depends on the experience of the individual student.*
3. a. Have the child return the candy or admit the misdeed if the candy has already been eaten, and work for the store-owner to make up for the cost of the candy. b. Have the boys help to clean the graffiti from the wall. c. Deduct the cost of missing supplies from employee paychecks *or* offer incentives for keeping supply costs low. *There are other examples of good answers for each of these items, these are just possible correct answers.*

Chapter 7

PART A
1. Memory
2. reconstructive
3. Ebbinghaus
4. Sperling
5. sensory
6. Attention
7. Short-term; encoding
8. Procedural or implicit
9. Declarative or explicit
10. declarative or explicit
11. semantic
12. episodic
13. biological
14. Lashley
15. hippocampus
16. frontal lobes
17. epinephrine (adrenaline)
18. neurons
19. Retrieval
20. priming
21. recognition
22. recall
23. encoding failure
24. TOT ("tip of the tongue")
25. (proactive) interference
26. persistence
27. Repression
28. anterograde
29. Schema

PART B
1. b
2. c
3. d
4. b
5. a
6. b
7. d
8. b
9. a
10. b
11. c
12. d
13. b
14. c
15. d
16. c
17. a
18. b
19. c
20. a
21. d
22. c
23. b
24. d
25. d

PART C
1. F; Memory
2. F; reconstructively, putting details together according to schemas
3. F; Ebbinghaus
4. T
5. F; Sensory memory to short-term (working) memory
6. T (or consolidation)
7. F; declarative (or explicit)
8. T
9. T
10. T
11. F; The experiences on the first day of school
12. F; failed
13. T
14. F; memory retrieval center
15. T
16. T
17. T
18. F; Recall remembering
19. T
20. F; Schacter
21. F; Transience
22. F; little empirical evidence
23. F; infantile amnesia
24. T
25. F; some protective effect

PART D

1. absent-mindedness (or encoding failure)
2. bias
3. transience (or decay)
4. retrograde amnesia
5. persistence
6. anterograde amnesia (mild dementia)
7. absent-mindedness
8. absent-mindedness (encoding failure)
9. misattribution
10. proactive interference

Chapter 8

PART A

1. thinking (or cognition)
2. Concepts
3. implicit (or procedural)
4. Natural
5. Compensatory
6. Heuristics
7. Availability
8. overconfidence
9. anchoring
10. Mental set
11. syntax
12. IQ
13. Binet and Simon
14. g
15. The Wechsler scales
16. savant syndrome
17. creative skills
18. environment
19. Hereditability
20. bound
21. free
22. valid; valid
23. internal
24. Goddard
25. 80; 89

PART B

1. a
2. b
3. b
4. d
5. b
6. d
7. b
8. d
9. a

10. a
11. c
12. c
13. c
14. d
15. d
16. b
17. c
18. a
19. b
20. b
21. c
22. b
23. d
24. a
25. d

PART C

1. T
2. F; declarative (or explicit)
3. F; are not
4. T
5. F; Algorithms are
6. T
7. T
8. F; Vygotsky
9. F; Linguistic relativity
10. T
11. F; Francis Galton
12. T
13. F; primary mental abilities
14. F; Howard Gardner
15. T
16. F; Flynn effect
17. F; 7
18. F; one
19. T
20. F; predictive
21. T
22. F; convergent
23. T
24. F; high average
25. F; college

PART D

Thinking

1. prototype
2. cognitive map
3. atypical example
4. algorithm
5. heuristic
6. insight
7. representativeness bias
8. availability bias
9. confirmation bias
10. functional fixedness

Language

1. symbols
2. abstraction
3. syntax
4. phonemes
5. memes
6. nativism
7. poverty of stimulus
8. suggestibility
9. euphemism
10. linguistic determinism

Scientists in the History of Intelligence Theory and Testing

1. Binet
2. Spearman
3. Anastasi
4. Guilford
5. Cattell
6. Thurstone
7. Gardner
8. Sternberg
9. Kamin
10. Jensen

Intelligence Theory and Testing

1. psychometric
2. g
3. crystallized
4. linguistic
5. creative
6. hereditability
7. valid
8. norms
9. representative
10. standard deviation

Chapter 9

PART A

1. Developmental psychology
2. prenatal
3. optimal
4. cephalocaudal
5. germinal
6. CNS stimulants (teratogens)
7. CNS depressants (teratogens)
8. Fontanels; sutures
9. manipulation of mental representations
10. egocentric
11. Theory of mind
12. concrete operations

13. Imaginary audience
14. Holographic speech
15. 4
16. postconventional
17. Carol Gilligan
18. basic trust versus mistrust
19. young adult
20. warmth; control
21. Erikson
22. identity diffusion

PART B

1. a
2. a
3. b
4. d
5. a
6. d
7. b
8. c
9. c
10. a
11. a
12. c
13. a
14. c
15. c
16. c
17. b
18. c
19. b
20. c
21. a
22. d
23. c
24. d

PART C

1. T
2. F; milestone
3. T
4. F; embryonic period
5. T
6. F; second
7. F; rolling over
8. T
9. F; assimilation
10. T
11. F; preoperational
12. F; imaginary audience
13. T
14. F; productive language
15. T
16. T
17. T
18. T
19. F; a temperament
20. T
21. F; Permissive
22. F; Authoritarian
23. T
24. F; physical health and mental activity affect cognitive decline

PART D

PRENATAL DEVELOPMENT

Stage	Time	Changes
First trimester: germinal period	Week 1	Cell divisions and implantation occur at the end of week 1.
First trimester: embryonic period	Weeks 2 to 7	"Floor plan" for baby, central nervous system develops rapidly, body areas become visible.
First trimester: fetal period	Weeks 8 to 12	Development of sex organs; appearance of reflexes, small movements, and heartbeat.
Second trimester	Months 4, 5, and 6	Nervous system cell migration, growth of organ systems and hardening of bones.
Third trimester	Months 7, 8, and 9	All organ systems in place and developed; baby puts on weight and increases in length; maturation of the central nervous system continues.

MAJOR MILESTONES OF CHILDHOOD COGNITIVE DEVELOPMENT

Age	Skill	Description
8 months	Object permanence	Child realizes that a hidden object still exists.
4 to 5 years	Theory of mind	Child realizes that others may have different thoughts than he or she does.
6 to 7 years	Conservation	Child understands that changing shape or type of container does not change mass.
12 and older	Hypothetical reasoning	Child asks "what if?" questions.
12 and older	Abstract reasoning	Teen can imagine and think about concepts such as truth, justice, and God and ask questions such as "Where does the universe come from?" and "What is the meaning of life?"

LANGUAGE DEVELOPMENT IN THE FIRST TWO YEARS OF LIFE

Age	Ability	Type of Ability (Receptive/Productive)
0 to 1 month	Recognizes difference between human voices and other sounds	Receptive
8 weeks	(1) Becomes sensitive to emotional cues in voices (2) Coos	(1) Receptive (2) Productive
4 months	Responds to his or her own name	Receptive
6 to 10 months	(1) Responds to vocal rhythm and intonation (2) Babbling (3) Jargon or conversational babbling	(1) Receptive (2) Productive (3) Productive
1 to 1½ years	(1) Follows simple commands (2) One-word or holographic speech	(1) Receptive (2) Productive
1½ to 2 years	Two-word or telegraphic speech	Productive

ERIKSON'S STAGES OF PSYCHOSOCIAL DEVELOPMENT

Stage	Age	Conflict	Resolution
Infancy	0 to 1 year	Basic trust versus mistrust	Caregivers who reliably meet the infant's needs foster a sense of trust in others.
Toddlerhood	2 to 3 years	Autonomy versus shame and doubt	Reasonable limits by care givers lead to a basic sense of independence in exploring the world.
Preschooler	3 to 6 years	Initiative versus guilt	Child learns to play and work with others, get needs met appropriately, and respects the rights of others. Child develops sense of purpose.
School age	6 to 12 years	Industry versus inferiority	Child feels competent in the eyes of society and his or her peers.
Adolescence	12 to mid-20s	Identity versus role confusion	Teen develops a stable sense of identity.
Young adult	Mid-20s to mid-40s	Intimacy versus isolation	Individual establishes satisfying long-term relationships.
Middle adulthood	Mid-40s to mid-60s	Generativity versus stagnation	Individual attains a sense that he or she is making useful contributions to the world and the future through family and work activities.
Late adulthood/ old age	Mid-60s onward	Ego integrity versus despair	Individual believes that his or her time in life has been satisfying and meaningful.

Chapter 10

PART A

1. Motivation
2. Charles Darwin
3. Fixed action patterns
4. Negative feedback
5. overjustification
6. Incentive
7. Self-actualization
8. Biological or physiological needs
9. a drop in blood glucose
10. Insulin
11. culture
12. the energy balance model
13. basal metabolism
14. Alfred Kinsey
15. hypothalamus; pituitary
16. Plateau
17. a refractory period
18. gender; sex
19. X
20. power
21. TAT
22. nACH
23. cultural factors (or culture)

PART B

1. a
2. a
3. c
4. a
5. c
6. d
7. c
8. a
9. d
10. a
11. a
12. b
13. b
14. b
15. d
16. b
17. b
18. d
19. c
20. a
21. d
22. a
23. a
24. c
25. d

PART C

1. F; Motivation
2. F; intrinsic
3. F; extrinsic
4. F; intrinsic
5. T
6. F; Optimum arousal
7. F; Incentive
8. F; Yerkes-Dodson
9. F; humanistic

10. F; safety; social
11. F; Self-actualization
12. F; do not have to be met
13. F; hypothalamus
14. T

15. F; set-point
16. F; slows down
17. T
18. T
19. F; Resolution

20. F; bisexual
21. F; penis; testicles
22. T
23. T
24. T

PART D

GENERAL THEORIES OF MOTIVATION

Theory	Description	Influenced Which School of Psychology
Instinct	Motivation is comprised of innate, biologically based drives for survival.	Psychoanalytic
Drive (homeostatic)	Motivation works to meet internal drives and maintain the body's state of homeostasis.	Biological/neuroscience
Incentive	Motivation is generated in response to external rewards.	Behaviorism
Psychological/ Humanistic	Motivation features an innate desire to meet a hierarchy of needs, from the most basic to the need to "self-actualize."	Humanistic

INFLUENCES ON HUNGER MOTIVATION

Type of Influence	Examples	Action
Hormonal	Insulin, glucagon, orexin, CCK, leptin	Work in digestive tract and bloodstream to influence levels of hunger in the short and long term.
Hypothalamic	Lateral, paraventricular and ventromedial regions	Starts up (lateral) and inhibits (short and long term) food intake.
Sociocultural	Diet that is favored in your culture; food that is available in your environment	Shapes human taste and preferences from a very early age.
Metabolic	Set-point or settling point; BMR	Regulates use of calories in repsonse to activity levels, age.
Dieting	Restricting food intake to a level of caloric consumption too low to meet all daily bodily needs	Lowering calorie intake in the absence of increased exercise can disrupt BMR in the long term
Evolutionary	Labor-saving technology combined with plentiful food in most wealthy world cultures	Many humans are becoming unhealthily overweight or obese.

Chapter 11

PART A

1. Emotion
2. autonomic
3. parasympathetic
4. opponent process theory
5. James-Lange
6. Schacter; Singer
7. universal
8. eustress
9. Seyle
10. resistance
11. change; change
12. appraisal; resources
13. nature of other events
14. chronic stress
15. posttraumatic stress disorder (PTSD)
16. a psychosomatic illness
17. Type A
18. Coping
19. Social support
20. reframing the problem
21. Sigmund Freud
22. increased
23. distraction/relaxation

PART B

1. b
2. a
3. d
4. b
5. b
6. d
7. b
8. a
9. b
10. d
11. a
12. b
13. d
14. a
15. c
16. d
17. b
18. a
19. d
20. d
21. a
22. b
23. a
24. a
25. d

PART C

1. F; are not
2. T
3. T
4. F; facial
5. F; acceptance
6. T
7. F; distress
8. F; sympathetic
9. F; chronic
10. F; alarm
11. F; appraisal
12. T
13. F; acute
14. F; Vietnam War
15. F; factitious
16. F; "nocebo"
17. T
18. T
19. F; Hardiness
20. F; constructive
21. T
22. T
23. F; catharsis
24. F; distraction from
25. T

PART D

Biological Basis of Emotions and Stress

1. autonomic nervous system
2. sympathetic nervous system
3. homeostasis
4. adrenaline
5. parasympathetic nervous system
6. opponent process theory
7. limbic system
8. amygdala
9. cerebral cortex
10. thalamus

Theories of Emotion and Stress

1. James-Lange theory
2. Ekman's theory
3. Lazarus's theory
4. two-factor theory
5. fight-or-flight theory
6. Plutchik's theory
7. Cannon-Bard theory
8. Type A/Type B
9. general adaptation syndrome
10. nocebo effect

Which Type of Coping Is It?

1. systematic problem solving
2. social support
3. humor
4. hardiness
5. relaxation
6. effective action
7. reframing
8. exercise
9. hobby
10. giving up

Chapter 12

PART A

1. social
2. individualistic
3. stable
4. fundamental attribution error
5. BIRGing; CORFing
6. attitude
7. the foot-in-the-door technique
8. sleeper effect
9. mere exposure effect
10. evolutionary
11. Prejudice
12. discrimination
13. brown-eyes/blue-eyes
14. normative social influence
15. Groupthink
16. Solomon Asch's
17. Kurt Lewin
18. Stanley Milgram
19. brutal; depressed/apathetic
20. Kitty Genovese
21. cooperative; competition
22. debriefed

PART B

1. d
2. c
3. b
4. d
5. a
6. a
7. b
8. d
9. b
10. a
11. c
12. a
13. b
14. c
15. c

16. a
17. a
18. d
19. d
20. d
21. b
22. d
23. a
24. d
25. c

PART C

1. T
2. T
3. F; outside the person
4. F; stable, internal
5. T
6. T
7. T
8. T
9. F; you will prevent something bad from happening
10. F; authority
11. T
12. F; social exchange theory
13. F; Stereotypes
14. T
15. F; Discrimination
16. T
17. T
18. F; social facilitation
19. F; individualistic; collectivistic
20. F; insecure (or unsure)
21. F; increase
22. F; no effect
23. F; Zimbardo et al.
24. T
25. T

PART D

Social Cognition:
Your friend says...
1. just world hypothesis
2. internal, unstable attribution
3. self-serving bias
4. BIRGing
5. internal, stable attribution
6. external, stable attribution
7. external, unstable attribution
8. CORFing
9. out-group homogeneity
10. cognitive dissonance

Social Cognition:
The advertisement says...
1. social proof
2. consistency
3. "good results"
4. reciprocity
5. authority
6. that's not all
7. door-in-the-face
8. foot-in-the-door
9. scare tactics
10. scarcity

Attraction and Person Perception
1. proximity (nearness)
2. similarity
3. stereotyping
4. mere exposure
5. social exchange
6. reciprocity of feeling
7. prejudice
8. discrimination
9. scapegoating
10. in-group/out-group

Classic Social Psychology Studies
1. power of the situation
2. prejudice
3. conformity
4. influence of expectations on performance
5. prejudice and perception
6. obedience
7. reducing intergroup prejudice
8. leadership style
9. diffusion of responsibility
10. cooperation

Chapter 13

PART A
1. Personality
2. psychoanalytic
3. behavior
4. psychoanalytic
5. pleasure principle
6. superego
7. neurosis
8. suppression
9. daydreaming
10. lifespan development

11. anal retentive; anal expulsive
12. castration anxiety
13. Jung
14. inferiority complexes
15. traits
16. McCrae; Goldberg
17. low in conscientiousness
18. social cognitive
19. internal
20. objective; projective
21. MMPI-2
22. Rotter Incomplete Sentences Blank

PART B
1. b
2. a
3. d
4. c
5. b
6. c
7. d
8. a
9. b
10. d
11. b
12. a
13. c
14. d
15. c
16. b
17. c
18. a
19. c
20. b
21. d
22. a
23. c
24. a
25. a

PART C
1. T
2. F; trait
3. T
4. F; psychosexual
5. T
6. F; ego
7. T
8. F; regression
9. T
10. T
11. T
12. F; oral
13. F; genital
14. F; animus; anima

15. F; basic anxiety
16. F; extraversion, emotional stability, and psychoticism
17. F; openness
18. F; high in neuroticism
19. T
20. T
21. T
22. F; positively
23. F; Projective
24. F; Rorschach
25. T

PART D

PERSONALITY THEORY

Personality Theory	Basic Principles	Psychologist(s) Associated with Theory
Psychoanalytic/psychodynamic	Personality shaped by early childhood experiences and unconscious forces.	Freud, Jung, Adler, A. Freud, Horney
Trait theories	Personality can be described and behavior predicted by use of a series of specific characteristics or traits	Allport, Eysenck, McCrae, Goldberg (Jung)
Humanistic	Healthy personalities feature a desire to have one's real and ideal self coincide, grow, develop and archieve one's full potential	Rogers, Maslow
Social cognitive	(1) Reciprocal determinism—personality is shaped through a dialog between behavior, social reaction and internal processing (2) Expectancy or perception of "locus of control"	Bandura, Rotter

PART E

Defense Mechanisms
1. repression
2. denial
3. projection
4. displacement
5. sublimation
6. rationalization
7. regression
8. undoing
9. daydreaming
10. reaction formation

Personality Theories
1. Freud
2. Jung
3. trait theory
4. Rotter
5. Rogers
6. Adler
7. Bandura
8. Freud
9. Freud
10. Horney

Chapter 14

PART A
1. Mental illness
2. neurology; psychiatry
3. exorcism
4. psychological
5. five (5)
6. II, two
7. Psychosocial stressors
8. Somatoform
9. personality disorders
10. anxiety
11. obsessive-compulsive anxiety disorder
12. seventy (70)
13. major depression
14. impulsive control
15. psychotic
16. delusions; hallucinations
17. Schizophrenia
18. disorganized
19. depression
20. drug therapy; supportive psychotherapy
21. M'Naghten
22. his or her own behavior
23. 1 percent

PART B
1. d
2. a
3. d
4. b
5. c
6. a
7. a
8. c
9. b
10. b

11. d
12. c
13. d
14. b
15. a
16. a
17. b
18. c
19. c
20. b
21. d
22. d
23. b
24. d
25. b

PART C
1. F; All; some
2. T
3. F; protection and compassion
4. T
5. F; psychosocial
6. T
7. F; physical or biological
8. F; Anxiety
9. F; Generalized anxiety disorder
10. F; are not related
11. T
12. F; seasonal affective disorder
13. F; bipolar disorder
14. T

15. T
16. F; negative
17. F; dissociative identity disorder (or multiple personality disorder)
18. F; 1 to 2
19. F; paranoid
20. F; more
21. T
22. F; Delusional disorder
23. T
24. T
25. F; be institutionalized for an indefinite period of time

PART D

HISTORY OF MENTAL HEALTH TREATMENT

Historical Period	Treatment Methods
Prehistory	Trephination, exorcism
Ancient Greece and Rome	Rest, exercise, nutrition
Middle Ages	Exorcism, persecution, execution
Eighteenth and early nineteenth centuries	Asylums for the poor; for some patients, moral model for treatment, offered protection and compassion: safe living arrangements, clean conditions, use of medications, and bleeding; hypnotism
Late nineteenth century	Emergency of scientific view of mental illness—Freud's talking cure, for example
Twentieth century to present time	Institutionalization, medication, psychosurgery, psychotherapy (most methods improving over the course of the century)

DIAGNOSTIC AND STATISTICAL MANUAL-IV-TR

Axis #	Disorders/Information	Specific Examples of Disorders or Information
I	Clinical/functional disorders	Mood, psychotic, impulse control, anxiety etc.
II	Personality disorders, mental retardation	Antisocial personality disorder, dependent personality disorder, Down's syndrome
III	General medical conditions	Diabetes, cancer, skin conditions
IV	Psychosocial stressors	School problems, legal problems, family problems
V	Global assessment of functioning	75 (marginally well); 15 (in need of intensive mental health care)

AXIS I DISORDERS

Group	Example(s)	Major Symptoms
Mood disorders	Major depression, bipolar disorder, dysthymia.	Irritability, mood swings, extreme sadness, periods of intense activity
Psychotic disorders	Schizophrenia, delusional disorder	Delusions, hallucinations, lack of or inappropriate emotional expression.
Anxiety disorders	Phobia, obesssive-compulsive disorder	Anxiety or fear out of proportion with the nature of the threat, obsessions, compulsions
Disorders that emerge in childhood	ADHD, autism	Hyperactivity and inability to concentrate in school, social withdrawal, impulse control problems, aggression
Impulse control disorders	Kleptomania, trichotillomania, Tourette's disorder	Stealing, pulling out hair, outbursts of aggression.
Eating and sleep disorders	Anorexia, bulimia, narcolepsy	Eating too much or too little, falling asleep suddenly and uncontrollably
Adjustment disorders	Adjustment disorder with depressed mood	Reaction to life stressor that persists for longer than is considered normal

AXIS II DISORDERS

Group	Example(s)	Major Symptoms
Cluster A personality disorders	Paranoid, schizoid, and schizotypal personality disorders	Odd or eccentric behavior
Cluster B personality disorders	Borderline, histrionic, narcissistic, antisocial personality disorders	Erratic or highly emotional behavior
Cluster C personality disorders	Avoidant, obsessive compulsive, dependent personality disorders	Anxious or fearful behavior
Mental retardation	Fetal alcohol syndrome, Down's syndrome	IQ score lower than 70 and problems managing daily living skills

Chapter 15

PART A

1. Psychotherapy
2. Clergy members
3. eclectic
4. Sigmund Freud
5. transference
6. behavioral therapy
7. classical conditioning
8. aversive (aversive counterconditioning)
9. modeling
10. thinking
11. Aaron Beck
12. unconditional
13. confidentiality
14. Inpatient psychiatric treatment
15. published
16. antipsychotic
17. seizures
18. lobotomies
19. TMS
20. Secondary prevention
21. Paraprofessionals
22. confidentiality
23. Psychiatric evaluation teams
24. released (deinstitutionalized)

PART B

1. a
2. b
3. b
4. a
5. b
6. d
7. c
8. c

9. b
10. c
11. d
12. a
13. c
14. c
15. d
16. c
17. d
18. b
19. a
20. c

PART C

1. T
2. T
3. F; Free association
4. F; maladaptive behaviors
5. T
6. F; reinforcements (rewards)
7. F; social psychology (observational learning)
8. F; Thought processes try
9. T
10. F; Aaron Beck

11. F; unconditional positive regard
12. F; Existential humanistic psychotherapy
13. F; does not make a great deal of difference
14. T
15. F; Tegritol (or Phenobarbital)
16. T
17. F; Hemispherectomies
18. F; TMS
19. T
20. F; unlicensed therapists
21. F; Under special circumstances
22. T
23. F
24. T
25. F; was not a successful movement

PART D

Which Type of Therapist Would Say This?

1. psychoanalytic or psychodynamic therapist
2. behavior therapist
3. rational-emotive therapist
4. behavior therapist
5. behavior therapist
6. person-centered therapist
7. cognitive-behavioral therapist
8. psychoanalytic or psychodynamic therapist
9. behavior therapist
10. existential humanist therapist

Which Therapy Concept Is It?

1. transference
2. token economy
3. reframing
4. participant modeling
5. exposure
6. unconditional positive regard
7. homework
8. free association
9. behavioral treatment plan
10. making meaning

PART E

PHARMACOTHERAPY (DRUG THERAPY)

Drug Class	Typical Brand Names	Neurotransmitters/ Brain Structures Acted On	Illnesses for Which It Might be Prescribed
Antipsychotic	Haldol, Mellaril, Risperidal, Thorazine	Dopamine (reduced); Serotonin (increased)	Schizophrenia, schizoaffective disorder, delusional disorder
Mood stabilizer	Lithium	Glutamate (reduced); increases volume of gray matter in cerebral cortex	Bipolar disorder
Anticonvulsant	Tegritol, Phenobarbital	Reduce firing of cortical neurons	Epilepsy
Antidepressant	Prozac, Elavil	Increases serotonin, epinephrine	Major depression, anxiety disorders
Antianxiety	Valium, Xanax	GABA (reduced), sympathetic nervous system activity (reduced)	Generalized anxiety disorder
Stimulant	Ritalin, cylert	Increase dopamine levels	ADHD

INDEX